DEATH
Investigator's
HANDBOOK

This book is dedicated to the investigator who

Knocks on one more door;
Misses one more hot meal;
Looks at the scene photographs one more time;
Makes one more phone call;
Makes one last try;

Solves one more case.

VOLUME TWO
Investigations

DEATH
Investigator's
HANDBOOK

Louis N. Eliopulos
Paladin Press • Boulder, Colorado

Death Investigator's Handbook:
Volume Two: Investigations
by Louis N. Eliopulos

Copyright © 2003 by Louis N. Eliopulos

ISBN 10: 1-58160-497-1
ISBN 13: 978-1-58160-497-9
Printed in the United States of America

Published by Paladin Press, a division of
Paladin Enterprises, Inc.
Gunbarrel Tech Center
7077 Winchester Circle
Boulder, Colorado 80301 USA
+1.303.443.7250

Direct inquiries and/or orders to the above address.

PALADIN, PALADIN PRESS, and the "horse head" design
are trademarks belonging to Paladin Enterprises and
registered in United States Patent and Trademark Office.

Visit our Web site at www.paladin-press.com

TABLE OF CONTENTS

PART II: INVESTIGATIONS · 133

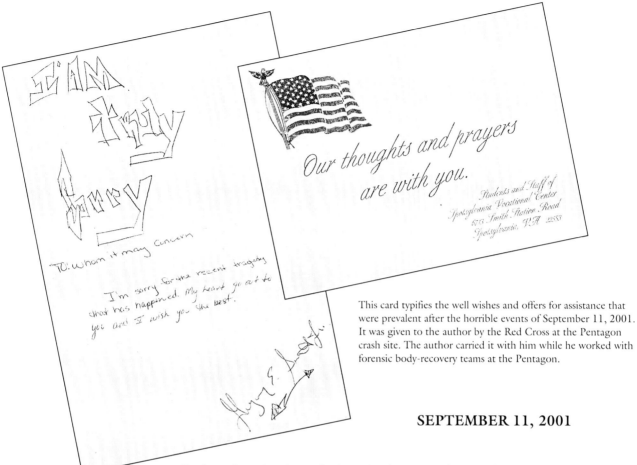

I'M truly Sorry

TO: Whom it may concern

I'm sorry for the recent tragedy that has happened. My heart go out to you and I wish you the best.

Our thoughts and prayers are with you.

Students and Staff of
Spotsylvania Vocational Center
6713 Smith Station Road
Spotsylvania, VA 22553

This card typifies the well wishes and offers for assistance that were prevalent after the horrible events of September 11, 2001. It was given to the author by the Red Cross at the Pentagon crash site. The author carried it with him while he worked with forensic body-recovery teams at the Pentagon.

SEPTEMBER 11, 2001

For all of my friends who called to check on me; for all of my fellow professionals who contacted me to volunteer their time and effort; for the homicide detective that called me and told me if it was his son who had died inside the Pentagon, he would want me to be the one to bring him out; for the school children who sent us notes and the people who brought flowers; for the Salvation Army and the Red Cross, which took care of our every want and need; to the church group from North Carolina who slept on the floor so that they could serve us hot meals—I say thank you.

Among the senseless tragedy and horrible carnage that occurred on September 11, 2001, I saw America at its very best. Deeply saddened, we collected our dead and grieved our terrible losses. And then, we moved on. I was never so proud to be an American. Your thoughts and prayers were not only heard but also deeply felt. I was so very proud to represent you.

—Lou Eliopulos
2003

ACKNOWLEDGMENTS

A very special thank-you for the continuous education and opportunity of working with the following true professionals of the forensic sciences:

Dr. Peter Lipkovic
Dr. Bonifacio Floro
Dr. William Maples
Dr. Arthur Burns
Dr. Margarita Arruza
Dr. Anthony Falsetti

Also, my profound appreciation to those individuals with whom I have shared the joy of solved cases and the agony and frustration of having a case remain unresolved:

Bruce Herring
William Hagerty
Dave Early
Tom Asimos
Robbie Hinson
Carol Dean
Pete Hughes
Jim Grebas
Mike Sullivan
Ralph Blincoe
Mark Fox
Sheri Blanton
Gerry Nance
Dayle Hinman
Dr. Jason Byrd
Brian Stamper

PUBLISHER'S NOTE

PART II

INVESTIGATIONS

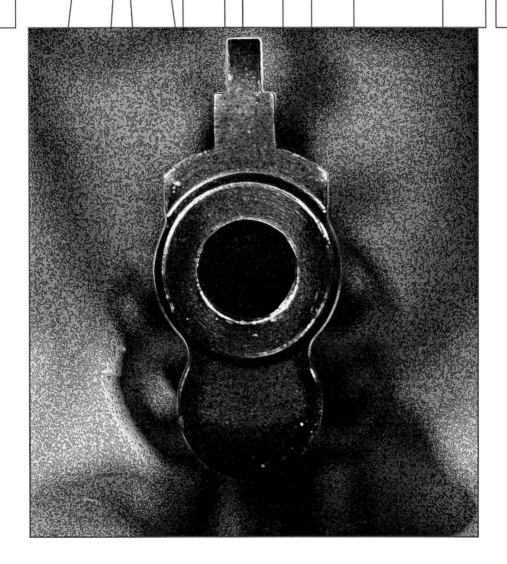

The three factors that solve crime

1. Physical evidence

2. Witness statements

3. Confessions

CHAPTER 14: THE CANVASS

The canvass is a questioning of the neighborhood that begins after a crime has been committed in an effort to develop witnesses to some aspect of the case. A witness may not claim to have knowledge of the specific event but may have seen a suspicious vehicle, have knowledge of the background of the victim, or have heard a gunshot at a specific time.

The canvassing officers do not conduct thorough, in-depth interviews with individuals who may have knowledge of the incident. Keep in mind, the purpose of the canvass is to *find* individuals who may contribute information to the investigation. The actual in-depth interview normally is done by one of the investigators assigned to the case.

The area involving a crime should be drawn and areas identified that are adjacent to the crime-scene area and along the route of the approach or escape the suspect may have used. Identify every possible household and then begin the canvass. Any residents found to be absent should be duly noted.

A synopsis of the information supplied by each canvass attempt should be prepared and forwarded to the investigator assigned the case. This should include individuals who had no information concerning the case. The canvasser should supply the names and addresses of every person who was contacted.

Consider canvassing the area during the time or day in which the incident occurred.

The canvasser should be looking for the following:

1)   Eyewitnesses to the incident

2)   Individuals who have knowledge of the circumstances of the incident

3)   Individuals who have knowledge about the time of the incident or of the death

4)   Individuals who may have knowledge about the decedent, including these:
      a) Identification
      b) Habits
      c) Friends and associates

5)   Individuals who may have knowledge about the suspect of the incident, including these:
      a) Identification or description
      b) Vehicle description
      c) Friends, associates, and accomplices

6)   Individuals who may have information concerning the motive of the killing

After the canvassing officers have established that an individual may have some knowledge about the particular incident, the witness is then ready for the interview.

CHAPTER 15: INTERVIEWING

THREE STEPS

Interviewing a witness is a three-step process of preparing, questioning, and closing.

1)   Preparation
   a) The initial process involves steps by the investigator to get potential witnesses involved in the investigation. Some people will have no hesitation about getting involved in the investigation, while others will be less than enthusiastic. Interviewing skills begin at this very elementary level.
   b) Approaching potential sources of information
      i) Always act in a professional and courteous manner. Treat every individual with respect.
      ii) Stay away from crowds and asking the crowd for information. Try to deal with each potential source individually, away from the crowd.
      iii) Try to make the source feel as comfortable as possible. Where the interview is conducted may help in this regard. For obvious reasons, people will feel least comfortable being interviewed at the police station. The most comfortable setting for most people to be interviewed is in their own homes. The circumstances of the case and the potential importance of the witness will normally dictate if the person is transported to the investigator's office.
      iv) Try to accommodate each individual but also attempt to conduct the interview under your conditions if at all possible. Once you have approached a potential source, making an appointment for a future interview can cause all sorts of problems. The source may be talked out of his initial cooperative mood by family members and co-workers who remind him of the problems that may arise from getting involve in the investigative and court processes (e.g., loss of time from work, threats).

2)   Questioning
   a) In an effort to relieve tension, let the witness tell the complete story of what happened without interruption. It is perfectly all right to take notes during the interview. Most witnesses expect the investigator to take notes and may consider him disinterested if he does not.

3)   Closing
   a) The closing the interview is very important. If the witness has pertinent information, the investigator would be well served to treat him very kindly: he may be a witness in future court action. In addition, this individual may have the potential for obtaining other information, or the investigator may wish to use this individual in the future as more information is developing with the investigation. Leave the witness with a positive image.

In considering this source as a court witness required to testify in this matter, the court generally imposes three conditions:

1)   Consciousness
          a) That the witness was conscious during the particular incident

2)   Presence
          a) That the witness was physically present during the particular incident

3)   Attentiveness
          a) That the witness was psychologically and mentally attentive at the time of the specific
              incident

The investigator should approach the information supplied by each witness with a critical eye to determine if it is accurate. This does not mean the that investigator should be critical of or cynical toward the witness. Questioning to establish the credibility of the witness and the information supplied should be done in a professional and straightforward manner and presented to the witness during the natural course of the interview. For example, consider the following:

1)   Physiological abilities of the witness
          a) This involves the five senses, with most important senses being the witness' ability to
              see and hear.
                  i) Does the witness require corrected vision lenses?
                  ii) Was the witness wearing those lenses at the time of the incident?
                  iii) Does this have an effect on the information supplied by the witness?

2)   External factors involving the witness
          a) Is the information contradicted by some external factors present?
                  i) May the witness have been too far away to see the details elaborated to the
                     investigator?
                  ii) Were the weather conditions on the date and time of the incident significant
                      enough to have caused a problem in the witness' account of what happened?
                  iii) Were there obstacles present at the scene that may have altered the subject's
                       view or ability to hear?
                  iv) Would lighting conditions at the scene have influenced the witness' account of
                      the event?
                  v) Would the time of day of the incident have influenced the information supplied
                     by the witness?

3)   The emotional state of the witness
          a) Is the witness in a fearful state, which may influence his recollection of what was
              seen or heard?
          b) Is the witness extremely angry, disgusted, or so prejudiced that his perceptive abilities
              may be affacted?
          c) Does the witness have an ax to grind against the suspect?

4)   Personal screening abilities
          a) Does this witness have special perceptions, knowledge, or talents that may make his
              information more reliable than that given by others?
                  i) Did the witness recognize the individual because he knows him or her?
                  ii) Is the description given of the gun carried by the suspect coming from a
                      witness employed as a gun dealer?

CHAPTER 16: SUSPECT DESCRIPTION

The following features can be used in compiling a description of a possible suspect observed by a witness:

Sex:	Male	Female
Race:	Caucasian	Negroid
	Mongoloid	Other
Age:	Under 16	16–20
	21–25	26–30
	31–35	36–40
	41–45	46–50
	Over 50	
Height:	Under 5"	5'1"–5'5"
	5'6"–6'	6'1"–6'3"
	6'4"–6'6"	6'7" +
Weight:	Under 100 lbs.	100–125
	126–150	151–175
	176–200	201–225
	226–250	256 + lbs.
Build:	Very thin	Thin
	Medium thin	Muscular
	Stocky	Heavy
Head shape:	Oval	Round
	Square	Rectangular
	Other	
Hair color:	Black	Brown
	Blonde	White
	Gray	Red
	Other	
Hair type:	Straight	Curly
	Bushy	Kinky
	Balding	Bald
Hair length:	Short	Medium
	Long	
Facial hair:	Mustache	Sideburns
	Partial beard	Goatee
	Full beard	

Complexion:	Light	Pockmarked
	Fair	Pimples
	Medium	Birthmark
	Dark	Other
	Ruddy	

Eye color:	Blue	Green
	Brown	Hazel
	Black	Other
	Gray	

Eye defects:	Crossed	Missing
	Squints	Cataracts
	Blinks	Glasses

Nose:	Small	Broken
	Medium	Hooked
	Large	Flattened
	Long	Other
	Wide	

Teeth:	Chipped	Good
	Gaps	Gold
	Stained	Protruding
	Decayed	Other
	False	

Scars:	Face	Arms
	Hands	Other

Tattoos:	Arms	Chest
	Back	Legs
	Buttocks	Other

Body piercing:	Ear(s)	Breast(s)
	Tongue	Genitalia
	Navel	Other
	Nose	

Posture:	Erect	Stooped

Speech:	Southern	Foreign
	Northern	Vulgar
	Lisps	Soft
	Nervous	Other
	Educated	

Clothing style:	Business	Casual
	Uniform	Dirty
	Flashy	Other

Articles of clothing:	Shirt/blouse	Jacket
	Pants/slacks	Shoes
	Skirt	Uniform
	Dress	Coat
Jewelry:	Necklace	Bracelet
	Watch	Rings
	Earrings	Other
	Medallion	

CHAPTER 17: INTERROGATION

INTERVIEW VERSUS INTERROGATION

1) Difference between interview and interrogation
   a) Interview is a nonaccusatory procedure where the primary focus is to collect information.
   b) Interviews are conducted at various locations. Interrogations are attempted in highly structured settings where privacy is essential.
   c) Note-taking is encouraged during an interview but should not be done during an interrogation.
   d) Interviews are conducted within a limited time frame (on an average of 15 to 40 minutes). An interrogation is not limited by time (to a reasonable extent).

LEGAL CONSIDERATIONS

1) Miranda warnings
   a) Before a person in police custody can be interrogated or otherwise deprived of his freedom in any way, he must be advised of his rights under *Miranda v. Arizona,* specifically the following:
      i) He has the right to remain silent.
      ii) Anything he says may be used against him.
      iii) He has the right to an attorney.
      iv) If he cannot afford an attorney, one will be provided to him at no cost.
      v) At any time during questioning, the suspect may change his or her mind and remain silent or request an attorney. (The last, or fifth, warning is subject to particular judicial interpretation by individual agencies. Many agencies do not include it as part of their interview procedures because federal and state courts have overwhelmingly held that it is not a Miranda requirement.

2) Miranda warnings do not have to be in writing; oral waivers are sufficient. Many departments require a suspect to not only sign a rights form but also initial each individual warning. In some departments, the Miranda warnings are included in the initial portion of any confession.

3) If at any time the suspect asks to consult with an attorney, the interview must cease. The interviewer cannot talk the suspect out of wanting to consult an attorney. The interview cannot be resumed until that individual contacts the police of his own volition or initiative, without any police persuasion or interference, and performs another waiver. Several states have ruled that the suspect's lawyer must be present when the waiver is executed.

4) Once Miranda warnings have been waived, it is not necessary to readvise the suspect of his Miranda warnings at any specific interval unless a considerable time has elapsed since the last questioning. No specific set time has been established for the readvisement of these warnings.

5) Trickery by the investigator will not necessarily nullify a confession. Indicating to a suspect that a co-offender has implicated the suspect, when in fact he has not, has been ruled by the U.S. Supreme Court to be legally permissible, providing the trickery poses no threat to the innocent.

6) Promises made to a suspect can nullify a confession if that promise presents a substantial risk of the investigator's receiving a false confession or makes an innocent person confess.

7) There are investigative procedures to minimize the effects of Miranda on cases where an interrogation has become important in solving the case.
    a) Try to create a noncustodial atmosphere.
        i) Tell the suspect he is not under arrest.
        ii) Ask the suspect to come in to the office to speak with the investigator.
        iii) Do not offer the suspect a ride to the police station.
        iv) Have a third party issue the Miranda warnings.

TWO PURPOSES OF THE INTERROGATION

1) To collect information

2) To obtain a confession or elicit an admission of guilt
    a) Catching the suspect in a lie and attempting to have the suspect admit to lying about some aspect of the incident
    b) Getting the suspect to admit to being at the scene or having been in contact with the decedent

PREPARATION FOR THE INTERROGATION

1) Isolate the potential subject. There should be no interruptions!

2) Avoid conducting the interrogation in an environment supportive of the subject. For example, don't interview the subject in his house or place of business.
    a) If you cannot have the subject leave his office, conduct the interview in a conference room. Don't let the subject be interviewed while he is sitting behind his desk.
    b) It is the responsibility of the interviewer to create a climate that promotes an effective interview.
        i) The more private the room setting, the more reliable the results of the interview or interrogation.
        ii) No barriers should exist between the interviewer and the subject.
            (1) If the subject is behind a table or desk, the interviewer may miss signs of anxiety displayed by the subject beneath the table.
            (2) If the subject tells a lie, the full effect of the deceptive act won't be displayed because of this barrier presented by the desk or table.
            (3) Place the chairs approximately 5 feet apart. Avoid using chairs that swivel, have wheels, or tilt back.

3) Know the facts of the case and the specific information that needs to be developed.

EVALUATING THE SUBJECT

1) Prior to interviewing the subject, the interviewer will have to evaluate the subject based on the following criteria:
    a) Subject's intelligence
        i) The more intelligent the subject, the more reliable behavioral symptoms will be.

> b) Emotional stability
> > i) Judgments can't be made on emotionally unstable individuals. Look for someone who goes back and forth in his emotions.
> c) Emotional maturity
> > i) The subject should be mature enough to have a basic understanding of right and wrong (e.g., children).
> d) Cultural differences
> > i) Consider cultural differences in what the interviewer may perceive as abnormal behavior.
> e) Drugs, alcohol, physical and medical conditions
> > i) A interviewee under the influence may have a diminished fear of the consequences.
> > ii) Prior to the interview, ask about medication he has taken and his prescription history.

INTRODUCTION

1) Always be polite, courteous, and professional during the interview.

2) Show that you're interested. Show that you are competent and confident. Show that you are dedicated to the case; let the subject know this is the most important thing that is scheduled for today.

3) Be understanding and sympathetic.

4) The opening statement is critical. The subject, if guilty, is on his guard, and anticipating the questions and replies.
> a) If the investigator begins the session by telling the subject, "We know what happened," his reaction may be, "Okay, prove it," or "Why do you need to talk to me, then?"
> b) If the investigator begins the session by saying, "We know you did it," the subject may be scared into silence or request an attorney.
> c) Keep in mind that the subject has agreed to talk with the investigators because he feels as though he can direct the investigation away from himself. It is to the investigator's advantage to get this person talking. Even if the subject never admits to the incident, he may give sufficient details or deceitful information, which may ultimately show his complicity in the incident.
> d) The investigator can usually gain the upper hand immediately into the session and throw the subject off his plan of action by asking unthreatening questions. Filling out a standard interview form is an efficient way to begin the session and have the subject begin talking and responding to questions provided by the interviewer. The unthreatening questions may cause the subject to drop his guard. He has been preparing his denials, and now his is answering questions about his date of birth and address.
> e) Establish a rapport with the individual but don't be overly friendly. Attempt to establish the personality type of thes individual.
> f) The critical stage in the interview process is entered when the general conversation turns to the subject's knowledge of the incident.

GETTING THE SUBJECT TO COOPERATE

1)   Getting the subject to cooperate is a function referred to as SOB.
        a) S—Stimulus. The stimulus is the technique used by the interviewer. It cannot be illegal (i.e., it cannot be something done to make an innocent person confess).
            i) Be flexible when supplying the stimulus. If the stimulus does not work, do you, the interviewer have the flexibility to back out and attempt another stimulus?
        b) O—Object. The object is the subject of the stimulus.
        c) B—Behavior. The result of the stimulus' acting on an object produces a behavior.

2)   Never get angry during the interview process. Anger simply means the interviewer has become the object and the subject has supplied the stimulus.
        a) If the subject gets angry, consider the displacement theory.
            i) Why is the subject angry? The subject may be angry that the police came to his office, not that he is being questioned about the crime. The subject is not denying the crime. It is not a bad technique to interview the subject when the subject is angry.

BEHAVIOR SYMPTOM ANALYSIS

1)   Many techniques are taught concerning the ability to read verbal and nonverbal responses for indications of deceptions. Kinesic Interview Techniques and Reid Interview Techniques are just two of the many available to the interviewer. It is not possible to detail all the indicators for deception the interviewer may come across in dealing with the interviewing of subjects. Behavioral attitudes looked at by interviewers include the following:
        a) Attitude
        b) Posture
        c) Eye contact
        d) Gestures
        e) Verbal answers

EXTERNAL FACTORS THAT ULTIMATELY INFLUENCE A SUBJECT TO COOPERATE

1)   Two factors will ultimately influence the ability of the subject to cooperate fully with the interview, especially when it comes to admitting responsibility for the incident.
        a) Social responsibility
            i) What does this person have to lose if admitting guilt? The more a person has to lose, the more the reliable the responses will be.
        b) Fear of consequences
            i) Don't scare the person into confessing. The interviewer wants to lessen the anxiety, not increase it.

INTERROGATION CHART
TRUTHFUL VERSUS DECEPTIVE BEHAVIOR (Buckley, Reid, 1992)

EVENT	TRUTHFUL	DECEPTIVE
Interview appointment	Tends to show up early.	Doesn't show up for appointment or shows late.
	Is much more cooperative.	Is not cooperative.
		Claims to have other appointments.
Nervousness	Tends to be nervous.	Tends to be nervous
	Calms down as interview progresses.	Calms down as interview progresses.
Anger	Angry. If asked what is making him angry, he will answer in specifics.	Angry. If asked what is making him angry, he will answer in nonspecifics. Won't calm down.
Fearful	Extremely nervous. If asked why he is here, will tell you. If you tell him why he is here, there will be an instant relief; he will sit forward in the chair and ask what you want to know.	Extremely nervous. Asked why he is here, he will play dumb.
Attitude	Composed.	Overly anxious.
	Self-assured, not cocky.	Seems confused. Asks for question to be repeated.
	No violent mood swings.	Women will have nervous laugh. Men will clear their throats.
Concern	Concerned. Wants you to know he is innocent.	Overly polite (Eddie Haskell syndrome).
	Understands the more time you waste with him, the more time will elapse in which the suspect will be at large.	Thanks you at the end of the interview. Will act as if it is no big deal.
		Will fall asleep in interview room.
Cooperation	Cooperates with investigation. Appears without attorney. Willing to prove innocence. Will take polygraph test.	Defensive. Will be quiet. Afraid he will say something to get himself in trouble.

Directness	Answers questions directly.	Evasive in answers. Noncommittal in response.
Openness	Open. Will volunteer information. Will narrow scope of investigation for you. Wants to narrow your list of suspects.	Complains. Have to give a reason why he doesn't cooperate. "This is costing me a lot of money to come down here." Does not want to eliminate any suspects.
Sincerity	Should sound as though they believe their own statement.	Guarded about what he tells you. Hand over mouth.
Perseverance	Unyielding. Gets more adamant and forceful in denials.	Defeated. Slumps head forward. Indicates sorrow he could not be more helpful.
Body position	Upright. Interested and alert. Barriers come down as interview progresses. Leans forward on occasion. Mirror image of interviewer. Casual posture changes.	Slouching. Wants to get farther away. Crossed arms and legs. Assumes runner's position. Lack of interest. Head in hand. Faces door Avoids facing interviewer. Erratic and rapid body changes. Head and body slump.
Personal gestures		Pulls up socks. Rubs and wrings hands. Scratches, strokes, and picks. Pulls on earlobes (I don't like what you're saying). Women pull and twirl hair. Dry mouth. May ask for a glass of water. Yawns, sighs. Body needs oxygen for fight or flight. Nail checks. Hands busy. Knuckle popping. Swinging of feet. Foot tapping. Leg bouncing. Sits on hands or feet.

Grooming gestures

Clothing adjustment.

Lint picking.

Watch winding.

CHAPTER 18: COERCED CONFESSIONS

The three basic components in solving homicides are physical evidence, witness statements, and confessions. That is, any one of these components may be used in combination or stand alone in obtaining a conviction involving a homicide.

In effect, there are many prisoners who may be imprisoned, and who have been in prison, after being found guilty based solely on their admissions made to police concerning a particular crime. The general consensus of the general public and the law enforcement community throughout the years has been that an innocent person, not subjected to torture and afforded all of his constitutional rights, would never confess to a crime he did not commit. In this day and age, through 24-hour continuous news coverage and the sophistication of the general public from watching law enforcement programs, the public no longer automatically accepts this. Law enforcement personnel remain steady in their original belief.

In essence, if a murder case is being prosecuted based largely on a confession supplied by the defendant, the detective should expect a challenge to a confession statement. The defense attorney will attack this confession from a three-pronged perspective: challenge the law, the facts of the case, and the detective personally.

CHALLENGING THE LAW

In the post-Miranda era, confessions have mainly been challenged on their legal status. Sophisticated defense attorneys, many of whom are former prosecutors, wage a multifaceted attack to keep their clients' confessions from being admissible. They hone their cross-examination techniques by attending professional conferences at which national and international experts instruct them on how to identify weaknesses in a criminal prosecution. The astute defense attorney maintains a network of available "forensic experts" willing to testify for a "professional" fee. Many of these "experts" sustain careers based solely on being expert witnesses.

Police detectives must testify in court and answer questions as to why they were wearing their weapons during the time of the interrogation (implying coercive tactics). The defense attorney may also question the detective about whether the door to the interrogation room contains a lock (implying that the subject was confined). The defense attorney may also question the detective as to whether there may have been a telephone book available to the detective while he engaged the suspect in conversation (implying that the detective physically attacked the suspect with the telephone book because it would not leave any marks).

If the detective did not videotape the confession, that can become a problem. If the confession was recorded on video, then *when* the camera began recording may become the issue. If confessions are normally captured on video or auditory tape, then confessions that were not recorded will become the major issue.

Defense attorneys and their coercion expert witnesses believe that videotaping is extremely helpful in dealing with involuntary and retracted confessions. If there are disagreements about the nature and scope of the interrogation, the defense attorney will argue that the absence of a videotape forces the court to believe one side or the other. Defense attorneys assert that if a video or audiotape had been created, then what actually took place could be known for certain.

Coercion experts would like to see the adoption of requirement that all interrogations be videotaped. The fact remains that under this close scrutiny, the evolution of interrogation practices works to undermine the very structure of its implementation. For example, in some clearly defined circumstances, police interrogators are allowed to lie to a suspect. An adept defense attorney eager to make his point that the police interrogators are liars can quickly capitalize on this intentional deception by the police. Likewise, a dedicated investigator who has spent his career seeking justice for a homicide victim, can sometimes be portrayed as overzealous and obsessed, anout-of-control detective who has lost his objectivity on this case. The defense attorney can suggest that his client was "railroaded" as a result of the investigator's obsession. Additionally, a police detective's efforts to control an interview can be represented as the detective's intimidation of the suspect that resulted in a coerced confession.

In reality, the defense attorney may not be unethical in vigorously defending his client. In fact, it has been the defense attorneys who have made us aware of cases in which innocent people have confessed to crimes they did not commit. We now know that innocent people have confessed, because modern forensic technology has allowed us the opportunity to further process physical evidence associated with particular crimes. For example, ABO serological evidence that was vaguely defining of a perpetrator has given way to DNA fingerprinting that, in this day and age, can sometimes be interpreted as mutually exclusive. In some of these cases, newly found innocent subjects had been sitting on death row.

Confessions have been problematical for the U.S. justice system. Fact finders must evaluate the reliability of a confession, first in terms of its admissibility and, if admitted, in terms of its weight. To do this, they must determine whether the confession was voluntary or was the result of pressure or inducement and whether the defendant was intellectually competent or was anxious, fatigued, mentally retarded, or unusually suggestible. The criterion for the admissibility of a confession has thus evolved into the quality of voluntariness. The aim of admitting into evidence only voluntary confessions is to prevent the introduction of unreliable evidence. The Supreme Court has kept the definition of voluntariness vague and imprecise and speaks of a comprehensive analysis of the totality of the relevant circumstances. (Kassin and Wrightsman, 1985).

Judges may exclude confessions where the coercion is blatant and obvious but not exclude confessions where the coercion is subtle and more readily disguised. Typically, confessions are excluded if they are elicited by physical violence or a threat of harm or punishment, promise of leniency, or without notifying suspects of their Miranda rights. (Kassin and Sukel, 1997).

Courts will usually consider the confession to be coerced if the confession was elicited by he following means:

1) Force
2) Prolonged isolation
3) Deprivation of food or sleep
4) Threats of harm or punishment
5) Promises of immunity or leniency
6) Failure to notify the suspect of his constitutional rights, unless exceptional circumstances exist
7) Police lies, fabricated evidence, or otherwise coercive behavior. (If it is demonstrated that police personnel did in fact lie, fake evidence, or otherwise coerce the confession, the fact finder must consider whether the police lies and deception would have made an innocent person confess).

The courts have allowed judges to make the determination as to the admissibility of the confession by evaluating whether it was voluntary.

1) The courts then suggest that the trial judge serves as a gatekeeper. The judge will decide whether to allow a confession to be admitted into evidence at trial. To this end, the judge may allow expert testimony about the circumstances of how the confession was elicited to be admitted into the trial. Because of the subjective nature of the judge's discretion, lying, deception, coercion, and fabrication of evidence may be allowed in one courtroom but prohibited in another.

2) Whatever the ruling at the trial level, admissibility of a confession can be challenged at an appellate level.

CHALLENGING THE FACTS OF THE CASE

The facts of the case are usually associated with the following.

1) Confession considerations
   a) Police are allowed to misrepresent or engage in deception with a suspect. For example, a suspect can be asked to explain his fingerprints' being found inside the victim's car. This may result in an admission by the suspect that he had been inside the victim's car when he had previously insisted he had never known or had contact with the victim. This may ultimately lead to a full confession by the suspect. In reality, there were no fingerprints of the suspect found in the victim's vehicle.

2) Police interrogations in which the police freely admit to deceiving suspects and lying to induce confessions
   a) The defense attorney will contend that the police have fabricated the results of the evidence examination, made false claims about witnesses to the crime, and falsely told the suspect whatever they thought would be successful in obtaining a confession.
   b) The defense attorney will imply that police interrogation tactics minimize the suspect's culpability, assuring him that his behavior was understandable and not really blameworthy, or telling him that if he described what happened, the detectives would help him in some way.
   c) Police will maintain that they are not doing anything wrong. The deceptive tactics are a necessary evil to obtain convictions of guilty persons. An innocent person will not fall for a trick if he had no part in the crime. Besides, the system, including the training academies and the courts, permit, if not encourage, deception during the investigation phase.

3) "The court observed that the 16 strategies for interrogation used by the police could actually be characterized into three major themes. The court found such practices inherently coercive.
   a) The first reattributes the implications of the situation by shifting the blame or minimizing the seriousness of the crime.
   b) The second attempts to frighten the individual by exaggerating the evidence available, telling the person that the interrogator knows he is guilty or stressing the consequences.
   c) The third makes an emotional appeal by showing sympathy, flattery, and respect, and by appealing to the best interests of the suspect." (Inbau and Reid, 1962).

4) The confession may later be retracted or challenged by the defendant's defense attorney.
   a) Judges and juries must assess the totality of the circumstances surrounding the defendant's confession. In most jurisdictions, expert testimony can be introduced by the defense to allow a jury to hear an explanation of how the defendant may have been led into giving a coerced confession.

5) Suspect considerations
   a) Police have long been familiar with the phenomenon of individuals confessing to murders they did not commit. Usually in those cases, the subject's demeanor is so bizarre that police immediately suspect that something is amiss. Such an individual is

summarily dismissed after police detectives ask the individual a couple of questions concerning the homicide. If the detective becomes so engrossed in solving this case that he ignores obvious conflicts between the suspect's story and the known facts, this case can become a problem and its resolution should be challenged.

    i) An example of a false confession situation is found during the early 1980s when two drifters, Otis Toole and Henry Lee Lucas were apprehended and suspected of killing more than 300 people across the United States. These individuals were killers, but to a much lesser extent than they boasted. However, some police officers, eager to clear their agency's unsolved homicides, ignored uncorroborated information from the two. Had the officers maintained their usual healthy skepticism, they would have been skeptical of Lucas' and Toole's confessions. It wasn't until some detectives who were critical of the way this case was progressing challenged the duo to prove their claims, causing their confessions to fall apart.

b) The police must consider whether the suspect was of sound mind and whether the confession was voluntary or coerced.

CHALLENGING THE DETECTIVE PERSONALLY

1) Defense attorneys may challenge the confession by attacking the credibility of the detective. This usually begins with the disclosure of the detective's interrogation training and confession case history. Prior allegations of inappropriate or physical force issues concerning the detective may also be the subject of review.

2) The defense attorney may accuse the detective of using such overtly coercive tactics as beating, intimidation, deprivation of personal contact with the outside world, and the lack of adequate food and bathroom breaks. The defense attorney may also attack the duration of the interrogation session.

3) The challenge to the interrogating detective could also examine the more subtle nature of his tactics. It could involve the following:

    a) Interrogation tactics of police versus the susceptible nature of a suspect

        i) Experts who testify on behalf of defense attorneys have examined certain methods of interrogation and claim those methods are inherently coercive.

        ii) There are certain fallacies associated with their assertions, including these:

            (1) Many times, a witness turns into a suspect not because of the way he responds to the pressure of the interview, but when he begins to lie about known information. This creates a red flag to investigators. People who lie about information on a case will bring attention to themselves and invite closer scrutiny by the detectives. To further assess this subject, misrepresentation of some material fact may be introduced by the interrogator relating to the investigative status of such things as evidence. This may be employed, not to test the physical or emotional resolve of the suspect, but to test, or question, his assertions, alibi, or motive. Whether the suspect is lying because of self-preservation, because he is guilty, because he likes to lie, or because he has a mental problem, he will evoke a much greater investigative interest. In these types of cases, determining the reason behind the fabrication may be just as important to a detective as learning who left their bloody fingerprint on the murder weapon.

(2) In contrast, there are many occasions in which an interrogating detective has lied to a suspect or witness to test the veracity of his assertion of guilt.

4) Coerced confessions and false confessions
    a) Coerced or nonvoluntary confessions must be distinguished from false confessions, since not all coerced or nonvoluntary confessions are false and not all false confessions are coerced. It is incorrect to assume that if a confession is coerced then it must be false.
        i) During the court proceeding, the defense attorney may introduce his expert witness to testify about coercive practices involving this particular confession. The defense attorney will argue that expert testimony should be allowed during this criminal trial to help jurors understand the circumstances that led to the nonvoluntary confession.

5) Interrogative suggestibility
    a) It is not uncommon for defendants to withdraw confessions made during the police interrogation. The defense attorney must offer believable reasons why an innocent person would have confessed in the first place. The defendant could supply those reasons when he takes the witness stand; however, a recanted confession should produce a fairly difficult cross-examination for the client. Instead, the defense will produce a "coercion expert" to testify on those reasons. The expert will cite the following:
        i) Coercive tactics
            (1) Police coercion, including deception and trickery, used to make criminals confess also run the risk of eliciting false confessions.
        ii) Interrogation stress
            (1) If a person has no experience with arrest and interrogation, he is more likely to become upset and strained by the interrogation.
                (a) A police interrogation is a highly stressful experience, especially when the individual is isolated and not in contact with familiar people. Isolation and confinement can cause a wide range of behavioral and physiological disturbances, including loss of contact with reality.
                (b) Stress can also arise from the suspect's submission to authority, represented by the interrogator. Certain suspects may obey instructions and suggestions that they would ordinarily reject.
        iii) Mental problems
            (1) There may be a problem in the interrogation of a person who may be mentally retarded or have some other serious mental problem.
                (a) Psychologists may be consulted prior to any interrogation of the suspect.
                    (i) The defense attorney may attack this process and imply to the jury that this was a malicious effort to use mental health professionals to probe, identify, and attack the mentally challenged defendant, thus making him more vulnerable and confused.
        iv) Immaturity of the suspect
            (1) Interrogations involving adolescents may lead to allegations of a coerced and false confession. Deceptive tactics, intimidation

accusations, and isolation issues appear to be much more of a concern to juries, especially when they involve an adolescent.
- v) Confusion
  - (1) A coercive interrogation expert may indicate that confusion could be at the root of the false confession.

6) "There are three types of false confessions:
- a) Voluntary
  - i) A confession made without external pressure
- b) Coerced-compliant
  - i) When the suspect confesses to escape an aversive interrogation, secure a promised benefit, or avoid a threatened harm
- c) Coerced-internalized
  - i) When the suspect actually comes to believe [he is] guilty of the crime."
  (Kassin, 1997; Kassin and Kiechel, 1996; Kassin and Wrightsman, 1985).

CONCLUSION

The ultimate standard for a reliably obtained, uncoerced confession is a professional interview conducted within the outlines of constitutional law. A confession should include details of the crime that have not been provided to the suspect under any circumstances.

The interrogating detective must maintain his objectivity when eliciting a confession. Overzealousness should not be confused with tenacity—tenacity solves cases; overzealousness causes problems. If the information obtained during the interrogation just doesn't add up, then the potential for a false or coerced confession should be considered.

CHAPTER 19: HOMICIDE INVESTIGATIONS

SIGNIFICANCE

The investigation of a homicide is the most detailed and significant undertaking of law enforcement agencies. Most people have resigned themselves to the possibility of crime entering their lives. In these day and times, they understand that they, or someone they know, may have their homes and vehicles broken into, or that they may be a victim of a robbery or an assault. They have grudgingly accepted crime as being part of their community and part of their lives. There are places they don't frequent, times of day or night they do not go into certain areas, and activities they refrain from doing or do only when accompanied by someone.

This acceptance of crime, however, does not extend to homicides. The general public will never understand homicide. Communities react in fear to a series of unsolved homicides affecting their city. People are outraged when a homicide occurs in their particular neighborhood or to an associate, friend, or relative. This nonacceptance by the general community is voiced through the media. This publicity causes additional community reactions and adds to the general feeling of insecurity, which is often expressed as dissatisfaction with the perceived inactivity on the part of law enforcement and other government agencies.

The ultimate manifestation of this vicious cycle results in sheriffs' and prosecuting attorneys' losing elections and police chiefs' being fired. No advertising budget is large enough for a chamber of commerce to promote a city that is perceived as dangerous. Few desirable businesses will relocate and bring employees, with children, into this seemingly dangerous environment. Homicides cannot be ignored, relegated to an insignificant, low-priority section of the department, or subject to budgetary restraints.

A homicide department should be staffed with the most qualified professionals of any department. New members must be broken in slowly and carefully monitored when they at first draw fairly innocuous death investigation cases before being allowed to work more difficult and complicated homicide investigations. Training with a formal and directed educational program should not only be initially intensive for new members, but should be a continuing process throughout the assignment of this individual.

HOMICIDE STATISTICS

1)   According to the FBI's *Uniform Crime Reports:*
         a) There is one murder every 25 minutes.
         b) Each year 21,000 murders occur.
         c) Murder makes up 2 percent of the violent crimes.
         d) The highest rates for murder occur in July and December.
         e) Most murders occur during the weekend.
         f) Most murders occur during the evening and night hours.
         g) The residence is the most common murder scene.
         h) Murder is a male-dominated crime.
         i) Fifteen percent of arrested murder suspects are females.

TABLE 1: HOMICIDE VICTIMIZATION, 1950–1999

YEAR	PER 100,000	TOTAL VICTIMS	YEAR	PER 100,000	TOTAL VICTIMS
1950	4.6	7,020	1976	8.8	18,780
1951	4.4	6,820	1977	8.8	19,120
1952	4.6	7,210	1978	9.0	19,560
1953	4.5	7,210	1979	9.7	21,460
1954	4.2	6,850	1978	9.0	19,560
1955	4.1	6,850	1980	0.2	23,040
1956	4.1	6,970	1981	9.8	22,520
1957	4.0	8,060	1982	9.1	21,010
1958	4.8	8,220	1983	8.3	19,310
1959	4.9	8,580	1984	7.9	18,690
1960	5.1	9,110	1985	7.9	18,980
1961	4.8	8,740	1986	8.6	20,610
1962	4.6	8,530	1987	8.3	20,100
1963	4.6	8,640	1988	8.4	20,680
1964	4.9	9,360	1989	8.7	21,500
1965	5.1	9,960	1990	9.4	23,440
1966	5.6	11,040	1991	9.8	24,700
1967	6.2	12,240	1992	9.3	23,760
1968	6.9	13,800	1993	9.5	24,530
1969	7.3	14,760	1994	9.0	23,330
1970	7.9	16,000	1995	8.2	21,610
1971	8.6	17,780	1996	7.4	19,650
1972	9.0	18,670	1997	6.8	18,210
1973	9.4	19,640	1998	6.3	16,910
1974	9.8	20,710	1999	5.7	15,533
1975	9.6	20,510			

Source: FBI, Uniform Crime Reports, 1950–1999.

2)   According to *Report to the Nation on Crime and Justice*, prepared by the Department of Justice in March 1988:
    a) The characteristics of homicide victims include these:
        i) Homicide victims are more often men than women.
        ii) Persons aged 25 to 34 are the most likely homicide victims.
        iii) Blacks are five times more likely than whites to be homicide victims.
    b) The lifetime risk of being a homicide victim is as follows:
        i) White males: 1 out of 179
        ii) Black male: 1 out of 30
        iii) White females: 1 out of 495
        iv) Black females: 1 out of 132
    c) Weapons used:
        i) Firearm: 59 percent
        ii) Handguns: 43 percent
        iii) Knife: 21 percent
        iv) Other: 13 percent

TYPES OF HOMICIDES

1)   The type of homicide is usually associated with the reason an individual was killed, or the motive. These can be numerous, and include the following:
    a) Jealousy
    b) Triangle situations
    c) Sex and sadism
    d) Revenge
    e) Personal gain
    f) Felony murder
    g) Self-defense
    h) Thrill killing
    i) Murder-suicide
    j) Anger
    k) Random killing

2)   Traditionally, the investigation of homicides is painted with a broad brush. That is, all homicides are treated equally. No distinction is made in investigative technique with regard to the various motives. For example, a homicide involving the shooting of a husband by his wife should not be investigated in the same way as a case in which the nude body of a woman is found mutilated along the side of a highway. The various general stages the investigation proceeds through may be similar, but the emphasis and direction of the investigation will vary according to the particular motive for the homicide.

3)   For investigative purposes, the various motives can be subdivided by the investigative techniques employed in making an arrest:
    a) Altercation homicides
        i) Altercation homicides involve the greatest amount of murders in any community. Most often the homicide is associated with a domestic incident between a husband and wife that escalates into an act of violence, ending in the murder of one of the participants. In a small number of these cases, the suspect may follow the initial homicide act by committing suicide.
        ii) Though not domestic in nature, similar circumstances involve acquain-

tances, associates, and friends who get into an argument, ultimately resulting in the death of one of the participants in the argument.

    iii) Altercation homicides are precipitated by an argument where some type of interaction, other than the homicide, occurred between the suspect and the victim. The relationship between the victim and and suspect may be one of the following:

        (1) Spouse

        (2) Common law

        (3) Offspring

        (4) Parent

        (5) Friend

        (6) Girlfriend or boyfriend

        (7) Acquaintance

        (8) Stranger

        (9) Business relation

        (10) Homosexual

        (11) Law enforcement

b) Contract murder

    i) This involves after other motives have been systematically eliminated. A suspect involved in hiring the hit man is usually the individual who has reason for or will benefit from the victim's death. The death may be for financial reasons or love of another.

c) Drug related

    i) Includes the following deaths where any drugs may be involved:

        (1) Robbery of drugs involving a user or dealer

        (2) Death by "hotshot"

        (3) Altered behavior of suspect due to the use of drugs

d) Robbery homicide

    i) This may involve the death of the victim or a suspect involving the commission of a robbery or burglary, including:

        (1) Kidnapping murder

        (2) Taxi driver murder

e) Sexual murder

    i) Includes any murder in which any overtone of the murder involves sex, including:

        (1) Rape

        (2) Lust murder

            (a) Sexual arousal and gratification being integral to the act of homicide

        (3) Serial

            (a) One or more subjects

            (b) Three or more victims

            (c) Three or more events

            (d) Three or more locations

            (e) Cooling-off period evident

            (f) Premeditation

            (g) Planning by the suspect evident

            (h) Suspect's fantasy involved

        (4) Incest

        (5) Homosexuality

         (6) Bondage
         (7) Prostitution
         (8) Necrophilia

f) Miscellaneous murders

    i) This is a catchall term used to explain those cases that do not initially appear to fit under the major classifications. They include the following types:

        (1) Terrorist
        (2) Innocent bystander murder
        (3) Hate crime
        (4) Altered behavior
        (5) Spree
            (a) One or more subjects
            (b) Two or more victims
            (c) One event (short or long in duration)
            (d) Two or more locations
            (e) No cooling-off period
        (6) Euthanasia
        (7) Mass murders
            (a) One subject
            (b) Four or more victims
            (c) One event
            (d) One location
            (e) No cooling-off period
            (f) Victims can be family
        (8) Hunting "accidents" involving shooting deaths
            (a) Many jurisdictions rule the case as a homicide even though the circumstances clearly indicate that it was unintentional.

INVESTIGATING A HOMICIDE

1) As previously stated, three things solve homicides: physical evidence, witness statements, confessions.

2) The homicide detective faces a multitude of duties to perform at the crime scene. Each event needs to be documented according to a routine procedure so that valuable information or observations are not overlooked.

3) Although each homicide is distinctive and unique, there are basic steps to be pursued at all crime scenes. The following checklist was designed to be used for violent deaths. Although extensive, it is not intended to be all inclusive. It is hoped that if the checklist is followed, all violent death investigations will meet minimum standards of competency. It is intended to be used not only as a guide for novice death investigators, but also as a handy checklist and a reminder of things that should be completed in thorough investigations by experienced death investigators.

4) An investigation follows a fairly well-defined, narrowing pattern, beginning with the discovery of the crime and culminating with the prosecution. All homicide investigations should follow an established regimen, known as the *pyramid process*. The following graphics illustrate this investigative procedure and the investigative checklist outlining each segment of the investigation.

WHAT HAPPENED + WHY IT HAPPENED = WHO DID IT

PROSECUTION

CASE
PREPARATION

IDENTIFICATION
AND ARREST

INVESTIGATIVE STAGE

POST-SCENE

THE CRIME SCENE

DISCOVERY OF THE HOMICIDE

The pyramid investigative technique of homicide investigation.

PROSECUTION

CASE PREPARATION
Review Evidence
Final Crime Theory
Reinvestigate
Demonstrative Evidence

IDENTIFICATION
AND ARREST
Bottleneck Case
Negative Evidence
Identification and Arrest of Suspect

INVESTIGATIVE
STAGE
Decedent Identification   Motive
Last-Hours Activities   Profiling
Opportunity   Computer Assistance

POST-SCENE
Cause of Death   Weapon Identification
Evidence Processing   Death Time Frame
Reconstruction   Updated Crime Theory

THE CRIME SCENE
Evidence Collection   Motive Development
Initial Crime Theory   Witness Development
Suspect Development

DISCOVERY OF THE HOMICIDE

DISCOVERY OF THE CRIME

1) Initial receipt of information
   a) Note date and time of original report
   b) Method of transmission
      i) Reporting party (e.g., officer, dispatcher)
      ii) Complete details

2) The crime scene
   a) Every investigation starts by asking this question: what happened?
      i) Begin the investigation by addressing this question. The common misconception on the part of death investigators is to ask who did this? This is wrong and will cause problems in all other areas of the case and will often result in cases going unsolved, being dropped by prosecutors, or having juries acquit the suspect.
      ii) Once the question of what happened is answered, the investigator should be concerned with "why." Why something occurred is establishing the motive of the crime.
      iii) Once you know what happened and why it happened, who did it becomes self-evident.
   b) Types of homicide scenes
      i) Residence
         (1) The preferred type of scene to work. The homicidal events are contained within four walls. The results of blood spatter and firearms are subject to analysis not only with the body but also within the particular areas involved.
         (2) The investigation has a basic, built-in starting point: to whom does this residence belong? Why is this victim in this residence? The scene is contained.
      ii) Vehicle
         (1) Similar to a residence in that the four walls usually contain the actions and their effects. The fact that a dead individual is inside a specific vehicle dictates that the starting points of the investigation are to whom the car belongs and why this subject is in it.
      iii) Outdoors
         (1) Worst-case scenario. Who the person is or why he is at this location is not necessarily related to the circumstances of the homicide. An article found at the scene can be discarded by anyone, not just someone who was part of the incident. Through-and-through bullets are not recovered in a vast majority of cases. Blood spatter and other evidence are affected by weather and other environmental factors. The scene is difficult to contain. The starting point is not well defined because the initial suspect and witnesses can be anyone.

THE CRIME SCENE: EVIDENCE COLLECTION

1) Establish a policy for crime-scene integrity.
   a) Do not touch, move, or alter anything at the scene until further documentation has been completed (observe, describe, record).

b) Do not use any telephone(s) located within the crime-scene area.

c) Coordinate activities at the scene and direct and direct investigators by fixing responsibility for the performance of certain duties.

d) Implement procedures to protect the evidence from damage by weather or exposure and the presence of police and other personnel.

e) Do not allow smoking by anyone at the crime scene.

f) Do not turn water on or off. Do not flush toilets. Do not use any facilities within the scene.

g) Consider obtaining a search warrant or consulting with the prosecuting attorney when needed for appropriate retrieval of evidence.

2)   Arrival at the homicide scene

       a) Record exact time of arrival.

       b) Record the exact address of the crime scene.

       c) Record the outside weather/temperature conditions.

       d) If outdoor scene, record outside lighting conditions.

       e) Interview the first officer and other police personnel at the scene to determine the sequence of events since their arrival. Include the following:

            i) Crime discovered by

            ii) Date and time of initial call

            iii) Complete details of first responding units

       f) Determine the scope of the patrol officer's initial investigation at the scene. Include the following:

            i) Protection of the crime scene

            ii) Notifications, alarms, Be On the Look-Out teletypes (BOLOs)

            iii) Preliminary investigative results

       g) Identify people who have been at the scene, including the following:

            i) Police officers and other law enforcement personnel

            ii) Ambulance and/or emergency personnel

            iii) Family (next of kin) and/or relatives and friends of the victim

            iv) Witnesses (keep key witnesses separated)

       h) Obtain victim information, including these:

            i) Name

            ii) Address

            iii) Sex and race

            iv) Date of birth and age

       i) Ascertain the location and number of victims.

       m) If this is a multiple murder, establish separate case numbers and provide for additional documentation.

       j) Have the responding patrol officer or crime-scene technician personally escort you through the scene to the body by a path least likely to destroy or disturb evidence.

       k) Consider wearing protective clothing, including:

            i) Shoe booties, especially if blood is present on the floor. Not only will it prevent the officer from tracking a biohazard into his vehicle, office, and home, but it may also be used to prevent inadvertent contamination of the scene by adding a bloody footprint(s) from one of the scene investigators.

            ii) Disposable coveralls

            iii) Latex gloves

            iv) Breathing filtered mask

            v) Eye protection

l) Record any alterations to the crime scene that are made as a matter of investigative necessity, emergency police response, or by emergency medical personnel. Consider these:

      i) Are lights turned on or off?

      ii) Are doors opened, closed, locked, unlocked, or broken?

      iii) Is the body moved from its original position?

      iv) What are the names of all parties who moved the body prior to and during the police presence at the scene?

      v) Are windows opened, closed, locked, unlocked, or broken?

      vi) Is any furniture moved?

      vii) Are any articles touched?

      viii) If appropriate, is the gas turned on or off?

      ix) Are any appliances running or on?

      x) If vehicles are involved, is the engine on or off?

      xi) Is the motor cold, cool, warm, or hot?

IMPLEMENT CRIME-SCENE CONTROL PROCEDURES

1) Determine the scope of and assess the general crime scene.

2) Identify and establish correct perimeters for the scene.

3) If the scene has been initially roped off or barricaded by first-responding patrol units, reevaluate and redo, if necessary.

4) Perimeters should be established by identifying the farthest reaches of evidence associated with the incident and then increase this area by 50 percent.

5) Establish outside and inside perimeters allowing only authorized personnel within each section.

    a) The inside perimeter is the immediate area associated with the body and other critical evidence.

    b) The outside perimeter is away from the critical processing area and is used to contain some of the police and other assisting personnel not really associated with the processing of the crime scene.

6) Assign patrol officers as needed to effectively safeguard the scene.

7) Update and expand crime-scene protection as necessary.

    a) Is this a multiple scene?

    b) Are there additional areas to protect?

    c) Establish a single path of entry and exit to the crime scene.

8) Implement procedures to safeguard all evidence found at the scene prior to collection.

9) Allow no entry to the crime scene except to authorized personnel who have a legitimate purpose for being at the scene (part of the crime-scene processing or associated with the actual investigation).

10) Initiate a crime-scene log.

    a) Assign a police officer to record people present at the scene. Include the following:

      i) Police officers and other law enforcement personnel.
      ii) Ambulance or emergency personnel
      iii) Family (closest next of kin) or relatives and friends of the victim.
      iv) All personnel and civilians involved in the investigation of the crime scene.
      v) Witnesses, including persons detained by the patrol officer(s).
          (1) Key witnesses should be separated.
      vi) Provide for witness security and availability.
      vii) Record arrival and departure times of all officials (e.g., medical examiner personnel, state attorney personnel, crime scene technicians).

11)   The crime-scene log should be delivered to the detective assigned to the case upon the release of the crime scene.

ESTABLISH A COMMAND POST OR TEMPORARY HEADQUARTERS

1)   Select a location out of the crime scene, preferably with two phones, one for outgoing telephone calls and one for incoming telephone calls.

2)   Notify communications or the station house of the telephone numbers established at the command post to facilitate communications between the various units concerned.

3)   Make notifications as necessary from this location including, but not limited to these:
      a) Crime-scene technicians
      b) Medical examiner or representative
      c) Additional investigators or law enforcement personnel
      d) State attorney's office
      e) Forensic anthropologist
      f) Tracker dogs

CRIME-SCENE PROCESSING

1)   The crime-scene search should not be undertaken until all photographs, sketches, measurements, dusting for prints, and written documentation have been completed (except in emergency situations).

CRIME-SCENE PHOTOGRAPHS

1)   The following photographs should be taken of the scene as soon as possible:
      a) Photos of the entire location where the homicide occurred
      b) Photos, including aerial photographs, of contiguous areas and sites
      c) Photographs (surreptitious) of the crowd or any bystanders
      d) Photos of all evidence at the scene
      e) Photos of suspect(s) or witnesses, if applicable
        i) Photos of suspect's clothing and shoes
        ii) Photos of any injuries (e.g., body, face, hands)

2)   Do not add any chalk marks or markers prior to taking the original crime-scene photographs. Markers can be added later on for close-up shots.

3)   Take photographs of general items and areas, working the camera into closer, specific shots.

4) Document crime-scene photographs by recording the following:
   a) Date and time photos are taken
   b) Exact location of photographs
   c) Description of item photographed
   d) Compass direction (north, south, east, or west)
   e) Focus distance
   f) Type of film and camera used
   g) Lights and weather conditions
   h) Number of exposures
   i) Identification of photographers

5) Eliminate extraneous objects, including any police equipment.

6) Show the relationship of the scene to its surroundings.

7) Outdoor scenes
   a) Photograph fixed objects as they relate to the scene at eye level.

8) Indoor scenes
   a) Photograph objects in the room such as doors and windows to "fix" the body and objects to the crime scene.

9) Use special photography equipment as needed.

10) Recommended crime-scene photographs:
   a) Front entrance of the building
   b) Entrance to the room or apartment where the deceased is found
   c) Two full-body views
   d) A general view of the body and crime scene from a 360-degree perspective
   e) A close-up shot of the body
   f) Photos of any visible wounds
   g) If body has been removed, photographs of the body's original location
   h) Photos of possible entrance or escape routes used
   i) Areas where any force used for entry or exit
   j) Area and close-up views of any physical evidence, such as bloodstains, weapons, shell casings, hairs, fibers, etc.
   k) Blood spatter with and without a ruler present
   l) Fingerprints (plastic, bloodstained, and latents), as well as any lifts, before removal of body
   m) Additional photographs after the body has been moved
      i) Areas beneath the body
      ii) Any additional evidence found beneath the body

CRIME-SCENE SKETCH

1) Make a simple line drawing of the crime scene, either in the investigative notebook or on a separate sheet of paper. The following information should be included:
   a) Measurements and distance
   b) A title block consisting of these:
      i) Name and title of sketcher
      ii) Date and time the sketch was made

iii) Classification of the crime
iv) Identification of the victim(s)
v) Agency's case number(s)
vi) Names of any persons assisting in taking measurements
vii) Precise address of the location sketched and compass north indication
viii) A legend to identify any objects or articles in scene
ix) A scale to depict measurements used

THE CRIME-SCENE SEARCH

1) Establish the perimeters of the crime scene and document this location by crime-scene photographs and sketches, including written documentation.

2) Reconstruct aspects of the crime in formulating the search.

3) Consult with the prosecuting attorney to obtain the legal basis for any search prior to the seizure of any evidence.

4) Visibly locate any physical evidence and determine which evidence should be gathered before any destruction or alteration takes place.

5) Establish the method of search based on your investigative theory, size of the area to be searched, and any other factors that arise while conducting this phase of the inquiry.

6) Areas that should be carefully examined:
   a) The point of entry
   b) The escape route
   c) The suspect, including his clothing and areas of injuries
   d) The location where any physical evidence or weapons may be located
   e) Contents of any trash cans
   f) Any vehicle used in the crime
   g) The suspect's residence
   h) The location where the actual assault leading to the death took place
   i) Location from which the body was moved
   j) Any area that appears to be disturbed or altered

DUST FOR FINGERPRINTS

1) Note that some areas to be processed may require the use of such chemical reagents as luminol, ninhydrin, cynoacrylate, or Amido black to effectively obtain latent print evidence. All involved parties sharing responsibility for processing the scene should consider any options associated with any choice of processing methods, especially if there is any potential risk for the destruction of evidence whenever chemical processing is a viable consideration.

2) The following areas should be processed for latent prints:
   a) Areas associated with the suspect's entry and exit
   b) Weapons or objects that may have been handled by the suspect. Consider these:
      i) Door handles
      ii) Faucets
      iii) Telephones
      iv) Windows

v) Glasses
vi) Light switches
vii) Newly damaged areas
viii) Objects that may have caused injuries or death
ix) Objects missing or moved from their original locations
x) Body, if appropriate

WITNESS DEVELOPMENT

1) Identify witnesses who may have information about the incident, victim, or suspect.
 a) Emergency medical personnel
  i) If emergency medical personnel were present before the investigator's arrival, determine if the crew or anyone else moved the body or any other items within the crime scene. If the scene or body has been altered in any way, note the following:
   (1) When were the alterations made?
   (2) What was the purpose of the movement?
   (3) What were the original positions, and where was the body or other items moved?
   (4) Identify the person who made the alterations.
   (5) Establish the time of death pronounced by emergency medical personnel.
 b) Canvass
  i) Canvass the immediate area, including possible escape route, by assigning sufficient personnel to locate any witnesses or persons who may have information about the homicide or death.
  ii) Assign a supervisor or coordinator to organize the canvass.
  iii) Use canvass control sheets.
  iv) Ensure that canvassers are provided with all information from the investigation and scene so that they may properly solicit information from prospective witnesses.
  v) If the circumstances warrant it, consider using a photograph taken of the victim while he was still alive.
  vi) Use the canvass questionnaire form and require official reports from canvassers indicating the following:
   (1) Negative locations (with no results and where no one is home)
   (2) Locations that have been canvassed, indicating number of persons residing therein
   (3) Positive locations for possible follow-up and a reinterview
   (4) Information relating to the incident being canvassed

2) Have investigators check vehicles and record registration numbers of autos in the immediate area.

SUSPECT DEVELOPMENT

1) Suspect at the scene
 a) If the suspect is arrested and present at the scene, make sure that he is immediately removed from the crime scene and not returned to the scene under any circumstances. Secure the clothing of the suspect. This procedure is necessary to prevent crime-scene contamination.

b) Safeguard all evidence found on the suspect, including blood, weapons debris, soil, proceeds of crime, etc.

c) Ensure that the suspect does not change clothes, wash his hands, or engage in any conduct that may alter or destroy evidence.

d) Record any spontaneous statements made by the suspect.

e) Do not permit any conversation between the suspect and any parties present.

f) Note any injuries to the suspect.

g) If the suspect is in custody at the scene and circumstances indicate that immediate interrogation of the suspect would be beneficial to the investigation, the following steps should be taken:

i) Advise the suspect of his rights under the Miranda ruling prior to any custodial interrogation (this should be done from a Miranda rights card or form, as dictated by department policy).

ii) Determine if the suspect is capable of understanding and fully understands his rights under Miranda.

iii) Obtain an intelligent waiver (by department policy) of these rights from the suspect prior to any questioning.

iv) Document this procedure in the investigative notebook.

v) Allow the suspect to make a full statement.

vi) Record this statement in writing and have the suspect sign it.

vii) Record the suspect's statement pursuant to departmental or task force policy, or after consultation with the prosecuting attorney (e.g., written, tape-recorded, court reporter).

viii) Keep the suspect isolated at all times from other suspects, witnesses, prisoners, and any other personnel not connected with the investigation.

ix) Advise any officers responsible for the transporting of the suspect not to engage the suspect in any conversation or questioning. However, if during transport the suspectmakes a statement, the officers should document this information, verbatim.

x) If the suspect is transported to the police station, he should be placed in a separate holding cell.

xi) Alibi statements should be documented and recorded in the investigator's notebook.

xii) Any self-serving or negative statements should also be recorded and documented in the event the suspect later changes his story.

MOTIVE DEVELOPMENT

1) Establish the best possible motive for the death to have occurred.
   a) Drug-related
   b) Other felony
   c) Hate/revenge
   d) Money/financial gain
   e) Sexual
   f) Terrorist/political
   g Gang
   h) Religious/ritual
   i) Racial
   j) Random

THE POST-SCENE INVESTIGATION

1) Cause of death
    a) Cause of death established through autopsy
    b) Medical examiner at the scene
        i) Record the time of arrival of the medical examiner.
        ii) Obtain a preliminary estimate on the time of death.
        iii) Obtain a preliminary cause of death after conferring with the medical examiner.
        iv) Obtain a preliminary opinion as to the possible weapon used to inflict the injuries to the decedent.
        v) Is there any weapon present that may be consistent with the suspected weapon?

    c) Description of the deceased
        i) A complete description of the body should be documented in the investigator's notes, including the following information:
            (1) The position of the body
            (2) Sex
            (3) Race
            (4) Appearance
            (5) Age
            (6) Build
            (7) Color of hair
            (8) Description of clothing
            (9) Presence or absence of any jewelry
            (10) Evidence of any injuries (e.g., bruises, bite marks, wounds, binding marks).
            (11) Condition of the body, including:
                (a) Livor mortis
                (b) Rigor mortis
                 (c) Decomposition (describe in detail)
                (d) Blood description including wet/dry status
                (e) Insect activity
                (f) Putrefacation
        ii) Is the condition of the body consistent with the known facts of the case?
        iii) Note and record (through observation and photographs) the condition of the victim's hands and feet for signs of evidence (e.g., defensive marks, hair, fibers, blood transfer).
        iv) What is the condition of the victim's pockets?
        v) What is the victim's apparent cause of death?
            (1) Gunshot wound
            (2) Stab wound
            (3) Blunt trauma
            (4) Strangulation
            (5) Burn
            (6) Poison
            (7) Asphyxiation/smother/suffocation
        vi) Arrange for transportation of the body.
        vii) Bag the decedent's hands with paper bags (not plastic) to preserve any trace evidence under the fingernails.
        viii) Use a new or laundered sheet to wrap the body prior to removal.

2)   Weapon identification
  a) If a weapon is found at the scene, do the following:
   i) Record where the weapon is located.
   ii) Safeguard the weapon for forensic identification.
   iii) Have the weapon photographed before further examination.
   iv) Determine if there is any blood or other trace evidence on the weapon.
   v) Determine if the weapon is from the premises.
   vi) Are the wounds consistent with the weapon?
   iv) Weapon identification verified through autopsy and crime lab examination.
    (1) If the weapon used in the homicide is missing and the suspect denies knowing anything about this weapon, listen closely to his explanation of his activities immediately after the homicide. The suspect will tell the interviewer of some place he traveled to that, if carefully considered, is not consistent with accepted activity. Look for the weapon at this location. The suspect feels compelled to rectify the possibility of the investigator's receiving information that he was at this location. The suspect takes the opportunity of the interview to insert a proactive excuse for being at this location. Although he may be cooperating with the police and admitting to some involvement with the homicide, the suspect will never totally implicate himself. For example, the suspect tells the interviewer that after he left the scene of the homicide his vehicle broke down on a bridge, but he was able to restart the vehicle and continue his drive home. The investigator should look for the murder weapon under the bridge.

  b) Firearms
   i) Do not attempt to unload.
   ii) Consider having the suspect's hands examined for the presence of gunshot residue analysis.
   iii) Are there any shell casings present?
   iv) Are any bullet holes or spent rounds?
   v) Determine how many shots were fired.
   vi) What is the position of rounds (live, spent, and misfires) within the revolver?
   vii) Is the safety on or off?
   viii) Is firearm loaded or unloaded? Is a live round chambered in the weapon?

3)   Time frame of death
  a) Time frame involving death as established through scene investigation, case development and autopsy examination
  b) Begin the investigation by establishing when the body was found and when the decedent was last known to be alive. This is the beginning window of establishing the time frame of the death.
  c) Other considerations that are less reliable:
   i) Rigor mortis
   ii) Livor mortis
   iii) Algor mortis (body temperature)
   iv) Stomach digestion

4)   Evidence processing
  a) All evidence collected at the crime scene(s), related areas, and body should be submitted for processing at the crime laboratory.

b) Developed latents should be submitted into AFIS.

c) All seroligical evidence should be submitted into CODIS (Combined DNA Index System).

5) Reconstruction components of the scene

    a) This involves a total analysis and understanding of what transpired by considering not only what is discovered but also what is missing.

    b) This requires the investigator to consider the operation, function, or behavior of such biological specimens (e.g., blood) and such objects as firearms and glass and how this behavior can be analyzed to explain what may have occurred, as well as what did not occur.

    c) The investigator attempts to establish the sequence of events by examining blood-stains, skid marks, tire treads, bullet holes in glass, fingerprints, and other evidence.

    d) The following questions must be answered before you can understand what may have happened.

        i) What are the major elements of the crime scene and the victim profile?

        ii) What is the extent of the crime scene?

            (1) How many locations are involved?

            (2) What is the time frame in which the crime occurred?

            (3) What were the locations and activities of the suspect and the victim at the time of the initial contact?

        iii) What is the motive of the crime?

        iv) What are the tools or weapons used?

            (1) What type of weapon was used?

            (2) What is the likelihood of associating the suspect with the crime?

            (3) What was the extent of force used (e.g., ligatures, degree of control, choice of weapon)?

        v) What are the motions, positions, and actions of the victim and the suspect?

            (1) Did the suspect lie in wait?

            (2) Did the suspect know the activities and schedule of the victim?

            (3) Did the suspect have other knowledge of the victim that implied familiarity?

            (4) Does evidence imply any physical characteristics of the perpetrator?

            (5) Was contact between the victim and the suspect prolonged or brief?

        vi) Was anything taken from the scene by the suspect or left behind belonging to the perpetrator?

        vii) Have you sought every alternative to the most obvious reconstruction, even if it seems implausible?

6) Updated crime theory

    a) Update the initial crime theory (what happened) based on the information being generated through the reconstruction of the crime scene and processing of the evidence.

INVESTIGATIVE STAGE

1) Decedent identification

    a) Little can be accomplished from an investigative standpoint until such time as the decedent is identified. Once the individual has been identified, then the activities of that person can be developed.

2)   Last-hour activities of decedent
        a) Knowing he last hour activities of the decedent can help identify individuals who had access to or were in the company of the decedent shortly before his death (i.e, opportunity). Unless proven otherwise, the last person who was with the decedent prior to his death is initially the investigator's best suspect.

3)   Development of motive
        a) With the discovery of the reason why (motive) the subject was murdered, the development of a suspect begins.

4)   Development of opportunity
        a) As you develop possible suspects, determining who had access (or opportunity) to commit the murder will eliminate some possibilities and solidify others.

5)   Computer assistance
        a) Consider using computer-assisted programs available to investigators in tracking leads, organizing homicides, supplying an inventory for processed evidence, and linking the information to other cases.
        b) Consider using Violent Criminal Apprehension Program (VICAP) for developing other cases that may be similar in other jurisdictions.

6)   Profiling of case
        a) Seek profiling assistance in cases involving the following:
            i) Sadistic torture in sexual assaults
            ii) Evisceration
            iii) Postmortem slashing and cutting
            iv) Motiveless fire setting
            v) Lust and mutilation murders
                (1) Ritualistic crimes
                (2) Rapes

IDENTIFICATION AND ARREST

1)   Bottleneck case
        a) The investigation up to this point consists of a vast amount of collected information. The investigator now directs the investigation, or bottlenecks the case, toward the suspect, who should be obvious.

2)   Negative evidence
        a) The investigation continues by following through on information developed regarding alibis, self-defense possibilities, and whether the intent of the suspect was influenced by his mental state or the use of drugs or alcohol. Checking the decedent's criminal background and prior associations with the suspect could also prove useful.
            i) Organized criminals have a "golden rule" involving old homicides: The death of a victim in an old homicides is always blamed on an ex-con who has died.
            ii) Check out the veracity of witnesses' statements.
            iii) Arrest suspect(s) and accomplices (if any).
                (1) Probable cause should now be sufficient to arrest the suspect.

CASE PREPARATION

1) Reinvestigate as necessary.
   a) Loose ends need to be tied together at this point in preparation for trial.

2) Review evidence.
   a) The evidence and its analysis should be reviewed to determine the significance of each piece of evidence.

3) Finalizel crime theory.
   a) What happened, how it occurred, when it happened, what was the motive, who was involved, and what were their activities should all be considered with regard to statements, confessions, and physical evidence.
   b) Demonstrative evidence is prepared.
      i) Professionally prepare any exhibits, models, and photographs to be used during the trial, which will simplify and make understandable investigative aspects about the case.

PROSECUTION OF THE CASE

1) The investigation should be conducted as a pyramid process, with the top of the pyramid associated with the prosecution of the person who is responsible for the murder. This is the ultimate goal of any investigation. As with any building process, the top tier can only be as strong as each successive layer. The entire building's strength is directly related to the strength of the foundation (crime-scene processing).

2) It's not what you think; it's not what you know. It's not what you suspect; it's what you can prove!

CHAPTER 20: ALTERCATION HOMICIDES

CONSIDERATION

1) Altercation homicides occur as a result of an altercation, argument, disagreement, or fight between the victim and the suspect.

2) This is the most common and the most easily solved type of homicide because the development of a motive will usually produce a suspect.

3) The difficult cases are ones in which the suspect attempts to conceal what has occurred by altering the circumstances of the homicide, for example:
   a) The body of a spouse or mate is discovered in a vehicle after being reported missing. The vehicle is recovered in a fairly public area.
   b) The companion is reported to have been shot after an accidental discharge of a firearm.
   c) The victim is reported to have committed suicide.
   d) The victim is reported to have been killed as an act of self-defense.
   e) Victim is found dead at home or office, an apparent victim of a home or business burglary turned homicide.
   f) The victim is reported missing, with foul play suspected. No body has been recovered.
   g) The victim's body is found dumped or buried, but he had not been reported missing by his companion.

4) These types of homicides include all domestic homicides and may include the decedent and the suspect in various relationships, including:
   a) Decedent versus spouse
      i) Common law
      ii) Offspring
      iii) Parent
      iv) Friend
      v) Girlfriend/boyfriend
      v) Acquaintance
      vi) Stranger
      vii) Business relation
      viii) Homosexual companion

PRIMARY FOCUS OF THE INVESTIGATION

1) Investigator is faced with three possibilities in investigating an altercation type of homicide.
   a) The suspect admits to the killing.
   b) The suspects admits to the killing but indicates it was a result of self-defense or some other less culpable type of activity.
   c) The suspect denies the killing, blaming it on some other suspect or factors.

2) Reconstruction of what occurred is critical. Preservation of the scene is necessary to correctly analyze and understand the significance of the following:
   a) Blood spatter

      b) Gunshot wounds and trajectories
      c) Gunshot powder
      d) Footprints
      e) Fingerprints

3)   Develop motive.

4)   Eliminate accident and suicide possibilities.

5)   Eliminate other homicide motives, including drug, robbery, and sex.

NOTIFICATION

1)   An on-call pathologist notification is optional unless:
      a) Conflicting information is developed concerning the reported incident.
      b) Reconstruction of the events is paramount in understanding what may have occurred.
      c) Time frame with regard to the death appears important.
      d) Insight into the type of weapon used would assist investigators at the scene.

SCENE PHOTOGRAPHS

1)   Follow the death-scene photographic guidelines for homicides. In addition, pay particular attention to the following.
      a) The extent of the crime scene. Cover all areas that appear to be involved in the assault.
      b) Photograph any indications or inconsistencies of time frame associated with the incident and death.
         i) Meal preparations
         ii) Interruption of victim's activities
         iii) Newspaper present/uncollected
      c) Photograph any area in which it appears the initial contact between the involved parties may have occurred.
      d) Show the area, through photographs, as being:
         i) Remote
         ii) In public view
         iii) Concealed or hidden
      e) Photograph any blood spatter that may indicate the movements or activities of the participants.
      f) Photograph areas where shell casings, live rounds, or expended projectiles have been recovered.
      g) Photograph any possible weapons found at the scene.
         i) Do not neglect other weapons or potential weapons at the scene, which may become significant as the investigation progresses.
            (1) Knives
            (2) Blunt objects (e.g., bats, canes, pipes, hammers, ashtrays).
            (3) Firearms
            (4) Ligatures
      h) Photograph any indications of a struggle, including:
         i) Broken glass
         ii) Overturned furniture
         iii) Restraints

i) Photograph any areas indicating a possible forced entry.

j) Photograph any indications of a robbery, including:

    i) Rifled drawers, cash boxes, jewelry boxes, etc.

    ii) Pockets turned inside-out

    iii) Contents of wallets or purses strewn about

    iv) Jewelry missing from the victim

k) Photograph any indications of drugs, drug paraphernalia, or alcohol containers.

l) Photograph any indications of the number of people who may have been present, including, for example:

    i) Drinking glasses, plate settings, etc.

m) Photograph the body. Include these:

    i) Any blood spatter present

    ii) Disturbance to clothing after bloodletting, unconsciousness, or death

    iii) Movement of body after death

    iv) Pockets turned inside out or jewelry obviously missing

    v) Wounds

SCENE INVESTIGATION

1) On a case where the suspect may have attempted to mislead the investigators, examine the scene and body to determine whether the assault appears personal or anonymous. For comparison, are the events of the incident as told by the possible suspect indicative of a personal or anonymous assault?

2) Reconstruction is critical.

a) Determine the activities and the movements of the participants.

    i) Interpret blood spatter.

    ii) Interpret gunpowder residue.

    iii) Interpret bullet trajectories and recoveries.

    iv) Note locations of recovered casings.

    v) Note locations of footprints.

    vi) Note locations of recovered latent prints.

    vii) Note location of overturned furniture.

    viii) Note location of broken glass.

b) Any indication that the perpetrator was lying in wait for the victim?

c) Does the scene indicate whether the attack was rapid or prolonged?

d) Can any conclusions be drawn from this assault about the suspect's stature?

3) Determine the possible weapon(s) used in the assault.

a) Was weapon brought to the scene or normally kept at the incident location?

b) Does the weapon have everyday household functions not normally associated with a murder weapon?

c) Was weapon left at the scene?

d) Where is the weapon normally kept?

e) Did use of the weapon require the suspect to be in close contact with the victim or at a distance?

4) Was anything taken from the scene? What is the status of victim's possessions, such as:

a) Vehicle

b) Jewelry

> c) Credit cards
> d) Wallet or purse
> e) Money
> f) Checkbook

5) Develop a time frame for the incident.
   a) Condition of the body
   b) Scene indicators
      i) Preparation of meals
      ii) Interruption of activities
      iii) Newspapers present/uncollected

6) Body examination
   a) Is there any indication the body may have been undressed or redressed after bloodletting, unconsciousness, or death?
   b) Is there any indication decedent may have received any observed injuries postmortem?

BODY TRANSPORT FROM SCENE

1) Bag (paper) the decedent's hands and transport to the MEO/morgue.

2) If blood spatter may be significant in this particular case, precautionary measures should be taken to preserve the spatter on the decedent's clothing.

BODY PROCESSING AT THE MEO/MORGUE

1) Examine the body closely. Look for tan lines, pale areas, or abrasions where a watch, ring, or necklace may have been prior to or during the incident.

2) Examine the clothing for tears, missing buttons, or any other indications of a struggle.
   a) Separately bag each item of clothing after it has been air-dried.

3) If this is a gunshot case:
   a) X-ray the area of the body involved.
   b) Complete a neutron-activation swabbing of decedent's hands.
   c) Collect the projectile.

4) Collect major case prints, including palm prints.

5) Collect a tube of blood.

6) If evidence suggests that the decedent may have been in a close physical confrontation with his assailant, collect fingernail scrapings and clippings.

FOLLOW-UP INVESTIGATION

1) Develop complete background information on victim.
   a) Who had a reason to kill this person?
   b) Sources:
      i) Family members

ii) Business associates
iii) Neighbors
iv) Other associates and friends
v) Courthouse records
vi) Criminal records

2)   Develop complete background of possible suspect(s).
        a) Sources:
            i) Family members
            ii) Business associates
            iii) Neighbors
            iv) Other associates and friends
            v) Courthouse records
            vi) Criminal records

3)   Types of information to develop:
        a) Length of association between victim and suspect
        b) Type of association between suspect and victim
        c) Problems in this relationship
            i) Previous threats
            ii) Previous assaultive behavior
            iii) Previous visits to this location by the police
            iv) Court actions filed or anticipated to be filed
            v) Lovers' triangle

4)   Tracing of weapon, purchase of ammunition, etc., (if applicable)

5)   Trace the activities of the suspect and victim leading up to the homicide.

CHAPTER 21: CONTRACT MURDERS

CONSIDERATIONS

1) A contract murder is usually committed through a third party for the purpose of improving a suspect's financial or domestic situation.

2) The motive in a contract murder is usually developed during the course of an investigation and is often not suspected during the initial processing of the scene. In spite of this, investigation will not be hindered with a thorough processing of the scene.

3) Caution should be taken in a suspected contract murder when dealing with the family until the family members or their associates can be excluded as potential suspects.

4) Initial suspicion of a contract murder usually results from information received by the police. Investigators should suspect contract murder if there are no indicators of other possible motives present at the death scene.

5) In financially based contract murders, you should consider not only the financial status of the decedent at death, but also the net worth or financial status of the decedent's estate, including life insurance policies, business assets, and other properties.

6) A contract murder case may start to develop in three different ways:
   a) The homicide scene appears exceptionally well organized. The suspect appears l knowedgeable about what he is doing.
   b) The missing person, fairly prominent, is found dead.
   c) The follow-up investigation has eliminated all other motives. The most logical motive appearsto be that the victim's death served to benefit another person.

PRIMARY FOCUS OF INVESTIGATION

1) Opportunity on the part of the person suspected of arranging the murder is of less importance in the majority of murder-for-hire cases because another party will have actually committed the murder. The suspect will normally have a great alibi, proving that he could not have been at the scene at the time of the murder. Therefore, investigators can usually establish the time frame of the decedent's death from the suspect's alibi.

2) Develop all sources of money. Include life insurance policies, stocks and bonds, savings accounts, checking accounts, businesses, etc.

3) Follow the money! Investigation should concentrate on who would benefit from the subject's death.

4) Detail all indications that the homicide was planned.
   a) Use of keys
   b) Items used to control victim that may have been brought to scene (duct tape, rope, etc.)
   c) Execution-style method of killing the victim
   d) Type of weapon used to kill the victim

      e) Interruption of the subject's activities at an opportune time
           i) The subject was the most vulnerable.
           ii) The subject was the most isolated.
           iii) The subject was made to go to a location where he would be isolated or vulnerable.

5) Develop who had knowledge of the decedent's activities and habits, and who had access to areas in which the decedent was found.

6) Document problems that may have been solved in the event of the decedent's death.

7) Develop associates of the decedent's who may have been responsible for requesting the contract murder.

NOTIFICATION

1) If a contract murder is suspected, a major case squad should be initialized.

2) A forensic pathologist/medical examiner should be requested at the scene.

3) There should be full-lab capabilities.

SCENE PHOTOGRAPHS

1) Follow the death-scene photographic guidelines for the particular situation of the case. In addition, give particular attention to the following:
      a) Overall of area
           i) Include aerial photographs.
           ii) Take photographs that demonstrate the area to be:
                (1) Remote
                (2) In public view
                (3) Concealed
           iii) Show all areas thought to be involved in the assault.
           iv) Photograph any area depicting the origin of or the initial contact of the involved parties.
      b) Photograph any blood spatter that indicates movement of the participants.
      c) Photograph signs of a struggle, as opposed to an execution-style homicide.
      d) Photograph areas where expended shell casings are found.
      e) Photograph any indications or inconsistencies of time frame associated with the incident and death:
           i) Meal preparations
           ii) Interruption of victim's activities
           iii) Newspaper present/uncollected
      f) Photograph any possible weapons found at the scene.
           i) It is important not to neglect other weapons or potential weapons also noted at the scene; these may become significant as the investigation progresses.
                (1) Knives
                (2) Blunt objects (e.g., bats, canes, pipes, hammers, ashtrays)
                (3) Firearms
                (4) Ligatures

g) Photograph any indications of a struggle, including:
    i) Broken glass
    ii) Overturned furniture
    iii) Restraints
h) Photograph any areas indicating a possible forced entry.
i) Photograph any indications of a robbery.
    i) Rifled drawers, cash boxes, jewelry boxes
    ii) Pockets turned inside-out
    iii) Contents of wallets or purses strewn about
    iv) Jewelry missing from the victim.
j) Photograph any indications of drugs, drug paraphernalia, or alcohol containers.
k) Photograph any indications of the number of people who may have been present, including:
    i) Drinking glasses or plate settings
l) Photograph the body, including:
    i) Any blood spatter present
    ii) Disturbance to clothing after bloodletting, unconsciousness, or death
        (1) Out-of-place or inappropriate placement of clothing
        (2) Torn clothing
        (3) Missing or torn-off buttons
    iii) Movement of body after death
    iv) Pockets turned inside-out or jewelry obviously missing
    v) Wounds

SCENE INVESTIGATION

1) Identify the decedent.

2) Is a residence, business, or vehicle involved?
    a) Who owns residence, business, or vehicle?
    b) Are there survivors/witnesses?
    c) Why was decedent at this location?
    d) What is the time frame when the decedent was at this location?
        i) Condition of the body
        ii) Scene indicators
            (1) Preparation of meals
            (2) Interruption of activities
            (3) Newspapers present/uncollected

3) Reconstruction
    a) Determine the activities and movements of the participants.
        i) Interpret blood spatter.
            (1) Examine for transfer patterns that may have been made by the suspect.
            (2) Consider the possibility and process blood present at the scene that may have originated from the suspect.
        ii) Interpret gunpowder residue.
        iii) Interpret bullet trajectories and recoveries.
        iv) Note locations of recovered casings.
        v) Note locations of footprints.

vi) Note locations of recovered latent prints.
vii) Note locations of overturned furniture.
viii) Note locations of broken glass.
b) Is there any indication that the perpetrator lay in wait for the victim?
c) Does the scene indicate if the attack was rapid or prolonged?
d) Can any conclusions be drawn about the suspect's stature (e.g., height of blood spatter, control of victim) with regard to this assault?

4) Evidence of struggle?
a) Overturned furniture
b) Broken glass
c) Torn clothing, missing buttons, etc.

5) Determine any areas of physical evidence that the suspect(s) may have caused or come into contact with during the incident.

6) Determine the possible weapon(s) used in the assault.
a) Was the weapon brought to the scene or normally kept at the scene of the crime?
b) Does the weapon have an everyday household function not normally associated with a murder weapon?
c) Was the weapon left at the scene?
d) Where is the weapon normally kept?
e) Did use of the weapon require the suspect to be in close contact with the victim or at a distance?
f) Note the number, caliber, and location of all casings found at the scene.

7) Examine the body of the decedent.
a) Note any areas of injury indicative of torture or beating that may have been made while trying to get information from the victim or establish control.
b) Interpret blood spatter on the body or clothing of the decedent.
c) Is there any indication the body may have been undressed or redressed after bloodletting, unconsciousness, or death?
d) Is there any indication that the decedent may have received any of the injuries postmortem?

8) Was anything taken from the scene? What is the status of victim's possessions, such as:
a) Vehicle
b) Jewelry
c) Credit cards
d) Wallet or purse
e) Money
f) Checkbook

BODY TRANSPORT FROM SCENE

1) Bag (paper) the decedent's hands and transport to the MEO.

2) If blood spatter is present and may turn out to be significant in this case, precautionary measures should be taken to preserve the spatter on the decedent's clothing.

BODY PROCESSING AT THE MEO/MORGUE

1) Examine the body closely. Look for tan lines, pale areas, or abrasions where a watch, ring, or necklace may have been prior to or during the incident.

2) Examine the clothing for tears, missing buttons, or any other indications of a struggle.
  a) Separately bag each item of clothing after it has air-dried.

3) If a gunshot case:
  a) X-ray the area of the body involved.
  b) Complete a neutron-activation swabbing of decedent's hands.
  c) Collect the projectile.

4) Collect major case prints, including palm prints.

5) Collect a tube of blood.

6) If evidence suggests that the decedent may have been in a close physical confrontation with the assailant, collect fingernail scrapings and clippings.

FOLLOW-UP INVESTIGATION

1) Identify all sources of financial worth involving the decedent.
  a) Insurance policies
    i) Check for the following:
      1) Life insurance
      2) Key-man insurance policy
      3) Credit life policies
    ii) Develop insurance information, including:
      (1) Date of issue
      (2) Face amount of policy
    iii) Any riders or exclusions to the policy
      (1) Accidental death benefits (double indemnity): the policy pays twice the face amount if death is classified as an accident or a homicide.
      (2) Suicide clause: policy will not pay if subject's death is determined to be a suicide.
(3) Beneficiary of the policy
  b) Personal property
    i) Real estate, including homes
    ii) Vehicles
    iii) Stocks, bonds, bank accounts
      (1) Any suits and judgments?
      (2) Any tax liens or IRS investigation?
    iv) Businesses and partnerships

2) Develop complete domestic history.
  a) Background and status of marriage(s)
    i) Date of marriage(s)
    ii) Number of marriages
    iii) Background of spouse(s)
  b) Background and status of divorce(s)
  c) Background of all children or children of spouse not related to the decedent (stepchildren).
  d) Develop any lovers' triangle situations.

3)   Develop complete business history.
        a) Type of business
        b) Decedent's responsibilities
        c) Condition of business
            i) Financial
                (1) Any audits in recent past?
                (2) Suits and judgments?
                (3) Tax liens?
        d) Partner(s) information
        e) What effect does the decedent's death have on the business?

4)   Criminal history of the following:
        a) Decedent
        b) Decedent's family
        c) Associates of decedent

5)   Develop the decedent's activities immediately leading up to his death.
        a) Were these activities routine and predictable?
        b) Who else knew of these activities?
        c) Was decedent called to a rendezvous?
        d) Was someone responsible for having the decedent go to the place in which the homicide occurred?
        e) Was decedent responsible for adversely influencing someone's life?
            i) Testifying against someone?
            ii) Having criminal charges filed against someone?
            iii) Bringing about a financial loss to someone??
            iv) Affecting someone's domestic life?
            v) Contributing to a business failure?

CHAPTER 22: DRUG-RELATED HOMICIDES

CONSIDERATIONS

1) A drug-related homicide is a death in which the primary impetus in the original contact between the assailant and the victim was for the acquisition of drugs.
    a) The decedent may be the seller or the abuser of the drug.

2) A drug homicide will often appear motiveless during the initial handling. The victim may be discovered collapsed in the streets or in a vehicle that has just been involved in an accident. Either at the initial discovery of the body or upon cursory treatment, a bullet wound may be found.

3) Reasons why drug-related homicides occur:
    a) A drug rip-off where buyer attempts to get drugs for free
    b) A money rip-off where an effort is made to steal the money belonging to the buyer or seller of the drugs
    c) Substitution of a nondrug substance for the illicit drug
    d) A dispute over drug territory
    e) Nonpayment of money owed for drugs

4) The best possible scenario, in terms of solving a homicide, is for the death to take place in a residence. The least favorable scenario is a street death.

PRIMARY FOCUS OF INVESTIGATION

1) Develop witnesses to the incident.
    a) The canvass is exceedingly important.
        i) Isolate the people who may have witnessed the incident. Avoid attempts to interview whole groups of people, especially in settings such as bars. Avoid asking people to come out of these groups and volunteer information. Obtain a list of the people in the group setting. Interview them some other time, alone, if possible.
        ii) If feasible, attempt to locate possible witnesses during the time of day the incident is believed to have occurred.
        iii) Develop from the canvass potential sources who are known to be "busybodies, porch-sitters, or window-gawkers.
        iv) From canvass interviews develop potential sources who leave or arrive at home or at work at the approximate time of the incident.
        v) Consider possible "invisible" witnesses who may have witnessed the incident (e.g., pizza delivery workers, newspaper delivery people, city work crews).
        vi) The canvass should include areas adjacent to the incident location and areas used as a possible escape route by the suspect.
        vii) The canvass interview should not be limited to addressing potential eyewitnesses to the incident, but should also include the acquisition of background information about the neighborhood, especially in those cases where the decedent is believed to have come to this area to purchase drugs.
        viii) During the canvass interview, the interviewer should stress the importance of residents' cooperating as it relates to the welfare of their neighborhood.

ix) Don't burn your bridges. Leave the door open to future calls. Leave a business card so the subject can contact you at a later date if he has a change of heart about getting involved or he learns of information following the interview.

2) Identify the decedent.
    a) What reason did the decedent have for being at this location?

3) Rope off the area and limit access to the scene immediately!
    a) The scene will normally be a well-traveled area. Limiting access will assist the investigator in understanding what may be evidence or what may have been left at some other time before the occurrence. Items such as tire treads, foot impressions, cans, or cigarette butts may be significantly involved.

4) Develop and collect evidence.

5) Reconstruct the incident.

NOTIFICATION

1) Medical examiner pathologist should be requested if the following may be necessary:
    a) Time frame since death
    b) Type of weapon causing death
    c) Possible activities associated with bloodletting

SCENE PHOTOGRAPHS

1) Follow the death-scene photographic guidelines for the particular situation of the case (e.g., outdoor, indoor, or vehicle scenes). In addition, give particular attention to the following:
    a) Make an overall photograph of area.
        i) Include aerial photographs
        ii) Show remoteness of area (if applicable)
    b) Photograph any blood spatter present at the scene that may indicate movement of the decedent during bloodletting.
    c) Photograph areas of the scene that tend to depict any activity of the injured party during bloodletting.
    d) Photograph signs of struggle as opposed to an execution-style homicide.
    e) On those cases where it appears the victim may have been killed for demonstrative purposes, be sure to include the following:
        i) The body viewed from the area of discovery
        ii) The body viewed from a 360-degree perspective
        iii) Areas on or adjacent to the body that may indicate movement of the body after death (e.g., drag marks, disheveled clothing, inappropriate blood spatter)

SCENE INVESTIGATION

1) Identify the decedent.

2) Determine why the decedent was at this location.

3)   Attempt to make a preliminary identification of the weapon involved. Is the weapon from the crime scene?

4)   Determine activities of the decedent immediately preceding and during the injury process leading to death.

5)   Determine any areas of physical evidence that the suspect may have caused or come into contact with during the event.

6)   Interpret blood spatter present at the scene.
       a) Examine for transfer patterns that may have been made by the suspect.
       b) Consider the possibility and process blood present at the scene that may have originated from the suspect.

7)   Determine if anything is missing.
       a) Vehicle
       b) Jewelry
       c) Credit cards
       d) Wallet or purse
       e) Money/checkbook

8)   If residence or vehicle is involved, determine the following.
       a) Who is the owner of the residence or vehicle?
       b) What reason did the decedent have in being at this location?
       c) Were there other people inside the residence or vehicle?
       d) Any indication of forced entry? How did the suspect or victim gain entry to the residence?
       e) Document any areas indicative of a struggle (e.g., overturned furniture, broken glass)
       f) If vehicle is involved, what is the status of the vehicle?
            i) Is the car running?
            ii) Was it involved in an accident? Detail the accident.
            iii) What is the position of all parties?

BODY TRANSPORT FROM SCENE

1)   Bag the decedent's hands (paper) and transport to the MEO.

2)   If blood spatter may be significant in this case, precautionary measures should be taken to preserve the spatter on the decedent's clothing.

PROCESSING AT MEO

1)   Search the body for drugs in underwear, socks, and other out-of-the-way places.
       a) Be extremely cautious when searching the decedent. Be alert for syringes, razor blades, and other sharp items present in pockets, bras, etc.

2)   If this is a gunshot case, do the following:
       a) X-ray the area of body involved.
       b) Do a neutron-activation swabbing of the decedent's hands.
       c) Collect the projectile.

3)   Collect major case prints.

4)   Collect a tube of blood.

5)   Collect, air-dry, and separately pack each item of clothing.

6)   If the decedent may have been involved in a close physical struggle with his assailant, collect fingernail clippings.

FOLLOW-UP INVESTIGATION

1)   Develop intelligence concerning drug activities and the individuals involved in them in this neighborhood.
      a) Is the drug dealing territorial?
          i) Develop whose territory.
          ii) Are any changes ongoing?
      b) Check drug-related incidents, arrests, and field interrogation cards in this particular area.
      c) Check robbery, burglary, and assault-type incidents and arrests involving this particular area.
      d) Check previous homicides in this particular area. Look for any similarities, such as:
          i) Description of suspect(s)
          ii) Type and caliber of weapon
          iii) Modus operandi
          iv) Description of vehicle(s) involved
      e) Consider any confidential informants who may be utilized.
      f) Learn everything about this neighborhood.

2)   Conduct postevent saturation.
      a) If decedent was an apparent visitor to the area where the incident occurred, consider the following:
          i) Complete the initial processing of the scene and leave the area.
              (1) Ignore the area in an effort to allow the drug activities to resume normal activities as soon as possible.
              (2) Coordinate activities with vice to target drug arrests in this particular area.
              (3) Interview arrested individuals for information concerning the homicide.

3)   Solicit media assistance.
      a) Historically, a large number of drug-related homicides have been solved because of police receiving information generated by media coverage of the incident.
          i) Coordinate with the police information officer to release certain information concerning the case to the media. The more people who see or hear the broadcast or read a news article on the incident, the better the chances of reaching a witness who has not yet been found.
              (1) Avoid releasing run-of-the-mill information because it won't get adequate coverage.
              (2) The best possible media report will describe the incident in a way that elicits some kind of sympathy. Expressing the brutal or senseless nature of the homicide or stressing the tragedy from the perspective

of the victim, the victim's family, or the neighborhood is one way that
may produce telephone calls.
 ii) Try to keep the story alive or push for a follow-up news story, especially in
 those cases where it is believed that juveniles committed the murder.
 iii) Once the information has been released to the media, prepare for phone calls.
  (1) Limit the number of people who will be fielding the incoming calls.
  (2) Prepare an interview sheet of pertinent questions.
  (3) The lead detective should review the information received from every
  call.

4)   On homicides where it appears that the decedent's death may have been orchestrated to serve as
   an example to others, work the case as an altercation-type homicide. The type of case is
   illustrated by what happened to the body, for example:
   a) Victim mutilation
    i) Throat cut
    ii) Tongue or eyes removed
    iii) Multiple gunshot wounds
    iv) Weapon prominently displayed (e.g., butcher knife sticking out of decedent's
     chest
    v) Victim prominently displayed for effect
    vi) Head amputation (not to be confused with head and hands amputated to
     thwart identification efforts)
   b) Investigative emphasis should be concerned with the collecting of background
    information on the decedent, specifically:
    i) Develop decedent's associates
    ii) Develop decedent's activities leading up to his death
    iii) Develop information about who may have been angry with the decedent.
     (1) Whom did the decedent rip off?
     (2) To whom did the decedent owe money?
     (3) Who needed to orchestrate the decedent's death as a demonstration
      or as a warning to others?

5)   Open channels of communication with the family of the decedent. If possible, notify the next of
   kin in person. Keep the family updated and assured of your interest in the case: family contact is
   exceedingly important. Family members can get information and talk to people the
   police cannot. They are an excellent source of leads.

CHAPTER 23: ROBBERY-RELATED HOMICIDES

CONSIDERATIONS

1) A robbery-related homicide occurs during the commission of a robbery where the initial intent was simply robbery.

2) Reconstruction of what may have occurred is critical because robbery is a very modus operandi–influenced event.
    a) Discrepancies in the suspect's activities or pattern may be altered through the evolution of improved techniques and with the continuing experience of the perpetrator.

3) Determine whether the decedent is the victim or the perpetrator of the robbery.

PRIMARY FOCUS OF INVESTIGATION

1) Distinguish the type of robbery by the location in which it occured or originated.
    a) Determine the initial approach site of the suspect.
        i) Business
            (1) Is business near an expressway or well into a neighborhood in which an effective escape may be somewhat compromised?
        ii) Residence (including home burglaries)
        iii) Street

2) Determine how and why victim may have been selected as a target.
    a) Did the general public have common knowledge about the cash and valuables in the victim's possession?

3) Develop the time frame of the robbery.

4) Determine what happened.
    a) How was entry gained?
    b) Was planning evident?
    c) Determine the type of weapon(s) used.
    d) What other tools did the perpetrator bring to the scene?
    e) Did the perpetrator attempt to conceal his identity (e.g., mask, gloves)?
    f) Develop the vehicle(s) used by perpetrator in arriving and leaving the scene.

5) Develop the modus operandi of the suspect.

6) Determine the experience of the suspect(s).
    a) Indication of problems in controlling the victim
        i) Type of restraints used (e.g., handcuffs, ropes, duct tape)?
        ii) Were restraints brought to the scene or already at the scene?
    b) Efficiency with which the victim was killed
        i) Experienced
            (1) Quick, efficient means of death will b evident.

(2) If gunshot was involved, it will be from close range: usually one or t two shots to the head.

(3) There was little or no movement precipitating death.

ii) Inexperienced

(1) The following is evidence of a struggle:

(a) Scene in disarray

(b) Clothing of victim torn and disheveled

(2) If gunshot, it may be distant shot.

(3) There may be multiple gunshot wounds.

(4) There may be blood spatter leading to body.

(5) There may be blood letting indicating that the victim may have been upright for an extended period.

(6) More than one weapon was used, with each successive weapon becoming increasingly less efficient (e.g., victim is initially shot, followed by a beating with a blunt object).

7) Why was the victim killed?

a) Victim attempted to escape.

b) Victim attempted to thwart the robbery.

c) Victim attempted to resist or did not heed instructions.

d) Victim was killed as an example.

e) Victim was killed to eliminate a possible witness.

i) Execution style

ii) Victim restrained

8) Determine what is missing.

NOTIFICATION

1) A medical examiner/pathologist should be requested if any of the following is necessary to understand the case:

a) Time frame since death

b) Type of weapon responsible for injuries.

c) Possible activities associated with bloodletting.

SCENE PHOTOGRAPHS

1) Follow the death-scene photographic guidelines for homicides. In addition, pay particular attention to the following:

a) Make an overall photograph of the area.

i) Include aerials to show relationship to expressways or the remoteness of the area.

b) Photograh any blood spatter present at the scene that would indicate the movements or activities of participants.

c) Photograph signs of a struggle versus execution-style homicide.

d) Photograph any possible weapon found at the scene.

e) Photograph areas where shell casings or expended rounds were discovered.

f) Photograph any areas of physical evidence that the suspect may have caused or come into contact with during the incident.

g) Photograph the body, noting any particular areas associated with these:

           i) Restraints
           ii) Beating or torture type injuries
           iii) Blood spatter present on the decedent's body or clothing
      h) Photograph areas indicating a possible forced entry.
      i) Photograph indications of a robbery.
           i) Rifled drawers and possessions
           ii) Opened cash and jewelry boxes
           iii) Strewn contents of purses or wallets
           iv) Pockets turned inside-out

SCENE INVESTIGATION

1)   Identify the decedent.

2)   Determine why the decedent was at this location.
      a) Determine the time frame in which decedent was at this location.

3)   Attempt to make preliminary determination of the weapon used.
      a) Note number, caliber, and location of all casings found at the scene.

4)   Determine activities of the decedent immediately preceding and during the injury process leading to the death.

5)   Determine any areas of physical evidence that the suspect(s) may have caused or come into contact with during the incident.

6)   Interpret blood spatter at the scene.
      a) Examine for transfer patterns that may have been made by the suspect.
      b) Eliminate the possibility of or process blood present at the scene that may originate from the suspect.

7)   Examine the body of the decedent.
      a) Note any areas of injury indicative of torture or beating that may have been an effort by the perpetrator to acquire information from the victim or establish control.
      b) Interpret blood spatter present on the body or clothing of the decedent.

8)   Determine what is missing.
      a) Vehicle
      b) Jewelry
      c) Credit cards
      d) Wallet/purse
      e) Money
      f) Checkbook

9)   Is there evidence of struggle?
      a) Overturned furniture?
      b) Broken glass?

10)   If residence or business involved, determine the following:
      a) Who owns residence or business?
      b) Are there survivors/witnesses?

BODY TRANSPORT FROM SCENE

1) Bag (paper) the decedent's hands and transport to the MEO.

2) If blood spatter may be significant in this case, precautionary measures should be utilized to preserve the spatter involving the clothing of the decedent.

PROCESSING AT THE MEO/MORGUE

1) Examine the body closely for tan lines, white areas, or abrasions where a watch, ring, or necklace, or other piece of jewelry may have been prior to the robbery.

2) Examine clothing for tears adjacent to pocket areas. Look for other tears in the clothing and missing buttons that may indicate a struggle.
   a) Collect, air-dry, and separately pack each item of clothing.

3) If it is a gunshot case, do the following:
   a) X-ray area of body involved.
   b) Complete a GSR swabbing of the decedent's hands.
   c) Collect the projectile.

4) Collect major case prints.

5) Collect a tube of blood.

6) If evidence suggests the decedent may have been in a close physical confrontation with his assailant, collect fingernail scrapings and clippings.

FOLLOW-UP INVESTIGATION

1) Meet with the family, business associates, friends, etc., of the decedent. Establish items that may be missing.
   a) Watches
      i) Type, style, and serial number
      ii) Jewelry
   b) Description. Was a photograph taken for insurance purposes?
   c) Credit cards
      i) Type and credit card number
   d) Checks
      i) Bank of issue and account number
   e) Cellular phone
   f) Vehicle
   g) Electronic equipment
      i) Manufacturer, type of equipment, and serial number

2) Analyze case for modus operandi
   a) Common areas of consideration for establishing similar modus operandi
      i) Victim selection
      ii) Entry/approach method used
      iii) Time frame of incident
      iv) Area selected

v) Weapon/ammunition used

vi) Notes used or things said by perpetrator during the robbery

vii) Description and number of suspects.

viii) Use/description of getaway vehicle

ix) What was taken? What was ignored?

3)   Develop witnesses to the incident.

         a) The canvass is exceedingly important.

CHAPTER 24: SEX-RELATED HOMICIDE

CONSIDERATIONS

1) A sexual homicide is recognizable because of the condition of the victim or the scene.
    a) The decedent may lack clothing.
    b) The decedent may have sexual organs exposed or injured.
    c) The decedent may be positioned in a provocative pose.
    d) The decedent may have foreign objects inserted into his cavities.
    e) Examination may indicate evidence of vaginal, anal, or oral sex.
    f) The scene may show evidence of substitute sexual activity or masturbation.

2) No other type of case has the potential for causing as much serious external pressure resulting from media coverage as a sexual homicide. Political and public interference and criticism may very easily get out of hand. It is imperative to establish quick control of the investigation and to create a channel for release of information to the public through media sources.

3) The crime scene becomes extremely important because the physical evidence may reveal behavioral traits of the murderer.

PRIMARY FOCUS OF INVESTIGATION

1) Identify the decedent.

2) Determine the location of the initial assault.

3) Determine how the target (victim) was selected.

4) Establish the activities of the victim.
    a) Immediately preceding death
    b) Normal activities of the decedent

NOTIFICATION

1) Major case squad initialization

2) Forensic pathologist/medical examiner

3) Full-lab capabilities

SCENE PHOTOGRAPHS (OUTDOOR SCENE)

1) Follow the guidance set forth in Chapter 9.

SCENE PHOTOGRAPHS (INDOOR SCENE)

1) Follow the guidance set forth in the section on photographs in Chapter 19. In addition, cover the following areas.
    a) Demonstrate the resistance and assaultive nature of the scene. A sexual homicide is an

act of violence. The resistance demonstrated by the condition of the scene, and the victim may be most helpful in developing a modus operandi and psychological profile of the offender. Include the following possibilities:

b) Photograph the point of entry. Include anything that was broken to gain access.

c) Photograph bloodletting at the scene.

d) Photograph eyeglasses on the floor.

e) Photograph any rifled purse with the contents strewn on the floor.

f) Photograph rifled drawers, jewelry boxes, and any other evidence of ransacking of the premises.

g) Photograph clothing torn and strewn about and buttons ripped from garments.

SCENE INVESTIGATION (OUTDOOR)

1) Follow the guidelines set forth in Chapter 9.

SCENE INVESTIGATION (INDOORS)

1) Determine the point of entry. Begin fingerprinting here.

    a) If the point of entry is a window, process the window for fingerprints. Don't forget the window ledge or any other areas the perpetrator may have needed to touch to gain access to the residence.

    b) A common entry source is a bathroom window. Note any articles that may have been moved out of the way to gain entry (e.g., shampoo bottle) and dust for fingerprints if possible.

2) Dust for latents on the underside of toilet seats.

3) Process for prints any items that appear to have been thrown out of the assailant's path.

4) Look for footprints outside, adjacent to the point of entry.

5) If a bed was used during the assault, use ultraviolet light to check for semen, urine, or saliva stains.

    a) Collect any sheet on the bed by folding it inward.

    b) If there is fecal matter on sheet, consider the possibility of anal assault.

6) Look for other items in the residence that may have been used as a semen receptacle.

7) If eyeglasses are found at the scene, process them for prints. They are often removed by the assailant.

8) Check clocks for interruption of power, which may give initial insight into the time frame of death.

    a) Check alarm clock status.

9) Record the status of electrical appliances, including lights, television, oven, heater, air conditioner, etc.

10) Check the status of the telephone (after processing for prints).

a) Has the line been cut?
b) Check the last-number-dialed feature.

11) Check the status of the answering machine.
   a) Listen to the tape for time feature.
   b) Listen to the tape for caller feature.
   c) Collect the tape.

12) Determine the possible weapon used. Is the weapon from the crime scene?

13) Check bathrooms and kitchen sink. The perpetrator may have cleaned up prior to leaving. Clothing and towels may reveal semen or pubic hair.

14) Check the toilet bowl for evidence. Kleenex or toilet paper may contain evidence.

15) Determine what victim was doing at the time of the attack.

16) Collect the decedent's address book.

17) Collect any cash register receipts from the time frame that is starting to develop.

18) Determine what is missing. Check the status of victim's possessions:
a) Vehicle
b) Jewelry
c) Credit cards
d) Checkbook

BODY TRANSPORT FROM SCENE

1) Check the body for any possible bitemarks. If present, follow the guidelines delineated in Chapter 68 on bitemark protocol.

2) Have the ET collect any obvious foreign material (e.g., hairs and fibers) that may get lost in transporting the remains.

3) Bag (paper) the hands of the decedent.

4) If the decedent is found face down, leave hinm in that position. Turning the victim over for the purpose of transporting may cause semen (if present) to run from the vaginal area into the anal area, thereby creating a false positive when anal swabbings are completed.

5) Carefully wrap the body in a clean sheet. Transport the remains to the MEO.

PROCESSING AT MEO/MORGUE

1) Check for semen stains and additional fibers.

2) Consider checking the body for latent prints.

3) If the body is covered with debris from the scene, brush the material off the body onto the sheet.

4)   Collect the sheet (fold inward) used to transport the body.

5)   Collect the bags used in covering the decedent's hands during transporting to the MEO.

6)   Pull head hair standards.

7)   Collect pulled and combed pubic hair standards.

8)   Collect left- and right-hand fingernail scrapings.

9)   Collect oral, anal, and vaginal swabbings on females (six swabbings per orifice).

10)   Collect anal and oral swabbings on males (6 swabbings per orifice).

11)   Consider collecting penis swabbing for presence of saliva.

12)   Collect a tube of blood.

13)   Collect major case prints on the decedent.

14)   If a firearm is involved, perform a neutron-activation swabbing of the decedent's hands. Collect the projectile.

15)   Collect, air-dry, and separately pack any clothing recovered.

16)   If the decedent is a skeleton or badly decomposed, the pathologist may consult a forensic anthropologist before conducting the autopsy. The significance of finding knife marks on the bone under microscopic examination may be markedly reduced because of the pathologist's use of a scalpel in the area during the autopsy.

FOLLOW-UP INVESTIGATION

1)   Identify the decedent.

2)   Reconstruct the scene.
3)   Develop the activities of the decedent preceding her death.

4)   Develop full background on the victim.
          a) Courthouse records
          b) Family interviews
          c) Criminal records
          d) Employer and co-workers
          e) Friends
          f) Former and/or current spouse(s)
          g) Neighbors

5)   Develop any suspicious activities in the neighborhood of the scene.
          a) Previous police responses to the scene and to the neighborhood

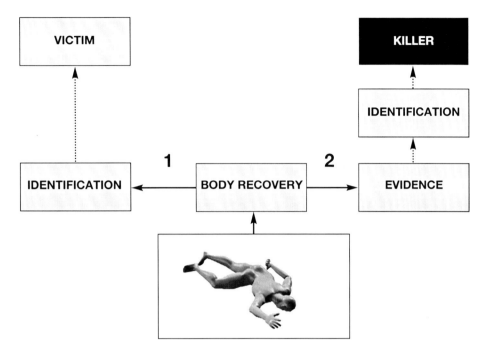

Body dumped, stranger-to-stranger homicide.

SUSPECT'S AND VICTIM'S ACTIVITY CHART

The following charts demonstrate the process an investigation should take when a stranger-to-stranger murder has occurred and a sexual motive to the case is fairly obvious.

Upon discovery of an unknown person with no identification, the homicide investigation actually assumes a two-pronged effort. The first effort (1) deals with working the area, and adjacent to the area, where the victim's body was recovered. This is referred to the *primary scene*. The homicide investigation begins here with the discovery of the victim's body.

The second direction the investigation pursues (2) is a vigorous effort to identify the decedent.

As the two-pronged investigation progresses, evidence processed at the scene may begin to be associated with a perpetrator. Items such as tire tracks, foot impressions, latent prints, and trace evidence such as semen, hair, and fiber may link this scene to other crimes or to a particular suspect.

In the second area of investigative direction, the successful identification of the victim can now be used to develop last-hour activities of the victim. Identification of the perpetrator may be accomplished through this alternative route by developing investigative detail of the victim's activities at the time these activities were interrupted by or had intersected with the killer's activities.

The ideal solution to an investigation of this type would be to successfully identify the killer through the processing of the evidence, as well as linking the victim with the killer through the activities of both parties.

As this type of case progresses, it is not unusual to develop a separate body recovery, death scene, assault site, and initial contact site. Likewise, all four sites may be one and the same. If separate sites are developed through the course of the investigation, the possibility of developing evidence linking the sites with the killer is distinct. Identification and processing of these sites, along with any conveyances that may have been used in transporting the victim, may be paramount to the resolution of the case.

CRIMINAL INVESTIGATIVE ANALYSIS

A sexually motivated homicide is one of the most difficult type of case to solve. The stranger-to-stranger

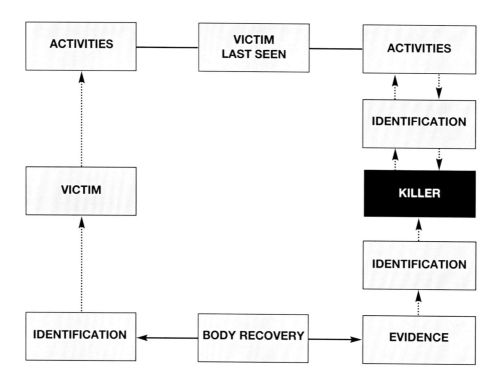

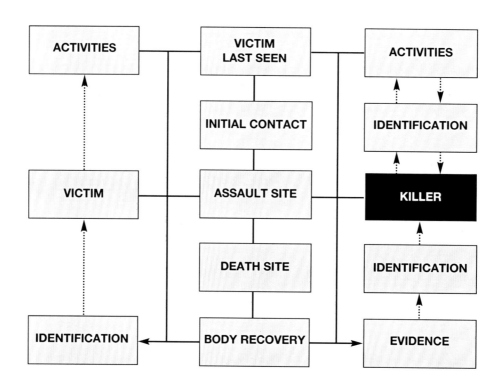

relationship between the perpetrator and the victim often found in these cases compounds the difficulty. Traditional methods of investigation using motive development as the primary impetus of the investigation are often unsuccessful; this crime is one in which opportunity, not motive, plays the greater role.

Investigating a case with the primary emphasis on motive development involves conducting a thorough background development of the victim. The emphasis of the probe is to develop and identify the individual or individuals who may be angry with, or would benefit from, the death of the victim. Once this has been established, the investigation bottlenecks toward this identified individual in developing the opportunity for him to have committed the crime and any evidence collected from the scene that may link that person to the particular scene or the incident.

Investigating a case in which the opportunity to have killed an individual is more important than the motive to kill, from a solvability perspective. For example, the death of a young female prostitute found dumped along an interstate may be sexually motivated. By classic investigation standards, finding who was angry with the victim or who would benefit from her death will not bring that investigator any closer to solving the case. In fact, the case will probably remain unsolved because the investigator will never find the suspect pool he is searching to contain the correct collection of suspects. Assuming the investigator is competent, lead after lead will prove unproductive. Eventually the case will be suspended, pending further developments.

In fact, once the victim has been identified and the preliminary stage of the investigation appears to have eliminated relatives, lovers, and associates of the victim as suspects, the investigation must turn toward identifying who had the opportunity to commit the murder. At what point did the subject's activities cross paths with the killer?

In those investigations where the perpetrator is not known, it stands to reason that his activities will, likewise, not be known. How does the investigation begin? At the only place it can. It must start at the point at which the only information is known—it must begin with the victim and the scene.

What were the victim's activities, how was the victim selected as a target, and what was done to the victim are three areas to explore. The significance of the scene, how it was selected, and the evidence it has provided are other avenues that need to be developed. One investigative tool—which has proven invaluable in understanding the triangular relationship between the victim, the scene, and the killer—involves the use of criminal investigative analysis. That is, a psychological assessment of the crime involves the identification and interpretation of certain types of evidence that would indicate the personality type most likely to have committed the crime.

CRIMES THAT CAN BE PROFILED

1) Sadistic torture in sexual assaults

2) Evisceration

3) Postmortem slashing and cutting

4) Motiveless fire setting

5) Lust and mutilation murders

6) Ritualistic crimes

7) Rapes

CRIMES THAT CANNOT BE PROFILED

1) "Smoking gun" homicides

2) Robberies

3) Drug-induced crimes

4) Any other crime not motivated by psychopathy or sexual perversion

5) Homicides in which the decedent has not been identified

PROFILING ASSISTANCE

1) The identification of a suspect

2) The interrogation strategy

3) The prosecution strategy

4) Presentence parole considerations.

WHY SERIAL MURDERERS KILL

1) Visionary/hallucinatory
   a) He hears voices directing him to kill specific groups of people.

2) Mission oriented
   a) The serial killer feels compelled to eliminate a certain group of people. The most often targeted groups are
   i) Prostitutes
   ii) Homosexuals

3) Hedonistic
   a) Killing is done for a thrill. Strangulation is a prevalent mode of death with these suspects: strangling someone is the most personal way to kill. The hedonistic killer may include the following:
      i) Thrill seeker
         (1) He derives pleasure from the murder.
      ii) Lust murderer
         (1) He relates the murder to sexual arousal and gratification.
      iii) Seeker of creature comforts
         (1) Homicide is used to further the killer's desire for creature comforts and the "good life."

4) Power/control oriented
   a) The power to let someone live or cause his death is the major impetus behind the power/control murderer.

ELEMENTS OF PROFILING

1) The following are some of the considerations the investigator should evaluate when assessing the relationship of the victim, suspect, and the crime scene.

2) Victim typology

3) Victim procurement
    a) Was the victim killed at the body-recovery site or killed somewhere else and dumped at this location?

4) Weapon
    a) Type of weapon used?
        i) Be cautious in attempting to analyze the particular weapon used in the death. For example, a .22-caliber gun may be chosen for use by a professional hitman to kill someone. Some other person may choose a small-caliber weapon because he is uncomfortable with a large-caliber weapon.
    b) Was the weapon brought to the scene or was it part of the scene?
        i) A weapon brought to the scene indicates planning.

5) Assaults against the victim/injuries
    a) Were the injuries before (ante), during (pari), or after (post) death?
    b) Were there any attacks to the face or eyes?
        i) May indicate that the victim and killer know one another: the killer attempted to depersonalize the victim.
    c) Was there biting, vampirism, cannibalism, defecation, etc.?

6) Tools of the crime
    a) Spontaneous versus planned offense?
    b) Indications of control through use of bindings, handcuffs, etc.?

7) Presence of evidence
    a) Does it appear that the perpetrator attempted to remove or destroy evidence. Consider not only common such findings as obvious cleaning up of blood, but other actions that may not be so obvious, for example:
        i) Cleaning of the body with bleach or bathing the victim may be an effort to remove evidence.
        ii) Chunks of flesh removed from the victim may indicate the perpetrator's removing his bite mark injuries prior to leaving the decedent.

8) Disposal of body
    a) If the body has been dumped, is there any indication that an attempt was made to conceal the body or leave it out in the open?
    i) Many considerations are involved.
        (1) For example, for a dead body found deep in the woods, not publicizing the find and staking out the area may eventually result in the suspect's returning to the scene.
            (2) Is the body dumped in the open because the perpetrator wants the body to be found or because of panic?
    b) Concealment of the remains
        i) The perpetrator may be concerned about the evidence he left on the body, or

he may fear that once the victim is identified and his activities are traced backward, the killer's identity will be readily apparent. This may indicate that the perpetrator has prior criminal experiences or is otherwise familiar with the evidence acquisition process. Examples of concealment include these:

> (1) Hands and head are removed and not present with the remainder of the remains.
> (2) The body is set on fire.
> (3) The body is thrown into water.
> (4) The body is buried.

   c) Display the remains.

> i) The body appears posed for responding investigators. This is sometimes referred to as the "Boston strangler" position, referring to the way the Boston strangler left his victims.
>
> ii) This may indicate that the perpetrator is taunting the family, police, or community.

9) Changes in modus operandi as crimes continue

   a) Is the perpetrator becoming more sophisticated as the homicides continue? Is there evidence of additional planning?

   b) Is there increased violence with or mutilation of the victims?

> i) This may indicate that the perpetrator has just been interviewed by the police if more violence has been observed on the latest discovered victim than on the earlier decedents.

   c) Typology of victim change

> i) The perpetrator becomes more confident.
>
> ii) The target becomes more difficult to get to because of media coverage, which allows potential victims to become more cautious, and because of increased police presence.

10) Postoffense behavior seen in the perpetrator

   a) Changes clothing and cleans himself.

   b) Cleans personal auto if used during the commission of the crime.

   c) Establishes an alibi.

   d) Maintains rigid demeanor, conduct, or appearance.

   e) Begins or increases use of alcohol and drugs.

   f) Is preoccupied with media accounts related to the crime.

   g) May give personal item taken from victim to significant person in his life.

   h) Shows employment tardiness, heavy use of sick leave, is fired or changes employment.

   i) Seeks legitimate reason or purpose for leaving the area.

   j) Returns to place of assault or disposal site.

   k) Experiences insomnia and depression.

   l) Experiences explosive episodes of rage and anger.

   m) Attends funeral of victim(s).

   n) Attends burial of victim(s).

   o) Is cooperative with investigators.

   p) Shows no overt change in appearance.

   q) Has short-term interest in religion.

   r) Maintains newspaper clippings related to the case.

   s) Remains in the area.

   t) May talk in third person about the crime

REQUESTING THE ASSISTANCE OF THE CRIMINAL INVESTIGATIVE ANALYSIS UNIT

1) Contact the local FBI office to begin the process. In addition, there are a number of state and local law enforcement specialists who have attended the FBI Academy and have been specially trained in analysis.

2) The specialist in criminal personality profile assessment requests that the particular case be worked up as follows:
   a) Case background
      i) Synopsis of the crime
      ii) Initial complaint reports and follow-up investigative reports
      iii) Detailed interviews of witnesses and any other pertinent information (unnecessary to include copies of follow-up reports where no information was gained)
      iv) Investigating officer's reconstruction of the sequence of events
      v) Copies of (or synopsized review of) local media attention to the crime
   b) Photographs (color, if possible)
      i) Complete photographs of the crime scene
      ii) Photograph of the victim before the incident
      iii) Autopsy photographs detailing the depth and extent of the wounds
      iv) If body found inside a building, photographs of the other rooms
      v) If available and appropriate, aerial photographs
   c) Crime-scene sketch (to include distances and directions)
   d) Map with plottings and key representing the following:
      i) Scale
      ii) Time/location victim was found
      iii) Location of the victim's residence
      iv) Location of the victim's vehicle (if pertinent)
      v) Location of the crime scene (if different from where the victim was found); also include any other related crime scenes.
      vi) Location of any other pertinent areas, for example
         (1) Evidence found
         (2) Attempts on other victims
      vii) Distances between all pertinent points
   e) Medical examiner's report (autopsy protocol)
      i) Toxicology and serology reports, including drugs, alcohol, presence or absence of sperm, etc.
      ii) Findings/impressions of the medical examiner about estimated time of death, type of weapon, suspected sequence of the delivery of the wounds and any other appropriate data available
   f) Neighborhood and complex (e.g., racial, ethic, social data and economic breakdown).
   g) Description of the victim's activity prior to death
      i) Where victim was last seen and by whom
   h) Background of the victim
      i) Age
      ii) Sex
      iii) Race
      iv) Physical description, including dress at time of incident
      v) Marital status/adjustment

vi) Intelligence, scholastic achievement/adjustment
vii) Lifestyle, recent changes
viii) Personality style/characteristics
ix) Demeanor
x) Residency, former and present, in relation to the crime scene
xi) Sexual adjustment
xii) Occupation, former and present
xiii) Reputation at home and work
xiv) Medical history, physical and mental
xv) Fears
xvi) Personal habits
xvii) Use of alcohol or drugs/social habits
xviii) Hobbies
xix) Friends and enemies
xx) Recent court action and prior record
xxi) Relatives in area, if practical
xxii) Names of all persons known to have seen victim during the 24 hours before incident
i) Complete list of evidence recovered

PSYCHOLOGICAL PROFILE

1) The following are factors usually addressed in a completed psychological profile of the perpetrator.
a) Age
b) Sex
c) Race
d) Marital status/adjustment
e) Intelligence
f) Scholastic achievement/adjustment
g) Lifestyle
h) Rearing environment
i) Social adjustment
j) Personality style/characteristics
k) Demeanor
l) Appearance and grooming
m) Emotional adjustment
n) Evidence of mental decompensation
o) Pathological behavioral characteristics
p) Employment/occupational history and adjustment
q) Work habits
r) Residence in relation to crime scene
s) Socioeconomic status
t) Sexual adjustment
u) Type of sexual perversion or disturbance (if applicable)
v) Prior criminal arrest history
w) Motive

VIOLENT CRIMINAL APPREHENSION PROGRAM (VI-CAP)

1) VI-CAP is a nationwide data information center designed to collect, collate, and analyze all aspects of the investigation of those violent crimes that meet the VI-CAP criteria.

2)   Purpose
        a) To identify similar pattern characteristics, including:
            i) Modus operandi
            ii) Victimology
            iii) Physical evidence
            iv) Suspect description
            v) Suspect behavior

3)   Goal
        a) To provide law enforcement agencies reporting similar-pattern violent crimes with information to initiate a multiagency investigation to identify and apprehend the offender

4)   General categories of crimes reported on the VI-CAP crime analysis report
        a) Homicides or attempts, solved or unsolved, especially these:
            i) Abductions
            ii) Apparently random
            iii) Apparently motiveless
            iv) Apparently sexually oriented
            v) Suspected to be part of a series
        b) Missing person cases, especially:
            i) Where circumstances indicate a strong possibility of foul play
            ii) The victim is still missing.
        c) Unidentified dead bodies, especially those those associated with this kind of case
            i) Where manner of death is known or suspected to be a homicide

5)   Special considerations
        a) VI-CAP accepts old cases (those from before June 1, 1985) for analysis, providing the following conditions exist:
            i) The cases contain elements of those crimes specific to VI-CAP analysis.
            ii) A VI-CAP report is completed and forwarded to the VI-CAP unit.
        b) If a submitted case is similar to a case on file, the involved investigators will be put in contact with one another. Specific information about the involved cases is never released by VI-Cap analysts.
        c) The information contained in VI-CAP is specifically exempt from the Freedom of Information Act.

VIOLENT CRIME LINKAGE ANALYSIS SYSTEM (ViCLAS)

1)   Similar in certain respects to the VI-CAP system used in the United States, ViCLAS was started by Canadian law enforcement.
        a) ViCLAS involves a questionnaire of 262 questions covering all aspects of a particular incident, including:
            i) Victimology
            ii) Modus operandi
            iii) Forensics
            iv) Behavioral information

2)   Purpose
        a) A computerized linkage analysis system designed to collate and compare data on serial-offense types of crime

3) Objectives
    a) The creation of a database for the collection of data on all homicides, sexual offenses, abductions, and all related attempts
    b) The comparison of cases leading to the identification of serial rapes and murders
    c) The monitoring of missing persons and the providing of potential identities for found human remains
    d) The examination of reported false allegation cases to identify any serial reports of this nature or to identify reports that are believed to be false but that are, in fact, genuine complaints

4) Types of cases
    a) All solved or unsolved homicides and attempted homicides
    b) All solved or unsolved sexual assaults or attempts
    c) Missing persons, where the circumstances indicate a strong possibility of foul play and the victim is still missing
    d) Unidentified bodies, where the circumstances indicate a strong possibility of foul play and the victim is still missing
    e) Unidentified bodies, where the manner of death is known or suspected to be a homicide
    f) All non parental abduction and attempted abductions
    g) False allegations of sexual assault or attempted murder

5) ViCLAS used by other entities
    a) Belgium
    b) Netherlands
    c) Germany
    d) Austria
    e) Sweden
    f) Australia
    g) United Kingdom
    h) New Jersey State Police

GEOGRAPHIC PROFILING

1) This is a fairly new investigative support technique designed to provide assistance in cases of serial violent crime.

2) The process is based on the analysis of the locations of a connected series of offenses, the characteristics of the neighborhoods in which they have occurred, and the psychological profile of the offender, in an attempt to determine the most probable areas in which the offender might live or work.

3) Geographic profiling is best understood as an information management strategy that can be used to prioritize suspects and locations, and then to help suggest new investigative tactics when traditional methods have not been successful.

SEXUAL QUESTIONNAIRE

On sexual homicides occurring at the decedent's home where it appears the assailant may have had some knowledge of the victim's activities and the security of the residence, the following information should be collected from relatives and friends to help establish a list of possible suspects.

1)   Neighbors
           a) Was the decedent having any problems with neighbors?
           b) Did the decedent spend any time with any particular neighbors?
           c) Was any neighbor seen hanging around the decedent's residence?

2)   Grocery store
           a) Identify store and location of the grocery store where decedent normally shopped for groceries.
           b) Are groceries ever delivered?

3)   Drugstores
           a) Identify store and location
           b) Were medications ever delivered?

4)   Dairy delivery?

5)   Any recent purchases delivered to the home?

6)   Television repaired recently?

7)   Large appliances repaired recently?

8)   Telephone problems or installations recently?

9)   Church
        a) Were any problems associated with decedent's church activities?

10)   Newspaper delivered to residence?

11)   Door-to-door salesmen
           a) Insurance
           b) Books
           c) Vacuum cleaners
           d) Bibles
           e) Magazines
           f) Jewelry
           g) Storm windows and doors
           h) Photo studios

12)   Had any survey takers come to the residence recently?

13)   Had the decedent been receiving any unusual phone calls recently?

14)   Did the decedent speak of any unusual or strange event prior to her death?
15)   Did the decedent recently purchase an automobile?

16)   Did the decedent frequent one particular service station? If yes, identify.

17)   Had the decedent recently used a credit card? If yes, develop the details.

18)   Did the decedent speak of any unusual visitor who had visited shortly before her death?

19)   Had the decedent suffered any break-ins recently?

20)   Had the decedent noticed anything unusual in her home shortly before her death?

21)   Had the police been called to this decedent's residence during the time shortly before the death?

22)   When the decedent traveled, did she drive a personal vehicle, take a taxi, or ride a bus?

23)   Did the subject exercise by jogging or walking?
            a) If yes, identify routine such as day and time.

24)   Has there been any change in the person who delivers mail?

25)   Did the decedent visit any bars or taverns?

26)   Did the decedent visit any restaurants regularly?

27)   Describe the social activities of the decedent.

28)   Was the decedent recently hospitalized?

29)   Identify decedent's doctor.

30)   Identify decedent's dentist.

31)   Did the decedent frequent any place on a regular basis?

32)   Had the decedent noticed anyone watching or loitering near her employment or residence?
            a) Any complaints concerning "Peeping Toms"?

33)   Had the decedent spoken of any unusual areas visited recently?

34)   Identify the decedent's life insurance company.

35)   Identify the decedent's health insurance company.

36)   Identify the decedent's dry cleaner. Does it make home deliveries?

37)   Identify the decedent's bank accounts.

38)   Had the decedent suffered a death in the family recently?
            a) Identify the funeral home.
            b) Identify the cemetery.

39)   Did the decedent (or apartment complex in which the decedent lived) have a regular scheduled exterminator?
            a) If yes, identify.

40)   Did the decedent have pizza delivered?

41)   Did the decedent park in a particular parking area at work?
         a) Did the decedent have her vehicle parked by valet recently?

42)   Did the decedent have her car repaired recently?
         a) If yes, identify repair shop.

43)   Is the decedent's gas meter outside the dwelling?

44)   What was the date the electric meter was read?

45)   Did the decedent have any repairs made to her dwelling recently?

46)   Had the decedent had any repairs made to her office recently?

CHAPTER 25: COLD-CASE INVESTIGATIONS: SOLVING UNRESOLVED HOMICIDES

THE COLD-CASE CONCEPT

Beginning with the surge of homicides during the mid-1980s and continuing until the early 1990s, many police departments found themselves unable to cope with the vast amount of resources, education, and technology required to adequately attack the onslaught of new drug-related, robbery-elated, and sexually motivated homicides. To compound the problem, many of these new cases were stranger to stranger, which are the most difficult to solve. The sheer impact of the number of all these new cases, and the difficulty in solving them, added to the gradually increasing numbers of unsolved homicides.

With the additional pressure on departments to keep up with this ever-increasing case load, many of the older detectives retired or had themselves reassigned. New detectives were no longer groomed during their police careers to become homicide detectives. The homicide detective was no longer the best and the brightest of any given department. Administrators were forced to bring in investigators with very little experience to fill empty slots and deal with runaway case loads. As a result, the number of unsolved homicides skyrocketed, and solvability and clearance rates dipped to all-time lows.

Departments attempted to adjust to this crack cocaine, gang-related homicide era by increasing the number of detectives assigned to the homicide division. As the alarming number of homicides began to decrease during the early 1990s, administrators were reluctant to reduce the number of homicide detectives for fear the lower crime numbers were temporary. Given the lessened case loads, police departments throughout the nation began to have their homicide detectives look at some of the older cases that had not been solved. Some of the detectives were eventually assigned to a permanent squad responsible for reviewing, analyzing, and providing one more concentrated effort to solve the unresolved cases. The detectives began working on cold cases, and their groups came to be cold-case squads.

The advent of these squads necessitated new protocol, whose considerations are outlined in this chapter.

PRIMARY FUNCTIONS OF A COLD-CASE INVESTIGATION UNIT

1) Investigation of unresolved murders

2) Assisting other law enforcement agencies with homicide cases and investigative leads

3) Training of other federal, state, and local law enforcement agencies interested in leaning the application of the cold-case methodology

ESTABLISHING A COLD-CASE HOMICIDE UNIT

1) Develop unit methodology.
    a) Cold cases are not investigated the same way as a "hot" homicide case.

SELECTION OF THE COLD-CASE INVESTIGATOR

1) A cold-case investigator should have a great deal of experience as a detective. He will be called

upon to work a case that has resisted regular efforts and attention to be solved. After all, if the solution to the case had been easy, it more than likely would have been solved already.

2) Cold cases are often very prolonged investigations, which require perseverance. Additionally, all of the problems experienced in "hot" homicide investigations are multiplied many times in the investigation of a cold-case homicide.

3) Detectives chosen for the cold-case unit should be experienced in homicide investigations and be very familiar with such things as statutes of limitations and degrees of murder.

4) The three most important features involving selection of cold-case detectives are these:
    a) Detective's experience
        i) In testifying in court
        ii) In handling informants
        iii) In undercover operations and investigations
    b) Detective's tenacity and patience
    c) Detective's interviewing and interrogation skills

5) The cold-case detective should also possess the following qualities:
    a) Being creative, innovative, and open to suggestion
    b) Being a good listener
    c) Having excellent oral and written communication skills

CATEGORIZING AND SELECTING THE COLD CASE

1) If your department is just starting a cold-case squad, do not choose the most difficult and baffling cases. Select the easier cases initially. Anticipation is going to run high, and administrators will want to have positive results quickly.
    a) Initially, select those cases where a latent print from the crime scene has not been entered into AFIS or a sperm specimen believed to belong to the perpetrator has not been entered into CODIS.
    b) As administrators realize the quick success of these types of cases and see the department's positive media coverage, they may develop a more solid and prolonged commitment to the cold-case concept. Once this has been achieved, the more difficult and time-consuming cases can be attempted.

2) The actual selection of the cases worked may be out of the control of the cold-case detectives. Administrative officials may wish to offer the cases they perceive as most troubling to the department.

3) Keep in mind that as the successes of the cold-case squad are reported, media coverage will develop additional leads and potential witnesses to come forward with information about other homicides. Some of these leads in unsolved homicides will be tantalizing and will draw the investigative attention of the detectives to the point of distraction.
    a) It is critical that the detectives in cold cases maintain their focus on the cases at hand.
    b) One case at a time would be an excellent ratio for each detective assigned to a cold-case squad.

SOLVABILITY RANKING OF CASES

5 Case has physical evidence to be processed that may be from the perpetrator.

4 Case has a fairly obvious suspect developed. Case contains promising leads.

3 Suspect is fairly well developed, but no indication in files of any promising lead(s). May require a confession to solve.

2 Case has no specific suspect. Investigation will be extensive.

1 Snowball's chance in hell.

After reviewing the entire case file, the cold-case reviewer can then assign a number reflecting the solvability ranking potential of the case.

ANALYZING THE CASE SELECTED

1) Don't operate in a vacuum. Realize if you are the only person working a case, all that you will bring to the case is what you have learned through your experience and education. Although that may be considerable, it will never match the levels of other experienced detectives and experts associated with death investigation. In consultation, consider using the talent and expertise of the following:

    a) Blood spatter experts
    b) Psychological profilers
    c) Prosecutors
    d) Crime-scene personnel
    e) Crime laboratory personnel
    f) Arson and other specific crimes experts
    g) Medical examiners/forensic pathologists
    h) Child abuse (medical) experts
    i) Firearm examiner experts
    j) Forensic anthropologists
    k) Forensic botanists
    l) Forensic entomologists

TIME, TECHNOLOGY, AND TENACITY

1) Time

    a) The passage of time is usually a liability in a homicide investigation. With cold-case investigation, the passage of time becomes an asset.

   i) The first 48 to 72 hours is the most critical in working a hot homicide.
   (1) Identifying and interviewing witnesses while the crime is fresh is an important consideration when working a hot homicide case.
   ii) The longer a hot homicide stays unsolved, the more likely it will stay unsolved.
  b) The passage of time becomes an ally to cold-case investigation because of the following:
   i) The normal passage of time causes relationships and associations to change.
   ii) These changes in relationships are vital to cold cases because witnesses may now be willing to provide information they weren't in the past.
    (1) Witnesses who may have been close to the suspect in the past may not be now. In some cases, they may even be adversaries.
    (2) A witness may have been afraid of the subject at the time of the murder. Time may have made the witness stronger or the subject weaker.
    (3) A witness may now need help with another aspect of the criminal justice system.
  c) A witness may have matured, married, found religion, or changed his life in any in any number of ways that affect his honesty and integrity.
  d) A witness may not mind getting involved now.
  e) A witness simply may not have been asked the right questions the first time he was interviewed.
  f) All potential witnesses must be located and interviewed.

2) Technology
  a) Fingerprint technology
   i) ALS
    (1) Cyanoacrylate latent fingerprint development system
    ii) AFIS
  b) DNA analysis
   (1) CODIS
  c) Firearms examination
   i) DrugFire and IBIS databases
  d) Lead development databases

3) Tenacity
  a) The continual application of creative methods and untraditional investigative techniques is the key to developing new information that will benefit the investigation.
  b) The newly assigned investigator must analyze, assess, and then attack the old case.

MEDIA CONSIDERATIONS

1) When a law enforcement agency makes an arrest on a cold case, that department will usually receive positive press. Although this should never be a consideration in law enforcement work, this media coverage can assist the cold-case program and the specific agency through the following considerations:
  a) Solving a cold case is usually good news, and, as such, coverage presents a positive image for the department.
  b) The agency is presented in a light of, "We don't ever give up!"
  c) Solving a case produces leads on other unresolved cases. People who watch or read the

news accounts of a successful cold-case resolution may contact the department with information about another such case.
   d) Unidentified witnesses watching or reading the media account may contact authorities and relate information concerning the solved case, which may assist in the prosecution of the case.

ADMINISTRATIVE SUPPORT

1)   The cold-case homicide unit can only work efficiently if its members are allowed to to work exclusively on old, unresolved homicides.
   a) If the detectives are continual put into the rotation of duty calls or if they are assigned current cases, their effectiveness in working on a cold case will be severely affected.

INVESTIGATIVE STEPS

1)   Review
   a) To conduct a thorough analytical review of the case file, the following questions should be addressed:
      i) Are all reports, case notes, and related documentation still available?
      ii) Are there complete autopsy files and photographs?
      iii) Are main characters (e.g., witnesses, suspects) still alive and can they be located?
      iv) What evidentiary items still exist?
      v) What, if any, new technological advances can be applied to the investigation?
      vi) Can the case be solved?

2)   Organization
   a) Completely organize or reorganize the case file. Prepare the following.
      i) Three-ring binders containing these:
         (1) Reports in chronological and alphabetical order
         (2) All evidence related reports
         (3) All case notes (alphabetical and chronological).
         (4) Reports and notes on key individuals
         (5) Prosecution reports
      ii) Time lines
      iii) Time correlation charts
      iv) Statement and information cross-check charts
      v) Lists of inconsistencies and unanswered questions
      vi) Comparison graphs or charts
      vii) Maps of key areas

3)   Evidence
   a) Contact the evidence custodian and make sure that the evidence can be located.
   b) Personally go to the evidence facility and verify that the evidence is present.
      i) Do not assume the evidence is in custody even if you are told that it is.
   c) Inventory and list the evidence yourself before you go any further with the investigation.
      i) Seek the assistance of a forensic consultant or experienced criminalistics expert when conducting an inventory and forensic review of the evidence.

4) Prosecutor
    a) Involve a prosecutor at the earliest possible time in the investigation for the following considerations:
        i) The degree of murder that may be applicable
        ii) Statute of limitations
        iii) Whether the law has changed since the date of the offense
        iv) What legal issues exist
        v) Miranda issues

5) Reconstruction
    a) Reconstruct all aspects of the crime by establishing what happened, why it happened, how it happened, and when it happened. Consider the following:
        i) Study the original crime scene. Examine all photographs, autopsy protocol, interviews, interrogations, statements, police reports, case notes, and any other related piece of documentation.
        ii) Revisit the crime scene.
        iii) Interview all original officers, investigators, crime-scene technicians, and the medical examiner.
        iv) Consult with forensic and psychological experts.
        v) Hold team brainstorming sessions.
        vi) Resubmit all the evidence to the forensic laboratory for additional examinations or reexaminations. Obtain contemporary evaluations for the original analysis.
        vii) Develop this:
            (1) What happened + Why it happened = Who did it

6) Investigation plan
    a) Formulate an investigation plan for the resolution of the case. Consider the following:
        i) Traditional considerations
            (1) Telephone records
                (a) Tolls, local, and cellular
            (2) Personal and work computer searches and seizures
            (3) Issuance of subpoenas or court orders
                (a) Grand jury subpoena
                (b) Forthwith subpoena
                (c) Subpoena duces tecum
            (4) Cellmate informants
                (a) Cellmate listening posts
                (b) Prison escorts, correctional staff (e.g., nurse, counselor)
            (5) Codefendants and accomplices in previous criminal cases
            (6) Forensic considerations
            (7) Probate and civil court actions
                (a) Judgments, probate (wills), law suits, etc.
        ii) Untraditional considerations
            (1) Mail cover
            (2) Trash pull
            (3) Surveillance considerations
                (a) Physical and electronic
            (4) Consensual oral/wire electronic interceptions
            (5) PIN register/wire taps (Title 11)

        (6) Informant development
        (7) Passive listening posts
        (8) Psychological profiling
        (9) Use of props
        (10) Analytical review and link analysis
        (11) Computer database utilization
            (a) Lexis/Nexis, CDB Infotek, etc.
        (12) Criminal intelligence sources
            (a) NCIC, NLETS, FinCEN, etc.
        (13) Offline NCIC checks
        (14) Undercover application considerations

7) Background investigation
    a) Conduct background checks on all suspects, subjects, witnesses.
        i) Look for criminal arrests.
        ii) Identify changes in associations and personal relationships.
            (1) Determine if the change in the relationship could be beneficial to the investigation.
    b) It is essential that these background investigations be conducted before conducting any interviews relative to the cold-case murder investigation.

8) Family
    a) Contact the victim's family and determine if any of them can assist the investigation.
        i) Be extremely cautious!
            (1) Be careful not to prematurely raise their hopes.
            (2) Be sure they are not suspects or in any way responsible for the murder.
        ii) The victim's family is usually a great source in developing the victimology.
        iii) The family is an excellent source for providing props that may prove beneficial in the interrogation or interviewing strategy.

9) Victim
    a) Develop victimology information about the decedent.

VICTIM INFORMATION

✔ Physical description of the victim	✔ Occupation
✔ Marital status	✔ Physical and mental history
✔ Residency in relation to the crime scene	✔ Use of alcohol or drugs/social habits
✔ Lifestyle/ recent changes	✔ Friends and enemies

      b) Review the medical examiner's file.
          i) Develop the person who made the identification of the deceased.
          ii) Collect all information about an insurance inquiry into the death.
          iii) Identify individuals who contacted the medical examiner and inquired
              about obtaining a copy of the decedent's autopsy report.
          iv) Collect any newspaper articles concerning the death that may be contained in
              the file.
          v) Identify the doctor who performed the original autopsy on the victim.

10)   Motive
      a) There is a 70-percent possibility that the victim was killed by someone who knew him
        and who would have wanted him killed. These types of cases are the easiest to solve.
        They involve motives usually associated with a domestic or altercation type of
        situation where revenge or anger may have been the determining factor in the death.
        They may also involve the contract killing of the victim. Staged scenes and
        concealment of the corpse may have been implemented to hinder or conceal the true
        motive of the murder and, hence, the logical identification of the perpetrator.
          i) Determine who has benefited the most from the death of the victim.
              (1) Were there financial incentives in the death of the victim?
                  (a) Life insurance benefits paid?
                     (i) Credit life on the victim's mortgage, automobile, etc.?
                    ii) Was the decedent having domestic problems?
      b) There is a 30-percent possibility that the victim was killed by a stranger. These motives
        usually involve robbery, sexual assault, drugs, terrorism, or random acts of violence.
        These are the most difficult cases to solve.

11)   Interview
      a) The investigation begins by interviewing the witnesses and associates on the periphery
        of the investigation.
          i) The investigation should delay as long as possible the public knowledge of a
              reopened investigation. Surprise is an ally in the investigation. It is especially
              beneficial when the suspect is first encountered if he is unaware of the
              ongoing investigation.
          ii) Peripheral witnesses can also supply the investigation with information about
              the suspect's changing relationships and associations.
          iii) The following individuals are considered potential peripheral witnesses:
              (1) Friends
              (2) Acquaintances
               (3) Co-workers
               (4) Neighbors
               (5) Cellmates
               (6) Club/organization members
               (7) Girlfriends/boyfriends
               (8) Co-defendants
               (9) Employers
               (10) Adversaries
              (11) Social services personnel
               (12) Family members
              (13) Church congregation members
               (14) Former spouse(s)
      b) Before interviewing any major witnesses, determine whether their situation is different
        now from that when the homicide occurred.

          i) They may be in jail, on probation, or in need of help with some other aspect of the judicial system.

          ii) They may have straightened out their lives, gotten married, or found religion.

   c) Approach the interview phase of the investigation like a chess match. Be cognizant of all potential ramifications before conducting each interview. Consider how a witness may react upon being approached for an interview by homicide cold-case detectives. Consider who this witness may contact as a result of being interviewed. Prepare for that possibility and consider how to take advantage of this potential situation for the benefit of the investigation.

   d) In most cold cases, preserving the element of surprise until the showdown interrogation with the suspect is incredibly important. Therefore, interviews of important witnesses who investigators believe will tell the main suspect about the interviews should not be scheduled, if at all possible, until interviews can be conducted simultaneously with the main suspect. Of course, this stratagem is contingent upon available manpower and resources.

   e) During the entire interview process, maintaining control and direction is essential. No investigative step should be taken without a clear objective.

          i) An investigative lead sheet should be used in a cold case investigation just as it is used in a hot homicide case.

             (1) The case agent/lead investigator should monitor and evaluate every lead that is accomplished.

          ii) Team conferences are important. One detective can do much of the investigation on the case; however, conferences with the rest of the team and supervisors also provide a sounding board for and insight into the investigation.

          (1) Once a definite suspect is identified, the entire team should be used to develop an operation plan and provide suggestions on the eventual showdown with the suspect.

   f) There may be occasions when the case agent or lead investigator may not be the best person to conduct certain interviews. The most effective interviewer should be considered at the time the main suspect and key witnesses need to be interviewed.

          i) Ego must be put aside to determine who is best suited to conduct or assist in the key interviews. Do not let attitudes or egos prevent the investigation from taking the best possible approach at the most critical interviews.

   g) Preparation for the interviewers and interrogators is critical. The methods, themes, and strategies used by the interviewers should be well thought out and practiced by those participating in the interview.

   h) Consider the following when preparing the interview room for the witness:

          i) Audio/video coverage

          ii) Use of props, including photos, maps, charts, evidence, recordings, etc.

12) Continuation of the investigation

   a) Do not stop your investigation after the arrest. The actions and movements of the subject or those close to him can be very telling about their involvement in the case. Monitor the subject's contacts and correspondence.

13) Prosecution of the cold case

   a) Remember the ultimate goal is the successful prosecution of the responsible perpetrators of the homicide.

          i) Cooperation with the prosecutor, established when the cold case is activated, is a continuing process, ending at the conclusion of the trial or the plea bargain.

EXCEPTIONAL CLEARANCE

1)   Cases can be resolved through avenues other than the arrest and prosecution of the guilty party. Sometime cases are exceptionally cleared. That is, there are times when an arrest cannot be made, but the case can be closed because of an exceptional circumstance associated with the case. For example, a homicide should not remain unsolved simply because the perpetrator has died. Under this and other special circumstances, the homicide case can be closed. This closure is usually referred to as *exceptionally cleared*. A case may also be considered exceptionally cleared if the statute of limitations has run out on the murder charge and a suspect has been identified.

      a) For an exceptional clearance to be declared, an exceptional investigative effort must have taken place. The homicide investigation must proceed until such evidence has accumulated that would have likely convicted the suspect in a court of law. A prosecutor may be consulted to determine if this threshold has been achieved.

PROSECUTORIAL CONSIDERATIONS

1)   Prosecutors may be somewhat reluctant to support an effort to reopen an old, unsolved murder case. Hot-homicide cases are difficult enough to prosecute successively. Cold cases bring their own set of prosecution problems. How the prosecutor is approached becomes very important.

      a) Be sure to make that prosecutor part of the investigative team.

      b) Make the case visual for the prosecutor. Use presentation boards, story boards, slides, or PowerPoint presentations.

COLD-CASE PITFALLS

1)   Remember, cold cases are difficult to solve. If it was an easy case, it wouldn't be unsolved.

2)   Administrators of police agencies are sometimes reluctant to devote manpower, resources, and time on cases in which they are more than likely not receiving any outside pressure to have a detective work on and solve. The case may have long ago been forgotten.

      a) If a department accepts the necessity for a cold-case unit, the administrative staff may be reluctant to allow cold-case detectives to work cold cases exclusively.

3)   Ultimately, what enable a cold-case program to succeed are the same dogged determination and perseverance that are necessary to solve these most difficult cases.

To the living we owe respect; to the dead, we owe the truth.

—Voltaire

The logo and motto of the Naval Criminal Investigative Service, noted as one of the premier agencies in the entire world for dogged determination in the investigation of unresolved (cold-case) homicides.

PERPETUAL CALENDAR

20th Century (1901–2000) Year Correlation

1901 - 2	1911 - 0	1921 - 6	1931 - 4	1941 - 3
1902 - 3	1912 - 8	1922 - 0	1932 - 12	1942 - 4
1903 - 4	1913 - 3	1923 - 1	1933 - 0	1943 - 5
1904 - 12	1914 - 4	1924 - 9	1934 - 1	1944 - 13
1905 - 0	1915 - 5	1925 - 4	1935 - 2	1945 - 1
1906 - 1	1916 - 13	1926 - 5	1936 - 10	1946 - 2
1907 - 2	1917 - 1	1927 - 6	1937 - 5	1947 - 3
1908 - 10	1918 - 2	1928 - 7	1938 - 6	1948 - 11
1909 - 5	1919 - 3	1929 - 2	1939 - 0	1949 - 6
1910 - 6	1920 - 11	1930 - 3	1940 - 8	1950 - 0
1951 - 1	1961 - 0	1971 - 5	1981 - 4	1991 - 2
1952 - 9	1962 - 1	1972 - 13	1982 - 5	1992 - 10
1953 - 4	1963 - 2	1973 - 1	1983 - 6	1993 - 5
1954 - 5	1964 - 10	1974 - 2	1984 - 7	1994 - 6
1955 - 6	1965 - 5	1975 - 3	1985 - 2	1995 - 0
1956 - 7	1966 - 6	1976 - 11	1986 - 3	1996 - 8
1957 - 2	1967 - 0	1977 - 6	1987 - 4	1997 - 3
1958 - 3	1968 - 8	1978 - 0	1988 - 12	1998 - 4
1959 - 4	1969 - 3	1979 - 1	1989 - 0	1999 - 5
1960 - 12	1970 - 4	1980 - 9	1990 - 1	2000 - 13

21st Century (2001–2100) Year Correlation

2001 - 1	2011 - 6	2021 - 5	2031 - 3	2041 - 2
2002 - 2	2012 - 7	2022 - 6	2032 - 11	2042 - 3
2003 - 3	2013 - 2	2023 - 0	2033 - 6	2043 - 4
2004 - 11	2014 - 3	2024 - 8	2034 - 0	2044 - 12
2005 - 6	2015 - 4	2025 - 3	2035 - 1	2045 - 0
2006 - 0	2016 - 12	2026 - 4	2036 - 9	2046 - 1
2007 - 1	2017 - 0	2027 - 5	2037 - 4	2047 - 2
2008 - 9	2018 - 1	2028 - 13	2038 - 5	2048 - 10
2009 - 4	2019 - 2	2029 - 1	2039 - 6	2049 - 5
2010 - 5	2020 - 10	2030 - 2	2040 - 7	2050 - 6
2051 - 0	2061 - 6	2071 - 4	2081 - 3	2091 - 1
2052 - 8	2062 - 0	2072 - 12	2082 - 4	2092 - 9
2053 - 3	2063 - 1	2073 - 0	2083 - 5	2093 - 4
2054 - 4	2064 - 9	2074 - 1	2084 - 13	2094 - 5
2055 - 5	2065 - 4	2075 - 2	2085 - 1	2095 - 6
2056 - 13	2066 - 5	2076 - 10	2086 - 2	2096 - 7
2057 - 1	2067 - 6	2077 - 5	2087 - 3	2097 - 2
2058 - 2	2068 - 7	2078 - 6	2088 - 11	2098 - 3
2059 - 3	2069 - 2	2079 - 0	2089 - 6	2099 - 4
2060 - 11	2070 - 3	2080 - 8	2090 - 0	2100 - 5

Virtual   Calendar   0

January						
S	M	T	W	T	F	S
1	2	3	4	5	6	7
8	9	10	11	12	13	14
15	16	17	18	19	20	21
22	23	24	25	26	27	28
29	30	31				

February						
S	M	T	W	T	F	S
			1	2	3	4
5	6	7	8	9	10	11
12	13	14	15	16	17	18
19	20	21	22	23	24	25
26	27	28				

March						
S	M	T	W	T	F	S
			1	2	3	4
5	6	7	8	9	10	11
12	13	14	15	16	17	18
19	20	21	22	23	24	25
26	27	28	29	30	31	

April						
S	M	T	W	T	F	S
						1
2	3	4	5	6	7	8
9	10	11	12	13	14	15
16	17	18	19	20	21	22
23	24	25	26	27	28	29
30						

May						
S	M	T	W	T	F	S
	1	2	3	4	5	6
7	8	9	10	11	12	13
14	15	16	17	18	19	20
21	22	23	24	25	26	27
28	29	30	31			

June						
S	M	T	W	T	F	S
				1	2	3
4	5	6	7	8	9	10
11	12	13	14	15	16	17
18	19	20	21	22	23	24
25	26	27	28	29	30	

July						
S	M	T	W	T	F	S
						1
2	3	4	5	6	7	8
9	10	11	12	13	14	15
16	17	18	19	20	21	22
23	24	25	26	27	28	29
30	31					

August						
S	M	T	W	T	F	S
		1	2	3	4	5
6	7	8	9	10	11	12
13	14	15	16	17	18	19
20	21	22	23	24	25	26
27	28	29	30	31		

September						
S	M	T	W	T	F	S
					1	2
3	4	5	6	7	8	9
10	11	12	13	14	15	16
17	18	19	20	21	22	23
24	25	26	27	28	29	30

October						
S	M	T	W	T	F	S
1	2	3	4	5	6	7
8	9	10	11	12	13	14
15	16	17	18	19	20	21
22	23	24	25	26	27	28
29	30	31				

November						
S	M	T	W	T	F	S
			1	2	3	4
5	6	7	8	9	10	11
12	13	14	15	16	17	18
19	20	21	22	23	24	25
26	27	28	29	30		

December						
S	M	T	W	T	F	S
					1	2
3	4	5	6	7	8	9
10	11	12	13	14	15	16
17	18	19	20	21	22	23
24	25	26	27	28	29	30
31						

Years that use Calendar 0

20th Century	1905	1911	1922	1933	1939	1950	1961	1967	1978	1989	1995
21st Century	2006	2017	2023	2034	2045	2051	2062	2073	2079	2090	

Virtual   Calendar   1

January							February							March							April						
S	M	T	W	T	F	S	S	M	T	W	T	F	S	S	M	T	W	T	F	S	S	M	T	W	T	F	S
	1	2	3	4	5	6					1	2	3					1	2	3	1	2	3	4	5	6	7
7	8	9	10	11	12	13	4	5	6	7	8	9	10	4	5	6	7	8	9	10	8	9	10	11	12	13	14
14	15	16	17	18	19	20	11	12	13	14	15	16	17	11	12	13	14	15	16	17	15	16	17	18	19	20	21
21	22	23	24	25	26	27	18	19	20	21	22	23	24	18	19	20	21	22	23	24	22	23	24	25	26	27	28
28	29	30	31				25	26	27	28				25	26	27	28	29	30	31	29	30					

May							June							July							August						
S	M	T	W	T	F	S	S	M	T	W	T	F	S	S	M	T	W	T	F	S	S	M	T	W	T	F	S
	1	2	3	4	5						1	2	1	2	3	4	5	6	7				1	2	3	4
6	7	8	9	10	11	12	3	4	5	6	7	8	9	8	9	10	11	12	13	14	5	6	7	8	9	10	11
13	14	15	16	17	18	19	10	11	12	13	14	15	16	15	16	17	18	19	20	21	12	13	14	15	16	17	18
20	21	22	23	24	25	26	17	18	19	20	21	22	23	22	23	24	25	26	27	28	19	20	21	22	23	24	25
27	28	29	30	31			24	25	26	27	28	29	30	29	30	31					26	27	28	29	30	31	

September							October							November							December						
S	M	T	W	T	F	S'	S	M	T	W	T	F	S	S	M	T	W	T	F	S	S	M	T	W	T	F	S
						1		1	2	3	4	5	6				1	2	3								1
2	3	4	5	6	7	8	7	8	9	10	11	12	13	4	5	6	7	8	9	10	2	3	4	5	6	7	8
9	10	11	12	13	14	15	14	15	16	17	18	19	20	11	12	13	14	15	16	17	9	10	11	12	13	14	15
16	17	18	19	20	21	22	21	22	23	24	25	26	27	18	19	20	21	22	23	24	16	17	18	19	20	21	22
23	24	25	26	27	28	29	28	29	30	31				25	26	27	28	29	30		23	24	25	26	27	28	29
30																					30	31					

Years that use Calendar 1

20th Century	1900	1906	1917	1923	1934	1945	1951	1962	1973	1979	1990
21st Century	2001	2007	2018	2029	2035	2046	2057	2063	2074	2085	2091

Virtual   Calendar   2

January

S	M	T	W	T	F	S
		1	2	3	4	5
6	7	8	9	10	11	12
13	14	15	16	17	18	19
20	21	22	23	24	25	26
27	28	29	30	31		

February

S	M	T	W	T	F	S
					1	2
3	4	5	6	7	8	9
10	11	12	13	14	15	16
17	18	19	20	21	22	23
24	25	26	27	28		

March

S	M	T	W	T	F	S
					1	2
3	4	5	6	7	8	9
10	11	12	13	14	15	16
17	18	19	20	21	22	23
24	25	26	27	28	29	30
31						

April

S	M	T	W	T	F	S
	1	2	3	4	5	6
7	8	9	10	11	12	13
14	15	16	17	18	19	20
21	22	23	24	25	26	27
28	29	30				

May

S	M	T	W	T	F	S
		1	2	3	4	
5	6	7	8	9	10	11
12	13	14	15	16	17	18
19	20	21	22	23	24	25
26	27	28	29	30	31	

June

S	M	T	W	T	F	S
						1
2	3	4	5	6	7	8
9	10	11	12	13	14	15
16	17	18	19	20	21	22
23	24	25	26	27	28	29
30						

July

S	M	T	W	T	F	S
	1	2	3	4	5	6
7	8	9	10	11	12	13
14	15	16	17	18	19	20
21	22	23	24	25	26	27
28	29	30	31			

August

S	M	T	W	T	F	S
				1	2	3
4	5	6	7	8	9	10
11	12	13	14	15	16	17
18	19	20	21	22	23	24
25	26	27	28	29	30	31

September

S	M	T	W	T	F	S
1	2	3	4	5	6	7
8	9	10	11	12	13	14
15	16	17	18	19	20	21
22	23	24	25	26	27	28
29	30					

October

S	M	T	W	T	F	S
		1	2	3	4	5
6	7	8	9	10	11	12
13	14	15	16	17	18	19
20	21	22	23	24	25	26
27	28	29	30	31		

November

S	M	T	W	T	F	S
					1	2
3	4	5	6	7	8	9
10	11	12	13	14	15	16
17	18	19	20	21	22	23
24	25	26	27	28	29	30

December

S	M	T	W	T	F	S
1	2	3	4	5	6	7
8	9	10	11	12	13	14
15	16	17	18	19	20	21
22	23	24	25	26	27	28
29	30	31				

Years that use Calendar 2

20th Century	1901	1907	1918	1929	1935	1946	1957	1963	1974	1985	1991
21st Century	2002	2013	2019	2030	2041	2047	2058	2069	2075	2086	2097

Virtual Calendar 3

January

S	M	T	W	T	F	S
			1	2	3	4
5	6	7	8	9	10	11
12	13	14	15	16	17	18
19	20	21	22	23	24	25
26	27	28	29	30	31	

February

S	M	T	W	T	F	S
						1
2	3	4	5	6	7	8
9	10	11	12	13	14	15
16	17	18	19	20	21	22
23	24	25	26	27	28	

March

S	M	T	W	T	F	S
						1
2	3	4	5	6	7	8
9	10	11	12	13	14	15
16	17	18	19	20	21	22
23	24	25	26	27	28	29
30	31					

April

S	M	T	W	T	F	S
		1	2	3	4	5
6	7	8	9	10	11	12
13	14	15	16	17	18	19
20	21	22	23	24	25	26
27	28	29	30			

May

S	M	T	W	T	F	S
				1	2	3
4	5	6	7	8	9	10
11	12	13	14	15	16	17
18	19	20	21	22	23	24
25	26	27	28	29	30	31

June

S	M	T	W	T	F	S
1	2	3	4	5	6	7
8	9	10	11	12	13	14
15	16	17	18	19	20	21
22	23	24	25	26	27	28
29	30					

July

S	M	T	W	T	F	S
		1	2	3	4	5
6	7	8	9	10	11	12
13	14	15	16	17	18	19
20	21	22	23	24	25	26
27	28	29	30	31		

August

S	M	T	W	T	F	S
					1	2
3	4	5	6	7	8	9
10	11	12	13	14	15	16
17	18	19	20	21	22	23
24	25	26	27	28	29	30
31						

September

S	M	T	W	T	F	S
	1	2	3	4	5	6
7	8	9	10	11	12	13
14	15	16	17	18	19	20
21	22	23	24	25	26	27
28	29	30				

October

S	M	T	W	T	F	S
			1	2	3	4
5	6	7	8	9	10	11
12	13	14	15	16	17	18
19	20	21	22	23	24	25
26	27	28	29	30	31	

November

S	M	T	W	T	F	S
						1
2	3	4	5	6	7	8
9	10	11	12	13	14	15
16	17	18	19	20	21	22
23	24	25	26	27	28	29
30						

December

S	M	T	W	T	F	S
	1	2	3	4	5	6
7	8	9	10	11	12	13
14	15	16	17	18	19	20
21	22	23	24	25	26	27
28	29	30	31			

Years that use Calendar 3

20th Century	1902	1913	1919	1930	1941	1947	1958	1969	1975	1986	1997
21st Century	2003	2014	2025	2031	2042	2053	2059	2070	2081	2087	2098

Virtual Calendar 4

January

S	M	T	W	T	F	S
				1	2	3
4	5	6	7	8	9	10
11	12	13	14	15	16	17
18	19	20	21	22	23	24
25	26	27	28	29	30	31

February

S	M	T	W	T	F	S
1	2	3	4	5	6	7
8	9	10	11	12	13	14
15	16	17	18	19	20	21
22	23	24	25	26	27	28

March

S	M	T	W	T	F	S
1	2	3	4	5	6	7
8	9	10	11	12	13	14
15	16	17	18	19	20	21
22	23	24	25	26	27	28
29	30	31				

April

S	M	T	W	T	F	S
			1	2	3	4
5	6	7	8	9	10	11
12	13	14	15	16	17	18
19	20	21	22	23	24	25
26	27	28	29	30		

May

S	M	T	W	T	F	S
					1	2
3	4	5	6	7	8	9
10	11	12	13	14	15	16
17	18	19	20	21	22	23
24	25	26	27	28	29	30
31						

June

S	M	T	W	T	F	S
	1	2	3	4	5	6
7	8	9	10	11	12	13
14	15	16	17	18	19	20
21	22	23	24	25	26	27
28	29	30				

July

S	M	T	W	T	F	S
			1	2	3	4
5	6	7	8	9	10	11
12	13	14	15	16	17	18
19	20	21	22	23	24	25
26	27	28	29	30	31	

August

S	M	T	W	T	F	S
						1
2	3	4	5	6	7	8
9	10	11	12	13	14	15
16	17	18	19	20	21	22
23	24	25	26	27	28	29
30	31					

September

S	M	T	W	T	F	S
	1	2	3	4	5	
6	7	8	9	10	11	12
13	14	15	16	17	18	19
20	21	22	23	24	25	26
27	28	29	30			

October

S	M	T	W	T	F	S
				1	2	3
4	5	6	7	8	9	10
11	12	13	14	15	16	17
18	19	20	21	22	23	24
25	26	27	28	29	30	31

November

S	M	T	W	T	F	S
1	2	3	4	5	6	7
8	9	10	11	12	13	14
15	16	17	18	19	20	21
22	23	24	25	26	27	28
29	30					

December

S	M	T	W	T	F	S
	1	2	3	4	5	
6	7	8	9	10	11	12
13	14	15	16	17	18	19
20	21	22	23	24	25	26
27	28	29	30	31		

Years that use Calendar 4

20th Century	1903	1914	1925	1931	1942	1953	1959	1970	1981	1987	1998
21st Century	2009	2015	2026	2037	2043	2054	2065	2071	2082	2093	2099

Virtual   Calendar   5

January							February							March							April						
S	M	T	W	T	F	S	S	M	T	W	T	F	S	S	M	T	W	T	F	S	S	M	T	W	T	F	S
					1	2		1	2	3	4	5	6		1	2	3	4	5	6					1	2	3
3	4	5	6	7	8	9	7	8	9	10	11	12	13	7	8	9	10	11	12	13	4	5	6	7	8	9	10
10	11	12	13	14	15	16	14	15	16	17	18	19	20	14	15	16	17	18	19	20	11	12	13	14	15	16	17
17	18	19	20	21	22	23	21	22	23	24	25	26	27	21	22	23	24	25	26	27	18	19	20	21	22	23	24
24	25	26	27	28	29	30	28							28	29	30	31				25	26	27	28	29	30	
31																											

May							June							July							August						
S	M	T	W	T	F	S	S	M	T	W	T	F	S	S	M	T	W	T	F	S	S	M	T	W	T	F	S
						1			1	2	3	4	5					1	2	3	1	2	3	4	5	6	7
2	3	4	5	6	7	8	6	7	8	9	10	11	12	4	5	6	7	8	9	10	8	9	10	11	12	13	14
9	10	11	12	13	14	15	13	14	15	16	17	18	19	11	12	13	14	15	16	17	15	16	17	18	19	20	21
16	17	18	19	20	21	22	20	21	22	23	24	25	26	18	19	20	21	22	23	24	22	23	24	25	26	27	28
23	24	25	26	27	28	29	27	28	29	30				25	26	27	28	29	30	31	29	30	31				
30	31																										

September							October							November							December						
S	M	T	W	T	F	S	S	M	T	W	T	F	S	S	M	T	W	T	F	S	S	M	T	W	T	F	S
												1	2		1	2	3	4	5	6				1	2	3	4
			1	2	3	4	3	4	5	6	7	8	9	7	8	9	10	11	12	13	5	6	7	8	9	10	11
5	6	7	8	9	10	11	10	11	12	13	14	15	16	14	15	16	17	18	19	20	12	13	14	15	16	17	18
12	13	14	15	16	17	18	17	18	19	20	21	22	23	21	22	23	24	25	26	27	19	20	21	22	23	24	25
19	20	21	22	23	24	25	24	25	26	27	28	29	30	28	29	30					26	27	28	29	30	31	
26	27	28	29	30			31																				

Years that use Calendar 5

20th Century	1909	1915	1926	1937	1943	1954	1965	1971	1982	1993	1999
21st Century	2010	2021	2027	2038	2049	2055	2066	2077	2083	2094	2100

Virtual   Calendar   6

January							February							March							April						
S	M	T	W	T	F	S	S	M	T	W	T	F	S	S	M	T	W	T	F	S	S	M	T	W	T	F	S
						1			1	2	3	4	5			1	2	3	4	5						1	2
2	3	4	5	6	7	8	6	7	8	9	10	11	12	6	7	8	9	10	11	12	3	4	5	6	7	8	9
9	10	11	12	13	14	15	13	14	15	16	17	18	19	13	14	15	16	17	18	19	10	11	12	13	14	15	16
16	17	18	19	20	21	22	20	21	22	23	24	25	26	20	21	22	23	24	25	26	17	18	19	20	21	22	23
23	24	25	26	27	28	29	27	28						27	28	29	30	31			24	25	26	27	28	29	30
30	31																										

May							June							July							August						
S	M	T	W	T	F	S	S	M	T	W	T	F	S	S	M	T	W	T	F	S	S	M	T	W	T	F	S
1	2	3	4	5	6	7				1	2	3	4						1	2		1	2	3	4	5	6
8	9	10	11	12	13	14	5	6	7	8	9	10	11	3	4	5	6	7	8	9	7	8	9	10	11	12	13
15	16	17	18	19	20	21	12	13	14	15	16	17	18	10	11	12	13	14	15	16	14	15	16	17	18	19	20
22	23	24	25	26	27	28	19	20	21	22	23	24	25	17	18	19	20	21	22	23	21	22	23	24	25	26	27
29	30	31					26	27	28	29	30			24	25	26	27	28	29	30	28	29	30	31			
														31													

September							October							November							December						
S	M	T	W	T	F	S	S	M	T	W	T	F	S	S	M	T	W	T	F	S	S	M	T	W	T	F	S
				1	2	3							1			1	2	3	4	5						1	2	3
4	5	6	7	8	9	10	2	3	4	5	6	7	8	6	7	8	9	10	11	12	4	5	6	7	8	9	10
11	12	13	14	15	16	17	9	10	11	12	13	14	15	13	14	15	16	17	18	19	11	12	13	14	15	16	17
18	19	20	21	22	23	24	16	17	18	19	20	21	22	20	21	22	23	24	25	26	18	19	20	21	22	23	24
25	26	27	28	29	30		23	24	25	26	27	28	29	27	28	29	30				25	26	27	28	29	30	31
							30	31																			

Years that use Calendar 6

20th Century	1910	1921	1927	1938	1949	1955	1966	1977	1983	1994	
21st Century	2005	2011	2022	2033	2039	2050	2061	2067	2078	2089	2095

Virtual   Calendar   7

January							February							March							April						
S	M	T	W	T	F	S	S	M	T	W	T	F	S	S	M	T	W	T	F	S	S	M	T	W	T	F	S
1	2	3	4	5	6	7				1	2	3	4					1	2	3	1	2	3	4	5	6	7
8	9	10	11	12	13	14	5	6	7	8	9	10	11	4	5	6	7	8	9	10	8	9	10	11	12	13	14
15	16	17	18	19	20	21	12	13	14	15	16	17	18	11	12	13	14	15	16	17	15	16	17	18	19	20	21
22	23	24	25	26	27	28	19	20	21	22	23	24	25	18	19	20	21	22	23	24	22	23	24	25	26	27	28
29	30	31					26	27	28	29				25	26	27	28	29	30	31	29	30					

May							June							July							August						
S	M	T	W	T	F	S	S	M	T	W	T	F	S	S	M	T	W	T	F	S	S	M	T	W	T	F	S
		1	2	3	4	5						1	2	1	2	3	4	5	6	7				1	2	3	4
6	7	8	9	10	11	12	3	4	5	6	7	8	9	8	9	10	11	12	13	14	5	6	7	8	9	10	11
13	14	15	16	17	18	19	10	11	12	13	14	15	16	15	16	17	18	19	20	21	12	13	14	15	16	17	18
20	21	22	23	24	25	26	17	18	19	20	21	22	23	22	23	24	25	26	27	28	19	20	21	22	23	24	25
27	28	29	30	31			24	25	26	27	28	29	30	29	30	31					26	27	28	29	30	31	

September							October							November							December						
S	M	T	W	T	F	S	S	M	T	W	T	F	S	S	M	T	W	T	F	S	S	M	T	W	T	F	S
						1		1	2	3	4	5	6					1	2	3							1
2	3	4	5	6	7	8	7	8	9	10	11	12	13	4	5	6	7	8	9	10	2	3	4	5	6	7	8
9	10	11	12	13	14	15	14	15	16	17	18	19	20	11	12	13	14	15	16	17	9	10	11	12	13	14	15
16	17	18	19	20	21	22	21	22	23	24	25	26	27	18	19	20	21	22	23	24	16	17	18	19	20	21	22
23	24	25	26	27	28	29	28	29	30	31				25	26	27	28	29	30		23	24	25	26	27	28	29
30																					30	31					

Years that use Calendar 7

20th Century	1928	1956	1984	
21st Century	2012	2040	2068	2096

Virtual Calendar 8

January

S	M	T	W	T	F	S
	1	2	3	4	5	6
7	8	9	10	11	12	13
14	15	16	17	18	19	20
21	22	23	24	25	26	27
28	29	30	31			

February

S	M	T	W	T	F	S
				1	2	3
4	5	6	7	8	9	10
11	12	13	14	15	16	17
18	19	20	21	22	23	24
25	26	27	28	29		

March

S	M	T	W	T	F	S
					1	2
3	4	5	6	7	8	9
10	11	12	13	14	15	16
17	18	19	20	21	22	23
24	25	26	27	28	29	30
31						

April

S	M	T	W	T	F	S
	1	2	3	4	5	6
7	8	9	10	11	12	13
14	15	16	17	18	19	20
21	22	23	24	25	26	27
28	29	30				

May

S	M	T	W	T	F	S
			1	2	3	4
5	6	7	8	9	10	11
12	13	14	15	16	17	18
19	20	21	22	23	24	25
26	27	28	29	30	31	

June

S	M	T	W	T	F	S
						1
2	3	4	5	6	7	8
9	10	11	12	13	14	15
16	17	18	19	20	21	22
23	24	25	26	27	28	29
30						

July

S	M	T	W	T	F	S
	1	2	3	4	5	6
7	8	9	10	11	12	13
14	15	16	17	18	19	20
21	22	23	24	25	26	27
28	29	30	31			

August

S	M	T	W	T	F	S
				1	2	3
4	5	6	7	8	9	10
11	12	13	14	15	16	17
18	19	20	21	22	23	24
25	26	27	28	29	30	31

September

S	M	T	W	T	F	S
1	2	3	4	5	6	7
8	9	10	11	12	13	14
15	16	17	18	19	20	21
22	23	24	25	26	27	28
29	30					

October

S	M	T	W	T	F	S
		1	2	3	4	5
6	7	8	9	10	11	12
13	14	15	16	17	18	19
20	21	22	23	24	25	26
27	28	29	30	31		

November

S	M	T	W	T	F	S
					1	2
3	4	5	6	7	8	9
10	11	12	13	14	15	16
17	18	19	20	21	22	23
24	25	26	27	28	29	30

December

S	M	T	W	T	F	S
1	2	3	4	5	6	7
8	9	10	11	12	13	14
15	16	17	18	19	20	21
22	23	24	25	26	27	28
29	30	31				

Years that use Calendar 8

20th Century	1912	1940	1968	1996
21st Century	2024	2052	2080	

Virtual   Calendar   9

January

S	M	T	W	T	F	S
		1	2	3	4	5
6	7	8	9	10	11	12
13	14	15	16	17	18	19
20	21	22	23	24	25	26
27	28	29	30	31		

February

S	M	T	W	T	F	S
					1	2
3	4	5	6	7	8	9
10	11	12	13	14	15	16
17	18	19	20	21	22	23
24	25	26	27	28	29	

March

S	M	T	W	T	F	S
						1
2	3	4	5	6	7	8
9	10	11	12	13	14	15
16	17	18	19	20	21	22
23	24	25	26	27	28	29
30	31					

April

S	M	T	W	T	F	S
		1	2	3	4	5
6	7	8	9	10	11	12
13	14	15	16	17	18	19
20	21	22	23	24	25	26
27	28	29	30			

May

S	M	T	W	T	F	S
			1	2	3	
4	5	6	7	8	9	10
11	12	13	14	15	16	17
18	19	20	21	22	23	24
25	26	27	28	29	30	31

June

S	M	T	W	T	F	S
1	2	3	4	5	6	7
8	9	10	11	12	13	14
15	16	17	18	19	20	21
22	23	24	25	26	27	28
29	30					

July

S	M	T	W	T	F	S
		1	2	3	4	5
6	7	8	9	10	11	12
13	14	15	16	17	18	19
20	21	22	23	24	25	26
27	28	29	30	31		

August

S	M	T	W	T	F	S
					1	2
3	4	5	6	7	8	9
10	11	12	13	14	15	16
17	18	19	20	21	22	23
24	25	26	27	28	29	30
31						

September

S	M	T	W	T	F	S
	1	2	3	4	5	6
7	8	9	10	11	12	13
14	15	16	17	18	19	20
21	22	23	24	25	26	27
28	29	30				

October

S	M	T	W	T	F	S
			1	2	3	4
5	6	7	8	9	10	11
12	13	14	15	16	17	18
19	20	21	22	23	24	25
26	27	28	29	30	31	

November

S	M	T	W	T	F	S
						1
2	3	4	5	6	7	8
9	10	11	12	13	14	15
16	17	18	19	20	21	22
23	24	25	26	27	28	29
30						

December

S	M	T	W	T	F	S
	1	2	3	4	5	6
7	8	9	10	11	12	13
14	15	16	17	18	19	20
21	22	23	24	25	26	27
28	29	30	31			

Years that use Calendar 9

20th Century	1924	1952	1980	
21st Century	2008	2036	2064	2092

Virtual   Calendar   10

January
S	M	T	W	T	F	S
			1	2	3	4
5	6	7	8	9	10	11
12	13	14	15	16	17	18
19	20	21	22	23	24	25
26	27	28	29	30	31	

February
S	M	T	W	T	F	S
						1
2	3	4	5	6	7	8
9	10	11	12	13	14	15
16	17	18	19	20	21	22
23	24	25	26	27	28	29

March
S	M	T	W	T	F	S
1	2	3	4	5	6	7
8	9	10	11	12	13	14
15	16	17	18	19	20	21
22	23	24	25	26	27	28
29	30	31				

April
S	M	T	W	T	F	S
			1	2	3	4
5	6	7	8	9	10	11
12	13	14	15	16	17	18
19	20	21	22	23	24	25
26	27	28	29	30		

May
S	M	T	W	T	F	S
					1	2
3	4	5	6	7	8	9
10	11	12	13	14	15	16
17	18	19	20	21	22	23
24	25	26	27	28	29	30
31						

June
S	M	T	W	T	F	S
	1	2	3	4	5	6
7	8	9	10	11	12	13
14	15	16	17	18	19	20
21	22	23	24	25	26	27
28	29	30				

July
S	M	T	W	T	F	S
			1	2	3	4
5	6	7	8	9	10	11
12	13	14	15	16	17	18
19	20	21	22	23	24	25
26	27	28	29	30	31	

August
S	M	T	W	T	F	S
						1
2	3	4	5	6	7	8
9	10	11	12	13	14	15
16	17	18	19	20	21	22
23	24	25	26	27	28	29
30	31					

September
S	M	T	W	T	F	S
	1	2	3	4	5	
6	7	8	9	10	11	12
13	14	15	16	17	18	19
20	21	22	23	24	25	26
27	28	29	30			

October
S	M	T	W	T	F	S
				1	2	3
4	5	6	7	8	9	10
11	12	13	14	15	16	17
18	19	20	21	22	23	24
25	26	27	28	29	30	31

November
S	M	T	W	T	F	S
1	2	3	4	5	6	7
8	9	10	11	12	13	14
15	16	17	18	19	20	21
22	23	24	25	26	27	28
29	30					

December
S	M	T	W	T	F	S
		1	2	3	4	5
6	7	8	9	10	11	12
13	14	15	16	17	18	19
20	21	22	23	24	25	26
27	28	29	30	31		

Years that use Calendar 10

20th Century	1908	1936	1964	1992
21st Century	2020	2048	2076	

Virtual   Calendar   11

January

S	M	T	W	T	F	S
				1	2	3
4	5	6	7	8	9	10
11	12	13	14	15	16	17
18	19	20	21	22	23	24
25	26	27	28	29	30	31

February

S	M	T	W	T	F	S
1	2	3	4	5	6	7
8	9	10	11	12	13	14
15	16	17	18	19	20	21
22	23	24	25	26	27	28
29						

March

S	M	T	W	T	F	S
	1	2	3	4	5	6
7	8	9	10	11	12	13
14	15	16	17	18	19	20
21	22	23	24	25	26	27
28	29	30	31			

April

S	M	T	W	T	F	S
				1	2	3
4	5	6	7	8	9	10
11	12	13	14	15	16	17
18	19	20	21	22	23	24
25	26	27	28	29	30	

May

S	M	T	W	T	F	S
						1
2	3	4	5	6	7	8
9	10	11	12	13	14	15
16	17	18	19	20	21	22
23	24	25	26	27	28	29
30	31					

June

S	M	T	W	T	F	S
		1	2	3	4	5
6	7	8	9	10	11	12
13	14	15	16	17	18	19
20	21	22	23	24	25	26
27	28	29	30			

July

S	M	T	W	T	F	S
				1	2	3
4	5	6	7	8	9	10
11	12	13	14	15	16	17
18	19	20	21	22	23	24
25	26	27	28	29	30	31

August

S	M	T	W	T	F	S
1	2	3	4	5	6	7
8	9	10	11	12	13	14
15	16	17	18	19	20	21
22	23	24	25	26	27	28
29	30	31				

September

S	M	T	W	T	F	S
		1	2	3	4	
5	6	7	8	9	10	11
12	13	14	15	16	17	18
19	20	21	22	23	24	25
26	27	28	29	30		

October

S	M	T	W	T	F	S
					1	2
3	4	5	6	7	8	9
10	11	12	13	14	15	16
17	18	19	20	21	22	23
24	25	26	27	28	29	30
31						

November

S	M	T	W	T	F	S
	1	2	3	4	5	6
7	8	9	10	11	12	13
14	15	16	17	18	19	20
21	22	23	24	25	26	27
28	29	30				

December

S	M	T	W	T	F	S
			1	2	3	4
5	6	7	8	9	10	11
12	13	14	15	16	17	18
19	20	21	22	23	24	25
26	27	28	29	30	31	

Years that use Calendar 11

20th Century	1920	1948	1976	
21st Century	2004	2032	2060	2088

Virtual   Calendar   12

January

S	M	T	W	T	F	S
					1	2
3	4	5	6	7	8	9
10	11	12	13	14	15	16
17	18	19	20	21	22	23
24	25	26	27	28	29	30
31						

February

S	M	T	W	T	F	S
	1	2	3	4	5	6
7	8	9	10	11	12	13
14	15	16	17	18	19	20
21	22	23	24	25	26	27
28	29					

March

S	M	T	W	T	F	S
		1	2	3	4	5
6	7	8	9	10	11	12
13	14	15	16	17	18	19
20	21	22	23	24	25	26
27	28	29	30	31		

April

S	M	T	W	T	F	S
					1	2
3	4	5	6	7	8	9
10	11	12	13	14	15	16
17	18	19	20	21	22	23
24	25	26	27	28	29	30

May

S	M	T	W	T	F	S
1	2	3	4	5	6	7
8	9	10	11	12	13	14
15	16	17	18	19	20	21
22	23	24	25	26	27	28
29	30	31				

June

S	M	T	W	T	F	S
			1	2	3	4
5	6	7	8	9	10	11
12	13	14	15	16	17	18
19	20	21	22	23	24	25
26	27	28	29	30		

July

S	M	T	W	T	F	S
					1	2
3	4	5	6	7	8	9
10	11	12	13	14	15	16
17	18	19	20	21	22	23
24	25	26	27	28	29	30
31						

August

S	M	T	W	T	F	S
	1	2	3	4	5	6
7	8	9	10	11	12	13
14	15	16	17	18	19	20
21	22	23	24	25	26	27
28	29	30	31			

September

S	M	T	W	T	F	S
				1	2	3
4	5	6	7	8	9	10
11	12	13	14	15	16	17
18	19	20	21	22	23	24
25	26	27	28	29	30	

October

S	M	T	W	T	F	S
						1
2	3	4	5	6	7	8
9	10	11	12	13	14	15
16	17	18	19	20	21	22
23	24	25	26	27	28	29
30	31					

November

S	M	T	W	T	F	S
		1	2	3	4	5
6	7	8	9	10	11	12
13	14	15	16	17	18	19
20	21	22	23	24	25	26
27	28	29	30			

December

S	M	T	W	T	F	S
				1	2	3
4	5	6	7	8	9	10
11	12	13	14	15	16	17
18	19	20	21	22	23	24
25	26	27	28	29	30	31

Years that use Calendar 12

20th Century	1904	1932	1960	1988
21st Century	2016	2044	2072	

Virtual   Calendar   13

January							February							March							April						
S	M	T	W	T	F	S	S	M	T	W	T	F	S	S	M	T	W	T	F	S	S	M	T	W	T	F	S
						1			1	2	3	4	5				1	2	3	4							1
2	3	4	5	6	7	8	6	7	8	9	10	11	12	5	6	7	8	9	10	11	2	3	4	5	6	7	8
9	10	11	12	13	14	15	13	14	15	16	17	18	19	12	13	14	15	16	17	18	9	10	11	12	13	14	15
16	17	18	19	20	21	22	20	21	22	23	24	25	26	19	20	21	22	23	24	25	16	17	18	19	20	21	22
23	24	25	26	27	28	29	27	28	29					26	27	28	29	30	31		23	24	25	26	27	28	29
30	31																				30						

May							June							July							August						
S	M	T	W	T	F	S	S	M	T	W	T	F	S	S	M	T	W	T	F	S	S	M	T	W	T	F	S
	1	2	3	4	5	6				1	2	3								1			1	2	3	4	5
7	8	9	10	11	12	13	4	5	6	7	8	9	10	2	3	4	5	6	7	8	6	7	8	9	10	11	12
14	15	16	17	18	19	20	11	12	13	14	15	16	17	9	10	11	12	13	14	15	13	14	15	16	17	18	19
21	22	23	24	25	26	27	18	19	20	21	22	23	24	16	17	18	19	20	21	22	20	21	22	23	24	25	26
28	29	30	31				25	26	27	28	29	30		23	24	25	26	27	28	29	27	28	29	30	31		
														30	31												

September							October							November							December						
S	M	T	W	T	F	S	S	M	T	W	T	F	S	S	M	T	W	T	F	S	S	M	T	W	T	F	S
					1	2	1	2	3	4	5	6	7				1	2	3	4						1	2
3	4	5	6	7	8	9	8	9	10	11	12	13	14	5	6	7	8	9	10	11	3	4	5	6	7	8	9
10	11	12	13	14	15	16	15	16	17	18	19	20	21	12	13	14	15	16	17	18	10	11	12	13	14	15	16
17	18	19	20	21	22	23	22	23	24	25	26	27	28	19	20	21	22	23	24	25	17	18	19	20	21	22	23
24	25	26	27	28	29	30	29	30	31					26	27	28	29	30			24	25	26	27	28	29	30
																					31						

Years that use Calendar 13

20th Century	1916	1944	1972	2000
21st Century	2028	2056	2084	

CHAPTER 26: SUICIDE INVESTIGATION

CONSIDERATIONS

1) A suicide should be investigated with all the thoroughness and tenacity of a homicide. Some investigators find that their investigations into probable suicides often produce more criticism and second-guessing than homicide investigations because of the following:
    a) There is a still the social stigma to the act of suicide placed on the family of the decedent.
    b) Family members and friends feel guilty because they did not intercede to prevent the suicide from occurring, or believe that others may think that they did not.
    c) The determination of suicide may result in significant financial repercussions to the family, such as the nonpayment of insurance death claims.

2) Suicide findings are not the logical conclusion of the finding that a death is not a homicide. Suicide must be proved. Clear and convincing evidence must be established through investigation. Evidence must be developed establishing that the suspect who committed the act is the decedent.

3) The quickest way for an investigator to get into trouble is to develop the false assumption that his function is to investigate only homicides. Once a suicide is believed to have occurred, the job of the investigator is concluded.

PRIMARY FOCUS OF INVESTIGATION

1) Is it possible that the decedent could have committed suicide?

2) Is it probable that the decedent committed suicide to the logical exclusion of homicide or accident?

3) Establish the opportunity and the conditions for the decedent to have self-inflicted his injuries.

4) Develop and detail all indications of intent on the part of the decedent.

5) Develop motive.

NOTIFICATION

1) No special requirements of notification are required unless circumstances at the scene do not readily point to suicide.

SCENE PHOTOGRAPHS

1) In general, scene photographs should detail the following:
    a) All evidence found at the scene
    b) All demonstrations of the decedent's efforts to commit suicide.
    c) All demonstrations depicting the nature of the decedent's injuries to be self-inflicted.
        i) Include blood spatter.
        ii) Include gunpowder residue.

iii) Include the position of decedent's body in relation to the unlikely position an assailant would have had to assume.

2) Follow specific requirements for photographs found in later chapters on specific means of death.

SCENE INVESTIGATION

1) Begin the investigation with the physical situation of the scene.
   a) Establish who may have had access to the decedent. Eliminate these individuals as suspects (e.g., gunshot residue kit of hands, blood spatter targeting, position of the decedent).
   b) Was the decedent secured and alone at the time of the injury? Document how the decedent was found. What steps were necessary to access the body (e.g., was it necessary to break into the apartment?)?

2) Eliminate various homicide motives.
   a) Robbery related
   b) Sex related
   c) Drug related
   d) Domestic or altercation related

3) Eliminate accidental nature of the injuries.
   a) For example, no gun-cleaning kit was found with the decedent if the cause of death was a gunshot wound, the decedent was not wearing a swimsuit when the body was recovered from a body of water, the decedent was not working on the car in the garage if death was by carbon monoxide poisoning.

4) Demonstrate the intent of the decedent:
   a) For example, did the decedent have to go somewhere and get a gun, find ammunition for the gun, wrap it in a pillow to muffle the sound, prop it on furniture, devise a trigger pull mechanism?
   b) Note(s) found at scene
   c) Instructions, money, or personal possessions from the decedent found at scene and directed to another individual
   d) Items placed to make the decedent more comfortable or to prevent soiling of the area immediately containing the decedent's body or body fluids
   e) Indication that the decedent knew the potential lethality of his actions (e.g., a pharmacist dying of an overdose or a marksman shooting himself while cleaning his weapon)
   f) Precautions taken to avoid rescue (e.g., locking doors, going to a remote area, arranging to be alone)

5) Establish the time frame of the death.

6) Follow specific instructions pursuant to the mechanism of death as described in Chapter 28.

BODY TRANSPORT FROM SCENE

1) Preserve all evidence associated with the mechanism of death.
   a) Hangings should be transported with noose and knot areas intact and still in position when possible.

247 · SUICIDE INVESTIGATION · 247

b) Gunshot wound victims should have their hands bagged for transportation.

c) Preserve any significant areas of blood spatter on the decedent's body or clothing.

2)   Check specific instructions pursuant to the mechanism of death contained in Chapter 28 on other deaths.

PROCESSING AT MEO

1)   All decedents should be fingerprinted. Major case prints may be considered in those cases where latent prints from a scene may be necessary to prove or disprove suicide.

2)   Follow specific requirements as delineated under the specific mechanism of the death.

FOLLOW-UP INVESTIGATION

1)   Conduct known-acquaintance interviews. Avoid asking the witnesses if the decedent would have killed himself. Instead seek the following information from sources.

    a) Develop how long the decedent and the witness knew each other.

       i) When did the witness meet the decedent?

       ii) How often would he visit with the decedent?

       iii) Describe the nature of their association.

    b) Develop background information on the decedent.

       i) What was occurring in his life leading up to his death?

       ii) Was the subject undergoing any changes? Describe.

    c) Develop any possible gestures that may indicate suicide.

       i) Unexplained dispersing of personal possessions or arranging for care of pets or children.

       ii) Utterances of farewell or of finality or indications of impending doom (e.g., "I won't be here to be kicked around, anymore." "You'll miss me when I'm gone."

       iii) Expressions of despair indicating mental anguish (e.g., "It doesn't matter, anymore." "What's the use?")

       iv) Distressful comments indicating physical torment (e.g., "I can't go on.")

       v) Deliberate efforts to learn more about death or the mechanism to produce death (e.g., asking a firearms salesperson about killing power of certain weapons, researching the effects of drugs, checking related books out of the library)

       vi) Previous suicide attempts

       vii) Previous suicide threats

       viii) Preoccupation with relatives or friends who have died

    d) Describe any physical changes affecting the subject.

       i) Include frequency, severity, and duration.

          (1) Physical complaints

          (2) Sleep

          (3) Appetite

          (4) Indigestion

          (5) Nausea

          (6) Bowel disturbance

          (7) Decreased sex drive

    e) How does this source explain the death?

f) Who else may know something of this case? Who was the decedent's closest confidant?

2)   Background of the decedent
       a) Financial
              i) Source of income
              ii) Did the decedent live within his income?
              iii) Recent losses?
                     (1) Suit(s)
                     (2) Investments
                     (3) Gambling losses
              iv) Bank account standing
                     (1) Bouncing checks?
              v) Being behind on payments on loans?
              vi) Status of these:
                     (1) Mortgage
                     (2) Electric bill
                     (3) Water bill
              vii) Any problems with IRS?
              viii) If employed, did subject handle money for employer?
                     (1) Audit underway?
                     (2) Any claim against bonding company?
              ix) If self-employed, condition of the business
                     (1) Pressed by creditors?
                     (2) Delinquent on rent?
                            (3) Delinquent on payroll?
       b) Domestic situation of subject
              i) Married, separated, widowed, divorced, or estranged
                     (1) Any recent changes?
                     (2) In receipt of any recent subpoena?
                     (3) Any changes in alimony or child support?
                     (4) Recent anniversary?
              ii) Any lovers' triangle situation?
              iii) Recent death or preoccupied with death of a family member or close friend?
              iv) Any pending criminal charges? Note dates of court appearances.
              v) Any added responsibilities because of injury or loss of family member?
       c) Health
              i) Any health impairments or diseases?
              ii) Any recent medical examination in which subject may have been told of serious problems?

CHAPTER 27: PSYCHOLOGICAL AUTOPSIES

WHAT IS A PSYCHOLOGICAL AUTOPSY

1) A psychological autopsy is a clinical/investigative tool that helps clarify the manner of death in a suicide, homicide, or accidental death by focusing on the psychological aspects of the death.
    a) Its primary purpose is to understand the circumstances and state of mind of the victim at the time of death.

2) The term *equivocal death analysis* is often used synonymously with *psychological autopsy*.

3) A psychological autopsy should never be used simply to support what is already known in a particular case. The psychological autopsy should not be allowed to supersede the harder scientific evidence.

4) Psychological autopsies must not only be grounded in scientific principles (be they physical or behavioral), but they must be conducted by those professionals with a broad range of experience with death investigation.
    a) All too often, psychological autopsies are conducted by those who have great expertise in suicides but lack understanding and experience in the fields of homicide and accidental death (Gelles, 2000).

5) The procedure involves the following:
    a) Reconstruction of the lifestyle and circumstances of the victim
    b) Details of behaviors and events that led to the death of the individual

6) The psychological autopsy is speculative. It is an opinion.

PREANALYSIS CONSIDERATIONS

1) The current trend in performing psychological autopsies is to have the case first analyzed by a forensic scientist or crime-scene specialist.
    a) A forensic review of the scientific information developed through the death-scene investigation may provide additional insight into the behavioral and motivational intentions of the subject.
    b) In many cases a solid forensic analysis can be a substitute for, or a supplement to, a psychological autopsy in clarifying the behavior of the decedent and the manner of death.

FORENSIC SCIENCE INVESTIGATIVE CONSIDERATIONS

1) In starting the forensic investigative analysis of a psychological autopsy, two questions must be at the forefront of assessing the case:
    a) First, what happened? That is, have the investigators significantly answered the question of what may have happened at the scene?
    b) Second, is it possible for the decedent to have committed suicide?

2) Just as a medical examiner determines the manner of death based on the best available information, the accuracy of a psychological autopsy is contingent on the most accurate information being supplied in the case study. The assessment of this critical information by a forensic scientist allows for the assumptions made by the psychologist to be reduced to a minimum and, thus, lends more credibility and accuracy to the interpretation provided in the psychological autopsy.

3) Discovery of the death
    a) Factors to be considered in assessing the initial effectiveness of the death investigation include the following:
        i) How soon the body is discovered
            (1) It is at this level in the death investigation that the first indicators of the manner of death may begin to appear. The security of the death scene and the isolation of the decedent within it may preclude the possibility of any other consideration for another person to have affected the decedent's death. With the self-infliction issue determined, what remains, then, is to establish whether the manner of death is a suicide or an accident.
        ii) The length of time it takes the first responding police units to arrive at the scene
            (1) At the discovery of the body phase, efforts by the subject to avoid rescue may become apparent. Many cases involve the discovery of the body once a family member or friend of the decedent arrives home from a shopping trip or the usual workday. Other cases have the decedent seeking the relative privacy of his own room or the locked security of a bathroom door.
        iii) The length of time it takes police detectives to arrive at the scene

4) The second level of information a forensic scientist examines is the death-scene investigation itself. The expert begins looking at the information collected by death-scene investigators. He determines whether the evidence at the scene was recognized, collected, and processed in an effort to answer the basic question of any death scene. That is, what happened?
    a) It is at this level, that the quality of the investigation, from an analytical standpoint, becomes apparent. Reviewing the photographs of the scene and the evidence that was collected or omitted from collection gives the reviewer some initial insight into the thoroughness and sophistication level of the investigation.
        i) If, for example, two Polaroid photographs were all that were taken of the death scene, then the analysis of this case should be ever diligent and the scrutiny level of any supplied material should be high.
        ii) The photographs taken of the crime scene may give the forensic reviewer some insight into whether or not the scene investigators had an understanding of what transpired or had determined what transpired at the scene that day.
        iii) An additional indicator for reviewing the overall quality of the scene processing is how closely the scene investigative teams' work product complied with the definition of evidence usually associated with crime-scene reconstruction specialists. That is, "evidence is anything which is added to the scene, is missing, moved, or removed entirely from the scene, or which contributes information to the who, how, when, where, why, [and what happened] of a crime" (Rynearson, Chisum, 1991).
            (1) Not only is the physical and trace evidence at the scene important in understanding what happened, but what *isn't* at the scene is also

critically important. The void made visible by the surrounding dust on the top of a counter may give investigators reason to believe an item was stolen at or around the time of the subject's death. This may be an important factor in deciding the manner of death or, at the very least, the motive for the killing. Likewise, the identification of any void in blood spatter radiating in a 360-degree pattern from a shotgun wound to the victim's head, may be quite compelling for a determination that the wound was self-inflicted.

5) In addition to evidence collection and development of the initial theory as to what may have happened, the death-scene examination should also begin to indicate the development of motive associated with the death and the identification of information sources for the investigator.

    a) Although motive development is more closely associated in the investigation of homicides, with the possibility of a self-inflicted death it becomes more focused on why the subject may have wished to end his life. In the absence of a suicide note at the scene, certain other indicators, or red flags, may draw the investigator's attention. These environmental factors include not only the possible weapon, but may also include medications, prescription vials, oxygen containers, a wheel chair, -ostomy appliances, prostheses, or a hospital bed.

6) Other forensic considerations include the following:
    a) Cause of death
    b) Evidence processing
       i) This may allow the weapon or mechanism of death to be identified.
    c) Time frame of death
       i) Information sources should assist the investigation in establishing a time frame for the death. "Collectively, this information is used to update and further enhance the theory of what happened to the decedent. This will enable the forensic scientist to form opinions relative to the sequence of events occurring before, during, and after the death event" (Rynearson, Chisum 1991).
    d) Reconstruction of the incident
       i) Reconstructing a death scene is similar to assembling a puzzle, with the information available corresponding to the puzzle pieces. A puzzle with only a few pieces that fit together easily makes assembly relatively simple. But when there are many pieces and several are missing or misleading, the puzzle can be difficult or even impossible to put together. Therefore, having a large quantity of accurate information will enable the reconstructionist to fit the pieces of the scene together more accurately.

USES FOR A PSYCHOLOGICAL AUTOPSY

1) The psychological autopsy serves as an adjunctive aid to the pathologist or medical examiner-coroner in determining the manner of death.
    a) It can provide an additional dimension to assess the circumstances, behaviors, and motivations of the decedent prior to his demise.

2) The psychological autopsy can also function as a consultative aid to lawyers and litigants in regard to the disposition of civil suits and insurance claims.

3) The report should always emphasize that the results are a speculative review of events and

conclusions regarding the personality of the deceased. Therefore, the report is subject to considerable variability and should be viewed only as an investigative aid.

CONDUCTING THE PSYCHOLOGICAL AUTOPSY

1) There are several questions that are to be answered when conducting this procedure. The primary questions include these:
   a) How and when did the individual die?
   b) Why did it happen at that particular time and place?
   c) What is the most probable manner of death?
   d) What were the decedent's intentions at the time of death?

2) Secondary questions would include these:
   a) What was the deceased like?
   b) What occurred in his life that could have contributed to his demise?
   c) What in his life could have been stressful?
   d) What were his reactions to those stresses?

3) The psychological autopsy attempts to understand the deceased's personality characteristics, motivations, and intentions.

THE CASE REVIEW

1) The following case material should be reviewed
   a) Crime-scene photographs and videotapes
   b) Crime-scene descriptions and drawings
   c) Demographic information about the decedent. Collect important identifying and demographic information:
      i) Name, age, and date of birth
      ii) Gender and race
      iii) Marital status
      iv) Occupation and level of education
         (1) The combination of occupation and education gives insight into socioeconomic status of the deceased.
      v) Home address (where the victim was living at the time of death)
      vi) Description of the death-scene location (address and scene description—e.g., friend's house, parent's home)
      vii) Data detailing the status of relationships and support systems
   d) Description of the details of discovery
      i) Develop whether the decedent made provisions for rescue, written communications, and communication of suicidal intent, written or oral.
         (1) Communication to whom?
   e) Details about acts of violence that accompanied the death and all other psychologically relevant details obtained from the scene (e.g., sexual paraphernalia, documents)
   f) Environmental conditions
   g) Forensic evidence, including a forensic science analysis
   h) Autopsy and toxicology reports
   i) Interviews with witnesses
      i) These should involve interviews with those individuals who were proximal to the decedent around the time of death.
         (1) Witnesses to individuals who have a history with the decedent, ranging from parents to close friends.

ii) The interview information may be distorted, specifically following the death of a friend or loved one.

(1) Often relatives and friends do not like to describe negative things about the deceased.

(2) Relatives and friends may overcompensate in their responses as a means to defend against guilt and anger directed toward the deceased.

(3) There is a natural defensiveness to accepting the death of a loved one, especially a child. "The denial is often powerful and a primary component in the distortion of information. Far too frequently the suicide of a loved one is so disturbing to a relative or friend that they must believe that it was an accident or in some cases a homicide" (Gelles, 2002).

iii) The following are general guidelines for conducting interviews of friends, associates, and family members of the deceased.

(1) The credibility of the reference is partially based on the frequency, duration, and quality of the relationship with the deceased. Sample questions to ask during the interview include:

(a) How long did you know the deceased?

(b) When did you first meet?

(c) How often did you associate with the deceased?

(d) How close was your relationship?

(e) What was the nature of your relationship (e.g., friend, relative, peer, co-worker)?

iv) The overall assessment of the decedent should be established by going over the following areas with individuals who can offer insight into the decedent's pattern of behavior, personality, and lifestyle.

(1) Personal interests and hobbies:

(a) What types of activities did the decedent enjoy during recreational and free time?

(b) How did he relax?

(c) What were his most enjoyable activities?

(2) Coping style:

(a) How did he react to stress, change, transition, loss, frustration, rejection, and criticism?

(b) Did he express his feelings openly?

(c) How did he deal with anger?

(3) Interpersonal relationships (inquiring across the developmental spectrum: childhood, school years, adolescence, adulthood):

(a) Did the decedent have many relationships or few?

(b) Was the nature of his relationships mostly acquaintances or closer relationships?

(c) Was the decedent a socially inclusive or reclusive individual?

(d) Would he have a focused group of friends or wide variety of friends with different interests and affiliations?

(4) Communication style:

(a) Did the decedent communicate openly, or was he more inhibited?

(b) Did he tend to verbalize thoughts and feelings or act them out behaviorally?

        (c) Were his communications spontaneous or more reflective?

(5) Marital/dyadic relationship history:

        (a) Describe marital status.

        (b) Describe any mental conflict or trouble in the relationship.

        (c) Explain the number and length of marriages.

        (d) Current living arrangements.

        (e) Number age, and sex of children.

            (i) Where do the children live?

        (f) Any changes in relationship with spouse and children; and threats or actual divorce or separation?

        (g) Were there any recent deaths in the family?

        (h) Was there a history of abusive behavior?

        (i) What was the overall quality of the current relationship?

        (j) Give a dating history.

(6) Family of origin history:

        (a) Describe parental marital, family medical, family psychiatric hospitalization and treatment, and family suicide history.

        (b) Provide number, ages, and sex of siblings.

        (c) Was there a family history of sexual abuse or other forms of child abuse or family violence?

        (d) Was there a family history of alcoholism or substance abuse?

        (e) Was there a history of family separations due to deployment, incarceration, or other circumstances?

            (i) Describe each separation, from whom at what age and for how long.

        (f) Give the death history of the victim's family (e.g., suicide, cancer, other fatal illnesses, accidents, ages of relatives at death, other details).

(7) Past problems:

        (a) Describe any troubles, pressures, tensions, or anticipated problems during the past year.

        (b) List and describe any observed or expressed symptoms of depression.

        (c) List any immediate danger signals that had been communicated.

(8) Work history:

        (a) State the victim's occupation and length of time in current position.

        (b) Identify any recent demotions, promotions, or difficulties with colleagues or supervisors.

        (c) State perceived level of work satisfaction (poor to excellent).

        (d) State the victim's employment history (e.g., jobs lost, retirement, promotion) and the frequency of job change and reasons for change or termination.

(9) Military history:

        (a) Identify periods and time in military service.

        (b) Indicate if the decedent was involved in any combat or exposed to any traumatic incidents.

        (c) Describe type of discharge.

        (d) Identify any awards or medals received, or any known disciplinary action while in the military.

(10) Medical history:
- (a) Describe any significant illness and treatment.
- (b) Describe any recent change or loss in health status.
- (c) Describe any injuries, accidents, or hospitalizations.
- (d) List current medications and history of compliance.
- (e) Indicate if the decedent was HIV positive.

(11) Psychiatric history:
- (a) Identify any psychiatric history, including diagnosis, hospitalization, and forms of psychotherapy.
- (b) Indicate the length and dates of treatment.
- (c) Identify any prescribed medication or other treatment (e.g., electric shock treatment).
- (d) State evidence of personality disorder or significant problems with anger, impulsive, emotional modulation, self-destructive or self-defeating behavior, or self-mutilation.

(12) Alcohol history/drug abuse history:
- (a) Describe the role of alcohol or drugs in the victim's overall lifestyle.
- (b) Identify the victim's behavior changes during periods of alcohol or drug abuse (e.g., hostile, altercations, loss of consciousness).
- (c) State the victim's usual alcohol consumption and evidence of addiction to alcohol, number of detoxifications, DUI arrests, blackouts, frequency of intoxication, and work-related alcohol abuse.
- (d) State whether the victim was enrolled in alcohol and drug abuse programs (inpatient or outpatient treatment).
- (e) Identify drugs victim used, if any.
- (f) Determine if the victim was addicted to drugs.

(13) Financial status:
- (a) Describe the victim's financial situation (e.g., recent losses, successes, or failures).

(14) Legal status:
- (a) Describe any current or past legal or criminal actions against the victim.
- (b) State the victim's criminal record (e.g., number and length of jail or prison terms, nature of the offenses).
- (c) State if the victim had been accused of any sexual misconduct or spousal abuse.

(15) History of prior suicide attempts:
- (a) Provide dates and descriptions of prior attempts and threats.
- (b) Were there provisions for rescue in any past attempts or gestures?
- (c) Give the circumstances surrounding attempts—were there precipitants or catalysts?
- (d) Include type of medical or psychological intervention received after suicide attempt (e.g., dates and length of treatment, type of treatment, hospitalization on an inpatient psychiatric unit).

(16) Interviewees' explanation of the death:
- (a) Ask interviewees how they explain what happened.

(17) Initial reviews of interview data should focus on the identification of the following:
  (a) What was the decedent's familiarity with the weapon or method associated with the death?
  (b) Was the death scene visited prior to the death?
  (c) Did the decedent rehearse the method?
  (d) Did the lethal method correlate with the decedent's lifestyle (e.g., guns and hunting, drowning and boating, swimming, fishing)?
  (e) Were any noticeable behavioral or emotional changes observed in the deceased?
  (f) How did he cope with problems in his life?
  (g) What changes were noticed in the deceased's mood?
  (h) When did these changes occur?
  (i) What was going on in his life at that time?

(18) Intent is a critical factor in evaluating the likelihood of suicide. Questions should include these:
  (a) What problems, difficulties, and concerns did the deceased have?
  (b) When did they start?
  (c) How much of a problem was that for him?
  (d) How did he demonstrate his problems with a particular issue?

(19) It is also important to ask the interviewees whether they were aware of any direct or indirect suicidal preoccupation. For example, "I'll kill myself." "I can't cope anymore." "The world would be better without me." "The voices are telling me to kill myself." "I can't stand it anymore." More subtle clues include giving possessions away, saying good-bye, talking about prolonged sleep and escape, and planning for survivors.

(20) It is important to ask about the frequency, intensity, and duration of any of the following symptoms.
  a) Sleep difficulties:
    (i) Trouble falling asleep, recurrent awakenings, early-morning risings, abrupt awakening in the morning accompanied by anxiety or restlessness
  (b) Physical complaints:
    (i) Low back pain, muscular tension, abdominal pain, diarrhea, constipation, vomiting, jaw pain. Were they treated, when, and by whom? List any over-the-counter or prescribed medications used.
  (c) Headaches:
    (i) Persistent or recurring
  (d) Appetite:
    (i) Decreases, lack of pleasure for favorite foods, weight loss without dieting; changes in eating patterns, overeating
  (e) Indigestion:
    (i) Continual heartburn, gas, cramps, nausea.
  (f) Libido:

(i) Decreased sex drive. Were there changes in
the level of sex drive (e.g., decrease or
increase; lack of pleasure, or ability to
perform); evidence of any autoerotic activity;
articles of pornography or sex aids

(g) Hypomania:
   (i) A definitive pattern of agitation and
      overactivity

(h) Paranoia:
   (i) A pattern of communications and behavior
      associated with feelings of persecution.
      Desperation associated with self-preservation.

(i) Realistic fears:
   (i) Communication of anxiety or fear associated
      with someone or some group

(21) Questions elaborating on the above conditions should include these:
   (a) How severe were they?
   (b) How often did they occur?
   (c) How long did they last?
   (d) When did they first occur, and were there any changes in this
      pattern?
   (e) When was the last time you saw the deceased?
   (f) Finally, ask interviewees if they have any additional comments.

j) Time line detailing the decedent's last series of behaviors.
  i) The time line helps to outline a series of events and behaviors that are
    particularly helpful for understanding motivation and what a person
    may have been doing at a particular place during a particular time
    under certain environmental conditions.
  ii) Those individuals associated with the decedent immediately before his
    death may be helpful in the construction of a time line documenting
    and accounting for as much time and as many events as possible. The
    following information may be useful in the collection of data for the
    time line.
    (1) Personality and lifestyle prior to death (2-week period before
       death):
       (a) Describe the basic personality (e.g., relaxed, intense,
          jovial, gregarious, withdrawn, outgoing, morose,
          bitter, suspicious, angry, hostile, combative).
       (b) Describe any noted recent changes in the victim's
          mood or symptoms of mental illness.
       (c) Describe the victim's recent changes in behavior, such
          as eating, sleeping, sexual patterns, drinking, driving,
          taking medications, social relationships, or hobbies.
    (2) Describe the victim's reaction to stress and typical stress
       reactions (e.g., impulsive, withdrawn, overly assertive, hostile).
    (3) Interpersonal relationships:
       (a) Describe intensity and frequency (e.g., many versus few,
          casual or intense).
    (4) Describe any recent uncharacteristic behavior
       including gambling, promiscuity, fighting, and
       withdrawal from friends.

(5) Describe the victim's friendship group.

(6) Describe manner in which time was spent.

(7) Describe recent agency contacts:

    (a) Document any contacts with mental health professionals, chaplain, physician, legal assistance, relief and family advocacy programs, and so on.

(8) Ask the interviewee to provide a detailed description of the deceased when he last saw him alive.

    (a) Include behavior, appearance, and activity.

9) Ask for references to provide confirmation of other interviewees who may have had association with the deceased or saw him prior to death.

    (a) Other individuals can provide information not previously developed.

k) Record review, including the following:

  i) Personal records

    (1) Letters or diaries

    (2) Videotapes and audio recordings made by the decedent

    (3) Medical and mental health records

      (a) Mental health clinics and or professionals often keep separate files on patients that may include information that has not been filed in a medical record.

    (4) If the victim has spent any time in military or civilian prison, records of contact and initial evaluations can be helpful.

    (5) Financial records

    (6) Computer records, including:

      (a) E-mail

      (b) Web sites most recently and most frequently visited

      (c) A decedent's computer can provide very valuable information about state of mind, interests and motivations. The computer offers a whole new arena in which to act fantasies and wishes, behaviors and impulses without scrutiny and with anonymity.

l) Additional record considerations

  i) Family advocacy or child welfare records

  ii) Police records, prison records, court records, or other documents about the decedent that offer insight into a discernible pattern of behavior

    (1) These records create a historical track of events that have occurred in the decedent's life and offer some insight into potential problems or situations that may have contributed to his death.

m) Any other information that will allow the clinician to offer insight into the following areas associated with the decedent's life

  i) Features of the decedent's personality, including:

    (1) Style of coping

    (2) Reaction to stress

    (3) Temperament

    (4) Attachment and interpersonal relationships

  ii) Trauma in the decedent's life

    (1) Impact on personality development and coping

  iii) Any medical or mental disease process

(1) Include substance use and abuse.
iv) Family history in regard to ages and causes of death of deceased family members
v) A 12-month time line constructed to detail the last hour, days, and weeks of the decedent's life
vi) Circumstances and communications prior to death that may explain how the individual died
vii) Differentiating accidental death or suicide in details associated with self-inflicted wounds and intent

SPECIAL PHRASES AND CRITERIA ASSOCIATED WITH SUICIDE (ROSENBERG ET AL., 1988)

1) Types of evidence of intent may appear in the following forms:
   a) Verbal expressions
      i) May include written diary notes, computer files, audio recordings, and videotaped messages
   b) Nonverbal expressions
      i) May include drawings or a very recent, potentially lethal attempt in which a timely discovery led to rescue

2) Preparations for death inappropriate to or unexpected in the context of the decedent's life.
   a) Examples include unexplained giving away possessions and making provisions for the future care of children or pets.

3) Expressions of farewell or the desire to die or an acknowledgment of impending death:
   a) "I won't be here to be kicked around anymore."
   b) "You were real important to me."
   c) "Have a good life."
   d) "You'll be sorry when I'm gone."
   e) "I can't stay around to face the future."

4) Expressions or actions signalling hopelessness:
   a) "It just doesn't matter anymore."
   b) "It wouldn't make any difference if I . . ."
   c) "What's the use of . . .?"
   d) Giving up activities or medical treatments that are clearly necessary to sustain life

5) Expressions of great emotional or physical pain or distress:
   a) "This pain is killing me."
   b) "I can't stand it anymore."
   c) "I cannot live like this."
   d) "It is too much for me to take."

6) Effort to procure, or learn about, means of death or rehearse fatal behavior:
   a) Recently purchasing firearms or ammunition
   b) Stockpiling potentially lethal drugs
   c) Purchasing rope
   d) Obtaining access to a high place

7) Precautions to avoid rescue:
    a) Locking doors
    b) Going to a prearranged, scheduled place
    c) Telling lies about one's whereabouts
    d) Arranging to be alone

8) Evidence that the decedent recognized high potential lethality of means of death
    a) For example, a pharmacist or physician taking an overdose of a highly lethal drug or the decedent's researching different drugs to determine their degree of lethality

9) Previous suicide attempt:
    a) Previous attempts include self-destructive acts carried out with the goal of killing oneself or with awareness that the consequences could be lethal.
    b) The more recent attempts and those with a high potential lethality may be more significant indicators of intent.
        i) Previous attempts, however, need not be recent or potentially highly lethal. Furthermore, the methods used in the previous attempts may differ.

10) Previous suicide threat:
    a) Examples of threats include playing with a gun and threatening, "I'm going to shoot myself."

11) Stressful events or significant losses (whether actual or threatened). Examples may include:
    a) The loss of a relationship with a significant other
    b) An intangible loss
        i) Examples may include not being elected to a desired office or being passed over for a promotion, loss of self-esteem, or financial losses.
    c) Anticipating difficult changes may constitute severe stress, even when those changes represent "desired" transitions, such as leaving for college or getting promoted at work.

12) Serious depression or mental disorder:
    a) Depression is not associated with a brief period of sadness. It is a mental disorder characterized by a serious and pervasive loss of pleasure and loss of interest in one's usual activities that lasts at least 2 weeks.
        i) Additional signs of depression are excessive guilt ruminations, loss of energy, loss of appetite, or a marked change in weight.
    b) Because depression is usually a recurrent disorder, a past history of depression may indicate a persistent problem.
    c) A person may commit suicide when he appears to be recovering or getting more energy.
    d) Depression or another mental disorder need not have been diagnosed by a mental health professional.
    e) Signs of impairment by a mental disorder might include:
        i) Inability to care for oneself
        ii) Inability to maintain relationships
        iii) Previous psychiatric hospitalization
    f) Other mental disorders include a manic state or manic-depressive illness, difficulty controlling impulses, psychoses, substance abuse disorders, and organic mental disorders.

g) A person with a mental disorder may commit suicide in response to a perceived command that was part of a hallucination (e.g., "My mother is calling me to join her in heaven." "The space creatures told me that if I did not kill myself they would torture me.").

THE WRITTEN REPORT

The written report is a presentation of the data and an analysis presenting the opinion of the clinician. Psychological autopsy reports have no standardized guidelines. The following outline is a suggested framework.

1) Disclaimer
  a) The report should include a series of statements emphasizing the limitations of the technique.

2) Introduction
  a) This part of the report should introduce the technique and the method used to evaluate the data.
  b) It should indicate who has requested the psychological autopsy, the organization that conducted the investigation, the nature of the forensic consultation and analysis, the data that was reviewed, and whom the psychologist interviewed.
      i) For example, the introduction should mention the use of crime scene data, investigative interview, available records reviewed, and whom the psychologist personally interviewed.

3) Identifying information
  a) Include name, age, address, marital status, occupation and any other details.

4) Forensic analysis
  a) Type of analyses completed

5) Description of the events leading to the death
  a) The presenting problem should reflect in sequence the details of the death and pertain to facts involving:
      i) The crime scene, investigative summary, events known to precede the death, and a time line of events 4 hours to 12 months prior to the death.

6) Past history
  a) This section should reflect as comprehensively as possible the decedent's past psychosocial history, including development, past medical illness and psychiatric history (psychotherapy and suicide attempts), family constellation and history, and educational and occupational history.
  b) Death history of the family should be included in this section (e.g., cancer, accident, illness, suicide, ages at death).

7) Personality assessment
  a) This section should describe the personality factors, typical patterns of reaction to stress, periods of maladjustment to interpersonal relationships, coping style, hobbies, interests, perversions, substance use and abuse, and fantasies or thoughts (dreams) or fear of death or suicide.

8)   Opinion/formulation
       a) This section should reflect the reconstruction of the factors and events that contributed to the death.
            i) This is the section in which the clinician offers a hypothesis about the death.
            ii) This section integrates the recent events as they related to the past history and personality formulation of the deceased.
            iii) In this section, hypothesis for and against suicide or accidental death can be expressed. Assessment of intention and a rating of lethality is offered.
            iv) The mental health professional strives to highlight the major issues associated with the personality, behavior, and motivation as they relate to the death but does not offer a manner-of-death determination. The medical examiner or coroner solely determines the manner of death.

CHAPTER 28: SMALL-AIRCRAFT CRASHES

CONSIDERATION

1)   Involves the crash of a light aircraft, not a commercial aircraft. For commercial crafts, consult the section on mass disasters.

2)   Initial responding units need to secure the area. No item should be handled. Bodies should be sent directly to the MEO, where a systematic check of the decedent's pockets and itemizing of the valuables should be conducted. In no case should a wallet or jewelry be removed from the body at the scene.

3)   This will be a joint investigation involving several agencies. The final disposition of this case will depend on the work conducted by several agencies. Cooperation, communication, and the sharing of information are a must.

PRIMARY FOCUS OF INVESTIGATION

1)   Identification of the remains

2)   Determination of the manner of death
          a) Accident versus suicide versus homicide

3)   Reconstruction of the events precipitating the crash will focus on three areas that may have, individually or collectively, been responsible for the aircraft to crash.
      a) Pilot error or health
      b) Mechanical failure of the craft
      c) Weather conditions

NOTIFICATION

1)   Notify the pathologist on call.
          a) Develop information and advise how many people may be on board, the accessibility of the crash site, and whether any potential hazards may be associated with recovery.

2)   If multiple deaths are involved, contact forensic odontologist to arrange gathering dental response team.

SCENE PHOTOGRAPHS

1)   The overall crash site area

2)   The path of the plane prior to coming to rest

3)   Any identification information about the airplane, such as the "N" (U.S. registration) number

4)   Damage involving the exterior of the plane

5)   Damage to the interior of the plane

a) Photograph areas that have crushed in around the decedents and may be responsible for some of the areas of injuries that will be noted during the autopsy examination.

6)   Photograph the decedent in relation to the crash site.

7)   Shoot close-ups of identifying characteristics of the decedent, including:
        a) Clothing
        b) Jewelry
        c) Hair
        d) Tattoos (observable)

8)   Photograph observable identifying items (e.g., purses, wallets) in relation to other debris, victims, and plane wreckage.

SCENE INVESTIGATION

1)   Determine date and time found.

2)   What is the date and time of the crash?

3)   Develop any eyewitnesses to the incident.

4)   Describe events preceding the crash.

5)   Is the flight chartered, personal, or scheduled?

6)   Is the aircraft single- or multiengine?

7)   Describe the weather conditions during the time in which the crash is believed to have occurred.
        a) If excessive winds were present or a thunderstorm was in progress, attempt to develop the reported miles per hour of the wind gusts.
        b) Did the en route weather change after the aircraft had taken off?

8)   Describe the lighting conditions at the time of the crash.

9)   Describe the terrain of the crash site.

10)   Was the aircraft landing, taking off, in flight, or between destinations at the time of the crash?

11)   What is the distance to the nearest airport?

12)   Was the aircraft in radio contact at the time of the crash?

13)   Was a distress message sent?

14)   Did the airplane burn, explode, break up on impact, or turn over?

15)   Describe the damage to the aircraft.

16)   Victim(s):

a) Describe each victim's position in the aircraft as left versus right side and identify row number, if available.
    i) Was any victim thrown from the aircraft?
b) Note the status of seat and shoulder harness with regard to each person.
c) Designate whether each victim was a pilot, copilot, student pilot, or passenger.
    i) How was it determined who the pilot may have been?
d) Describe each victim, including clothing, injuries, and identifying marks. Describe any identification found in the clothing of the remains.

17) Aircraft condition
    a) Any indication the aircraft may have malfunctioned?
    b) Did fire occur as a result of the crash?
    c) Describe damage to the propellers.

18) Pilot information
    a) What was the rating of the pilot, copilot, or student pilot?
    b) How many years of experience for each?
    c) How many hours of flying time for each?
    d) Develop the date of the last physical examination for the pilot.
    i) Identify the physician who performed the physical examination.

19) Any evidence of drugs aboard the aircraft?
    a) Drugs found?
    b) Drug residue found?
    c) Seats removed from the aircraft?
    d) Suspicious circumstances involving the flight of the aircraft?

BODY TRANSPORT FROM SCENE

1) If identification of the passengers is not obvious because of the injuries involved, refer to each with a corresponding letter (e.g., Body A, Body B).

2) Do not attempt to associate scattered belongings and body parts with a particular decedent while at the scene. Record the recovery location and treat each item as a separate entry.

3) Place each decedent in a separate body bag. Do not remove any valuables or identification from the remains.

4) Transport all to the morgue.

PROCESSING AT MEO/MORGUE

1) Do not assign a medical examiner number if dealing with pieces of remains. A case number will be assigned after further processing.

2) Implement full identification procedures if multiple bodies are involved and severe mutilation has occurred.
    a) Fingerprint the decedent.
    b) Prepare postmortem dental charting.
    c) Form an antemortem information-gathering team.

266 · DEATH INVESTIGATOR'S HANDBOOK · 266

3)   Collect specimens required by the National Transportation Safety Board (NTSB).

FOLLOW-UP INVESTIGATION

1)   Concentrate activities in identifying decedents.
        a) If multiple deaths are involved:
            i) Make arrangements for obtaining a manifest or passenger list.
            ii) Collect antemortem identification information:
                (1) Fingerprint
                (2) Dental
                (3) DNA

2)   Update aircraft crash information.
        a) Mechanical history of the plane
        b) Condition of equipment at the time of the crash
        c) Preliminary findings on the cause of the crash as developed by investigators

3)   Develop pilot health history, if necessary.

CHAPTER 29: ALCOHOL-RELATED DEATHS

CONSIDERATIONS

1)   An alcohol-related death is directly attributed to the acute, short-term ingestion (accidental death) or long-term effect of drinking alcohol (natural disease).

2)   Alcohol-related diseases eventually prove fatal to individuals who refuse to seek medical attention or take care of themselves. Alcoholics tend to be antisocial, preferring to live alone. The death investigator will be challenged in developing information on these decedents because of their lonely lifestyle. This lack of initial information may confuse the death investigator at first, causing him to mistake the unusual alcohol-related bleeding or injuries with foul play.
          a) Alcoholism and its manifestations
                    i) Alcohol is a poison. The person who drinks is protected from the effects of the poison (alcohol) by the detoxification action of his liver.
                    ii) Although all organs (e.g., liver, heart, brain, upper gastrointestinal tract) suffer as a result of chronic alcohol abuse, natural deaths usually involve the following:
                              (1) Bleeding into the gastrointestinal tract from a peptic ulcer or bleeding tendencies
                              (2) Epileptic seizures with loss of respiratory function
                              (3) Cardiac rhythm disturbances (ventricular fibrillation) associated with malnutrition
                              (4) Infections such as pneumonia
                              (5) Necrotizing pancreatitis

3)   It's not unusual for the family, friends, or neighbors of the decedent to relate a fairly extensive history of alcohol abuse but a more recent history of abstinence. What has probably occurred was that the subject was in ill health and decided to give up drinking.

PRIMARY FOCUS OF INVESTIGATION

1)   To determine the manner of death

2)   To determine if the alcohol-related death resulted from short-term consumption (acute), causing a toxic level of alcohol (accidental manner of death) versus the effects associated with long-term, constant consumption (natural manner of death)

NOTIFICATION

1)   A pathologist is not required at the scene unless:
                    a) The manner of death may be confused, or an attempt appears to have been made by the decedent or some other interested party to alter the circumstances of death.
                    b) The decedent's identification may be affected because of decomposition.

SCENE PHOTOGRAPHS

1)   Photograph the entire area of the involved scene showing the condition of premises.

2)   Photograph any areas indicating movement and activities of the decedent immediately before death.

3)   Photograph any indications of security or any absence of foul play that suggest the scene is of a natural death.

4)   Photograph any items or areas of the scene that may indicate the time frame involved in the death.
        a) Newspapers collecting on front porch, food preparation, etc.

5)   If alcohol containers, drugs, or drug paraphernalia is found at the scene, photograph these items.

6)   Photograph the decedent's body relative to the position within the scene area.

7)   Photograph the body to show consistency or inconsistency of time frame changes on the decedent (e.g., rigor mortis, lividity, skin slippage, blistering).

8)   Document the absence of injuries to the decedent's remains through photographs.

9)   If decedent has injuries that could have resulted from collapsing to the floor, photograph any item the subject may have struck during the collapse. Take close-up photographs of the injuries.

10)   Take an identification photograph of the subject.

SCENE INVESTIGATION

1)   Scene of the death
        a) Give general description of the scene. Make special note of the condition of the premises.
        b) Describe the amount of empty, partially filled, and filled alcohol containers at the scene. Be sure to check the trash can.
        c) Describe the decedent and any indication of previous movement of the decedent within the scene.
        d) Describe the absence of foul play associated with the death of the decedent. For example:
            i) Describe the security of the residence.
                (1) How was entry gained?
                (2) Any indication the site has been rifled?
                (3) Any indication the VCR, television, stereo, or other item has been taken?
            ii) Describe the security the decedent took to secure his personal effects (e.g., wallet, purse, jewelry, checkbook).
        e) Describe medications found at the scene.
            i) Medications observed relative to the body.
        f) Describe any activity or item indicative of the time frame of the subject's death (e.g., newspapers collecting on front porch, food preparation).

2)   Circumstances of the death
        a) How was death discovered?
        b) When was decedent last seen alive?

    c) Describe activities of decedent shortly preceding death.

    d) Describe the terminal episode.

3)   History of the decedent

    a) Develop any complaints the decedent may have made prior to his death.

    b) Develop the decedent's past medical history, including all physicians.

    c) Develop the decedent's social history, including alcohol and drug habits.

    d) Develop any changes in the decedent's household, eating, sleeping, and work habits.

    e) Develop the decedent's prescriptive medication history.

4)   Body examination

    a) Describe position of the decedent's body.

    b) Describe clothing worn by the decedent. Is the clothing appropriate under the circumstances of the incident?

    c) Describe the time frame factors associated with the examination of the decedent's remains (e.g., rigor mortis, lividity). Are these time frame factors consistent with the information known about the subject's death?

    d) Describe any areas of injury observed on the decedent. Are there any items or conditions present, or could the final activities of the decedent have caused the injuries (e.g., collapsing from a standing position and striking the head on the floor or a table).

    e) Describe the appearance of the decedent, including:

        i) Jaundiced?

        ii) Unkempt?

        iii) Weight in proportion to height?

TRANSPORTING REMAINS

1)   Collect all prescriptive medications associated with the decedent and transport them with the remains.

PROCESSING AT MEO

1)   Fingerprint the decedent.

FOLLOW-UP INVESTIGATION

1)   Because of decomposition factors, if it appears there may be a problem in the identification of the decedent, take the following actions.

    a) A search should be conducted of the subject's residence in an attempt to locate background information on the subject that may assist in the identification of the decedent:

        i) Appointment books listing physicians and dentists

        ii) Personal telephone books listing doctors and dentists

        iii) Telephone book with hand-written telephone numbers written on the front or back cover or in the section listing dentists

        iv) Canceled personal checks listing payments to doctors or dentists

2)   If it appears that there may be a problem in locating the next of kin:

    a) A search of the decedent's residence should be conducted to develop the following:

        i) Personal address book that may include listing of next of kin or people with similar last names who may be related

        ii) Christmas or birthday cards, which may have been sent by relatives

iii) Current or past employers, insurance papers, family bible, or other items that may identify family members or friends of the decedent who may have knowledge of family members.

ETHANOL CONCENTRATIONS (WECHT, 1991)		
Blood Ethanol Level	Common Signs and Symptoms	Drinks in 1 hour by 150-lb. Man
0.01	Little effect	
0.10	Decreased inhibitions Decreased attention span Altered judgment Impaired memory	5–8
0.20	Uncoordination Slurred speech Confusion Staggering	10–15
0.30	Visual disturbances Marked uncoordination Stupor	15–20
0.40	Depressed or abolished reflexes Coma Possible death	20–25
0.50	Possible death	25+

These beer cans were found on the night stand of a hotel room occupied by an individual who had checked himself out of a hospital, against medical advice, after he was told to stop drinking and smoking. He was found dead in the bathroom. If decedent's death was a result of acute ethanol toxicity, his death would be ruled as an accident. If subject died as a result of chronic alcoholism, his death would be ruled as natural.

CHAPTER 30: DEATH BY ASPHYXIA

CONSIDERATIONS

1)   Asphyxia occurs when the body is deprived of oxygen.

2)   Asphyxia normally occurs rapidly, involving only a matter of minutes.

3)   There are several means of achieving an asphyxial condition.
        a) Hanging
            i) Body weight provides the force on a suspending rope or ligature.
            ii) Most hangings are suicidal. Accidental hanging is uncommon, and homicidal
                hangings are extremely rare.
            iii) Suspension of the body completely off the ground is not necessary to effect a
                hanging. The weight of an individual's head and shoulders (approximately 30
                pounds) is enough to interrupt oxygen intake while lying, slumped, kneeling,
                or reclining.
            iv) A typical suicide by hanging involves very little premeditation. Common
                household items are used for suspension (e.g., extension cords, belts, ties).
                The subject usually uses a simple slip or fixed knot.
            v) Inspection of the decedent's neck will reveal an inverted-V abrasion and
                furrow caused by the article used to suspend the individual. This rope or other
                suspension article commonly rides up past the hyoid cartilage (Adam's apple)
                at the front of the neck. At the point of suspension away from the neck, the
                rope will have pulled away from the subject, thus causing an incomplete
                encirclement.
                (1) The prominence of the abrasion/furrow is directly related to the type
                    of article used for suspension. The use of a sheet, blanket, or other
                    soft material may cause the abrasion/furrow to be indistinct or, in
                    some cases, not visible.

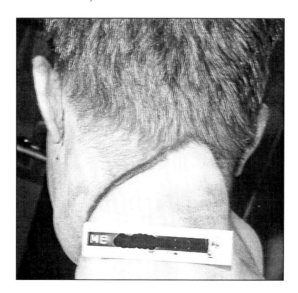

Inverted-V abrasion.

vi) Instinctive attempts to gain release may result in the appearance of small, linear abrasions around the rope site on the neck. These small abrasions are a result of fingernail scraping. On some occasions, the actual fingers of the decedent may become trapped between the suspension article and the neck.

vii) Mechanism for death

(1) After pressure is applied to the neck, unconsciousness occurs within a matter of seconds, although the heart may continue to beat for up to 15 or 20 minutes.

(2) The blood supply to the brain and airways are both compromised in a hanging. Circulatory interruption is more critical.

(3) Pressure to the base of the neck and area where the tongue attaches frequently causes the lower jaw to open and the tongue to protrude between the teeth. With death, the moisture on the tongue dries, causing the tongue to become discolored when exposed to the air.

(4) Fracturing the neck is rare, except in those cases where the drop is far enough to allow the full, suspended weight of the individual to fall upon the point at which the rope is attached to the neck. Referred to as a *judicial hanging*, this hanging requires a drop of approximately 7 feet or more. Autopsies usually reveal a fractured neck occurring in the area between the third and fourth or fourth and fifth cervical vertebrae.

(5) Since the pressure of the hanging is fairly evenly distributed around the neck by the very length of the supporting object, focal internal bleeding is relatively rare. Fractures of the hyoid or thyroid cartilage are occasionally seen, although they are more common in cases involving the elderly where this cartilage has lost much of its pliability due to the aging process.

(6) As circulation ceases, blood begins to settle in the lower parts under the influence of gravity and may, on occasion, produce focal leaking into tissue, which are referred to as Tardieu spots (small vessels leaking into tissue).

TONGUE AND NECK ORGANS AT AUTOPSY

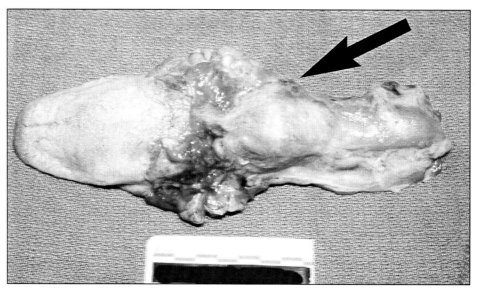

Examination of the neck organs and tongue are important in suspected strangulation cases. Areas of hemorrhaging (see arrow) may establish that strangulation has occurred.

b) Manual strangulation
  i) Manual strangulation involves pressure being applied to the neck by hands or forearms.
  ii) The manner of death is predominantly a homicide. The assailant will be physically stronger, generally, than the victim.
  iii) Suicide by manual strangulation is impossible since the application of manual pressure to one's own neck will cease upon reaching an unconscious state.
  iv) Manual strangulation deaths involving accidents are rare.
  v) Mechanism of death
    (1) Bluish discoloration (cyanosis) of the face may be noted along with small hemorrhages (petechiae) on the skin of the face, scalp and eye regions.
    (2) There are usually markings on the neck appearing as small, linear abrasions. It is often assumed that these are left from the fingernails of the perpetrator, although it is probably more commonly associated with the fingernail marks of the decedent as he attempts to dislodge the hand or arm gripping his throat.
    (3) Bruising may be observed on the decedent's neck, chin, and shoulder areas as a result of the struggle.
    (4) At autopsy, the pathologist may find hemorrhaging involving the short (strap) muscles of the neck and in the area around the hyoid gland in front of the larynx (voice box). The focal pressure of the tips of the fingers involving the gripping hand causes this.
    (5) Fracture of the hyoid bone and other neck cartilage is common but not always present.

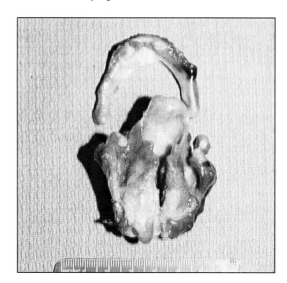

The hyoid.

    (6) Manual strangulation involving the forearm (sometimes referred to as *mugging* or a *chokehold*) may be evidenced at autopsy by focal hemorrhaging in the area between the front of the neck bones (cervical vertebrae), the esophagus, and the trachea.
c) Ligature strangulation
  i) In this mode of death, some force other than body weight applies the constricting pressure.

ii) Most deaths are by homicidal means, but there are some suicides and accidental deaths caused by ligature strangulation.

(1) Suicides are effected by the individual's placing a ligature around his neck and pulling the item tight. When unconsciousness occurs, the article, suitably applied, does not slip and ultimately leads to the person's death if the events are not interrupted by other sources.

iii) Concealable and common articles are usually used.

iv) In homicide cases, the victims tend to be people less able to defend themselves from a more aggressive assailant.

(1) Male victims may be related to homosexual activity.

v) Mechanism of death

(1) The prominence of the furrow/abrasion around the neck is directly related to the width and softness of the article used to do the strangulation.

(2) Bruising and linear abrasions may be made on the neck as the victim struggles in his efforts to dislodge the article.

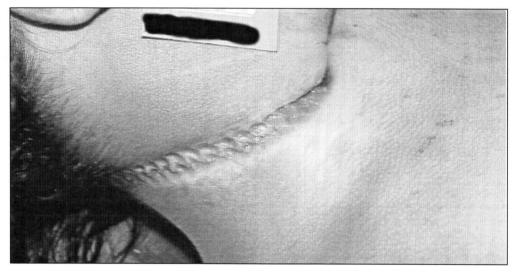

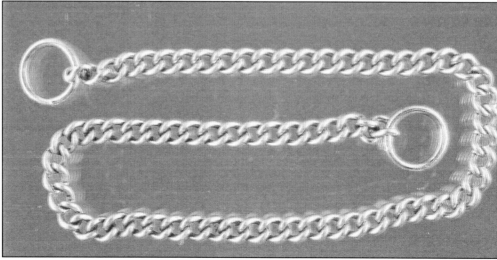

Identifying the weapon used in a ligature strangulation is incredibly important to death investigators. Prominent markings on the neck may indicate a particular weapon.

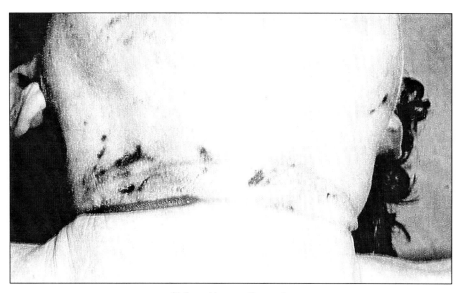

Nail markings on the neck.

(3) The face is usually congested because the article frequently encircles the entire neck at least once and possibly several times. The terminal event will most likely occur with the victim in a horizontal position on the floor. This horizontal position is conducive to the flow of blood traveling to the face and neck. It becomes trapped in this area by the encircling article. Because of this, small hemorrhages may be observed on the face and around the eyes of the decedent.

(4) Death is caused primarily by the disruption of the circulation of blood to the brain; however, airway disturbance may also be a factor.

(5) The ligature mark tends to be at about the same level around the neck and not pulled upward on one side as one would see in hanging deaths.

vi) Be aware of the possibility of innocent neck markings that appear on certain cases being misinterpreted as ligature markings.

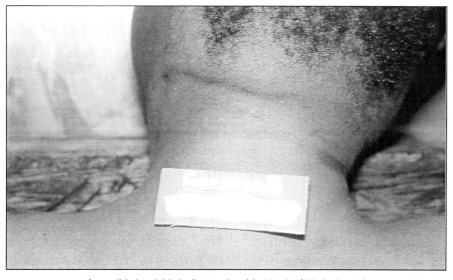

A possible homicide by ligature is evident by the fairly horizontal furrow abrasion on this decedent's neck.

(1) People who died with their heads propped up on pillows, especially the elderly, may appear to have ligature marks on their necks. In fact, these marks are simply creases caused by the head being propped up on the pillows. This may also be seen upon examining bodies in funeral homes where the head of the decedent may have been propped up on a block.

(2) On decomposing bodies, swelling involving the skin of the neck may bring the skin of the neck into contact with clothing (collars) or jewelry. The impression of these items on to the skin of the neck may be misinterpreted as ligature markings.

(3) In children, prior drooling into the folds of their neck, combined with refrigerating the body and propping of the head onto an adult-sized head block prior to autopsy, may produce markings on the neck resembling ligature markings.

d) Smothering (suffocation)

i) In deaths caused by smothering, asphyxia occurs from obstruction of the respiratory openings, usually by covering the nose and mouth of the decedent or placing him in a container with too little oxygen.

ii) Unless a gag is found, some item such as sand packed into the airway, or a plastic bag is found over the decedent's head, autopsy findings will usually be inconclusive. Therefore in these types of cases, the circumstances of the death, developed through careful investigation, may be more important than the autopsy findings.

(1) If a plastic bag is found over a decedent's head, it should be noted that it is not necessary for the bag to be completely sealed. The bag needs only to be placed in such as a way as to affect the normal exchange of gases.

(2) Any time a plastic bag is found over an individual's head, the initial suspicion should be huffing or sniffing, where a foreign substance is placed inside the bag for abusive purposes. Huffing involves a wide range of substances, including glue, freon, toluene, and White-Out.

(3) Death may occur from:

(a) Lack of oxygen

(b) Sudden abnormal beat of the heart associated with a halogenated hydrocarbon

(c) A combination of the above

(4) Whenever a bag is encountered under these circumstances, it should be immediately placed into a paint can and sealed for toxicological testing.

e) Choking

i) Choking requires an obstruction within the airway.

ii) Death is usually accidental and brought about by intoxication, senility, or such illnesses as Parkinson's disease.

iii) Homicides are associated with gags that slip or swell as a result of the absorption of saliva. Choking homicides may also be seen in infants, especially unwanted newborn babies.

iv) There are two important considerations about asphyxial deaths due to choking:

(1) It is often incorrectly diagnosed by inexperienced physicians who find stomach contents in the upper airway.

(a) Regurgitation of stomach contents sometimes occurs during the period immediately preceding death. This is more closely associated with disorganized muscle activity and has nothing to do with the actual cause of death.

(b) Stomach contents may flow into the upper airway and be seen during autopsy. This results from the carrying and moving of the decedent after death.

(2) A cafe coronary (a death caused by a particle of food, referred to as food bolus, obstructing the airway) can be incorrectly diagnosed as a heart attack.

(a) Alcohol consumption is a common finding in these deaths.

f) Traumatic "crush" asphyxia

i) In this asphyxial type of death, an external compressive force prevents the chest from engaging in normal respiratory movements.

ii) Most of the deaths associated with this method are accidental in manner, but a few homicides have been reported. Intoxication, senility, and natural illnesses or disability often contribute to death.

iii) Autopsy examination may or may not show internal evidence of such injuries as rib fractures.

iv) External examination of the body may show lines of pressure on the skin, with forcible redistribution of blood noted. This will appear as an intense congestion of the head and neck and possibly the limbs, depending on the position of the weight and the posture of the individual during the incident.

g) Postural asphyxia

i) Postural asphyxia occurs when a person's bodily position results in a partial or complete airway obstruction. It usually involves the following:

(1) The decedent is discovered in a position not conducive to breathing. Normally this results from a restrictive or confining position; however, it may also involve simple flexion of the head onto the chest, a partial or complete airway obstruction, or neck compression.

(2) Investigative information indicates the decedent inadvertently placed himself in this confining position without the deliberate action of another person.

(3) The reason the decedent couldn't extricate himself from this confining position is usually associated with alcohol, dementia, or some other disabling condition.

(4) There is an absence of any other possible cause of death.

h) Drowning

i) Drowning is smothering with or without choking in water.

i) Asphyxiating gases

i) Asphyxia can occur if an individual breathes an atmosphere that contains:

(1) Insufficient oxygen to support life

(2) Poisonous gases

(3) Carbon monoxide

ii) It is usually associated with a suicide or an accidental manner of death.

j) Autoerotic death

i) In an autoerotic death, the individual attempts stimulate and enhance sexual activity by using some technique of oxygen deprivation (hypoxia). It may involve ligature strangulation, hanging, asphyxiating gases, or smothering.

ii) Death results when something unexpectedly goes wrong. This error in judgment usually occurs because the practitioner becomes unconscious and cannot resume the air flow, ultimately leading to asphyxiation.

    iii) These type of deaths are distinguished from suicides by the apparent presence of an escape mechanism to allow the practitioner to escape from the predicament he has placed himself in, providing unconsciousness does not occur.

    iv) The majority of victims are adolescents or young adults. They may be single or married.

    v) The practice is usually conducted when the practitioner is ensured privacy for an extended period.

    vi) Cross-dressing may also be observed.

    vii) If a rope is applied to the neck, a towel or other soft object is inserted between the rope and the skin to prevent marking the neck.

    viii) Erotic or sexually explicit material may be present.

    ix) Relatives who discover the body may tamper with the scene.

    x) Receptacles (e.g., tissue, rag) for semen may be present near the body.

PRIMARY FOCUS OF INVESTIGATION

1) What are the cause and manner of death?

2) What type of instrument or action caused the death?

3) How much time has elapsed since death occurred?

NOTIFICATION

1) A pathologist should be requested on all homicides or uncertain manner of death where the following details may be in question:
   a) Time frame since death
   b) Type of weapon causing the death
   c) Possible activities associated in effecting death

2) The pathologist should be requested on any case in which the manner of death is undetermined or confused, or the decedent or some other interested party appears to have altered the circumstances of the death.

SCENE PHOTOGRAPHS

1) Follow the death-scene photographic guidelines applicable to the particular circumstances of this case (e.g., outdoor, indoor, vehicle scenes). In addition, give particular attention to the following:
   a) Photograph any resistance that may have been demonstrated by the decedent:
       i) Torn clothing, including buttons ripped off
       ii) Defense injuries on neck, hands, arms, legs, and feet
       iii) Eyeglasses broken or thrown on the floor
       iv) Rifled purse, wallet, dresser drawers, jewelry box, safe, pulled-out pockets from decedent's pants, etc.
       v) Overturned furniture

b) Photograph any weapon present, including the following:
    i) Relationship of item(s) used to cause the death with the location and position of the body
    ii) Area where murder weapon may have originated
    iii) A close-up view of the murder weapon
    iv) If ligature is involved, photograph the knot around the decedent's neck and the knot used to attach the ligature to allow for suspension of the decedent (if applicable).

c) Photograph the body of the decedent, including:
    i) All areas of injuries involving the decedent
    ii) All areas of blood on the decedent's body; clothing; and feet, socks, or shoes (soles of feet or shoes)
    iii) All areas of blood immediately adjacent to the body
    iv) Body condition as it relates to the time frame of death
    v) Any inconsistencies with regard to the time frame of death, as evidenced by the condition of the remains
        (1) Rigor mortis
        (2) Lividity
    vi) Any transfer evidence observable on the decedent
    vii) Any indication of animal or insect activity involving the decedent's body
    vii) Any apparent efforts made by rescue workers to resuscitate the decedent

d) Photograph all evidence and items that may illustrate the circumstances of the incident.
    i) Directional evidence, including:
        (1) Blood spatter
        (2) Glass fractures
        (3) Footprints, tire tracks, etc.
        (4) If applicable, photograph the method used by the decedent to obtain height or access the area from which he jumped or attached the ligature necessary for suspension (e.g., ladder, chair).
        (5) If autoerotic death is suspected, photograph displaced mirrors or mirrors, which may have been positioned to reflect the participant's image during the autoerotic episode.
    ii) Any relational evidence present that may be connected to the incident. For example, a small pad of cloth in the decedent's hand or a small, opened vial of some unknown substance on the floor next to him.
    iii) Inferred evidence is evidence that is significant in its absence. For example, dust surrounding a clean area on top of a television set may indicate a VCR has been taken.

SCENE INVESTIGATION

1) Locate and develop information from essential informants, including these:
    a) Eyewitnesses
    b) Persons who found the body or were first at the scene
    c) Doctor, nurses, or emergency medical technicians who gave medical attention

2) From the original scene of the incident develop the following information:

a) Determine the exact time of incident.

b) Determine the exact time when the decedent was found.

c) Describe building, room, or place where the body was found.

d) What reason did the decedent have for being at this location?

e) Describe the exact position of the body.

f) Describe the clothing worn by the decedent.

    i) Note any tears, missing buttons, bloodstains, etc.

g) If present, describe the exact position of the possible weapon found on the scene.

h) Describe any other (possible) involved article and describe its location.

i) Describe any other items of potential evidence, including blood spatter, overturned furniture, ransacked drawers, and suicide note. Detail the locations of these items.

    i) If autoerotic death is suspected, note the placement of any mirrors located in the area the activity was believed to have occurred.

j) If smothering is suspected, check all trash cans for discarded plastic bags.

k) If the death is associated with hanging:

    i) Examine the area where the ligature is attached. Note any notched areas indicating possible prior acts or attempts.

    ii) Examine the ligature for any worn areas or napping. Is there any indication that the rope was used to hoist the weight (homicide) or pulled down (suicide or accident)?

    iii) If alive when found, did decedent make any comments?

3)   Weapon description

a) Describe the instrument believed to be associated with the injuries incurred by the decedent.

    i) Include measurements of possible weapon, type of weapon, and whether or not the item was brought to the scene or was from the scene originally.

    ii) Describe the type of edge visible on this item.

    iii) Who is the owner of this item?

b) If the article used to cause death is not present on the remains, is there an item in the area that may be involved? Is there any blood or other trace evidence visible on this item that may link it to the incident?

c) If a ligature is involved, examine the knot used to cause death and the knot used to attach the ligature to allow for suspension of the decedent (if applicable).

    i) Describe the knot(s).

    ii) Describe how a particular knot worked.

    iii) Does this particular knot or ligature preclude self-application by the decedent?

4)   Injury description

a) Describe the areas of apparent injury to the decedent.

    i) Inspect the hands and arms for defense marks.

5)   Circumstances

a) Describe what happened.

b) If there are any suggestions that the decedent's death may be accidental, describe them in detail.

c) What is the suspected murder weapon normally used for? Where is it normally kept? Where was it prior to the infliction of injury?

d) Describe events preceding the death. Detail any comments made by the decedent during this period.

BODY TRANSPORT FROM SCENE

1) If blood interpretation may be significant in this case, consider removing those items of clothing with bloodstains before transporting the remains (obtain prior approval from the on-call pathologist).

2) Check the remains for any trace evidence. If these items might be lost during transport, the evidence technician should collect them after photographing them.

3) Bag (paper) the hands of the decedent.

4) Place any item believed to have been involved in the possible abuse of an intoxicant into a metal paint can and seal the can immediately.

5) If a ligature is involved, cut it at a point that will not affect the knot around the neck of the decedent or the knot around the attached area. If at all possible, transport the ligature around the neck intact to the MEO.

PROCESSING AT THE MEO

1) If homicide is involved or suspected, or if suicide is not a certainty:
   a) Consider examining the body for latent or patent prints.
   b) Collect any trace evidence that may be present.
   c) Collect the bags used to cover the decedent's hands while being transported to the morgue.
   d) Collect fingernail scrapings and clippings from the decedent.
   e) Obtain pulled and combed hair standards from the decedent.
   f) Collect a tube of blood for typing purposes.
   g) Obtain major case prints.
   h) Collect, air-dry, and separately pack any item of clothing of the decedent.

2) If this is a homicide, collect whatever evidence is required, based on the motive indicated. For example, complete sexual swabbings are required if sexual homicide is indicated.

3) If the remains are skeletonized or badly decomposed, the pathologist may wish to consult a forensic anthropologist before conducting an autopsy.

FOLLOW-UP INVESTIGATION

1) If this is a homicide, follow the guidelines indicated by the motive.

2) If it is a suicide, follow the guidelines in Chapter 26.

3) If an accidental death is indicated:
   a) Reconstruct the events based on the evidence and statements made to the investigators.
   b) Obtain complete background information on the decedent, including:
      i) Financial (include status of insurance policies).
      ii) Health (include any psychiatric or physical problem that may have contributed to the incident)
      iii) Domestic
   c) Develop any similar incidents involving the decedent or someone known to him.

CHAPTER 31: BIOTERRORISM

The following is an overview of anthrax, as well as procedures that should be followed when responding to suspected anthrax or "suspicious white powder."

ANTHRAX BACKGROUND

1) Anthrax is a bacteria that forms spores. It was categorized as one of the first occupational hazards of ancient wool sorters and was a much more common infection years ago. There have been very few natural cases over the past hundred years. Only 18 confirmed inhalation cases have occurred between 1900 to 1976, and not a single case within the past 25 years—until October 1, 2001.

ANTHRAX INFECTION

1) Anthrax is produced by the bacteria *Bacillus anthracis*. A tough protective coat allows the bacteria to survive for decades as spores. Anthrax is dangerous because it is:
   a) Highly lethal
   b) One of the easiest biological agents to manufacture
   c) Relatively easy to develop as a weapon
   d) Easily spread in the air over a large area
   e) Easily stored and dangerous for a long period

2) Anthrax normally occurs in domesticated and wild animals, including goats, sheep, cattle, horses, and deer. A zoonotic disease, anthrax is also communicable to human beings, although once infected a human is not contagious. Anthrax can infect humans in one of three ways:
   a) Cutaneous anthrax, also known as "skin" anthrax, may be contracted by handling contaminated hair, wool, hides, flesh, blood, or excreta of infected animals, as well as manufactured products from infected animals, such as bone meal.
      i) Infection is introduced through scratches, abrasions, or wounds of the skin.
      ii) The mildest form of anthrax infection, cutaneous anthrax symptoms include itching, rash, and possible lesions near the site of infection. With proper treatment, cutaneous infection is fatal in less than 1 percent of all cases. Approximately 95 percent of human anthrax infections are cutaneous infections, and this form presents the greatest threat to personnel handling contaminated packages.
   b) Gastrointestinal anthrax is contracted by orally ingesting anthrax spores, usually by eating insufficiently cooked meat that has been infected.
      i) Symptoms include abdominal distress, rapidly developing fluid accumulation in the peritoneal cavity, cholera-like diarrhea, fever, and septicemia. Gastrointestinal anthrax infections are unlikely from handling contaminated packages.
   c) Inhalation anthrax is contracted by inhaling spores directly into the lungs.
      i) Such infections normally occur among workers handling infected animal hides, wools, and furs.
      ii) This mild disease can progress rapidly to respiratory distress and shock in 2 to 4 days, followed by a range of more severe symptoms, such as difficulty in breathing and exhaustion.
      iii) Death usually occurs within 24 hours of respiratory distress.

iv) Under natural conditions, inhaled anthrax is exceedingly rare, with only 18 cases reported in the United States in the 20th century.

v) It may be possible to contract inhalation anthrax infections from a contaminated package. However, in most cases deliberately causing such infections would require some method of rendering the anthrax spores as an aerosol. This is a fairly sophisticated procedure requiring specific expertise and the use of sophisticated technology.

ANTHRAX SYMPTOMS

1) There can be 1 to 6 days between exposure and symptoms.

2) Symptoms of inhalation anthrax include the following:
   a) There are viral-like aches and pains, fever, malaise, fatigue, cough, and mild chest discomfort, followed by severe difficulty breathing.
   b) The usual course is that a person gets infected, develops the symptoms, has a temporary recovery, and then has a worsening of symptoms.
   c) Typically, anthrax that has been inhaled gets into the smallest part of the lungs, the alveoli. Because they are so small (usually less than a few microns), the particles are able to enter the alveoli . From the alveoli, anthrax often releases toxins that can affect the lymphatic system. These toxins ultimately seep into the blood of its host.
      i) In more than half the cases, the infection also spreads to the brain.

3) The specific cause of death from anthrax is related to breathing difficulties, but mainly to the overwhelming, uncontrollable infection, also known as sepsis.

ANTHRAX TREATMENT

1) Treatment of anthrax
   a) Immediately starting a regimen of antibiotics 1 day after exposure appears to provide significant protection against death from anthrax, especially when coupled with active immunization. Penicillin, doxycycline, and ciproflaxin are all effective against most strains of anthrax, with penicillin being the preferred treatment for its natural form.
   b) Inhalation anthrax is fatal if untreated. A vaccine, formerly administered to military personnel in a deployable status, is known to protect against cutaneous anthrax and is also believed to be effective against inhalation anthrax.

ANTHRAX PROTOCOL

The following are the recommended precautionary measures and emergency procedures for handling a package suspected of being contaminated with a biological agent (U.S. Postal Service, 2001). This information may also be found on the U.S. Postal Service Web site (http://www.usps.gov/cpim/ftp/notices/not71.pdf).

1) Suspicious parcels
   a) Some of the characteristics of a suspect package include:
      i) Presence of any unusual material, especially a powder-like substance, either that is detectable on the outside of the package or that falls out when the package is opened.
         (1)Weaponized anthrax exhibits the consistency and fineness of talcum

powder and varies in color from white to off-white to brown. Less sophisticated anthrax is probably less consistent (lumpy) and more granular.

    ii) Restrictive endorsements such as "personal" or "private," especially when the addressee does not usually receive personal mail at the office or military command

    iii) Fictitious or nonexistent return addresses

    iv) Addresses written in distorted handwriting, with homemade labels, or cut-and-paste lettering.

    v) Improper titles with name or addressed to title only (a more common occurrence in military commands)

    vi) Protruding wires, aluminum foil, oil stains, or peculiar odor

    vii) Cancellation or postmark from a different location than return address

    viii) Excessive postage

    ix) Unprofessional wrapping with several combinations of tape

    x) Special instructions (e.g., "Fragile, handle with care" or "Rush: do not delay.")

2) Recommended preventive measures

    a) All personnel handling mail should wear rubber gloves.

    b) Keep large Zip-Loc plastic bags nearby for isolating suspicious mail and possibly contaminated clothing (see below).

3) Contaminated package emergency procedures

    a) If a package is suspected of containing a biological/chemical agent and mailing cannot be confirmed with the addressee or sender, take the following steps immediately:

        i) Avoid opening or handling the suspect package.

        ii) Isolate the package and evacuate the immediate area.

            (1) If you have already handled the package, isolate it by sealing it in a plastic bag. If the package has not been handled, simply evacuate the area immediately.

        iii) Ensure that all persons who have touched the package wash their hands thoroughly with soap and warm water.

        iv) Contact base security/local police and request assistance. Be sure to emphasize that you suspect a biological agent.

        v) Prepare a list of all persons who touched the package, including contact information. Be prepared to provide this list to authorities.

        vi) Place all items of clothing worn when in contact with the package in plastic bags. Seal the bags and be prepared to provide the bags to law enforcement agents.

        vii) As soon as practical, shower with soap and warm water.

        viii) If you are prescribed medication, take it until otherwise instructed.

        ix) Local authorities should notify the nearest state/federal authorities as dictated by standard operating procedure. Authorities are also encouraged to contact the Centers for Disease Control and Prevention (CDC) emergency response at commercial (770) 488-7100.

NOTE: Various companies have publicized their use of powders as part of their publishing/mailing procedures. It is a common practice in the publishing industry to apply a light coating of cornstarch to the cover and pages of glossy magazines and other printed materials. This process prevents the pages from sticking to each other during shipping. The fine white or light brown powder applied during the process is called printers' spray powder and is NOT toxic and poses NO health risk. One out of 160,000 envelopes goes out with a buildup of corn starch and is visible as a white powder.

BIOTERRORISM SYNDROMES
(Los Angeles Public Health, 2001)

ACUTE RESPIRATORY DISTRESS WITH FEVER

INHALATION ANTHRAX

Disease description:	Abrupt onset of fever, chest pain, respiratory distress without radiographic findings of pneumonia, no history of trauma or chronic disease, progression to shock and death within 24 to 36 hours
Differential diagnosis:	Dissecting aortic aneurism, pulmonary embolism, influenza
Initial lab and diagnostic test results:	Chest X-ray with widened mediastinum; gram-positive bacilli in sputum or blood

PNEUMONIC PLAGUE

Disease description:	Apparent severe, community-acquired pneumonia but with hemoptysis, cyanosis, gastrointestinal symptoms, shock
Differential diagnosis:	Community-acquired pneumonia, Hantavirus pulmonary syndrome, meningococcemia, rickettsiosis, influenza
Initial lab and diagnostic test results:	Gram negative bacilli or coccobocilli in sputum, blood, or lymph node; safety pin appearance with Wright or Giemsa stain

RICIN (AEROSOLIZED)

Disease description:	Acute onset of fever, chest pain, and cough, progressing to respiratory distress and hypoxemia; not improved with antibiotics; death in 36 to 72 hours
Differential diagnosis:	Plague Q fever, staphyloccoccal enterotoxin B, phosgene, tularemia, influenza
Initial lab and diagnostic test results:	Chest X-ray with pulmonary edema

STAPHYLOCOCCAL ENTEROTOXIN B

Disease description:	Acute onset of fever, chills, headache, nonproductive cough, and myalgia (influenza-like illness) with a normal chest X-ray
Differential diagnosis:	Influenza, adenovirus, mycoplasma
Initial lab and diagnostic test results:	Primarily clinical diagnosis

ACUTE RASH WITH FEVER

SMALLPOX

Disease description:	Popular rash with fever that begins on the face and extremities and uniformly progresses to vesicles and putsules; headache, vomiting, back pain, and delirium common
Differential diagnosis:	Varicella, disseminated herpes zoster, vaccinia, monkeypox, cowpox
Initial lab and diagnostic test results:	Clinical with laboratory confirmation; vaccinated, gowned and gloved person obtains specimens (scabs or swabs of vesicular or pustular fluid)

VIRAL HEMORRHAGIC FEVER (EBOLA)

Disease description:	Fever with mucous membrane bleeding, petechiae, thrombocytopenia
Differential diagnosis:	Meningococcemia, malaria, typhus, leptospirosis, borreliosis, thrombotic thrombocytopenic purpura (TTP), hemolytic uremic syndrome (HUS)
Initial lab and diagnostic test results:	Definitive testing available through public health laboratory

NEUROLOGIC SYNDROMES

BOTULISM

Disease description:	Acute bilateral descending flaccid paralysis beginning with cranial nerve palsies
Differential diagnosis:	Guillain–Barre syndrome, myasthenia gravis, mid-brain stroke, tick paralysis, Mg intoxication, organophosphate, carbon monoxide, paralytic shellfish, or belladonna-like alkaloid poisoning, polio, Eaton–Lambert myasthenic syndrome
Initial lab and diagnostic test results:	CSF protein normal; EMG with repetitive nerve stimulation shows augmentation of muscle action potential.

ENCEPHALITIS (VENEZUELAN, EASTERN, WESTERN)

Disease description:	Encephalopathy with fever and seizures and/or focal neurologic deficits
Differential diagnosis:	Herpes simplex, postinfectious, other viral encephalitides
Initial lab and diagnostic test results:	Serologic testing

CHAPTER 32: DEATH BY BLUNT TRAUMA

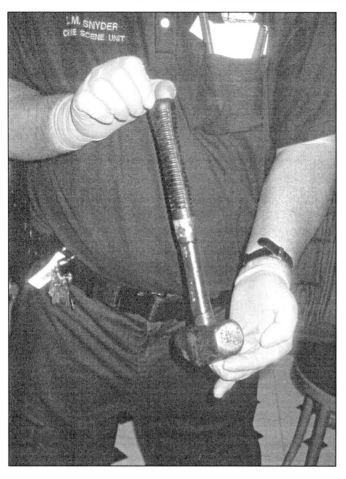

CONSIDERATIONS

1)   Deaths from a blunt injury can result from a suicide, an accident, or a homicide.
        a) Localized violence and the use of some weapons characterize homicidal deaths. It may
           involve one blow or multiple blows.
        b) Suicidal deaths from blunt injury are most often seen in persons who have jumped
           from high places or thrown themselves into the path of a moving vehicle.
        c) Accidental deaths due to blunt force are most often the result of a fall with injuries
           inflicted to the head and neck.

2)   Blunt injuries result from the application of force to the body over a large or small surface area
        resulting in damage to the tissues, but not necessarily accompanied by a penetrating wound.
        Blunt-force injuries can be divided into two different areas:
        a) Generalized injuries in which the entire body or a large segment of the body is
           affected. Incidents producing blunt trauma over a generalized area include automobile
           and airplane accidents, collapse of buildings, falls from a great heights, or explosions.
        b) Localized injuries involve a relatively small part of the body, although there may be
           occasions in which a collection of blows may involve a larger area of the body because
           of overlapping small areas of injuries. Localized injuries form the greatest majority of
           homicidal blunt-trauma activity.

3)   The extent of blunt force injury depends on four factors:
      a) The amount of force applied
      b) The length of time of the application of the force
      c) The size of the area over which the force is applied
      d) The elasticity of the organ receiving the force

4)   Type of injuries associated with blunt trauma
      a) Abrasions
          i) Normally, these cause superficial injury to the skin but may be associated with a more severe injury to the internal organs.
          ii) Abrasions may become important because at the site of the injury a patterned abrasion may be visualized. This patterned abrasion may be representative of the tool used to inflict the injury.

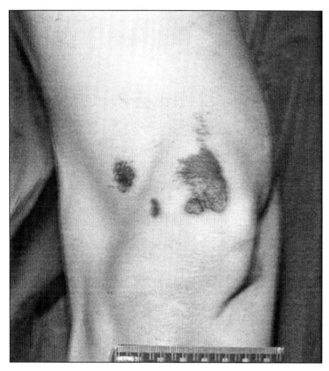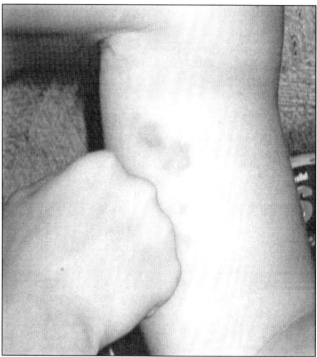

Examples of abrasion and contusion injuries.

      b) Contusions (bruises)
          i) A bruise is caused when small blood vessels break and the blood moves into the surrounding tissue.
          ii) The time frame for the colorization of a bruise is ambiguous and not a very good indicator of the time that has passed since the bruise was produced. How much blood is involved, what kind of circulation there is to the involved area, and how thick the skin is in the involved area all affect a bruise. The best conclusion that can be reached in interpreting the bruise is fresh (redness and swelling, bluish-black) versus an old bruise (blue-green, green, yellow, brown).
          iii) If bone is present under the soft tissue injured, the contusion may appear rapidly. If the force injures deeper tissues or causes fracturing of bones, the

contusions or ecchymosis may then become apparent at a later time. For this reason, blunt-trauma deaths involving suspected beating or child abuse cases may be better viewed if the body is retained for an additional day after the autopsy is performed.

c) Lacerations

    i) These occur when the blunt force applied to the soft tissue stretches the skin past the point of elasticity resulting in the tearing of the tissue.

BLUNT FORCE INJURY—MULTIPLE LACERATIONS

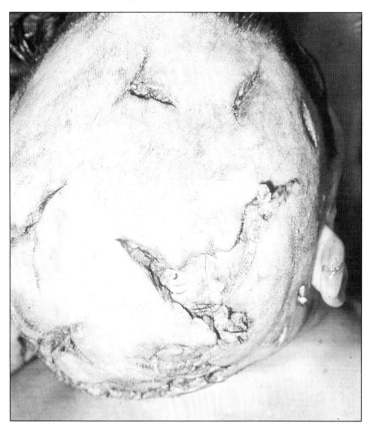

The pathologist often shaves the head of the victim to better examine wounds. Patterned injuries may be discerned, leading police to a particular weapon used to produce the injuries.

    ii) Lacerations of the scalp often resemble incised wounds. However, lacerations caused from blunt force can be distinguished from incised injuries caused by sharp instruments by closely examining the wound. Blunt-force lacerations characteristically have ragged margins, and within the depth of the wound there are bands of unsevered tissue connected to both sides of the wound.

    iii) The direction of the force causing the laceration may also be determined through examination of the wound.

d) Fractures

    i) Fracturing of the bone may occur as a result of the blunt force applied to the area.

FRACTURE INJURIES IN BLUNT FORCE CASES

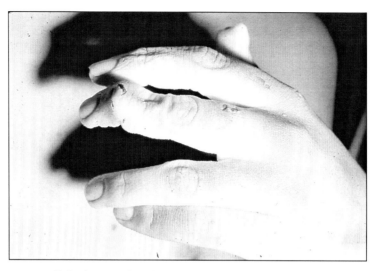

Defensive wounds to the hands, arms, feet, and legs are
sometimes present on victims as a result of blunt-force attacks.
A fractured finger is present on this decedent.

ii) Blood vessels and nerves may be injured in areas associated with the fracture.

iii) Bony fragments produced during the fracturing process may also produce contusions and lacerations.

iv) There is usually a considerable amount of hemorrhaging associated with a fracture caused by blunt force. Although fractures involving the extremities are not usually fatal, blunt-trauma fractures sustained to the head and chest area may be fatal due to injuries inflicted upon vital organs (e.g., brain, heart, lung, liver) in these areas. The complicating factor of hemorrhaging following fracture is particularly significant in injuries to the head: the space inside the cranial vault is limited, and the extravasated blood may cause fatal pressure on the brain.

5) Blunt trauma to the head is responsible for more homicides than blunt injury to all other parts of the body combined.

    a) The head is selected in a great majority of fatal assaults.

    b) The victim will strike his head against an unyielding surface when thrown, knocked, or in falling to the floor or pavement.

    c) The brain is more vulnerable to injury by blunt force, which would rarely be lethal if applied to other areas of the body.

6) The skull

    a) The skull has two major divisions: the face and cranial vault.

        i) The face is attached to its cranial vault only by a series of fragile struts of bone. These struts can break away, saving the cranial vault and brain from injury.

            (1) Most commonly fractured is the bit of bone that makes the nose stick out.

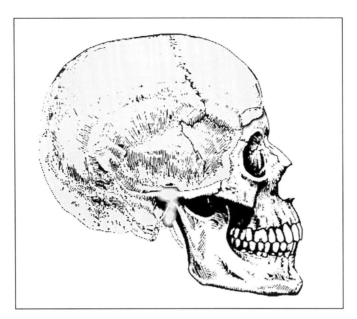

Two major skull divisions.

(2) Much more capable of absorbing lots of energy is the zygomatic arch, or cheekbone. It is fairly sturdy, but the arch tapers to a fine strut, where it is attached to the cranial vault. This strut is a thin column of bone at the outer edge of the orbit.

(3) The only other bone holding the face in place is the column between the upper teeth and the cranial vault. Composed mostly of the maxilla, it is full of holes, sinuses, and wafers of bone that are thinner than the average potato chip.

(4) Also part of the facial bones is the mandible, which is a hoop of bone.

    (a) Hoops and rings are naturally very strong, but when they break, they tend to break in at least two places and lose virtually all of their strength.

    (b) The mandible is extremely important because it also keeps the tongue out of the airway.

ii) The bony struts are fairly hardy but will fracture at specific points when hit by a strong force, allowing the face to move posteriorly and inferiorly.

    (1) These struts will absorb a tremendous amount of energy to protect the soft, vulnerable brain in its cranial vault.

        (a) The strong upper parts of the orbits tend to remain intact, and the jaw apparatus, with the all-important airway, tends to move as a block, helping to preserve the vital functions of respiration and, eventually, nutrition.

b) Immediately after trauma, fractured facial bones may indicate that the structures protected by the facial bones have been compromised.

    i) Of primary concern is whether the brain has been injured. If it has, the cranial vault may be broken. Signs of this include:

        (1) Cerebrospinal fluid (CSF) leaks

(2) Battle's sign (a bruise-like discoloration over the mastoid process caused by blood dissecting from a basilar skull fracture)

(3) Deformity

(4) Brain matter oozing out

ii) The airway may be compromised in several ways:

(1) Teeth may be broken.

(2) Blood or vomit may be aspirated.

(3) A fractured mandible can allow the tongue to occlude the pharynx, rendering a jaw thrust maneuver worthless, and making oral endotracheal intubation very difficult.

iii) Fractures about the nose that extend into the cranial vault can make nasogastric or nasoendotracheal intubation risky.

(1) The tube may have entered the cranial vault, which could have caused the death.

c) If the injured person is sent to a hospital, doctors will look for facial fractures to determine if there are more extensive injuries.

i) They will palpate and look for deformity at the usual fracture sites:

(1) Bridge of the nose

(2) Posterior portion of the zygomatic arch

(3) Prominent portion of the cheek

(4) Outer margin of the orbit

(5) Along the mandible

ii) Maxillary fractures may have left the upper teeth and palate unattached, or "floating."

(1) The doctor, having grasped the upper incisors and gently checking for motion, may have detected this.

(2) The doctor may have visibly examined the patient and observed that the upper incisors are posterior to the lower incisors or that the palate is blatantly crooked.

(3) Most of the facial structure serves to align the teeth; thus, in the injured person who may have still been conscious, the doctor may have simply asked the question, "Do your teeth still fit together when you bite down?"

d) Some signs of skull fracture may be altered over time.

i) A depressed cheek that is evident to a paramedic in the field may be obscured by edema by the time a physician sees the injured person.

ii) A battle's sign may take several hours to appear.

7) Think of the head as a helmet protecting the brain.

a) *Cranium* is from the Greek and means, roughly, helmet, and the structure of the cranial vault serves as a protective helmet for the brain. It comprises protective plates of bones, fused strongly together to form a natural helmet.

b) The brain is a fragile and easily damaged organ, susceptible to all sorts of injuries.

c) The cranial vault employs the same technology as a football helmet. Not only is its shape important in distributing forces, but it uses a packaging method to prevent injury to the brain.

i) The packaging follows a "hard, soft, hard, soft, hard" regimen.

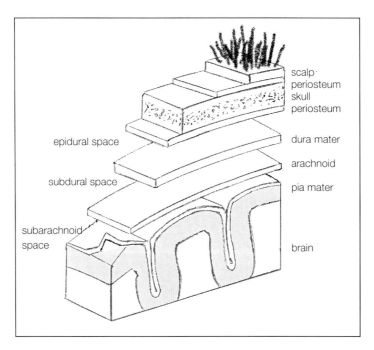

A cross section of the brain.

    (1) The hard skull is covered by a soft, thick, hair-covered scalp that is about as thick and resilient as a floor mat in a car.

    (2) The cranial vault itself is made up of three layers:

        (a) Two hard "tables" of bone sandwiching a soft middle layer of sinuses and a marrow-like, impact-absorbing layer, called *diploe.*

    (3) The brain is both surrounded and filled by fluid. The brain takes up about seven-tenths of the space inside the skull. The rest of the space is filled with blood vessels and CSF. The brain is filled with CSF that flows down around the cord and back up to surround the brain.

    (4) CSF flows around the outside of the brain, through a latticework of fibers. The density of CSF is precisely adjusted to buoy the brain and provide a remarkably effective hydraulic cushion. This fluid protects the brain from injury.

ii) The brain's protective mechanisms are highly interdependent. That is, if any element of protection is damaged, the entire system becomes more vulnerable.

    (1) A little crack in the skull, a minor concussion, a little bleeding around the brain or a minimal loss of CSF can lead to far more serious consequences if a second injury occurs.

    (2) The dura mater is a silvery, fiber-reinforced sheet of tissue whose texture, strength, and adhesion to the inside of the skull have a lot in common with duct tape.

        (a) *Dura mater* is a Latin word meaning "tough mother." It serves to protect the brain and to keep CSF where it belongs, providing a barrier against infection and a tamponade against hemorrhage.

8)   How the brain gets injured
        a) Because of frontal-lobe development, the cranium makes the head top-heavy.
            i) In deceleration injuries, the person tends to lead with the forehead, putting the frontal lobes at risk.
        b) The temporal lobes inhabit a fairly difficult area of the head. Each temporal lobe is tucked under the frontal and parietal lobes.
            i) Each side of the skull is divided into three chambers, or *fossae*. Fossa is Latin for ditch, and the middle ditch is where the temporal lobe lives. In front of this ditch is the sphenoid, or "wedge-shaped" bone, with the sharp end of the wedge pointing right at the temporal lobe.

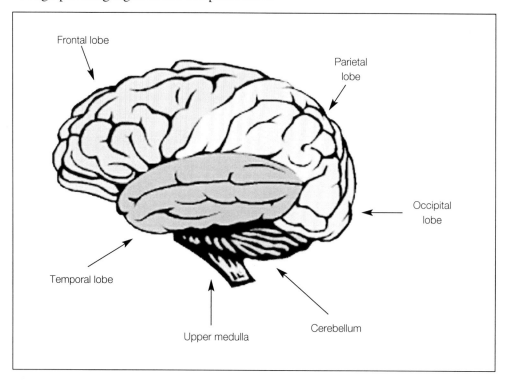

Lateral surface of the brain.

            ii) The floor of the middle ditch is full of lumps and bumps, and the back wall is an immobile mound of bone called the *petrous pyramid*. Injury occurs because the temporal lobes are housed in an area of the skull that is under a large mass of brain in a rough ditch of bone, between areas of hard and sharp bone.
            iii) The size of the temporal lobes accounts for another syndrome seen in head injuries: the epidural hematoma.
                (1) Inside the skull, in the area of the temple, the temporal lobe appears to have pushed the skull out laterally, making the temple area of the skull one of the thinnest and least-protected parts of the cranial vault.
                (2) The arteries in the dura mater are so large that they make grooves in the skull, one of which crosses over the thin, poorly protected temple area.
                    (a) With a blow to the temple, the thin skull can fracture along the groove and tear the artery. Arterial bleeding occurs between the dura mater and the skull—the classic epidural hematoma.

INTERIOR OF SKULL

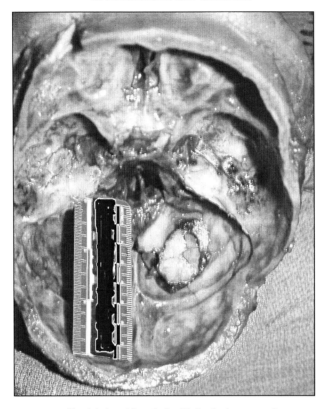

The interior of the skull, with the brain removed.

(b) This is the type of intracranial bleeding where the patient is usually rendered unconscious, followed by an improving level of consciousness (lucid interval), followed in time by blood collecting between the dura mater and the skull and crushing the brain. If hospitalized, the injured person may show a rising, then falling, Glasgow Coma Scale. He is at real risk for deterioration and death.

9)   Understanding blunt trauma injury
       a) The brain, fragile and oversized, is protected by the breakaway nature of the face in concert with the hydraulic and structural mechanisms of the cranial vault.
       b) Efforts to overcome those protective mechanisms, as well as to recognize the syndromes that occur when those mechanisms have been overwhelmed, are critical in understanding the significance of blunt-trauma injury and death.

10)   These are some of the types of injuries incurred as a result of fatal blunt head trauma.
       a) Injury to the scalp
          i) This may identify the weapon used.
          ii) This may indicate the direction and application of the force.
       b) Skull fractures
          i) Skull fractures do not need to be present for severe brain damage to have occurred.
          ii) The presence of skull fractures demonstrates that sufficient violent force was

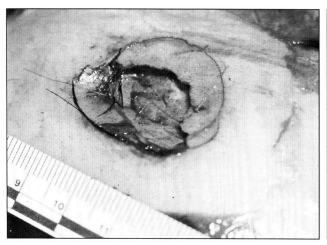 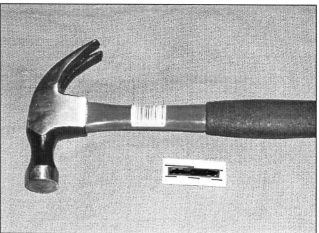

Distinctive blunt-trauma injury.

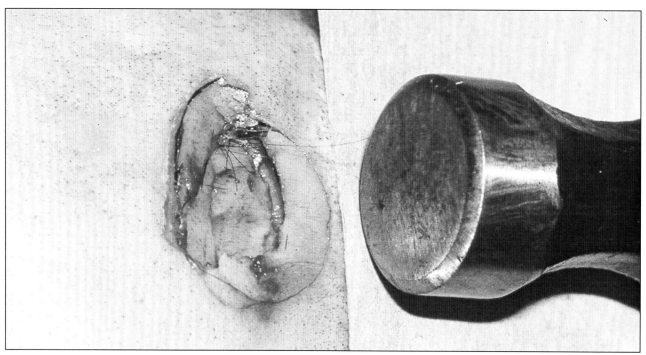

Blunt trauma caused by the action of a hammer to the head may leave a distinctive pattern on the skull of the victim.
Tool-mark identification may be used to determine the murder weapon.

applied to break bone. The nature of the skull fracture (whether patterned, nonpatterned, depressed, or nondepressed) may indicate to some extent the nature of the striking object.

iii) Types of skull fractures:

    (1) Linear

        (a) This accounts for more than 70 percent of all skull fractures.

        (b) In a linear skull fracture, a fracture occurs to the bone, but the bone does not move.

    (2) Depressed

        (a) This may be present with or without an accompanying scalp laceration.

(b) The force causing the fracture actually produces a sunken area in the involved portion of the skull.

    (3) Diastatic

        (a) These fractures occur along the suture lines of the skull.

    (4) Basilar

        (a) This is a fracture involving the base of the skull.

c) Spectacle hemorrhages

    i) As a result of contre-coup force, usually due to a fall in which the back of the head strikes the ground violently, the thin orbital plates, that separate the orbit from the lower surface of the frontal poles in the anterior cranial cavity will fracture, resulting in spectacle hemorrhages of the eyes.

d) Subarachnoid hemorrhages

    i) Traumatic subarachnoid hemorrhage is most often caused by the rotation of the brain within the subarachnoid space. Bleeding will result mainly because of the shearing of small subarachnoid vessels.

e) Subdural hematomas

    i) This is the most common form of significant traumatic intracranial bleeding.

    ii) Any force that indents the skull significantly or causes the brain to shift its position suddenly or to rotate in relation to the skull can create enough stretching force to lacerate bridging veins.

    iii) A fracture may or may not be present in a subdural hematoma.

f) Epidural hematomas

    i) This is almost always associated with a fracture.

    ii) The epidural is the most lethal of the intracranial hemorrhages.

    iii) Epidural hematomas may occur from blows delivered to a stationary head or from a falling head striking a stationary object.

g) Brain contusions

    i) Shearing forces occurring within the tissues at the moment of impact cause small bruises on the surface of the brain.

COUP/CONTRE-COUP EFFECT

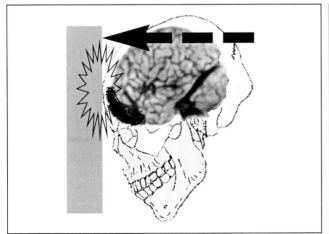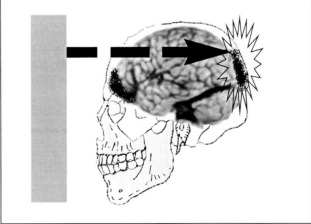

As the head is propelled forward, the brain travels with the skull. As the head drives into an object, tt suddenly stops its acceleration, but the brain continues forward, striking the stopped inside surface of the skull. This injures the adjacent surface of the brain, causing a coup injury. The head then bounces away from the nongiving surface. The brain, acting Jello-like, bounces away, striking the opposite surface of the skull. This causes a contre-coup injury.

        ii) This hematoma can be used to determine whether the injury was due to a stationary head being struck by a moving object or a moving head hitting on a stationary object.

        iii) The coup, contre-coup effect refers exclusively to contusions. Coup injury involves the area immediately adjacent to the direct blow. As the brain moves within the cranial vault, the brain strikes the opposite side of the skull, resulting in a contre-coup injury.

11) Injuries to the brain

    a) Causes:

        i) Falling onto and striking a surface area with the head

            (1) If the head strikes an object with sufficient force, the brain can move inside the skull so violently that it may tear some of the blood vessels, and even bruise the brain itself, if it hits the inside of the skull. This may occur without damage being sustained by the skull.

            (2) Blood begins to flow through the broken blood vessels in the brain. As with other areas of the body that get injured, swelling in the brain area occurs. Unlike with the rest of the body, there's no place for the swelling, or fluid, to go within the tightly confined space containing the brain. With the swelling, the flow of life-sustaining blood becomes affected. Initially, the brain stops making CSF and starts to reabsorb what is already there. The injured brain may even try to create more space by limiting the amount of blood flowing to the brain. If the damage is significant, the brain's compensatory mechanisms cannot keep up with the swelling. Intracranial pressure (ICP) will start to build, resulting in the brain's being pressed up against the inside of the skull.

        ii) Striking the head with a blunt object

        iii) Coming to a sudden violent stop

            (1) With a relatively large brain lying inside a relatively large head (the head and brain weigh anywhere from 16 to 22 pounds), and supported by a relatively skinny neck, brain injuries may occur within their own medium with deceleration forces.

    b) The brain may be injured even if there is no apparent injury to the outside of the head.

12) Signs of blunt-trauma head injury

    a) Loss of consciousness

    b) CSF or bleeding from nose or ears

        i) Any drainage of clear fluid or clear fluid mixed with blood from nose or ears indicates a crack in the skull.

    c) Excessive drowsiness

        i) The injured person may not be easily awakened, which may indicate that pressure is developing inside the head.

    d) Persistent vomiting

        i) Increasing intracranial pressure after a blow to the head may cause the injured individual to have persistent vomiting episodes.

    e) Unusual bruising

        i) Bruises around the eyes ("raccoon eyes") or behind and below the ears (battle's sign) indicate that bleeding may be occurring inside the head.

    f) Pupil irregularity

          i) A pupil that has grown larger and less responsive than the other indicates that pressure is developing on the side of the brain that controls the altered pupil.

    g) Loss of coordination

          i) An individual whose walking becomes unsteady or who has lost the ability to use his arms and legs normally may be experiencing increasing pressure on an injured cerebellum, the center of coordination.

    h) Speech difficulty

          i) If the victim has lost the ability to speak, or if his speech has become slurred, it may indicate an injury and subsequent increase in pressure to the injured person's cerebrum (where the speech control center resides).

    i) Severe headache

          i) A complaint of a headache that keeps getting worse is a sign of increasing pressure inside the victim's head.

    j) Double vision

          i) A complaint about double vision, or any failure of the eyes to move or focus normally, may indicate damage to the back of the brain, where messages from the eyes are interpreted, or that pressure has developed on the optic nerve.

    k) Seizure

          i) Increasing intracranial pressure may cause a seizure (convulsion).

PRIMARY FOCUS OF INVESTIGATION

1) Cause and manner of death?

2) Type of instrument used to cause the death?
    a) Did the weapon submitted as the fatal weapon cause the wounds?

3) How much time elapsed between when the wound was inflicted and when death occurred?

4) Were the injuries inflicted before or after death occurred?

NOTIFICATION

1) A pathologist should be requested on all homicides or deaths of uncertain manner where the following details may be in question:
    a) Time frame since death
    b) Type of weapon causing the death
    c) Possible activities associated with bloodletting

2) The pathologist should be requested on any case in which the manner of death is undetermined or confusing, or where it appears that the decedent or some other interested party attempted to alter the circumstances of the death.

3) If the body is badly decomposed or skeletonized, a forensic anthropologist may be desired at the scene.

SCENE PHOTOGRAPHS

1) Follow the death-scene photographic guidelines for the particular situation of the case (e.g., outdoor, indoor, vehicle scenes). In addition, pay particular attention to the following:
    a) Photograph any signs of resistance by the decedent.

    i) Torn clothing, including buttons ripped from clothing
    ii) Defense injuries of hands, arms, legs, and feet
    iii) Eyeglasses broken or thrown on the floor
    iv) Rifled purse, wallet, dresser drawers, jewelry box, safe, pulled-out pockets from decedent's pants, etc.
    v) Overturned furniture
b) Photograph any weapon present. Include the following:
    i) Relationship of weapon with location and position of body
    ii) Area where weapon may have originated
    iii) A close-up photograph showing the suspected weapon with and without a ruler present
    iv) Close-up photograph of any trace evidence observable on the suspected weapon.
c) Photograph the body of the decedent, including:
    i) All areas of injuries involving the decedent
    ii) All areas of blood on the decedent; his clothing; and his feet, socks, or shoes (soles of feet or shoes)
    iii) All areas of blood immediately adjacent to the body
    iv) Body condition as it relates to time frame of death
    v) Any inconsistencies with regard to the time frame of death, as evidenced by the condition of the remains
        (1) Rigor mortis
        (2) Lividity
    vi) Photograph any transfer evidence observable on the decedent.
    vii) Photograph any indication of animal or insect activity involving the decedent's body.
    viii) Photograph any apparent efforts made by rescue workers to resuscitate the decedent.
d) Photograph all evidence and items that may depict the circumstances of the incident.
    i) Directional evidence, including:
        (1) Blood spatter
        (2) Glass fractures
        (3) Footprints, tire tracks, etc.
    ii) Relational evidence or evidence present that may be connected to the incident, for example, a hat found on top of the kitchen counter that does not belong to anyone who lives at the residence
    iii) Inferred evidence is evidence that is significant in its absence, for example, dust surrounding a clean area on top of a television set may indicate that a VCR has been taken.

SCENE INVESTIGATION

1) Locate and develop information from the essential informants, including:
    a) Eyewitnesses
    b) Persons who found the body or were first at the scene
    c) Doctor, nurses, or EMTs who gave medical attention

2) From the original scene of the incident, develop the following information:
    a) What was the exact time of incident?
    b) What was the exact time when the decedent was found?

c) Describe the building, room, or place where body was found.
d) What reason did the decedent have for being at this location?
e) Describe the exact position of the body.
f) Describe the clothing worn by decedent.
    i) Note any tears, missing buttons, blood stains, etc.
g) If present, describe the exact position of possible weapon found on the scene.
h) Describe any other (possible) weapon and describe its location.
    i) Describe any other items of potential evidence, including blood spatter, overturned furniture, ransacked drawers, suicide note, etc. Detail the location of these items.
j) If alive when found, did the decedent make any comments?

3)   Develop a weapon description.
    a) Describe instrument believed to be associated with the injuries incurred by the decedent.
        i) Include measurement of possible weapon, type of weapon, and whether or not the item was brought to the scene or was from the scene originally.
        ii) Describe the type of edge visible on this item.
        iii) Who is the owner of this item?
    b) If the weapon was not inserted in the decedent when found, is there any blood or other trace evidence visible on this item?

4)   Develop a wound description.
    a) Describe the areas of apparent injury to the decedent.
    b) Inspect the hands and arms for defense marks.

5)   Detail circumstances.
    a) Describe what happened.
    b) Describe in detail any suggestion that the death may be due to accidental means.
    c) What is the possible crme weapon normally used for? Where is it normally kept? Where was it prior to the infliction of injury?
    d) Describe events preceding the death. Detail any comments made by the decedent during this period.

BODY TRANSPORT FROM SCENE

1)   If blood interpretation may be significant in this case, consider removing those items of clothing before transporting the remains (obtain approval from the on-call pathologist).

2)   Check the remains for any trace evidence. If these items may be lost during transport, the evidence technician should collect them after photographing them.

3)   Bag (paper) the hands of the decedent.

PROCESSING AT THE MEO/MORGUE

1)   If homicide involved or suspected, or if suicide is not a certainty:
    a) Consider examining the body for latent or patent prints.
    b) Collect any trace evidence that is present.

c) Collect the bags used to cover the decedent's hands while traveling to the morgue.
d) Collect fingernail scrapings and clippings from the decedent.
e) Obtain pulled and combed hair standards from the decedent.
f) Collect a tube of blood for typing purposes.
g) Obtain major case prints.
h) Collect, air-dry, and separately pack any items of the decedent's clothing.

2) Collect whatever evidence may be required based on the motive indicated, if homicide. For example, complete sexual swabbings if sexual homicide is indicated.

3) If the remains are skeletonized or badly decomposed, the pathologist may consider consulting a forensic anthropologist before conducting an autopsy.

FOLLOW-UP INVESTIGATION

1) If this is a homicide, follow guidelines indicated by the motive.

2) If it is suicide, follow guidelines listed under Chapter 26.
3) If an accident is indicated:
    a) Reconstruct the events based on the evidence and the statements made to the investigators.
    b) Obtain complete background information on the decedent, including these:
        i) Financial (include status of insurance policies)
        ii) Health (include any psychiatric or physical problems that may have contributed to the incident)
        iii) Domestic
    c) Develop any previous accidents involving the decedent

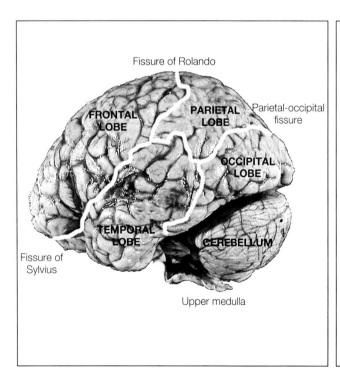

Brain sections, lateral view.

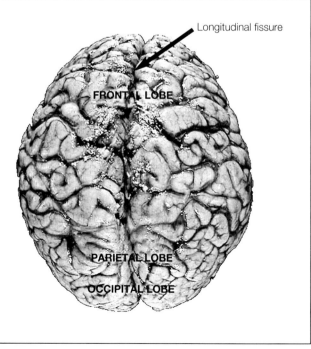

Upper surfaces of the brain.

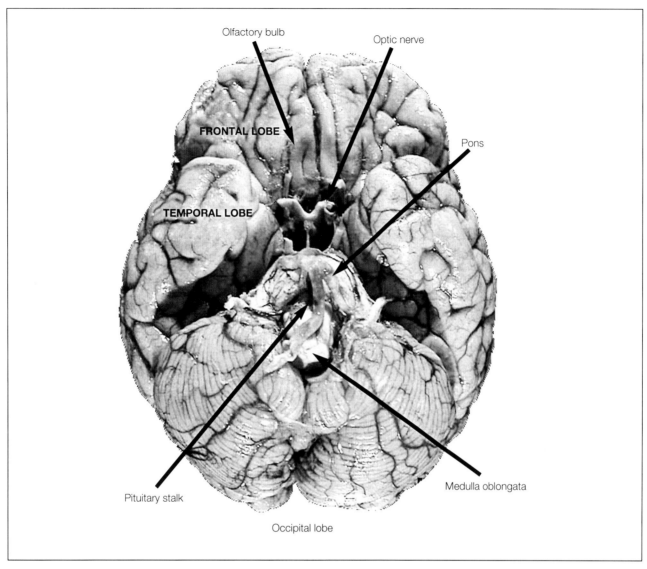

Olfactory bulb

Optic nerve

Pons

FRONTAL LOBE

TEMPORAL LOBE

Medulla oblongata

Pituitary stalk

Occipital lobe

Bottom view of brain.

CHAPTER 33: DEATH CAUSED BY CARBON MONOXIDE

CONSIDERATION

1) Incomplete or presumptive investigation will cause a multitude of problems for the investigator in this type of case.

2) Carbon monoxide is a colorless, odorless gas by-product formed through the incomplete combustion of any of the following:
   - a) Gasoline
   - b) Diesel fuel
   - c) Kerosene
   - d) Butane
   - e) Propane
   - f) Liquefied petroleum gas
   - g) Wood
   - h) Charcoal

3) No established fatal level of carbon monoxide exists. Heavy smokers may have a level of up to 13 percent.

4) Children, small pets, and people suffering from natural diseases are more susceptible to carbon monoxide poisoning.

5) Consider this as a presumptive cause when more than one body is present at the scene and it appears they succumbed to natural causes.

6) In the absence of fire, carbon monoxide poisoning is normally attributed to:
   - a) Accidental or deliberate inhalation of motor vehicle exhaust
   - b) Accidental or deliberate inhalation of carbon monoxide fumes generated by a heat-producing device, such as a heating stove or a charcoal-burning barbecue grill.

PRIMARY FOCUS OF INVESTIGATION

1) Accident versus suicide

NOTIFICATION

1) No special notification is required unless multiple deaths are involved.

SCENE PHOTOGRAPHS

1) Photograph the overall scene.

2) Photograph the source of the carbon monoxide.

3)   Photograph the body at the scene.
                a) Detail pink discoloration involving the decedent.
                b) Detail any grease or absence of grease on the hands of decedent.

4)   Photograph the presence or absence of any tools from the immediate scene.

5)   Photograph any special efforts by the decedent to ensure carbon monoxide intake.
                a) Hose connected to an auto exhaust pipe
                b) Sealed doors, windows, etc.

SCENE INVESTIGATION

1)   Describe the scene. Consider drawing a diagram of the scene showing positions of windows, doors, autos, etc.
2)   Describe activities leading up to the discovery of the body.

3)   What is the probable source of carbon monoxide?
                a) If an auto is involved:
                        i) Is ignition still on?
                        ii) Is motor running?
                        iii) What is the status of gas tank?
                        iv) What is the status of vehicle's battery?
                        v) Is there any indication that the vehicle overheated?
                        vi) Is the decedent inside a closed auto?
                                (1) Are doors to the auto locked?
                        vii) Is the decedent in a closed garage?
                        viii) What is the weather like? Could the decedent have shut the door for warmth? Could the wind have blown the door shut?
                        ix) Are any hoses or other apparatus present?

The "intent" of this subject is evidenced by the exhaust adaptation he made to his vehicle, found parked and running in the garage. The decedent was seated inside his vehicle, and the hose was routed to the passenger compartment.

          x) Was car in good mechanical condition? Was there any recent difficulty with it?

          xi) If tools were found spread out:

               (1) Were there grease marks on decedent's hands or clothing?

               (2) Did the car show signs that work had been done?

               (3) How was the decedent dressed?

               (4) Was the decedent mechanically inclined? Was it his custom to work on his vehicle?

     b) If the decedent is found inside a residence:

          i) Does the heating system use air movement to heat or cool?

          ii) Is the garage connected to the house?

          iii) Could a vehicle in the garage be a source of the carbon monoxide?

          iv) Are there any other dead or sick people in the house?

          v) Are there any dead animals in the house?

4)   Was a suicide note found?

5)   Describe the exact position of the decedent.

     a) Is there any indication that the decedent attempted to escape?

     b) Describe if a cherry/pink color is present on the remains.

6)   If it is a possible suicide, what is the motive?

7)   Is there any indication of alcohol?

8)   Develop health history of the decedent.

     a) Collect the decedent's prescriptions and transport with remains to the MEO/morgue.

TRANSPORTING REMAINS

1)   No special requirements

PROCESSING AT MEO/MORGUE

1)   Fingerprint the decedent unless a question exists as to whether or not the decedent was working on his vehicle at the time of death. If this situation exists, delay the fingerprinting until the pathologist has examined the hands.

2)   Notify the proper agencies involved if the source of the carbon monoxide is not known or if survivors may remain in the same odorless, colorless, poisonous environment. Consider having the police seal the involved location.

FOLLOW-UP INVESTIGATION

1)   If suicide is indicated, follow the guidelines in Chapter 26.

2)   Consult experts about possible leaks, equipment malfunction, or problems involving a design that may encourage carbon monoxide problems.

3)   If fire is involved, follow the recommendations in Chapter 41.

CHAPTER 34: CHILD DEATHS

CONSIDERATIONS

1) Four possibilities in dealing with the death of a child:
   a) Natural death with well-documented history
   b) Sudden infant death syndrome (SIDS)
      i) Most common cause of death for children under the age of 1 year old
      ii) SIDS profile:
         (1) The child is from an economically deprived family.
         (2) The child is 2 to 4 months of age.
         (3) The child appears well nourished and well developed.
         (4) There may be a medical history of a minor respiratory infection or colic during the day prior to the death
         (5) The child was well when last seen. Such victims are usually found in the morning.
      iii) SIDS is the diagnosis given to the death of an infant after negative findings are developed in three areas involving the case:
         (1) Examination of the death scene
         (2) A complete postmortem examination and medical history investigation
         (3) Case history investigation
      v) Increased incidence of SIDS:
         (1) Low socioeconomic-status households
         (2) Large families
         (3) Young mothers
         (4) Smoking mothers
         (5) Drug-addicted mothers
         (6) Cooler seasons of the year (fall and winter)
         (7) Midnight to 9 A.M.
         (8) Premature infants
         (9) Twins (tends to recur)
         (10) Males (3-to-1 ratio)
         (11) Tendency to recur in families
         (12) Mothers who receive little or no prenatal child care
   c) Accidental death of child
      i) Bed clothing (e.g., pillows, blankets, sheets), by itself, doesn't appreciably diminish the child's oxygen intake and cause the suffocation of the infant.
      ii) It is extremely rare for a child to be suffocated by an adult lying on top of it while sharing a bed unless the adult is impaired with alcohol or drugs.
   d) The child may die as a result of child abuse. The investigation should be directed toward identification of historical hints, social stresses, medical findings, and circumstantial risk factors, which predisposed the dead child to lethal child abuse or neglect.
      i) Battered-child syndrome
         (1) Most deaths occur before the age of 5.
         (2) Head injuries are the most common cause of death.

CHILD DEATH BY- SUFFOCATION

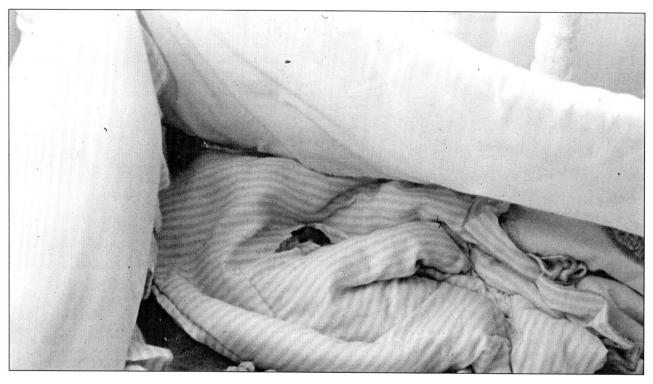

The child in this photo was believed to have suffocated in this makeshift crib. The parents had received the crib, without a mattress, as a gift. They purchased a crib mattress at a flea market. The mattress did not come up to the edges of the crib, so the parents stuffed this area with a comforter and sheet. During sleep, the baby turned over, landing facedown in this area. The mother of the child discovered the child dead. Lividity patterns on the face of the infant confirmed the baby's position in the crib.

(3) Injuries will involve:
    (a) External injuries
        (i) Cigarette burns are usually inflicted on palms of hands, soles of feet, and buttocks.
        (ii) Scalding is usually associated with the child's having wet the bed. Because the child is dipped into hot water, demarcation of the pattern will be noticeable on the skin.

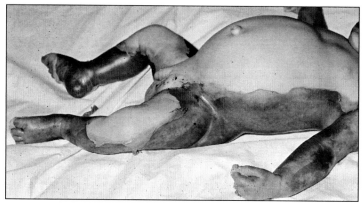

The demarcated skin appears as a red area that may be accompanied by blisters or skin slippage.

(iii) U-shaped bruising indicates an item such as a looped extension cord and is most often found on the back or buttocks.

(iv) Be alert for patterned bruises and items that may have caused them. Through normal activities, children get bruises over areas of prominence (e.g., chin, knees, elbows). Bruises found on the back, abdomen, and buttocks should be considered suspicious.

(v) Lips may be bruised, or the frenulum (the area where the lip and gum join) may be torn.

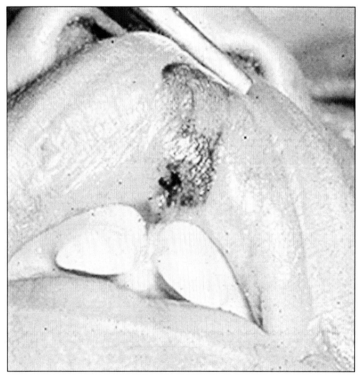

This damage to the frenulum, where the lip and gum join, may indicate trauma from with a direct blow or through forced feeding.

(vi) Bruising may be observed on the ears of the child.

(b) Internal injuries

(i) Subdural hematoma

(c) Skeletal injuries

(i) Rib fractures

(ii) Spiral fractures from twisting of extremities

(d) Ocular injuries

(i) Eyes blackened or containing subconjunctivae hemorrhage (i.e., blood in the white of the eye)

ii) Physical neglect

(1) Inadequate care, supervision, or protection from elements, for example:

(a) Leaving small children alone

(b) Leaving a child in a car during a hot day

(c) Inappropriate dress for the season

(d) Failure to take the child for medical care when it has been suffering from an extreme illness

PRIMARY FOCUS OF INVESTIGATION

1) Did the child die as a result of natural causes, accident, or child abuse? Deaths that result from child abuse are homicides.

2) Is death due to injury or complication of injury?
    a) What is the mechanism of that injury?
        i) Consider any item that may have contributed to the child's death.
    b) When did injury occur? Who had access to the child?
    c) What was the time of death?
    d) Does the lethal episode represent a single episode or the last of multiple episodes?

3) Document the medical history of the child.

4) Document the family history.
    a) Omissions made by the family are extremely important. For example, did family members deny any other deaths involving other children that you later develop to be true?
    b) Stress in the family is the most important element. In examining for family stress, look for these indicators:
        i) Social isolation with no or little support from family and friends
        ii) Inadequate medical care
        iii) Frequent moving and job changes
        iv) Financial problems
        v) Primary caregiver has no one to help with care of child
        vi) Spouse abuse
        vii) Alcohol or drug abuse
        viii) Low self-esteem

5) Develop any background or history of child abuse.

6) Look for triggers for abusive behavior.
    a) Persistent crying
    b) Refusing food
    c) Toilet training
    d) Disobedience

7) Identify red flags.
    a) Unexplained illness or injury
    b) Repeated physical abuse
    c) Delaying or failing to report injury
    d) Providing misleading information to medical attendants

NOTIFICATION

1) It is not necessary to notify the pathologist unless a homicide is suspected or other circumstances of the death become suspicious.

SCENE PHOTOGRAPHS

1) If homicide is involved or suspected, follow the guidelines involving the photographing of homicide scenes.

2) Photograph the scene to show the overall condition (e.g., well maintained versus unsanitary).

3) Photograph the decedent, including:
    a) Clothing
    b) Injuries
    c) Sanitary conditions
    d) Any indications of time frame for death

4) Photograph any item (e.g., furniture) that may have contributed to the death.

5) Photograph plastic bags found out of place and in proximity to the decedent.

6) If neglect is suspected, photograph the negative aspects of the situation, for example:
    a) Empty refrigerator and cupboards to demonstrate an lack of food
    b) Supply of clean diapers? Soiled diapers present?
    c) Infant formula present? Out of date?

SCENE INVESTIGATION

1) Identification
    a) Infant's full name
    b) Age
    c) Date of birth
    d) Race
    e) Sex
    f) Home address
    g) Social Security number

2) Circumstances of death:
    a) List scene address
    b) Describe condition of infant when found
        i) Dead
        ii) Unresponsive
        iii) In distress
        iv) Other
    c) Describe sequence of events before death
    d) Infant placed (date, time, location, by whom)
    e) Known alive (date, time, location, by whom)
    f) Infant found (date, time, location, by whom)
    g) Authorities (911) called (date, time, location, by whom)
    h) Infant injured (date, time, location, by whom)
    i) Identify actual death scene
        i) On scene
        ii) Emergency room
        iii) En route/dead on arrival

        iv) In-patient
        v) During surgery
    j) Place of fatal event
        i) Unwitnessed or witnessed in room or area
        ii) At home or away from home
        iii) Indoors or outdoors
        iv) In a vehicle or not

3)   Basic medical information:
    a) Identify health care provider for child
    b) Identify birth hospital, city and state
    c) Develop maternal illness or complications during pregnancy
    d) Identify major birth defects
    e) Was infant one of multiple births
    f) Gestation age at birth (weeks)
    g) Birth weight

APPROXIMATE WEIGHT PERCENTILES FOR GIRLS
(Barchart.com, 1999)

Percentile	3 (in months)	6	9	12	18	24
95	15	19	23	25	28	31
75	13	17	20	23	25	28
50	12	16	10	21	24	26
25	11	15	18	19	22	25
10	10	13	16	18	20	23

APPROXIMATE WEIGHT PERCENTILES FOR BOYS
(Barchart.com, 1999)

Percentile	3 (in months)	6	9	12	18	24
95	16	21	24	27	30	33
75	14	19	22	24	27	30
50	13	17	20	23	25	28
25	12	16	19	21	24	26
10	10	15	18	20	22	24

h)   Hospitalization of infant after initial discharge
    i) Emergency room visits during the past two weeks?
    j) Known allergies?
    k) Growth and weight gain normal for the child?

l) Exposure to contagious diseases in past 2 weeks?

m) Illness in past 2 weeks?

n) Lethargy, crankiness, or excessive crying in past 48 hours?

o) Describe child's normal eating habits.

     i) Any appetite changes in past 48 hours?

     ii) Infant ever breast-fed?

     iii) Date, time, and content of last meal?

p) Vomiting or choking in past 48 hours?

q) Fever or excessive sweating in past 48 hours?

r) Diarrhea or stool changes in past 48 hours?

s) Infant ever stopped breathing or turned blue?

t) Regular sleeping habits of child?

u) Vaccinations in past 72 hours?

IMMUNIZATION AGES OF CHILDREN (IN MONTHS)
(Barcharts.com, 1999)

Immunization	0–2	2	2–4	4	6	6–18	12–15	12–18
Hepatitis	B-1		B-2			B-3		
DTP		DTP		DTP	DTP			DTP or Dtap
Hemophilius B Hib		Hib		Hib	Hib		Hib	
Polio, OPV		OPV		OPV		OPV		
Varicella zoster VZV								VZV
MMR							MMR	

IMMUNIZATION TYPE

Hepatitis B vaccine	Immunizes against a virus that can cause chronic liver disease
DTP	Contains diphtheria and tetanus toxoids and an acellular pertussis (whooping cough) vaccine
Hemophilius B vaccine	Immunizes against bacteria that cause such dangerous ailments as meningitis
OPV vaccine	Immunizes against polio
VZV vaccine	Immunizes against chicken pox
MMR vaccine	Immunizes against measles, mumps, and rubella (German measles)

v) Infant injury or other condition not mentioned above

w) Medication history (medicine names and doses; if prescription, describe prescription date, prescribing physician, amount prescribed, amount remaining, and name of pharmacy)

    i) Home remedies

x) Emergency medical treatment

    i) None

    ii) CPR

    iii) Transfusion

iv) IV fluids

v) Surgery

y) Description of nature and duration of resuscitation and treatments to revive the child

z) Description of any known injuries or marks on child created or observed during resuscitation or treatment

4)   Household environment

    a) Type of dwelling?

    b) Number of bedrooms?

    c) Overall condition of the residence (e.g., clean, dirty, cluttered)?

    d) Number of adults living in household?

    e) Number of children living in household?

    f) Evidence of alcohol or drug abuse?

    g) Serious physical or mental illness in household?

    h) Police called to home in past?

    i) Prior contact with social services?

    j) Documented history of child abuse?

    k) Odors, fumes, or peeling paint in household?

    l) Dampness, visible standing water, or mold growth?

    m) Pets (e.g., rodents, birds, insects) in household?

5)   Infant and environment

    a) Incident occurred in crib, bed, or other (describe)?

    b) Child was sleeping alone, with others, info not available?

    c) Body position when placed?

    d) Body position when found?

    e) Face position when found?

    f) Developmental stage of child (e.g., able to crawl, walk)

    g) Was nose or mouth covered or obstructed?

    h) Describe postmortem changes when found (e.g., rigor, lividity, body temperature).

    i) Number of covers or blanket layers on infant?

    j) Describe sleeping and supporting surface.

    k) Describe child's clothing.

    l) Describe other items that were (or may have been) in contact with the child.

    m) Describe other items in crib or immediate environment.

    n) Describe devices operating in the room.

    o) Describe cooling/heating source in room.

    p) Was cooling/heating source operating?

        i) Thermostat setting?

        ii) Thermostat reading?

ACTIVITY ABILITY OF CHILDREN
(Barcharts.com, 1999)

Activity	50%	75%	90%
Rolls over completely in any direction	2 1/2 months	3 1/2 months	4 1/2 months
Sits alone for 30 seconds or more	6 months	7 months	8 months
Pulls self to stand using furniture	7 months	9 months	10 months
Stands alone for 10 seconds or more	10 1/2 months	13 Months	14 months
Walks well by self	12 months	13 1/2 months	14 months

       q) Actual environment temperature?
       r) Outside temperature?
       s) Items collected (consider collecting the following):
             i) Baby bottle
             ii) Apnea monitor
             iii) Formula
             iv) Medicines
             v) Diaper
             vi) Pacifier
             vii) Clothing
             viii) Bedding
       t) Draw a scene diagram (include north direction, windows and doors, wall lengths, ceiling heights, location of furniture, body location when found, location of other objects within room, location of heating and cooling supplies and returns).

6)   Caregiver information
       a) Mother (age, marital status, cohabiting history)
       b) Natural father (age, marital status, cohabiting status)
       c) Any other child deaths involving mother/father?
       d) Identify:
             i) Usual caregiver?
             ii) Last caregiver?
       e) Any other child deaths involving caregiver?
       f) Identify:
             i) The person who last placed the baby down before it was found dead?
             ii) Last witness?
             iii) Finder:
             iv) First responder?
             v) 911 caller?

TRANSPORTING REMAINS

1) No special handling is required unless case is believed to be a homicide or suspicious in nature.

2) If homicide is suspected, bag the hands of the decedent prior to transporting. Protect for trace evidence.

3) If bite marks are present on the child, follow guidelines suggested in Chapter 68 on bite mark protocol.

4) If child expired at a hospital, request copies of head and body X-rays before remains are transported.

5) Always carry the covered body of the dead child as though it were still alive. Complaints may arise from the parents of the child, neighbors, and the general public about the manner in which the child's remains are handled.

PROCESSING AT MEO/MORGUE

1) For identification purposes if the child is less than 2 years old, inked prints of the feet should be obtained.

2) If the case is suspected to be a homicide, obtain major case prints and trace evidence recovery, depending on the circumstances of the case.

3) If bite marks are present, consider obtaining a cast of the decedent's teeth to eliminate the possibility of self-infliction.

4) Take full-body X-rays.

FOLLOW-UP INVESTIGATION

1) Run a criminal records check on individuals involved with the immediate care of the decedent.

2) Run child protection agency inquiry history on the parents or other individuals responsible for the immediate care of the involved child.

3) If death is suspicious, consider interviewing the following:
   a) Other children in the household
   b) Other family members
   c) Teachers and counselors
   d) Neighbors

4) If case is determined to be a homicide, follow guidelines suggested under the homicide section appropriate to the possible motive (the majority will be altercations).

5) If death is found to be as a result of some product, report findings to the appropriate section of the U.S. Consumers Protection Agency (MECAP).

INJURIES ASSOCIATED WITH CHILD ABUSE

Always take into account the extent to which CPR efforts may have contributed to the injuries observed. In addition, be aware that a suspicious area on the child may be a Mongolian spot, a bluish discoloration found in the lower back at birth. It will usually get smaller in size and may disappear as the child gets older.

Body Area	Injury	Mechanism
Face: Lip	Contusion	Direct blow
Frenulum of lip	Laceration	Direct blow; forced feeding.
Tongue	Laceration	Forced feeding
Ear	Hematoma	Direct blow
Nasal septum	Deviation; hematoma	Direct blow
Eye	Hematoma, hyphema, subconjunctival hemorrhage	Direct blow
Head and central nervous system	Subdural hematoma	Direct blow. Shaking (may cause retinal hemorrhage or detachment). Consider traumatic until proven otherwise.
	Cephalhematoma	Hair pulling (especially prevalent with braids)
Thorax and abdomen	Hemothorax (blood collecting in the space between the lungs and chest wall)	Direct blow
	Pneumothorax (air in the chest cavity).	Direct blow
	Solid viscus (internal organs)	Direct blow
	Tears of mesentery	Direct blow
Skeletal system	Callus (new bone in the area of a fracture)	Old injury
Ribs	Fracture	Direct blow
	Spiral fracture	Twisting of extremity
Legs/arms	Avulsion (tearing) of muscle	Jerking of extremity

Body Area	Injury	Mechanism
Skin and subcutaneous tissue (palms of hand, soles of feet, or buttocks)	Small circular bones	Cigarette burns
Buttocks, feet, or hands	Scalding with clear mark of demarcation	Immersion in hot water (may be brought on by difficulties in toilet training)
Wrists, ankles, and mouth	Contusions and use of bindings	May indicate previous abrasions
Lower back	Contusions	Corporal punishment
All areas	Oval abrasions with marked pattern Patterned contusions	Bite mark Beating with a looped cord (U-shaped), buckle, heel of shoe (stomping), hand marks, etc.
Genitalia Hymen Vulva Fourchette Scrotum/penis Anus	Venereal warts, gonorrhea, syphilis Bite mark Laceration Hematoma Laceration Hematoma and/or swelling Laceration; poor sphincter tone	Remote sexual assault Possible sexual assault Possible recent sexual assault Recent sexual assault Recent sexual assault Twisting injury Possible sexual assault
General appearance: Weight Height	Subcutaneous fat absent; fatty liver, ascites, thymic atrophy; third percentile in comparison weight Third percentile in height comparison	Possible starvation Possible starvation

ABANDONED NEWBORN
STILLBORN INFANT OR FETUS

Consideration

1) The forensic pathologist will attempt to identify whether the decedent is a fetus or full-term infant.
    a) Was fetus or infant stillborn, or did the infant live after birth?

2) Why was decedent abandoned?
    a) Financial considerations?
    b) Concealed pregnancy?
    c) Homicide?
        i) Rag or other item stuffed into decedent's mouth?
        ii) Observed trauma?

COURT ILLUSTRATION OF CHILD ABUSE

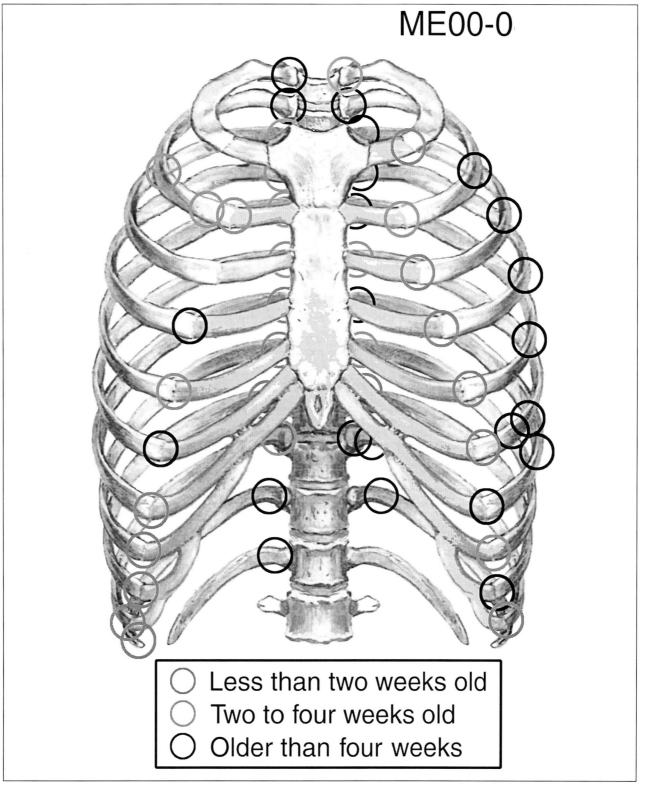

An example of a court exhibit prepared on a child-death murder case. The case had originally been signed out as a natural death. Following investigative suspicions, investigators exhumed the child's body, and a second autopsy revealed 52 rib fractures. The father of the child admitted to holding the child by his rib cage and crushing the child until he could feel the child's ribs break under his fingers. He was convicted of first-degree murder. (Drawing courtesy of Dr. Andrew Baker, Armed Forces Institute of Pathology.)

iii) Abandoned in an isolated location where the baby may have expired due to:
    (1) Exposure
    (2) Asphyxia (possibly placed in a plastic bag while alive)

Primary Focus of Investigation

1) Was infant or fetus born alive?
    a) Best indication is food found in the stomach of the infant during the autopsy examination.

2) Cause and manner of death?

3) Who are the parents of the fetus or infant?

4) Develop the time frame for the incident.

Notification

1) A pathologist at the scene is not required unless homicide is readily apparent.

Scene Photographs

1) Photograph the overall area. Detail the relative isolation of the area, if appropriate.

2) Photograph the remains from various angles detailing the remains with the area.

3) Shoot close-up photographs of the remains.

4) Shoot close-up photograph of the umbilical cord end.

5) Photograph the clothing or lack of clothing condition involving the decedent.

Scene Investigation

1) Be cautious in approaching the scene because the person who abandoned the remains may have left footprints or tire tracks.

2) Be cautious around the immediate area containing the remains for fingerprints left by the abandoning party.

3) Be alert for possible fingerprints left by the abandoning party on items containing and involving the remains, for example:
    a) Plastic bag containing the infant
    b) Paper towels used to wipe hands
    c) Diaper
    d) Bloody prints on items and on decedent

4) Describe the area. Is it frequented by others, or is it a fairly well isolated?

5)   Describe time frame of when infant was found. Work backward to a time established when the decedent was not present, for example:

        a) Tire tracks or footprints present after a rainstorm

        b) Trash can liner changed on a regular basis

        c) Items found with the decedent that may date the incident, for example:

            i) Cash register receipts showing date and time

6)   How was the body discovered?

7)   Describe the decedent. Does it appear to be fully developed?

8)   Describe any injuries observed on the remains.

Transporting the Remains

1)   In those cases in which physical evidence may be present, carefully wrap the remains in a shroud to preserve them for processing at the MEO/morgue.

Processing at the MEO/Morgue

1)   Take inked prints of the decedent's feet.

2)   If applicable, examine remains for fingerprints, which may have been transferred in the blood covering the remains.

3)   Cut and preserve the end of the umbilical cord, which would have been attached to the mother.

4)   Collect blood or other specimens for possible processing of DNA.

        a) If fetus is involved, the pathologist may wish to preserve the entire specimen. Do not place the specimen in formaldehyde; freeze it instead.

Follow-Up Investigation

1)   Utilize the media immediately.

2)   Identify the time frame of the incident. Seek witnesses who would have been at this location during the identified time.

CHAPTER 35: DELAYED-FATAL HOSPITAL CASES

CONSIDERATION

1) A delayed-fatal case involves the death of an individual after he has been removed from a scene and transported to a hospital.

2) The investigation into the decedent's death should not be predicated on the length of time this individual has survived; it should be based on the reason he was admitted to the hospital.
   a) For example, a hospitalized patient dies of pneumonia 2 months after being admitted to the hospital for a gunshot wound of the abdomen. As long as the patient's demise can be directly related to the event precipitating the admission and the eventual pneumonia, the death investigation concerns the original incident.

3) Distinguish, if you can, between injuries resulting from resuscitative measures performed by rescue and emergency room personnel and those resulting from the trauma associated with the original incident.

PRIMARY FOCUS OF INVESTIGATION

1) Work back case to determine the original circumstances involving the subject's admission to the hospital.

2) Develop background information on the subject, including health and social history.

3) Develop medical information about what happened to the subject while at the hospital and during transport by the rescue service.
   a) All treatment including surgery
   b) Medication
   c) Diagnosis

4) Identify and locate any evidence associated with the case.

NOTIFICATION

1) Notification is usually not necessary unless organ donation is requested, especially in those cases in which a homicide or questionable suicide may be involved. Consultation with the pathologist, prosecuting attorney, and detective handling the case may be required.

PHOTOGRAPHS

1) Upon arrival at the MEO or morgue, the decedent should be photographed with all bandages, tubes, lines, etc., still attached.

2) Photograph the decedent with all bandages, tubes, etc., removed.

3) Take an identification photograph of the decedent prior to the autopsy with all tubes, and bandages removed from the head area. Blood and any other fluids should have been wiped away prior to the photograph's being taken.

4)   Photograph all of the decedent's injuries, surgical incisions, and hospital-produced wounds with and without a scale being present.

INVESTIGATION

1)   Identify the hospital involved.

2)   Identify the reporting person.

3)   Get the full name of the decedent.
        a) Decedent's race and sex?
        b) Decedent's address and home telephone number?
        c) Decedent's date of birth?
        d) Develop decedent's next of kin.
                i) Next of kin's address and telephone number?

4)   Identify the attending physician.

5)   Identify the physician who pronounced the decedent.
        a) Develop the date and time of pronouncement.

6)   Was the family present at the time of death?
        a) If yes, identify family member.

7)   Identify how the subject was transported to the hospital from the scene.

8)   According to the hospital chart:
        a) Identify the location of the original incident.
        b) Identify the date and time of the original incident.
        c) Detail the circumstances of the original incident.

9)   Identify the law enforcement agency involved with the original incident.

10)   Identify the location of the subject's personal effects.
        a) Make arrangements to obtain clothing on all violent deaths, including motor vehicle deaths.
                i) Arrange to obtain the motorcycle helmet on a motorcycle crash victim.

11)   Attempt to obtain admission blood alcohol and drug screen results if done.

12)   Attempt to obtain admission blood and urine specimens of all accepted cases if still available.

13)   Has organ donation been requested?
        a) Has organ donation been authorized?

14)   Order a copy of the patient's medical chart, including:
        a) EMT or rescue report
        b) ER record
        c) X-ray reports, especially those reports relating to the injured area
        d) All doctors' notes

e) First and last 3 days of nurses' notes
f) All operative records
g) Admission summary
h) Discharge summary

BODY TRANSPORT FROM HOSPITAL

1) All tubes, lines, bandages, casts, braces, etc., should remain as placed and transported with the remains.
    a) Tubes and lines can be cut and tied off, but their placement should never be altered.
    b) Tubes and lines should be cut to allow for the length of tubing or line to be visible. A small length of tubing or line should never be left as a sharp stub.

2) Be extremely caution when transporting the remains.
    a) Body fluids may leak from the tubing, gurney, and body.
    b) Fluids may be present on the floor of the hospital facility.
        i) The investigator could slip and fall on the floor.
        ii) Body fluids can adhere to the investigator's shoes and be transferred to the floor of his car, office, or home.
    c) The body may be wrapped in a shroud, thereby hindering the handlers of the body from observing any potential sharp-item areas.

FOLLOW-UP INVESTIGATION

1) Conduct the investigation indicated using the guidelines appropriate for the particular type of death caused by the original incident.

TRAUMA SCORE CODES

The trauma score is used by rescue and ER personnel to establish a system to evaluate the severity of the condition of an arriving patient. The high scores are reflective of normal function; the low scores represent impaired function. The points are totaled and rated according to the Glasgow Coma Scale.

TRAUMA SCALE

Respiratory Rate

10–24 minutes	4
25–35 minutes	3
36 minutes or more	2
1–9 minutes	1
0 minutes	

Respiratory Expansion

Normal	1
Retractive/None	0

Systolic Blood Pressure

90 mm Hg or greater	4
70–89 mm Hg	3
50–69 mm Hg	2
0–49 mm Hg	1
No pulse	0

Capillary Refill

Normal	2
Delayed	1
None	0
TOTAL TRAUMA SCORE	1–16

GLASGOW COMA SCALE

Eye Opening

Spontaneous	4
To voice	3
To pain	2
None	1

Verbal Response

Oriented	5
Confused	4
Inappropriate words	3
Incomprehensible sounds	2
None	1

Motor Response

Obeys command	6
Localizes pain	5
Withdraw (pain)	4
Flexion (pain)	3
Extension (pain)	2
None	1

TOTAL GLASGOW COMA SCALE POINTS

14–15 =	5
11–13 =	4
8–10 =	3
5–7 =	2
3–4 =	1

SURGICAL INCISIONS AND HOSPITAL-PRODUCED WOUNDS

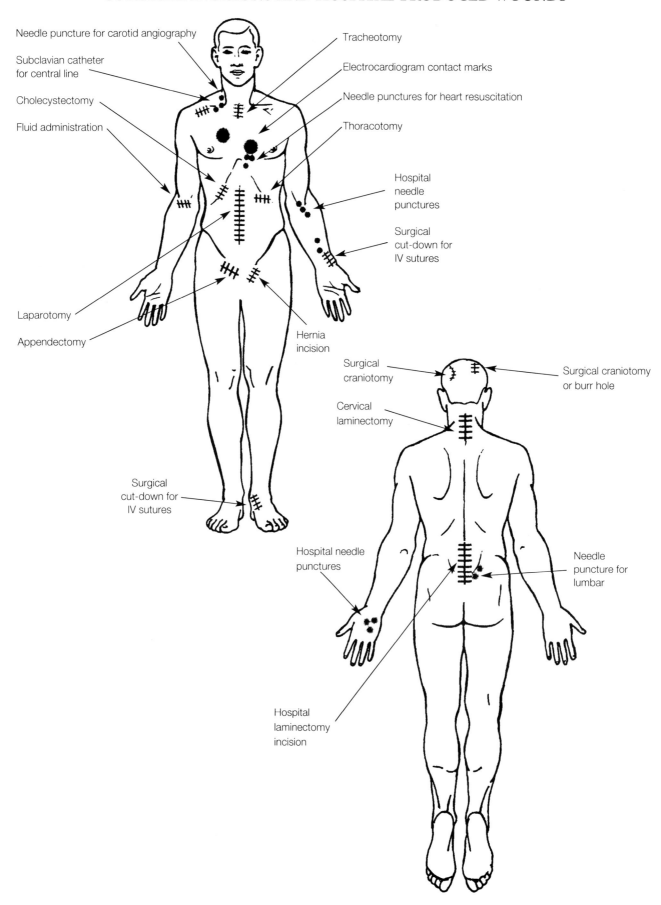

Needle puncture for carotid angiography

Subclavian catheter for central line

Cholecystectomy

Fluid administration

Tracheotomy

Electrocardiogram contact marks

Needle punctures for heart resuscitation

Thoracotomy

Hospital needle punctures

Surgical cut-down for IV sutures

Laparotomy

Appendectomy

Hernia incision

Surgical cut-down for IV sutures

Surgical craniotomy

Surgical craniotomy or burr hole

Cervical laminectomy

Hospital needle punctures

Needle puncture for lumbar

Hospital laminectomy incision

MEDICAL ABBREVIATIONS

A

a	artery
A	area, anterior
Ab, ab	abortion, antibody
abd	abdomen
ABP	arterial blood pressure
abs	absent
a.c.	before meals
AC & CHR	acute and chronic
acc	accident
accom	accommodation
ad lib	as desired
adm	admission
ADT	a placebo
alc, alcho	alcohol
amb	ambulatory
ann fib	annulus fibrosis
ant	anterior
A/P	anterior and posterior
aq	water
ARDS	adult respiratory distress syndrome
art	artery, arterial
ASCVD	arteriosclerotic cardiovascular disease
Ax	axilla, axillary

B

B	bath
Bab	Babinski sign
Bas	basal, basilar
bid	twice a day
BRP	bathroom privileges
B.S.	breath sounds

C

c	with
C	centigrade
C-I-XII	1st to 12th cranial nerve
Ca	cancer, carcinoma
card	cardiac
CBC	complete blood count
cc, c.c.	cubic centimeters
C.C.	chief complaint
CCI	cerebral cranial injuries
C.D.	contagious diseases
C.E.	cardiac enlargement
Cerv	cervix, cervical
cf	compare

CHF	congestive heart failure
cm	centimeter
CNS Dis	central nervous system disease
Coc	coccygeal
comf	comfortable
comm	communicable
comp	compound, compress
cons	consultation
COPD	chronic obstructive pulmonary disease
CR	cardiorespiratory system
cran	cranial
Cr.Ns.	cranial nerves
CSF	cerebrospinal fluid
C-V	cardiovascular
CVA	cerebrovascular accident

D

dehyd	dehydrated
depr	depressed
decr	decrease(d)
dis	disease
dist	distal
DM	diabetes mellitus
DOA	dead on arrival, date of admission
Dors	dorsal
D.P.	pulse (dorsalus)
DTRs	deep tendon reflex

E

ECG	electrocardiogram
EEG	electroencephalogram
EKG	electrocardiogram
elev	elevated
En	enema
ETOH	alcoholism
excess	excessive
ext	external
extr	extremities
extens	extension
ess	essentially

F

F	finger(s), female, or Fahrenheit
fem	femoral, femur
F.H.	family history
flac	flaccid
fl	flexor, flexion
FML	fatty metamorphosis of the liver
Fr, Frx	fracture
Fx	fracture

G	gt	drop(s)

H	h	hour
	H	hypodermic
	HASCVD	hypertension and arterioschlerotic cardiovascular disease
	H&C	hot and cold
	hern	herniated
	hg/gb	hemoglobin
	HHD	hypertensive heart disease
	hist	history
	H.S., h.s.	hour of sleep
	Ht	height, heart
	Hx	history
	hyst	hysterectomy, hysteria

I	i, ii, iii	1, 2, 3, etc.
	i.d.	during the day
	I.M.	intramuscular (injection)
	irreg	irregular
	irrig	irrigate, irrigation
	I.V.	intravenous
	IVD	intervertebral disc
	IVP	intravenous pyelogram
	IVU	intravenous urogram

J	jt	joint

K	K	potassium
	KJ	knee jerk
	KUB	kidney, ureter, bladder (X-ray)

L	L	liver, liter, left, lower, light, or lumbar
	lac	laceration
	lam	laminectomy
	lap	laparotomy
	lat	lateral
	L.E.	lupus erythematosus, lower extremity
	lg	large, leg
	lig	ligament
	L.L.E.	left lower extremity
	l & w	living and well
	L. lat	left lateral

LOA	left occipital anterior
LOP	left occipital posterior
L.P.	lumbar puncture
L.S.	lumbosacral
LSK	liver, spleen, kidney
Lt	light, left
L.U.E.	left upper extremity
lumb	lumbar

M

m	minims
M	male, mother, meter
max	maximum, maxillary
med	medial
min	minimal, minums
mm	muscles
MN	mononuclears
mod	moderate(ly)
monos	monocycles
M.S.	multiple sclerosis
Ms	murmurs
mss	massage
M.T.	muscles and tendons
multi	multiple
multip	multiparous (more than one pregnancy)
musc	muscle(s)

N

n	nerve
N_2	nitrous oxide
NBM	nothing by mouth
neg	negative
NPO	nothing per mouth
Ns	nerves
N.S.	nervous system
noc	night
norm	normal
nullip	nulliparous (no pregnancies)

O

OBS	organic brain syndrome
Occ(p)	occiput, occipital
occas	occasional
OPD	outpatient department
O.R.	operating room
orth	orthopedic

P

PA	posterior-anterior
P&A	percussion and auscultation
palp	palpate(d)
para i	has one pregnancy
p/c, p.c.	after meals
P.E.	physical exam
PEG	pneumoencephalogm
Per	perineal
pen	penicillin
P.F.	push fluids
P.H.	past/personal history
po	per oral
P.O.	postoperative
POC	product of conception
pos	positive
post	posterior
preop	preoperative
primip	primiparous (first pregnancy)
P.R.N.	in dosage, as required when necessary, as needed
pron	pronator (pronation)
prox	proximal
Pt	patient
Px	physical exam

Q

q	every
qd	every day
qn	every night
q2h	every 2 hours
qid	4 times a day
qns	quantity not sufficient
qs	quantity sufficient
qv	as much as you wish

R

R	right, rub
R, (R)	rectal (temperature)
rad	radial
RBC	red blood cells
rect	rectum, rectal
rehab	rehabilitation
resp	respiratory
RHD	rheumatic heart disease
R/O	rule out
RRE	round, regular, and equal
Rt	right
Rx	prescription

S		
	s	sine (without)
	SBS	shaken baby syndrome
	sens	sensory, sensation
	skel	skeletal
	sibs	siblings
	SIDS	sudden infant death syndrome
	sig	take (prescription)
	sl	slightly
	SLR	straight-leg raising (test)
	SOB	shortness of breath
	SOS	when necessary
	sp	spine, spinal
	ssp. cd.	spinal cord
	spec	specimen
	sp. fl.	spinal fluid
	spg	sponge
	spin	spine, spinal
	ss	one-half
	s.s.	soap suds
	st	stomach
	stat	immediately
	stom	stomach
	S.T.S.	serological test for syphilis
	subcut	subcutaneous
	sup	superior
	supin	supination
	surg	surgery
	sys	system

T		
	T	temperature
	T & A	tonsillectomy and adenoidectomy
	tab	tablet
	T.A.T.	tetanus antitoxin
	thor	thorax, thoracic
	thromb	thrombosis
	tid	3 times a day
	TPR	temperature, pulse, and respiration

U		
	uln	ulnar
	upper GI	upper gastrointestinal
	u/o	under observation

V		
	Vag	vaginal
	VC	vital capacity
	VD	venereal disease
	vent	ventral
	vol	volume

W		
	wd	well developed
	wf	white female
	wh ch	wheel chair
	wm	white male
	wn	well nourished
	wt	weight, weigh
X		
	x	times

CHAPTER 36: DEATH BY DROWNING

CONSIDERATION

1)   This includes apparent drowning in pools, rivers, lakes, oceans, and any other body of water.
        a) This includes near-drowning deaths.
            i) Near-drowning deaths are delayed-fatal deaths where the subject survives a drowning episode but later succumbs to complications associated with the incident.
                (1) An autopsy will usually disclose acute pulmonary edema. Later complications include pneumonitis, bronchopneumonia.

2)   This chapter does not include scuba deaths.

3)   Drowning death is a death diagnosed by exclusion. There are no gross autopsy findings of significance that directly indicate that an individual died as a result of drowning.
        a) If it is determined that the decedent did not die of drowning, what is the cause of death?
        b) In other deaths, bleeding from the remains can usually be used to assist in distinguishing antemortem versus postmortem injury. In a drowning death, this is made somewhat more difficult because the position of the head of a floating corpse allows for blood to congest in the head. Because of this possible bleeding, postmortem injuries sustained to the head may look as though the injured site could have been sustained while the victim was alive and in the water. This may not necessarily be true.

4)   Drowning is really an asphyxial death, usually requiring only that the nostrils and mouth (sources of breathing) to be immersed in water. Because of this requirement, people have died in relatively shallow areas of water such as bathtubs, shallow ponds, and 5-gallon buckets. In addition, there are other causes of death associated with a body being in a body of water.
        a) Hypothermia death results from the loss of body heat caused by the environmental condition involving temperature. "Death may result in individuals immersed in water with a temperature usually associated with a temperature less than 68°F. (Pounder, 1992).

5)   How drowning occurs
        a) The typical drowning process begins when a person grows tired, suffers some type of cramping, or is found in water in which he is unable to swim either through personal limitations or through environmental factors. Submersion in the water occurs.
        b) Holding the breath can only last until carbon dioxide requires the drowning person to aspirate. Since the person is now immersed in water, water is aspirated into the lungs.
        c) The gulping of water causes the victim to begin coughing and in some cases vomiting. This is followed fairly quickly by the loss of consciousness.
        d) Involuntary respiration resulting in the aspiration of water is a result of the deepening unconsciousness process.
        e) Respiratory failure will precede heart failure.
        f) Death can occur in as little as 2 to 3 minutes. It is usually irreversible if the drowning person has been submerged for more than 10 minutes (although there have been

cases, usually involving children, who have survived an extended period of submersion, usually in cold water).

6)   Effects of immersion
    a) Once unconscious, a body will usually sink in the water. In some cases, because the specific gravity of a body is very close to that of water, air trapped in clothing or other conditions may affect the buoyancy of the body.
    b) A body will usually remain at the bottom of the water source until the normal decomposition process begins to bloat the body with the formation of methane gas. This putrefaction process will either be accelerated or slowed, depending on the temperature of the water. The depth of the water will influence temperature of the water. Once a body breaks the surface, the traffic along the waterway will determine when the floating body is spotted.
    c) The clothing of the body, weights attached to the body, or injuries sustained to the body may affect the timing of the body's surfacing.

DROWNING VICTIM

A body at the bottom of a pool shows the areas exposed to abrading on bottom surfaces.

7)   Postmortem injuries
    a) Because the body is in a position where the hands, feet, and head assume a lower position than the remainder of the body (dead man's float), abrasions to these areas may occur as the body drifts along the bottom.
    b) These injuries involve a much greater area of the body and vary in location when the submerged body is subjected to wave action or strong tidal surges. The presence of other objects may greatly affect the severity of injuries. Passing motor boats, including rocks and the actions from propellers, may also cause postmortem injuries.
    c) Marine life will use the body as a food source. Smaller marine life will feed off the soft flesh areas of the face. Larger marine life can cause amputations and other injuries.

8)   Recovery of the drowning victim
    a) If search divers recover bodies, the body may be fairly well preserved. Water tends to retard the decomposition process in contrast to similar conditions on land. In addition, the deeper the water, the cooler the temperature.
    b) Body temperature
        i) "The body cools in water about twice as fast as in air (i.e., about 5°F per hour) and reaches the temperature of the water usually within 5 to 6 hours and nearly always within 12 hours" (Pounder, 1992).
        ii) The general formula (4-2-1 rule) used by forensic pathologists associated with the environment's effect on a decomposing body is as follows:

4 days buried = 2 days in the water = 1 day on land

        iii) Adipocere also begins to appear on bodies submerged in cold water for extended periods.
    c) Upon the body's removal from water, frothy foam may be exuded from the nose and mouth of the victim. This is a result of the combination of water, mucous, and air meeting in the structures of the lung. The fluid may also be tinged with blood as a result of some blood vessels' bursting during the process.
        i) This is an important finding because it may indicate that the subject was alive at the time he entered the water. Unfortunately, frothy foam is also observed in deaths associated with heart failure, drug overdoses, and head injury.
    d) Fluid is usually responsible for a significant weight gain in the lungs. Again, this is not significant if attempting to use this finding as a consequence of drowning only. Pulmonary edema associated with heart failure, drug overdoses, and head injury also causes a weight gain by the lungs.
    e) Foreign material may be found in the decedent's airways, lungs, and stomach. This may be cited as evidence that the subject was alive at the time he was immersed in the water. However, another explanation for this debris could be the passive flow of sand, silt, and plant material that is believed to occur in a dead submerged body.

9)   Diatoms
    a) "Diatoms, or *Bacillariophyceae,* are a class of microscopic unicellular algae of which about 15,000 species are known (approximately half live in fresh water and the other half in sea or brackish water)" [Pounder, 1992].
    b) The common thought process in understanding the relationship of diatoms to that of a drowning death involves the presence of these diatoms in the system of the decedent. For the diatoms to have had a chance to enter the subject's system and be present in tissues such as liver, brain, and bone marrow, that person must have been alive while in the water, thus giving the diatoms a chance to enter his circulation system.
    c) Problems with the diatom presence theory
        i) Contamination of the source material is always a consideration.
        ii) Diatoms are found everywhere and in just about everything. Having a particular diatom, unique to the particular waterway involved and found in the bone marrow of the decedent, is still rather speculative.
        iii) Even if the diatoms are acknowledged as being present in the victim's system and unique to that body of water—thus indicating that the victim must have been alive when entering the water—whether the death was an accident, a suicide, or a homicide still cannot be determined by the presence of diatoms alone.

iv) Some tests have found the presence of diatoms in the organ specimens of a decedent whose death did not involve the possibility of drowning; nor was the subject's body recovered from water. Speculation would thus indicate that diatoms might enter the circulation via the possible contaminants of food that the decedent had been eating or through the air he had breathed.

v) There are many lab personnel who believe that if the contamination issue is addressed, the presence of diatoms in the organs of a body recovered from an area of water is strongly indicative of the victim's being alive when he entered the water.

    (1) Part of the examination should involve collecting diatom specimens from the involved body of water. The diatoms found in the organ specimen and in the water should be the same type of diatom.

PRIMARY FOCUS OF INVESTIGATION

1) Determine if the death is a suicide, an accident, or a homicide.

2) Eliminate alternative causes of death.

    a) The critical focus of any body recovered from a water source is the answer to two questions:

        i) Was the decedent alive or dead upon entering the water?

        ii) Why did the person drown?

3) Determine the circumstances.

4) Identify the decedent, especially in those cases involving prolonged submersions.

NOTIFICATION

1) No special notification is required unless the scene investigation begins to indicate that the body may have been dead when placed in the water. The on-call pathologist should then be notified.

SCENE PHOTOGRAPHS

1) Overview of the area showing the body of water involved

2) Overview of body showing its condition

3) Close-up view of the face

4) Any other photographs significant to the circumstances (e.g., open gate, steps leading to the pool area, broken railing on dock)

5) Please note that after removing the body from the body of water, especially in cases involving prolonged submersion, the body will rapidly begin to decompose. Take as many photographs as possible immediately after recovery has been made, especially in those cases where identification appears to be a consideration.

SCENE INVESTIGATION

1)   Develop any eyewitnesses to the incident.
            a) Did the decedent call for help?
            b) Describe the actions of the decedent.

2)   How long before the body was recovered? How long has the decedent been missing?

3)   Any rescue efforts? CPR attempts?

4)   Describe the water.
            a) How deep is the water?
            b) What is the distance from the shore to the location the drowning was believed to have occurred?
            c) Any strong currents or undertow?
            d) Any stones or stumps?
            e) Any sudden drops or holes on the bottom?
            f) Was the water rough?

6)   Describe the weather conditions (e.g., foggy, rainy, clear) at the time of the incident.

7)   If the death resulted from a fall from boat, what type of boat?
            a) Was decedent the operator of or a passenger in the boat?
                    i) Was the decedent accustomed to using such boats?

8)   Decedent information
            a) What was the swimming capability of the decedent?
            b) Was the decedent familiar with the body of water involved?
            c) Was the decedent diving into the water?
                    i) A person diving into shallow water may strike his head against the bottom. This may cause the neck to hyperflex and result in the diver's losing consciousness. If not immediately discovered and properly handled, the diver may drown from loss of consciousness while being submerged. The injuries may be severe enough in their own right to cause death.
                    ii) Common autopsy findings may involve the findings of a hemorrhage in the deep muscles of the neck. Fracturing of the cervical vertebra of the neck may or may not be present.
                    iii) The impact of the dive may be present in the form of a bruise or abrasion on the face or forehead.
            d) Describe the clothing worn by the decedent.
                    i) Had the decedent removed his coat, shoes, or valuables prior to entering the water?
            e) Obtain the health history of decedent.
                    i) Describe the antemortem health condition of the decedent.

9)   Did the decedent have a history of a heart condition, fainting spells, vertigo, epilepsy, or high blood pressure?
            a) Obtain a drug abuse and prescriptive history of the decedent.

10)   Was there any evidence of alcohol?

    a) Were alcohol containers found that might be attributed to the decedent?

    b) Did any witnesses allude to the possibility of alcohol consumption?

    c) "Approximately two-thirds of adult males found drowning have consumed alcohol"(Pounder, 1992).

11) If swimming pool is involved:

    a) Was it in ground or above ground?

    b) Describe the security condition involving the pool.

    c) What efforts did the decedent have to make to gain entry to the pool?

12) If the decedent is a child, is this activity consistent with the child's age and development?

TRANSPORTING REMAINS

1) No special handling is required unless identification is anticipated to be a problem. If this is the case, expedite the handling at the scene and transport and store the decedent promptly.

PROCESSING AT MEO/MORGUE

1) If the death is not a homicide, fingerprint the decedent. If it is a homicide, do not fingerprint body until after the autopsy.

2) If it is a homicide, collect the following:

    a) Clothing (bag separately)

    b) Fingernail scrapings

    c) Head hair standards

3) Consider identification procedures if warranted.

FOLLOW-UP INVESTIGATION

1) If suicide may be indicated, follow the appropriate guidelines.

    a) The body may be found with stones in the pocket or weights tied to the body in some suicidal drowning cases.

        i) Like other cases involving bindings, the type of knot and how it is tied are both important considerations in determining if the death is a suicide.

2) If homicide may be indicated, follow specific guidelines relative to a possible motive.

    a) A homicidal drowning is fairly uncommon.

        i) It may involve a relationship between the assailant and the victim in which the assailant is stronger than the victim and overpowers him.

        ii) Disease, alcohol, or drugs may incapacitate a victim.

        iii) The victim may be taken by surprise or placed into a water situation where he is unable to swim or his ability to swim is greatly challenged by the water conditions.

    b) Water is often used as a means of disposing of a victim killed by other means at another location.

        i) This method may be used to conceal the body, even temporarily, or it may be used to wash away forensic evidence.

            (1) The sophistication of this action may imply to investigators that the killer is experienced with the criminal justice system (i.e., the perpetrator has a criminal history).

347 · DEATH BY DROWNING · 347

SUICIDE BY DROWNING

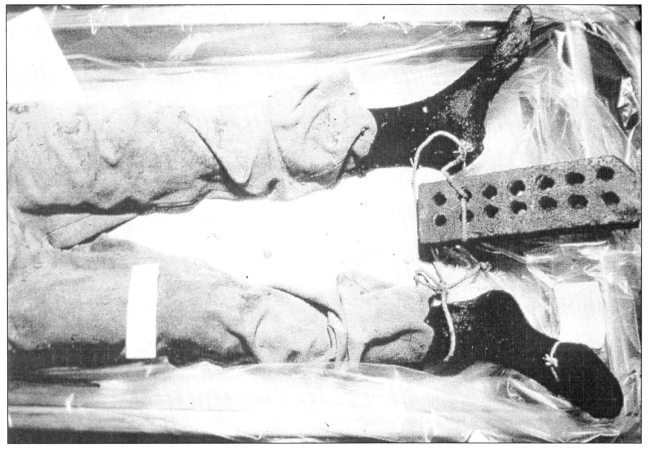

To combat any efforts of self-preservation, this suicide victim tied a block to his legs. He had left a note indicating his intentions.

HOMICIDE SUBMERSION IN WATER

The nude body of a young woman found in this lake alerted investigators to a possible body dump instead of a drowning. Careful consideration must be given to the removal of the victim from the lake in these circumstances.

CHAPTER 37: DRUG DEATH INVESTIGATION

CONSIDERATIONS

1) Drug-related deaths are not necessarily synonymous with a drug overdose death.

2) The circumstances of the death are extremely important in recognizing a possible drug-related death.

3) The case may involve insurance considerations with regard to life insurance policies.

4) The case may involve allegations about the prescribing habits of a particular doctor.

5) An overdose death of a user may bring murder charges to the individual who sold the drugs to the decedent.
    a) Cocaine-related deaths might involve particular behavior patterns before the subject's death.
    b) Cocaine is a stimulant and produces euphoria in the user. Some of the behaviors seen in the user/abuser include these:
        i) Hyperactivity
        ii) Paranoia
        iii) Delusions
        iv) Aggressive behavior
            (1) Police may respond to a scene where an individual is acting bizarre. As officers try to restrain him, the individual fights back with unusual strength, but ultimately he is restrained. Sometime after the initial struggle, the individual gets unusually quiet. When an officer checks on the individual, he is found to be dead.
        v) Mania
        vi) Hyperthermia
            (1) The user often becomes extremely warm and often takes off his clothes, sometimes even jumping into any nearby water.
        vii) Depression
            (1) The "cocaine blues" condition sometime results in suicide.
        viii) Cardiac problems associated with arrhythmias
        ix) Central nervous system problems associated with convulsions (epileptic-like seizures leading to respiratory arrest)

PRIMARY FOCUS OF INVESTIGATION

1) How much the drugs contributed to the death

2) The manner of death concerning possible overdose
    a) Natural
        i) Chronic overuse of medication resulting in diseased organs
    b) Suicide or accident associated with an acute overdose
        i) Deliberate versus unintentional overdose

3) The type of drugs involved

NOTIFICATION

1)   A pathologist is not required at the scene unless:
        a) The manner of death may be confused, or an attempt appears to have been made by the decedent or some other interested party to alter the circumstances of death.
        b) The decedent's identification may be affected because of decomposition.

SCENE PHOTOGRAPHS

1)   Photograph the entire area of the involved scene showing the condition of premises.

2)   Photograph any areas containing indication of movement and activities of the decedent immediately before his death.

3)   Photograph any indications of security or absence of foul play that suggest that the scene is most likely that of a natural death.

4)   Photograph any items or areas of the scene that may indicate the time frame of the death.
        a) Newspaper collecting on the front porch, food preparation, etc.

5)   If alcohol containers, drugs, or drug paraphernalia are found at the scene, photograph them.

6)   Photograph the decedent's body relative to its position within the scene area.

7)   Photograph the decedent to depict signs of consistency or inconsistency of time frame changes on the body (e.g., rigor mortis, lividity, skin slippage, blistering).

8)   Document the absence or presence of injuries to the decedent's remains through photographs.
        a) If decedent has injuries that may have resulted from collapsing to the floor, photograph any item he may have struck during the collapse.
        b) Take close-up photographs of the injuries the decedent may have incurred while collapsing.

9)   Photograph any indication of needle marks.
        a) Blood at injection site
        b) Needle track marks

10)   Photograph the presence of foam or foam residue around the nose or mouth of the decedent.

11)   Take and identification photograph of the subject.

SCENE INVESTIGATION

1)   Examine the scene of the death
        a) Give a general description of the scene. Make special note of the condition of the premises.
        b) Search for any medication, medication containers, or drugs. The search should include the following areas:
            i) Inside trash containers
            ii) Around the immediate surroundings of the decedent

          iii) Under the furniture

          iv) Under the bedding materials

     c) Examine the scene for any signs of recreational drug use.

          i) Roach clips

          ii) Burnt spoons

          iii) Burnt bottle caps

          iv) Cans with unusual holes cut into them

          v) Razor blades

          vi) Small mirrors

          vii) Tourniquets.

2)   Is there any indication of hyperthermia?

          a) Are there indications that the decedent may have thrown off his clothing and attempted to cool down with wet towels, ice, or showers, as sometimes seen in cocaine cases.

3)   Describe the decedent and any indication of previous movement by him within the scene.

4)   Describe any signs that point to the absence of foul play associated with the demise of the decedent, for example:

          a) Describe the security of the residence.

          b) How was entry gained?

          c) Is there any indication that the site had been rifled?

          d) Is there any indication the VCR, television, stereo, or anything else has been taken?

          e) Describe the security of the decedent's personal effects, including wallet, purse, jewelry, and checkbook.

5)   Describe any medication found at the scene.

          a) Where are the medications observed relative to the body?

6)   Describe any activity or item indicative of time frame of the subject's death e.g., (newspapers collecting on front porch, food preparation).

7)   Describe the circumstances of the death.

     a) How was death discovered?

     b) When was the decedent last seen alive?

     c) Describe activities of decedent shortly preceding death.

     d) Describe the terminal episode.

8)   Compile a history of the decedent.

          a) Develop any complaints the decedent may have made prior to his or her death.

          b) Develop the decedent's past medical history, including all physicians.

          c) Develop the decedent's social history, including drinking and drug habits.

          d) Develop any changes in the decedent's household, eating, sleeping, and work habits.

9)   Conduct a body examination.

          a) Describe the position of the decedent's body.

          b) Describe the clothes worn by the decedent. Are they appropriate under the circumstances of the incident?

          c) Describe the time frame factors associated with the examination of the decedent's remains (e.g., rigor mortis, lividity).

i) Are these time frame factors consistent with the information known concerning the subject's death?

d) Describe any areas of injury observed on the decedent.

    i) Are there any items or conditions present, or could the final activities of the decedent have caused the injuries (e.g., collapsing from a standing position and striking of the head on the floor or on a table).

    ii) Blood may be noticed around the mouth area. Lacerations or bite marks may be seen on the lower lip or tongue, suggesting a possible convulsion as sometimes seen with overdose deaths.

    iii) White foam, somewhat similar to that seen in drowning cases, may be seen coming from the nose or mouth of the decedent. The foam may have a bloody tinge.

        (1) Depending on the length of time until the discovery of the body, the foam may dry out and appear as a discolored, white crusty area around the mouth.

    iv) Does the subject have any obvious needle marks?

        (1) If yes, where are they located?

        (2) Do they appear fresh?

10) Gather specific drug information.

a) Why is there the suspicion of drug involvement in this case?

b) Is there any indication that the decedent was in the possession of drugs or drug-related materials? If yes, describe.

c) Did decedent have access to someone else's medication? If yes, identify that person and the medication that may be involved.

d) Describe any history of drug abuse involving the subject.

e) Describe current prescriptive medications taken by the subject. Itemize each as follows:

    i) Prescription name?

    ii) Date prescribed?

    iii) Doctor prescribing?

    iv) Quantity prescribed?

    v) Quantity remaining?

    vi) Note any apparent mixture of medications in the Rx vial.

    vii) Identify the location in which the medication was recovered.

    viii) Note any unlabeled vials and describe the contents.

f) Is there a particular drug suspected in the death? If yes, identify the drug.

g) Identify the last medication known to have been taken by the subject.

    i) Quantity taken?

    ii) Time taken?

    iii) Witness to the incident?

TRANSPORTING REMAINS

1) Collect all prescription medications associated with the decedent and transport them with the remains. Include all empty vials. They may be just as important as the filled vials.

2) If the decedent expired at a hospital, make every effort to collect his blood, urine, and gastric specimens taken when he was admitted to the hospital.

PROCESSING AT MEO/MORGUE

1)   Fingerprint the decedent.

FOLLOW-UP INVESTIGATION

1)   If it appears there may be a problem in the identification of the decedent because of decomposition factors, do the following:
      a) Search the subject's residence for background information that may help identify him. Look for the following:
         i) Appointment books listing physicians and dentists
         ii) Personal telephone books listing doctors and dentists
         iii) Telephone book with handwritten telephone numbers on the front or back cover or in the section listing dentists
         iv) Canceled personal checks listing payments to doctors or dentists
         v) Prescription medications (pharmacies are now using computers extensively to document patients' prescriptions. Computer printouts of the decedent's entire prescriptive history can be obtained, which could be valuable to the investigation for developing the decedent's doctors, medical history, and prescription medication history.

2)   There may be a problem in locating the next of kin.
      a) Search the decedent's residence for the following:
         i) Personal address book, which may include listing of next of kin or people with similar last names who may be related
         ii) Christmas or birthday cards that may have been sent by relatives
         iii) Contact information for current or past employers', insurance papers, the family Bible, or other items that may identify family members or friends of the decedent who may know family members

CHAPTER 38: DEATH BY ELECTROCUTION

CONSIDERATIONS

1)   Death by electrocution occurs when a person becomes part of the electrical circuit.

2)   To understand deaths involving electricity, it is necessary to have a basic understanding of electrical principles.
        a) Electricity is measured in amperes (the amount of electrical current), volts (the measure of force behind the electrical current), and ohms (the resistance of an object in having electricity pass through it).
            i) Ohms law defines the relationship of resistance to current flow to voltage by the following formulas:

> Amperes = volts ÷ ohms
>
> Volts = amperes x ohms
>
> Ohms = volts ÷ amperes

   b) Amperes (the amount of electric current) is the most important consideration in electrocution deaths. The following chart is generally accepted in describing the effects of amperes with regard to humans and other common electrical appliances (Wright, 1990).

AMPERE AMOUNT	EFFECT
0.001 ampere	Barely perceptible tingle
0.016 ampere	"Let go" threshold
0.020 ampere	Muscular paralysis
0.100 ampere	Ventricular fibrillation
1.200 amperes	100-watt lightbulb lights
2.000 amperes	Ventricular standstill
15.000 amperes	Common household fuse blows

   c) The resistance found in human skin protects humans from electrocution to a certain point. Resistance of human skin is accepted as follows (Frankel, 1980):

SUBSTANCE		RESISTANCE
Dry skin	=	100,000 ohms
Water- or sweat-soaked skin	=	1,000 ohms
Internal resistance of body	=	500 ohms

d) Therefore, it may be possible to predict the effects of electricity on a body by using Ohm's law. For example (Wright, 1980):

    i) Dry hand-to-hand contact with regular household current (120 volts) would be configured as follows:

1. amperes	=	volts ÷ ohms
2. amperes	=	120 volts ÷ 100,000 ohms = 0.001
3. 0.001 amperes	=	Barely perceptible tingle

3) Electrocution can result from four electrical conditions:

    a) Low-voltage (less than 1,000 volts) alternating current, or AC, (household electricity)

        i) Death normally occurs as a result of ventricular fibrillation as the heart attempts to beat in the rhythm of the electrical current, resulting in cessation of the heart's normal activity.

        ii) The chances of a fatality are greater if the heart and/or brain stem is in the pathway of the direct current (Wetli, 1988).

    b) Low voltage (less than 1,000 volts) direct current, or DC

        i) This type of current is supplied by a battery and is rarely fatal.

    c) High voltage (greater than 1,000 volts)

        i) The voltage can either be AC or DC.

        ii) The fatality is a result of the heat generated by the passage of high-velocity current.

        iii) High-voltage deaths usually involve contact with an uninsulated high-power line by a grounded source.

    d) Lightning

        i) It is the heat produced by the extremely high voltage that is most often responsible for the death of a person struck by lightning.

4) Burned tissue may be associated with an electrical death. The following should be considered:

    a) Appearance of electrical burns are dependent on four factors:

        i) The amount of current

        ii) The voltage

        iii) The area involved that is actually in contact with the energized source and ground

        iv) The length of time involving the contact

    b) In approximately 50 percent of low-voltage electrocution deaths, burns do not appear.

    c) Burns associated with high-voltage electrocution deaths are common.

    d) There are three types of electrical burns.

        i) Contact burns

            (1) These are produced by the particular electrified article at the point of contact with the subject

(2) Careful examination required because the burned area may appear as a transfer image of the article causing the death

(3) Burned skin or hair from the subject may be attached to the suspected item.

(4) Upon examination, skin may be charred or burned but the hair in this area is not singed.

ii) Arcing burns

(1) These are much more common in high-voltage incidents because the path of heat destruction may arc rather than take a direct course through the subject.

iii) Dendritic burns

(1) In cases involving extremely high voltage, the heat associated with the electrical incident produces immediate lividity and causes the disruption of red blood cells along the blood vessels, resulting in an image resembling tree branches on the body of the decedent.

PRIMARY FOCUS OF INVESTIGATION

1) In distinguishing natural deaths from low-voltage electrocutions deaths, low-voltage electrocutions deaths might not be discernible through autopsy. High-voltage deaths are fairly obvious.

a) Failure to distinguish electrical deaths from natural deaths may result in other loss of life if the dangerous article is not identified and removed.

2) Development of the circumstances of the death is critical.

a) Any scene in which a potentially grounded person was near a potential source of low voltage should be initially examined as a potential electrical death.

b) Any person who is heard to yell immediately preceding a collapse should be considered a potential electrocution victim. This behavior is atypical of any other type of death.

c) A person sustaining a fatal low-voltage electrocution may not be incapacitated immediately. As much as 15 seconds of consciousness, during which the victim undergoes ventricular fibrillation, may be sufficient time for him or someone else to turn off the involved tool or appliance. During this time, the individual may engage in conversation or some other activity prior to collapsing.

d) Any death that has a fairly certain time frame (e.g., one that is witnessed) yet in which early rigor mortis is established or present in one particular region of the body may indicate an electrical source as the mechanism of death. Electrical current accelerates the development of rigor.

3) Develop the manner of death.

a) Although most electrocution deaths are accidental in nature, a few may involve homicidal or suicidal actions.

4) Potential sources of the electrocution must be examined and collected, if possible, for detailed analysis.

5) Was faulty equipment responsible for the death?

6) Was the equipment used improperly?

NOTIFICATION

1) In electrocution deaths other than lightning strikes, pathologists may wish to come to the scene due to:
   - a) The complexity of the case and to understand what may have happened and what equipment may have been involved.
   - b) The death ultimately resulting in a civil lawsuit in which all factors of the case are scrutinized meticulously

2) The pathologist may wish to visit the scene involving multiple deaths.

3) The pathologist may wish to visit the scene in which the manner of death may be a suspected homicide.

4) Consideration may be given to having an electrical engineer's responding to the scene to test the suspected equipment or eliminate the possibility of the death investigator or others involved in the investigation from getting injured while attempting to learn what caused the injury.

SCENE PHOTOGRAPHS

1) Photograph the scene, including these:
   - a) Overall of scene
   - b) Body position relative to the scene
   - c) Electrical apparatus at the scene
   - d) Electrical damage present
   - e) Any indications of alcohol or drug abuse present at the site
   - f) If decedent has fallen from an elevated area, complete photographs of this structure:
      - i) Relative to the decedent's final resting place
      - ii) Decedent's original position, looking carefully for electrical burn marks at this location or any transferred skin

2) Photograph any indications of the decedent's activity immediately preceding the death.

3) Photograph any appliance, tool, cords, switches, and extension cords making up the electrical circuit suspected in the death.
   - a) If the item is to be taken apart, photograph each step involving the disassembly process.

4) Photograph the body, including:
   - a) Overall shot of the decedent
   - b) Any area of damage to decedent's clothing
   - c) Any injuries involving the decedent
      - i) If burning is present, photograph areas of injury, including those areas of electrical burns where the hair has not been singed.
      - ii) If dendritic pattern is present, photograph this immediately because this arborization pattern may disappear with time.
   - d) Any areas indicative of time frame of death

SCENE INVESTIGATION

1)   Scene examination
           a) Give a general description of the scene.
           b) Describe the location of the decedent within the scene.
           c) Describe any electrical apparatus that may be present and possibly involved in the decedent's demise.
           d) Describe any indication of electrical damage.

2)   Circumstances
           a) How was the death discovered?
           b) When was the decedent last seen alive?
           c) Describe activities of the decedent shortly before his death.
           d) Describe activities of the decedent at the time of his death.
                   i) Did the decedent shout or give any indication that something was wrong?

3)   History
           a) Develop any specific complaints concerning the health of the decedent leading up to his death.
           b) Detail the past medical history of the decedent. Include all physicians who may have knowledge of his health history.
           c) Develop complete social history of the decedent, including alcohol and drug habits.
           d) Develop his prescription medication history.

4)   Body examination
           a) Describe the observed position of the decedent's remains.
                   i) Note any information about whether the decedent was moved.
                   ii) Did the decedent fall? If yes, detail the decedent's fall from height.
           b) Describe clothing worn and note any damaged areas.
                   i) Include soles of shoes, if worn or knocked off the decedent.
           c) Note any efforts of resuscitation.
           d) Examine the decedent for any areas of apparent electrical burns.
           e) Note any other injuries.
           f) Note the condition of decedent's remains relative to time frame factors, especially involving rigor mortis and lividity.

BODY TRANSPORT FROM THE SCENE

1)   Collect and transport all clothing worn by the decedent at the time of the incident. If rescue efforts were made to revive the decedent, be sure to track down and collect the clothing that rescue attendants may have removed and discarded at the scene.

2)   If possible, collect all portable equipment and power cords involved in the suspected circuit, including extension cords.

PROCESSING AT THE MEO/MORGUE

1)   Fingerprint the decedent.
       a) Be cautious and alert to the possibility of burns or smoke marks on the hands, which may be very hard to discern. Keep in mind that people may first come in contact with electrical sources

through the use of their hands and fingers, so do not fingerprint the body until the pathologist has carefully examined the hands.

FOLLOW-UP INVESTIGATION

1) If low-voltage electrocution is suspected, conduct an examination of the suspected apparatus, including the following:

    a) Electrical outlet

        i) Check the outlet to determine if it is properly wired. An outlet tester using a series of lights is available to check the correct wiring, or a voltmeter can be used as follows:

            (1) Energized side (hot) to neutral should register at 120 volts.

            (2) Energized side to ground should register at 120 volts.

            (3) Neutral to ground should register at 0 volts.

            (4) Ground should be verified.

                (a) Most low-voltage electrocutions are caused in part by the defeat of the ground circuit (Wright, 1991).

        ii) Plugging a tool into a ground-hot reversed outlet can be the cause of death. Nothing else is required other than plugging in the tool or appliance, regardless of whether the tool is turned on or not (Wright, 1991).

    b) Wiring of equipment

        i) Check X-ray equipment, switches, and wiring. This may eliminate the need for disassembling the material, while also showing shorts and miswirings.

        ii) Test the continuity of the individual wires.

            (1) Each wire should register 0 ohms from end to end and infinity ohms from wire to wire.

        iii) Examine the plug and receptacle.

            (1) Energized line

                (a) The wiring plug should have the energized wire as the dark brass prong of the male plug.

                (b) The energized wire should be the smallest slot in the female receptacle.

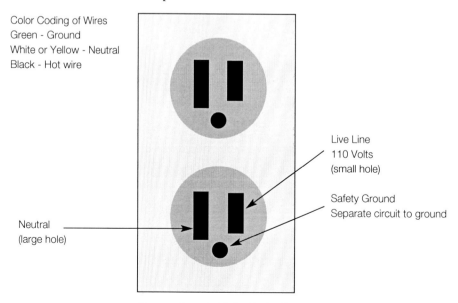

Common household electrical outlet.

(2) Neutral wire
      (a) The neutral wire should attach to the light prong on the male plug.
      (b) The neutral wire should be the larger slot on the female receptacle.
iv) Test the continuity of the appliance or tool with the switch on and off.

NOTE: Do not plug the appliance or tool into the live circuit. Testing can be done on an unplugged unit!

(1) The ground should read 0 ohms to the case.
(2) Neutral should read infinity ohms to all exposed parts of the tool.
(3) Energized wires should read infinity ohms to all exposed parts of the tool.

CHAPTER 39:
DEATH CAUSED BY EXPLOSIONS OR BOMBS

CONSIDERATIONS

1) There is a distinction to be made between an explosion death and a bombing death.
   a) Explosions can be the result of factors other than a bomb. A contained burn is an explosion. An explosion can be diffuse or concentrated.
      i) Diffuse explosions
         (1) These explosions involve ignition within a confined area and may involve natural gas, leaks, volatile liquid vapors, or dust from grains.
         (2) They tend to be accidental in origin.
         (3) They leave no crater or discoloration.
         (4) They may leave some clues on the structure as to the source of the ignition.
         (5) If the source for the ignition is lighter than air (e.g., natural gas), the involved structure will be pushed out near the top
         (6) If the source of the ignition is heavier than air (e.g., gasoline, kerosene), the walls of the structure will appear to be pushed out from the base of the structure.
         (7) The primary explosion will do the majority of the damage. There is little return force or implosion associated with a diffuse explosion.
      ii) Concentrated explosions
         (1) There is an explosion followed by an implosion. The initial force weakens the structure; the secondary force causes it to collapse.

2) To determine the nature of an explosion, the bomb expert looks for five effects associated with an explosion:
   a) Pressure
   b) Concussion
   c) Vacuum (implosion)
   d) Fragmentation
      i) Primary (part of the bomb)
      ii) Secondary (part of the environment)
   e) Heat

3) Explosives are classified into two groups:
   a) Low explosive
      i) This must be containerized to explode.
      ii) The explosion is the result of a burn rather than an explosion. Expanding gases and pressure associated with burning exceed the pressure of the container.
      iii) Injuries to the victim are usually caused by shrapnel.
      iv) No crater is associated with the use of a low explosive.
      v) There are two types of powder usually associated with low explosives:
         (1) Black powder
         (2) Smokeless powder
      vi) If only black powder or smokeless powder is involved in the blast, crime-scene technicians should be able to locate unburned or partially burned particles

that were blown outward from the center of the blast. Fragments of the container or the ignition device may also be found embedded in objects, bodies, or surfaces along the leading edge of the explosive force. These materials are very important from an evidence standpoint.

    vii) The powder can be placed in a capped, pressure-tight container (e.g., a metal pipe). Heat, impact, friction, or sparks can then set it off. Usually, the powder is ignited through a fuse.

        (1) The fuse used in a particular device may not be destroyed. Recovery of the fuse at the scene may lead to the identification of the manufacturer.

        (2) Time-delay devices usually contain electrical tag or permanent ink tape and wire used for hook-up purposes. These items frequently survive the blast. The tape may be a potential source for fingerprints or trapped hair belonging to the bomber. The wire may be traceable to a particular supply that may be found in the suspect's possession.

b) High explosive

    i) This type doesn't need oxygen to explode.

    ii) It doesn't need to be containerized.

    iii) It leaves a crater at the blast site.

    iv) It causes massive tissue destruction on the decedent.

    v) A high explosive actually comprises two actions: a primary and secondary explosion.

        (1) The primary explosion sets off (detonates) the secondary explosion. Detonation can be achieved through heat or shock.

        (2) Examples of primary explosives include blasting caps, detonating cord, and boosters.

           (a) Blasting caps become important because portions of the plastic-insulated lead-in wire often survive blasts. These wires may be useful in identifying the manufacturer of the particular blasting cap used.

        (3) A secondary explosive is used to shatter or destroy objects. It is usually set off by the shock of the primary explosive. Examples of secondary explosives include the following:

           (a) Nitroglycerin—used in making dynamite. There are four types of dynamite:

               (i) Straight dynamite

               (ii) Ammonia dynamite (less sensitive to shock than straight)

               (iii) Gelatin dynamite (water resistant)

               (iv) Ammonia-gelatin dynamite.

                    (b) Slurries or gels. These are becoming increasingly popular. They have the consistency of toothpaste, and are cheap, relatively safe, and easy to handle.

                    (c) Blasting agents.

                    (d) Binary explosives. These involve two nonexplosive chemicals that become explosive only when mixed.

                    (e) Military explosives. These have specific specifications for use, including being

relatively insensitive to heat, shock, friction, and bullet impact. They must have a high destructive power; must be lightweight and convenient to use; and must be able to be used in water. Examples include:
(i) Trinitrotoluene (TNT)
(ii) RDX (plastic explosives)
(iii) Composition C-3
(iv) Composition C-4

4) Since 1977, lot numbers have been inserted into explosives for tracing purposes.

5) Many commercial chemical supplies are relatively easy to purchase by individuals wanting to assemble homemade bombs. If the following supplies are observed in an individual's residence, consider the possibility of his being involved in the bomb-making business:
a) Aluminum powder
b) Charcoal
c) Chlorates
d) Magnesium
e) Nitric acid
f) Nitrates
g) Perchlorates
h) Sodium
i) Sugar
j) Sulfur
k) Sulfuric acid

6) It is estimated that 50 percent of bombing victims in the United States are the bombers themselves (Brodie, 1991).

7) Most bombings occur at night, thereby requiring two searches: a preliminary search that can be conducted immediately and a secondary search that is conducted during daylight hours.

PRIMARY FOCUS OF INVESTIGATION

1) Secure the scene.
a) Identify the immediate area in which the bomb exploded.
b) Identify the outer most area of the scene by locating the debris thrown the greatest distance and proceed by securing 50 percent more area.

2) Identify decedents.

3) Search the scene.
a) Identify and recover possible components of the bomb.
b) Obtain possible latent prints or DNA of the bomber on components of the bomb.

4) Try to determine whether the bombing was a random act or a selected method of death for a specific individual.

5) Could the decedent be the bomber?

6)   The scene of a bomb blast may be structurally unsound. Use extreme care in processing it.

NOTIFICATION

1)   Give full notification to the major case squad, including:
           a) The forensic pathologist
           b) The prosecuting attorney
           c) Bomb experts
                   i) The Bureau of Alcohol, Tobacco and Firearms (ATF) has a highly specialized
                      unit that will normally respond if requested and take full responsibility for
                      processing the scene correctly.
           d) The crime-scene analysis unit
           e) The forensic anthropologist
                   i) The anthropologist's presence desirable if there are multiple fatalities with
                      severe tissue destruction, resulting in scattered fragmentation of body parts.

SCENE PHOTOGRAPHS

1)   Shoot overall photographs, of the scene including:
           a) Aerial photographs of the scene
           b) Relationship of building or vehicle to other buildings, landmarks, and streets
           c) Overall area to show the path of the destructive force
           d) Address of incident
           e) Structural damage indicative of the force of the blast
           f) Overall shots of the area containing the decedent
           g) Shots of the crowd

2)   Photograph evidence of the bomb, including:
           a) Crater
           b) Coloration of the blast area
           c) Bomb components, including:
                   i) Fuse
                   ii) Wires
                   iii) Timing mechanisms
           iv) Batteries
           v) Blasting cap debris
           vi) Unexploded pieces of the bomb

3)   Photograph other evidence, including:
           a) Tire impressions
           b) Foot or shoe impressions
           c) Any articles left behind
           d) Any areas containing fingerprints
           e) Any areas containing tool marks

4)   Take decedent photographs.
           a) Photograph the decedent from all four sides.
           b) Show the relationship of each body part to one another and of each part to the scene.
           c) Take overall and close-up photographs of the decedent's injuries.
           d) Photograph decedent's hands and feet.

e) Photograph the area immediately under the decedent's body after it has been removed.

f) Photograph any evidence observable on the decedent's remains.

g) Photograph the full face of each victim (if possible) and any other views that may be useful in establishing identity.

SCENE INVESTIGATION

1) Determine the perimeter of the scene by locating the debris farthest from the explosion and the area in which the bomb appears to have exploded.

2) Sketch the scene.

3) Note any odors present.

4) Note the color of the blasted area.

5) If a crater is present:
   a) Measure its length, width, and depth.
   b) Collect debris in the crater; dig down under the surface for more evidence. Use sifting screens to assist the search; the largest fragments of the bomb may be at the bottom of the crater.
   c) Collect soil samples.

6) Search for pieces of the actual bomb (e.g., wires, clock, parts, paper, unexploded materials, batteries, parts of containers, fuse, and metal fragments).
   a) If the bomb was delivered in a package, for example, obtaining the name, postmark, and address information may be critical in identifying a subject.

7) Consider other areas of evidence:
   a) Tool marks—the suspect may have had to break in to the area to place the device.
   b) Fingerprints—the suspect may have touched other areas associated with the incident.
   c) Tire tread marks—consider whether the suspect may have accessed the area by driving a vehicle.
   d) DNA of the suspect (e.g., hair, blood) may be found on material used by the bomber to effect the attack. It may also be present as a result of his being injured during the attack.
   e) Fiber evidence

8) Identify the device used, including:
   a) Types and amount of explosives
   b) Brand names or other words observed
   c) Numbers, especially lot identification numbers
   d) Type of container used
   e) Type of initiating device

9) Identify witnesses from the area.
   a) Question witnesses.
      i) What did they hear or see before, during, and after the explosion?

BODY TRANSPORT FROM SCENE

1) No body should be removed from the scene until all involved agencies have evaluated the scene.

2) Appendages of body parts attached loosely by tendons or other tissue must be handled with care to keep the specimen intact. Carelessness in removing the bodies may cause a portion of the body to separate and become lost or commingled with other remains.
   a) Be especially careful in handling skin peeling away from fingers, toes, hands, and feet. Take whatever precautions are necessary to prevent the skin in these areas from disassociating.
   b) Body parts should be assigned numerical identification tags. No attempt should be made to associate parts of bodies to bodies at the scene.

3) Scraps of clothing or whole articles of clothing still clinging to the decedent should be secured with the remains of the decedent.
   a) Protect clothing during transport because it may contain residue that could prove useful in determining the bomb components.
   b) Do not attempt to piece together parts of clothing at the scene. Collect each item separately.

4) Never remove any article of clothing, jewelry, wallet, or other possession from the decedent or the decedent's clothes! Searching the clothes and removing the objects are completed at the morgue during the identification process.

5) Do the following with multiple fatalities or multiple body fragments:
   a) Tag the remains using a tag or permanent ink that is not affected by moisture.
   b) A record of each item removed should be maintained. This may assist in later efforts to identify the decedents or their body parts.

PROCESSING AT THE MEO/MORGUE

1) Take X-rays of the entire body because during the blast components of or evidence from the bomb may have been embedded into the body.

2) Separately bag all articles of clothing, being especially careful not to shake out or disturb any trace evidence present on the clothing.

3) Based on the damage involved, identification may be a problem. If visual identification is not possible, proceed with secondary measures of identification, including:
   a) Fingerprints
   b) Dental
   c) Radiographs
   d) DNA

FOLLOW-UP INVESTIGATION

1) Submit all recovered components to the crime lab for chemical analysis and latent fingerprint examination.
2) From the bomb expert obtain the following information:
   a) Reconstruction of the device by a bomb expert, based on the components recovered, may lead to a particular modus operandi involving previous bombings by the suspect;

supply investigators with leads for items purchased by the suspect to build the bomb; or serve as items to be placed in a search warrant of a potential suspect.
   b) What is the expertise of the bomber? Is there any indication of a military background?
   c) Is there any indication of where the bomb may have been made?
   d) Get final details on where the bomb was placed.
   e) Where did the components of the bomb originate?
   f) How was the bomb detonated?

3)   The investigation should continue by tracing various components recovered to vendors and, subsequently, to the purchaser of these items.

4)   Consider having the case profiled by the FBI Behavioral Science Unit.

5)   If a call was received about a bomb threat, interview everyone receiving the warning to obtain the following information:
   a) In detail, what did the caller say about the device?
   b) Did the caller give the address and other details about the location of the device?
   c) Did the caller describe the device?
   d) Did the caller explain how the bomb would explode?
   e) Did the caller describe what type of explosive was involved?
   f) Did the caller explain why he made the bomb?
   g) Did the caller say when the bomb was scheduled to explode?
   h) Did caller explain how to deactivate the bomb?
   i) Describe the caller's voice, including:
      i) Male or female?
      ii) That of a child, young adult, or elderly person?
      iii) Tone of the voice?
      iv) Accent?
      v) Familiar voice? If yes, can the source identify the caller?
   j) Any background noises associated with the phone call.

6)   If a suspect is apprehended shortly after the explosion obtain the following evidence if possible:
   a) Collect the suspect's clothing and submit it to the crime lab for explosive evidence.
      i) NOTE: Do not bring the suspect back to the explosion scene for identification purposes before collecting his clothes.
      ii) Do not have one of the scene investigators or evidence technicians who have been working the scene collect evidence from, or come in contact with, the suspect until after the suspect has been processed or the investigator or technician has changed clothes and showered. Defense attorneys will claim that explosive evidence could have gotten on the suspect's clothes through contamination from someone who was at the scene.
   b) Swab the suspect's hands with an acetone solution on cotton applicators.
   c) If the suspect may have used a vehicle, consider not only searching the vehicle but processing the vehicle for explosive materials or tools.

7)   Identify the decedent(s).
8)   Where was each decedent in relation to the placement of the bomb?
9)   Develop information about the bombing:
   a) Was it an anonymous act with a random victim?
      i) Terrorist action

        ii) Extortion attempt

        iii) Labor dispute

        iv) For thrills

     b) Was it a selected method of death for a specific individual?

        i) The bombing method may have been selected:

           (1) To establish an alibi for the individual responsible

           (2) As an effort to obliterate the identification of the victim or all evidence of the crime.

           (3) As a means of getting to an individual not normally approachable through conventional means.

10)   If the investigation appears to be determining that the decedent was an intended, not random, target, follow the guidelines listed Chapter 21 on contract murders.

CHAPTER 40: DEATHS CAUSED BY FALLS FROM HEIGHTS

CONSIDERATIONS

1) Fatal injuries can result from a fall from ground level or from a great height.

2) Fatal injuries occur as a result of deceleration and impact forces. Injuries are similar to those seen in driving-force type of incidents, such as in a car wreck where the driver or passenger is unrestrained. Fractured bones with lacerations to internal organs or the head area are commonly seen during autopsy examination.

3) A toxicological history should be included with each case; it may become significant in understanding why the decedent fell.

4) The physics involved are these:
   a) If a body, human or otherwise, falls in a vacuum, the mathematics involving the time and velocity of the fall are as follows:

$$t = \sqrt{\frac{2d}{g}}$$

$$v = \sqrt{2gd}$$

v = velocity in feet/seconds
d = distance fallen in feet

t = time in seconds
g = 32.14 feet/second^2

   b) When a person falls through the air, it does not take very long before the velocity increases to the point at which time air drag on the body becomes a significant factor, reducing the velocity of the fall while decreasing the distance fallen in a given time or increasing the time required for a given distance of fall. The relationship in air becomes increasingly complex because of the effect of body position, ratio of surface area to body weight, air drag, and air density, as well as additional effects associated with horizontal velocity, aerodynamics, and air swirling around tall buildings—among other considerations.
      i) At 50 feet or less, the rate of the fall is so close to a fall within a vacuum that air drag can be ignored.
      ii) Extended falls in air are less predictable. Between 50 and 1,500 feet, the rate of the fall increases in a nonlinear fashion. During the 10th to 12th second of a free fall, a terminal velocity is attained. After terminal velocity occurs, it will then take approximately 5 seconds to fall each additional 1,000 feet.
      iii) Terminal velocity is estimated to be approximately 110 miles per hour.

5) The combined effects of the surface that is struck and the bodily injuries effectively prevent any reliable estimate of the distance fallen.

DISTANCE FALLEN	TIME TAKEN	SPEED AT IMPACT	
(feet)	(seconds)	(fps)	(mph)
01	0.25	08.0	05.4
02	0.35	11.3	07.7
03	0.43	13.9	09.5
04	0.50	16.0	10.9
05	0.56	17.9	12.2
10	0.79	25.4	17.3
15	0.97	31.1	21.2
20	1.12	35.9	24.4
25	1.25	40.1	27.3
30	1.37	43.9	29.9
35	1.48	47.4	32.3
40	1.58	50.7	34.6
45	1.67	53.8	36.7
50	1.76	56.7	38.7

PRIMARY FOCUS OF INVESTIGATION

1)   Determine whether the death was an accident ,a suicide, or a homicide.
      a) If suicide is suspected, demonstrate efforts made by the decedent prior to jumping from heights.
      b) If an accident or homicide is suspected, demonstrate findings.

NOTIFICATION

1)   No special notification is required unless:
      a) It appears the manner of death is undetermined or confused, or the decedent or some other interested party appears to have altered the circumstances of the case.
      b) Multiple deaths may have occurred.
      c) Civil litigation involving great sums of money is a likely result of the death(s) involving the decedent(s).

SCENE PHOTOGRAPHS

1)   Shoot overall photographs of the scene. Show the relationship of the decedent to the area involved in the death.

2)   Show the distance involved in the decedent's fall.

3)   Photograph any areas that the decedent may have struck on the way down.

4)   Show the departure site from the landing site.

5)   Photograph the departure site, including:
       a) Windows, if any
             i) Status of window
            ii) Size of window
           iii) Height from floor to window and any other article at or near the window that
                may be involved in the incident
       b) Flooring of departure site, including any rug, obstruction, or slippery surface that
          may have influenced the incident
       c) Any items discarded or removed by the decedent prior to the fall

6)   Photograph the type of surface area struck by the decedent.

7)   Photograph the activities involving the decedent immediately preceding the fall.

8)   Photograph any indication of drug or alcohol use or abuse at the scene.

9)   Photograph the involved site from the perspective of all of the eyewitnesses.

10) Photograph any safety equipment in use and any failures associated with the use of this
     equipment.

11) Photograph the decedent, including:
       a) All injuries associated with the decedent
       b) The decedent's clothing, including shoes
       c) Any safety equipment worn by the decedent. Take close-up photographs of any broken
          hasps, torn straps, etc.

SCENE INVESTIGATION

1)   Physical description of site
       a) Provide an overall physical description of the area.
       b) What is the distance the decedent fell?
       c) If a building is involved, what is the height of the building?
       d) Describe the area in which the decedent began the fall.
             i) If a window is involved:
                  (1) Was the window opened, raised, or broken?
                  (2) How was the window normally kept?
                  (3) Were there any screens or venetian blinds?
                        (a) Had these been removed or raised?
                  (4) What is the exact height from the floor to sill?
                  (5) What is the exact size of the window?
                  (6) Describe any furniture, radiators, toys, or other obstacles near the
                      window that may be significant.
            ii) Describe the flooring of the departure area.
                  (1) Describe any obstruction, rug, or slippery condition that may have
                      influenced the incident.
           iii) Describe the surface area struck by the decedent.
            iv) Describe any object that the decedent may have struck before hitting the
                surface area where he was found.
       e) Describe any specific surface or apparatus used by the decedent prior to the fall.

        f) Are there any indication of alcohol, illicit drugs or paraphernalia, or prescriptive medication at the scene?

2)   Circumstances of the fall

        a) Develop any eyewitnesses to the incident and obtain statements.

        b) What reason did the decedent have for being at this site?

            i) Did the decedent have any special training or previous experiences in the type of activity leading to his death?

        c) Describe the activities of the decedent leading up to his death.

        d) Identify the person, business, or agency responsible for the area where the decedent fell to his death.

        e) Describe any special equipment, apparatus, or safety gear required for this particular area. Was this equipment being used?

        f) Does the decedent appear to have jumped, been pushed, or have slipped and fallen to his death?

3)   Victim description

        a) Describe any injuries observed on the decedent's body.

        b) What is the decedent's height?

        c) Describe decedent's clothing.

            i) Is the decedent wearing shoes? If yes, describe.

        d) Describe any safety gear worn by the decedent. What is the working status of this gear (e.g., broken clips, torn straps).

        e) Take complete measurements of decedent in relation to the area in which he landed. What is the distance from the body to the wall?

        f) Had the decedent removed his coat, hat, valuables, etc., prior to the fall? Was anything of this nature found at the point of departure?

        g) Any indication of drinking or drug abuse?

        h) Any indication of sudden illness?

            i) Develop medical history of the decedent, including psychiatric. Develop a listing of all medications prescribed.

BODY TRANSPORT FROM SCENE

1)   No special handling is required unless it is suspected that the decedent was pushed. If homicide is suspected:

        a) Bag (paper) the hands of the decedent.

        b) Protect the body to prevent the loss of trace evidence. Collect any trace evidence that may be lost during transport.

PROCESSING AT MEO/MORGUE

1)   If homicide is suspected:

        a) Collect, air-dry, and separately bag the clothing of the decedent.

        b) Collect fingernail scrapings.

        c) Collect head hair standards.

        d) Collect major case prints.

2)   If homicide is not suspected, fingerprint the decedent.

3)   Collect and retain any safety equipment associated with the remains for further disposition.

FOLLOW-UP INVESTIGATION

1)   If homicide is indicated, follow guidelines associated with the particular motive most closely related to the facts developing in the case.

2)   If suicide is indicated, follow the guidelines in Chapter 26 for suicide.

3)   If an accident is indicated:
       a) Reconstruct the events based on the evidence acquired and statements made to the investigators.
       b) Obtain complete background on the decedent, including:
              i) Financial (including status of insurance policies, current employment, etc.)
              ii) Health (including any psychiatric or physical problem that may have contributed to the incident).
              iii) Developing a complete domestic situation.
              iv) Developing any previous accidents or suicide attempts involving the decedent

CHAPTER 41: FIRE DEATH INVESTIGATION

CONSIDERATIONS

1) The investigation of a fire death, specifically concerned with how the victim died, usually involves a two-pronged approach. Death investigators will usually have to rely on another agency, normally the fire department, to conduct an investigation into the cause and origin of the fire. A follow-up investigation, usually conducted by a death investigator, delves into the motive for the death or the fire. Interested parties include homicide, the medical examiner, the state attorney's office, the fire department, and insurance agencies.

2) All fire-associated deaths should be treated as homicides until proven otherwise.

3) Postmortem artifacts are often confused for ante- or perimortem injuries.
    a) Skin will split and tear because the heated air dries out the skin and causes it to split. Tears should affect only skin and fat tissue; therefore, if muscle tissue is involved, foul play may be involved.
    b) Fire damage causes the body to assume a grotesque position called the "pugilist position," as a result of the muscles cooking in the heat.
    c) It is not uncommon to see the decedent's intestines sitting atop the body. Heated gas inside the intestine causes it to break through the weakened stomach walls.
    d) Tongues protrude.
    e) Fire-induced fractures are common, especially in the long bones.
    f) Granular, brown, mudlike material is often found between the bone and brain. This is caused by heated fluids on the brain. It is not an epidural hemorrhage. Dangerous overinterpretation can occur from this common phenomenon.
4) Most victims usually die as a result of carbon monoxide toxicity. Burns are usually secondary.
    a) The typical lethal situation result in a 40- to 50-percent carbon monoxide saturation. A house fire usually results in a carbon monoxide level of approximately 60 or 65 percent.
    b) A person who is breathing carbon monoxide and trying to get away will find any physical activity extremely exhausting because the muscle activity uses up the remaining oxygen in the body.
5) Victims can also die as a result of the following:
    a) Breathing hot air (superheated air) causes pulmonary injuries.
    b) The possibility of inhaling toxic fumes generated by burning materials, such as carpeting or drapes
    c) Oxygen deprivation caused by the fire

PRIMARY FOCUS OF INVESTIGATION

1) Identify the decedent.

2) Was decedent alive or dead at the time of the fire?

3) What is the cause of death? Did the fire cause the death?

4) Did the victim ingest some substance that impaired judgment to the point that escape from the fire scene was impossible?

5) Are there antemortem injuries associated with the death?

6) What are the postmortem injuries?

7) What is the manner of death?

8) What caused the fire?

NOTIFICATION

1) Notification to the pathologist should be made and his presence at the scene requested when:
    a) The fire appears to be set in an effort to conceal a homicide.
    b) A problem with the identification may exist because of the damage caused by the fire.
    c) Multiple deaths result

SCENE PHOTOGRAPHS

1) Follow the guidelines set forth in Chapter 5 on photographing a death scene. In addition, take photographs that show the following:
    a) The entire building from all sides (consider aerial photography)
    b) If possible, the fire in progress
    c) The area of the fire's origin (if several areas of origin appear to be present, try to photograph each area individually in detail and in relation to one another)
    d) The fire's direction (e.g., slow versus rapid nature of the fire, and the way in which the fire spread)
    e) The type of material that burned
    f) Location and condition of windows and doors, including whether they were locked or secured and whether items may have placed in front of them
    g) Spectators at the fire scene
    h) The presence or absence of any articles of values in the fire residue (e.g., televisions, computers)
    i) Any areas that appear to have been created to promote burning (e.g., flammable trailers leading from one room to the next; closet doors left open to facilitate burning of the closet's contents; paper left strewn on the floor; open transoms, ventilation systems, or fire doors to promote drafts)
    j) Electric clocks that may have stopped as a result of the fire and would indicate the time of the fire
    k) Remnants and condition of such fire prevention equipment as smoke detectors and sprinkler systems.
    l) Any evidence of movement by the decedent while the fire is blazing (e.g., footprints in soot, broken-out windows)
    m) The body as it is uncovered and the debris that is removed from over it
    n) Once the body has been removed, the underlying surface on which the body was lying
    o) The underside of the body initially hidden from view

SCENE INVESTIGATION

1) Describe the scene. If a structure is involved, include:
    a) The type of structure (e.g., single-family residence, trailer, vehicle)
    b) The type of construction (e.g., wood frame, concrete block, brick)

2)   Describe the type of fire (e.g., wood and furnishings, electrical, solvent, natural gas).

3)   What is the cause of the fire?

4)   Was the fire an arson?

5)   Describe the extent of the fire.

6)   Where did the fire start?

7)   Did the fire consume the immediate area around the decedent?

8)   What is the condition of the decedent's remains? Is the decedent burned beyond recognition?

9)   Is the decedent's clothing intact or consumed by the fire? Describe the clothing, if present.

10) Where were the exits in relation to the decedent's remains? What is the status of the exits (locked or unlocked)?

11) Detail any items found at the death scene that may be related to the fire (e.g., cigarettes, lighters, matches, alcohol containers, drugs or paraphernalia)

12) Give a physical description of the decedent (e.g., child, adult, male, female).

13) Describe the physical condition of the decedent.
         a) Detail his health history.
         b) Detail his alcohol history.
         c) Detail his drug history.
         d) Detail his medical history, including any physical infirmities.
         e) Did the decedent smoke?

14) What was status of the victim when first discovered (e.g., alive, dead)? If alive when found, when did he die (e.g, DOA, how many hours later)?

15) Is ther any suspicion that the fire may have been started to conceal another crime or the decedent's death?

BODY TRANSPORT FROM SCENE

1)   If the decedent has been burned, place the remains in a body bag. Preserve any remnant of skin from the hands for possible printing.

2)   If this a likely smoke inhalation death, no special procedures are necessary.

3)   Depending on the degree to which the decedent has been burned, the investigators may consider bringing in a special recovery team, including a forensic anthropologist.

PROCESSING AT MEO/MORGUE

1)   Full-body X-rays should be taken.

2) If arson is a possibility, clothing remnants should be collected and individually placed in a "paint" evidence can, which is then sealed.

3) An evaluation of fingerprints should be completed, if possible.

4) Teeth should be extracted or X-rayed for identification purposes, if necessary.

FOLLOW-UP INVESTIGATION

1) Cause and origin investigation commences.

2) It is important to understand that an arson investigation must be conducted to determine the cause of the fire. Normally a fire marshal or an arson investigator assigned to the fire department conducts this investigation. To better understand how this portion of the investigation is conducted, an example of cause and origin investigation is included.
    a) Discovery of the fire
        i) How was the fire discovered?
        ii) Who reported the fire? Has this person reported other fires?
        iii) Describe the weather conditions.
            (1) Are the conditions involving the structure consistent for the weather conditions (e.g., is the heater running even though it's the middle of the summer)?
            (2) Could weather conditions have caused or contributed to the fire (e.g., lightning, cold) or affected the spread of the fire (e.g., wind conditions)?
        iv) Did the fire department personnel notice any man-made barricades that may have delayed their arrival or affected their approach to the fire?
        v) Were any cars noticed speeding away from the scene?
        vi) How did the fire department gain access to the involved site? What were the conditions of doors and windows?
        vii) What was the color of the smoke, which may indicate the type of item burning (Factory Mutual System, 1979)? See the table below for the relationship between color of smoke and the product burning.

COLOR OF SMOKE	ITEM COMBUSTING
Black	Acetone, kerosene, gasoline, rubber, tar, oil (lube), coal, plastic
Black to brown	Turpentine
Brownish black	Lacquer thinner
Brown to black	Naphtha
Brown	Cooking oil
Gray to brown	Wood, paper, cloth
Greenish yellow	Chlorine gas
Yellow to brownish yellow	Sulfur, nitric acid, gunpowder, hydrochloric acid
White to gray	Benzene
White	Phosphorus

viii) What is the color of the flame noticed by the fire fighters? See the table below for examples.

COLOR OF FLAME	ESTIMATED TEMPERATURE OF FIRE
Red	900–1,650°F
Orange	1,725°F
Yellow	1,825–1,975°F
White	2,200°F
Blue white	2,550°F

ix) Did fire fighters notice a reaction when water struck the flames?

x) Did firefighters notice unusual conditions that may have facilitated the spread of the fire?

    (1) Separate fires?

    (2) Trailers leading from room to room?

    (3) Punched-out holes in the ceiling, exposing another floor to the spreading fire, or in the walls, enabling the fire to spread from room to room?

xi) Is there an absence of personal belongings in the ashes of the fire? What is the status of the family pet?

xii) Did firefighters notice any unusual odors?

b) Locating the point of origin

  i) The point of origin is found by identifying the materials involved, determining the ignition temperatures and approximate burning times, and locating any draft conditions in the area of origin that could have influenced the spread of the fire.

  ii) If a structure is involved, did the fire begin in the exterior or the interior of the structure?

    (1) Exterior

      (a) Examine the area of greatest destruction.

      (b) Look for openings or drafts that may have influenced the spread of the fire.

      (c) If there is a possible gas leak, is the valve on the gas source open or shut?

    (2) Interior

      (a) After photographs have been taken, reconstruct the fire scene by returning physical items of debris to their proper locations, and observe what changes to the structure and its contents were caused by the fire.

      (b) Find the area of greatest destruction.

        (i) The ceiling may assist in finding the area of greatest damage. Find the most damaged area of the ceiling. The point of origin may be directly underneath this spot.

      (c) Find the lowest point of burning.

c) Determining the direction of heat flow

  i) Light bulbs may swell and lose their shape. The side of the bulb facing the fire may be melted.

ii) Heat colors will be found on shiny metals subjected to the fire (e.g., ovens, toasters, irons), as shown in the table below.

COLORS	TEMPERATURE
Yellow	450°F
Brown to purple	550°F
Blue	600°F
Faint red	900°F
Dark cherry	1,100°F
Full cherry	1,400°F
Salmon	1,600°F
Lemon	1,800°F
White	2,200°F
Sparkling white	2,400°F

  iii) Window glass closest to the flames will be relatively soot free or clearer than windows farther away from the fire's point of origin.

  iv) Look for a fire pattern; a normal fire pattern burns in a V shape.

d) Determine the slow-versus-rapid burning nature of the fire.

  i) Overhead damage

    (1) Uniform overhead damage: slow burning

    (2) Extensive damage in one place: fast burning

  ii) Fire pattern

    (1) Wide angle V: slow burning

    (2) Narrow angle V: fast burning

  iii) Crazing of glass

    (1) Large cracks and heavy soot: slow burning

    (2) Irregular-shaped cracks and slight soot: fast burning

  iv) Alligatoring

    (1) A slight scraping of the wood surface that reveals undamaged wood: fast burning

    (2) A slight scraping of the wood surface that reveals more charred wood: slow burning

  v) Line of demarcation

    (1) A noticeable line dividing charred from uncharred present on a piece of wood from the fire: indication that the fire is fast burning

e) Determine the cause of the fire

  i) A fire requires a fuel source, a heat source, oxygen, and an event to bring them together.

    (1) Fuels

      (a) Flammable liquids

      (b) Combustible solids

      (c) Combustible gases

(2) Heat sources
    (a) Open flames
    (b) Hot surfaces
    (c) Electricity
    (d) Friction
    (e) Chemical reaction
    (f) Compression of gases

ii) Is there equipment in the area of origin that could have started a fire?

(1) Low-temperature or no-flaming heat sources
    (a) Light bulbs
    (b) Electric blankets
    (c) Electric irons
    (d) Steam pipes

(2) Electric motors of items found in the point of origin to be checked internally
    (a) Wire coating in the interior of the unit should not be burned away unless the motor had been burned out.
    (b) In motors with bronze-type bearings, if the shaft is found frozen to the bearings, it may indicate an electrical problem with the unit.
    (c) Possible friction problems can be detected by examining the pulleys. Motor belts should be worn at the contact area with the pulleys if friction was a problem. Fire damage to the middle of the belts normally indicates an external heat source problem.
    (d) Electrical appliances containing thermal controls should be examined. Sticking or fusing of the contact points may indicate overheating of the unit.

(3) Possible short of the electrical circuit
    (a) Examine the fuse panel for tampering.
    (b) It may be difficult to determine whether damage caused the fire or the fire caused the damage. Shorts caused during the heat of the fire will show decomposition and carbonization only on the side of the insulation exposed to the fire. Shorts caused by an overload condition will show decomposition and carbonization on both sides of the insulation.

(4) Smoking materials
    (a) These require a good insulation to cause flaming combustion.
    (b) Smoldering time can take from 1 1/2 to 3 or 4 hours.
    (c) Cigarettes' burning involving furniture is slow and smoldering. Heavy charring will be seen on the inside of the furniture and on the floor immediately under the involved furniture.

(5) Is there any indication of an explosion?
    (a) Gas leaks cause explosions. Is there any gas furnace or appliances? What is the status of the gas valves?
    (b) Are there any gas appliances in an unusual location?
    (c) Are there any loosened pipe fittings or piping sawed or cut in half?

(6) Was there spontaneous combustion?

(a) It takes a considerable amount of combustible material to produce spontaneous heating.

(b) Materials active in spontaneous combustion include these:

    (i) Aluminum shavings, filing, or powder

    (ii) Animal hides, skins, or manure

    (iii) Bronze, magnesium, steel, or zinc shavings or filings

    (iv) Hay or grain

    (v) Vegetable oil

iii) Examine for suspicious activities.

(1) Unusual location of normal, everyday items, which can be combustible.

    (a) Gas-soaked rags found under drapes

    (b) Piles of paper found on the floor

(2) Trailers between fires, such as string or cord soaked in gasoline or kerosene

(3) Candles or wax residue found near the point of origin

(4) Discarded matches in unusual places

(5) Accelerant containers and evidence of flammable liquids

    (a) Charring greater at the base of furniture, in floor crevices, and at corners of rooms

    (b) Ink blot patterns of burning visible on the floor

(6) Timing devices

(7) Chemicals unusual for occupancy

(8) Unexplained multiple fires

iv) Examine for incendiary devices

(1) Incendiary devices that include common household or hardware items

(2) Key ingredients: potassium chlorate and potassium permanganate, which can be purchased in chemical supply houses

(3) Potassium chlorate and sugar, which will burst into flames when in contact

(4) Potassium chlorate and Ivory Liquid dishwashing detergent

(5) Gasoline and sulfuric acid

(6) Candles (slow-burning), nontapered emergency variety

(7) Light bulbs with paper and string wrapped over the bulb

(8) Gulfwax with metallic sodium inside

(9) HTH (pool cleaner) and Score hair cream or HTH and brake fluid

(10) Incendiary instructions provided by two sources:

    (a) Military manuals (many arsonists have military experience)

    (b) *Anarchist's Cookbook*

3) Motive investigation for arson—fire investigation is a search not only for a specific heat source of fuel, but also an exploration into the psychology of those individuals involved in the event.

    a) Fraud

        i) The background check should include a search for the following red flags:

        (1) Unemployment/employment condition

        (2) Labor problems

        (3) Business reversals

            (a) Declining neighborhood

            (b) Tax problems

            (c) Competition

  (4) Lengthy illness resulting in emotional and financial problems

  (5) Expensive lifestyle beyond income

  (6) Stock market losses

  (7) Heavy indebtedness or bankruptcy

  (8) Sizable decrease or increase in property values

    (a) Was the value of the burned property compatible with the amount insured?

  (9) Zoning changes (e.g., expressway bypassing business)

  (10) Obsolescence

  (11) OSHA problems

  (12) Insurance claims record

    (a) Other total fire losses

      (i) Check with previous insurance carriers.

      (ii) Check police or fire reports.

      (iii) Check newspapers.

    (b) Relatives with large fire losses

  (13) Frequent changes in residence

  (14) Frequent changes in jobs

  (15) Property for sale

    (a) For how long?

    (b) Why?

ii) Suspicious activity (red flags)

  (1) Lack of injuries or burns suffered by the subject during the fire

  (2) Removal evidence by subject soon after the fire

  (3) Time of the fire (midnight to 6 A.M.)

  (4) Subject out of town visiting relatives

  (5) Pets removed prior to fire

  (6) Moving or transferring furniture prior to fire

  (7) Insurance policy and other important papers not burned in the fire

    (a) All receipts for purchases saved

  (8) Subject's claiming purchase of new items but has no recollection of where the items were purchased

  (9) Subject's house or office modest house but furnishings, clothing, or jewelry expensive

  (10) Unusual amount of cash or other property

  (11) Missing items (e.g., furnishings, personal items, valuables, contents of refrigerator or freezer)

iii) Where and how to locate red flags

  (1) Courthouse records

  (2) Neighbors

  (3) Employers

  (4) Banks

  (5) Creditors

  (6) Business competitors

  (7) Current or former employees or co-workers.

  (8) Statements from subject and witnesses

  (9) Examination of fire scene

  (10) Former spouses

  (11) Computers

  (12) Telephone/cell phone records

b) Pyromania

i) Very rare, this crime is usually done by a loner, loser-type, who normally does not use an accelerant.
c) Crime concealment
    i) Homicides
    ii) Suicides
    iii) Theft
d) Spite/revenge
    i) Most rapidly increasing form of arson
    ii) Usually done at night
    iii) Usually set with no regard for the peril to others
e) Civil disorders
f) Vandalism
g) Vanity
    i) Volunteer fireman or security guard who sets the fire and then puts it out

4)   Proving arson
    a) Investigation must prove that:
        i) The fire was set deliberately.
        ii) The fire was incendiary.
        iii) The suspect had a motive.
        iv) The suspect directly or indirectly caused the fire.

METAL	MELTING POINTS (F)	MELTING POINTS (C)
Aluminum	1,218	659
Brass	1,570–1,900	854–1,038
Bronze	1,290–1,890	699–1,032
Cast iron	2,000–2,800	1,093–1,538
Chromium	3,407	1,875
Copper	1,981	1,083
Gold	1,945	1,063
Iron	2,795	1.535
Lead	625	329
Magnesium	1,202	650
Nickel	2.651	1,455
Platinum	3.216	1,769
Silver	1,761	961
Solder	Varies	Varies
Stainless steel	2,462–2,822	1,350–1,550
Steel	2,552–2,882	1,400–1,583
Tin	449	232
Zinc	787	419

CHAPTER 42: FIREARM-RELATED DEATHS

CONSIDERATIONS

1) Developing the manner of death
   a) Is it homicide or suicide?
      i) Multiple gunshot wounds
         (1) Although multiple gunshot wounds do not necessarily rule out the possibility of suicide, a thorough and comprehensive autopsy examination can usually substantiate the likelihood of a homicide or a suicide.
      ii) Area of injury
         (1) The area of injury may preclude the possibility of self-infliction. For example, a person who has been shot in the back is most likely the victim of a homicide.
      iii) Distance from target to muzzle
         (1) The ability to establish the distance in which the shot was fired may allow the investigation to conclude that the death was a result of a homicidal act instead of being self-inflicted.
      iv) Trajectory of the projectile
         (1) The trajectory of the bullet established through autopsy examination may indicate a consistency or inconsistency with the initial speculation involving homicide versus suicide.
      v) Position at the time of injury
         (1) Reconstruction of the incident to show the victim's position may determine the likelihood of the person's being a suicide or homicide victim. For example, through examination and analysis of blood spatter, gunshot powder residue, and bullet trajectory, investigators may be able to show that the decedent was in the driver's seat of a vehicle at the time he was shot. For the decedent to have been shot by a perpetrator, the suspect would have had to be seated on the floorboards of the vehicle with his hand holding a gun and pointing at the suspect while the suspect's arm is through or under the steering wheel. The unlikelihood of this occurring lessens the chances of homicide.
      vi) Presence or absence of a weapon
         (1) The absence of the murder weapon in light of the serious nature of the wound (indicating total and immediate cessation of movement) may indicate a homicide.
   b) Gunshot wounds may also be inflicted accidentally.
      i) Gun-cleaning incident
      ii) Unloading of weapon
      iii) Accidental discharge of weapon while falling
      iv) Accidental discharge of weapon because of dropping the weapon

2) Classification of handgun or rifle gunshot wounds of entrance
   a) Gunshot wounds of long range
      i) No powder or soot is present at wound site.
      ii) Contact (abrasion) margin is present.

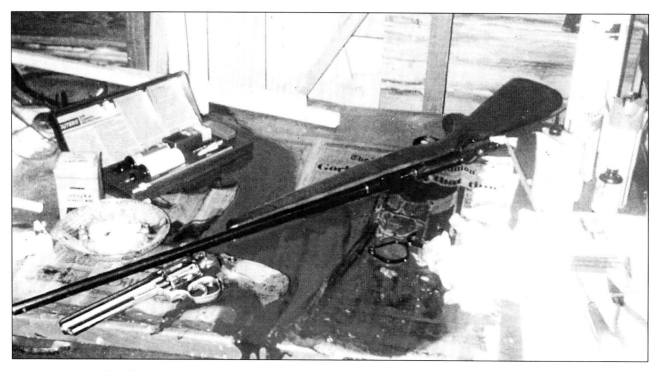

Investigators may encounter scenes involving gunshot fatalities in which a gun-cleaning kit is present.
The kit may have been placed there to conceal the correct manner of death.

CONTACT Soot and powder found within wound	INTERMEDIATE 1–24" soot and/or powder	DISTANT >24" or no powder present
Soot and burning powder accompany all contact shots. Because the barrel of the weapon is placed against the skin, the escaping soot and burning powder residue may be found in the wound.	Soot can also be present on intermediate targets. Tattooing or stippling created from burned gunpowder particles will be present on all intermediate targets.	Distant gunshot wounds will not be accompanied by soot or powder residue.

Gunshot wounds are classified into three categories: contact, intermediate, and distant.

(1) This is a discolored circle around the entrance wound caused by the pushing of the skin by the bullet on entrance.

(2) If the bullet enters the skin from a straight-on trajectory, the margin is symmetrical.

(3) If the bullet enters the skin at an angle, there is a wider abrasion margin at one area of the entrance wound closest to the direction in which the bullet traveled.

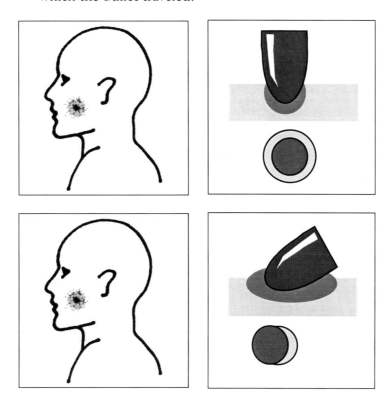

b) Gunshot wounds of intermediate range

    i) Hot gunpowder grains accompany the bullet to the wound site and are driven into the skin, leaving small red marks on the skin. This is referred to as stippling or tattooing of the skin.

        (1) Stippling occurs only when the victim is alive.

        (2) Stippling cannot be washed off the skin.

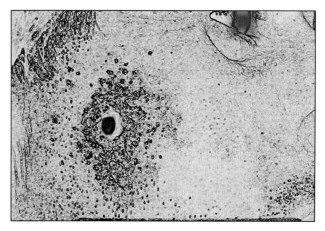

Example of tattooing from a close-range gunshot wound. The tattoo cannot be wiped off. Example of soot, which can be washed from the skin.

c) Gunshot wounds of short and close range
    i) Soot (also called soiling or smudging) is now present. This is a gray or black dense powder usually accompanied by stippling.
        (1) Be cautious in handling soot, which can be washed or wiped off the skin, leaving an altered wound with inconsistent features.
d) Gunshot wounds at contact range
    i) Loose fit (also referred to as near-contact)
        (1) A corona of soot may be present, where the weapon has not been placed directly against the skin.
        (2) A flare-up or leakage of soot may be present, where one edge of the weapon's barrel has been lifted ever so slightly away from the skin during firing of the weapon.
    ii) Contact (direct)
        (1) A corona of soot represents the size of the barrel of the weapon. The muzzle sight of the weapon may be stamped in the soot and visible on the skin.

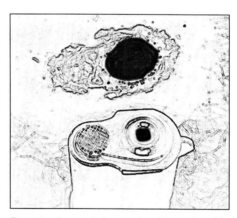

Example of a muzzle impression stamped on skin.

        (2) Soot and tattooing may not be present on external visualization of the wound. During autopsy examination, soot and powder will be present along the wound track.
        (3) The wound may appear pinkish because of carbon monoxide from the the firing of the weapon.
        (4) Searing of the skin at the wound site may be visible.

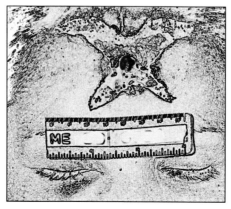

A stellate contact wound.

(5) Larger weapons may blow out the wound on contact shots, causing stellar lacerations at the entrance site.

(6) Radiating lacerations involving the mouth may indicate that the victim placed the weapon in his mouth and fired.

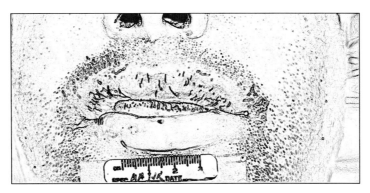

Lacerations surrounding the mouth may indicate an intraoral entrance wound.

3)   Other wounds caused by bullets
    a) Graze wound
        i) A graze wound is caused by a bullet that touches but does not enter the skin. As it passes along the skin, a furrow of abraded tissue may form. This abraded wound will have "shark teeth"-looking tears along the edges of the rut. The "teeth" will always point toward the direction from which the bullet came.

Example of a graze wound. The direction is established through the skin tears.
The tears point toward the direction of the shot.

    b) Keyhole-entrance wound
        i) A keyhole entrance wound has the characteristics of both an entrance and an exit site on the skull. The external beveling at the entrance site occurs when a bullet strikes the skull tangentially to the bony surface. This striking of the skull tangentially, as may occur in graze wounds, produces a keyhole defect where entrance and exit defects overlap.

4)   Classification of shotgun wounds
    a) The shotgun is primarily a close- to medium-range weapon. Most shotgun fatalities occur at a distance of less than 10 yards.

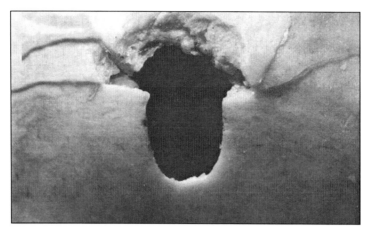

An example of a keyhole-entrance wound in the skull.

i) Distant range
    (1) The most reliable method for establishing range of fire is careful measurement of the wound pattern on the body.
    (2) At any given range, the degree of choke will have the greatest influence on pattern size.
    (3) A choke on a shotgun is a constriction of the bore of the weapon designed to provide smaller, denser shot patterns at longer ranges.
    (4) On a full-choked weapon, the generally accepted guideline for establishing distance from the muzzle is a 1-inch diameter of wound for every yard of distance. For example, a 3-inch diameter shotgun wound of entry would generally indicate that the shotgun was 3 yards (9 feet) distant at the time of fire.
    (5) On a shotgun in which no choke was present (e.g., sawed-off shotguns) a 1-inch diameter wound usually indicates 2 yards of distance between the wound and the muzzle of the weapon when fired.
    (6) As range increases, the shot pattern increases in size and decreases in density. Satellites (stray pellets) are present away from the main pattern.
ii) Intermediate ranges
    (1) The entry wound is circular with sharp margins.
iii) At increased range: the edges become scalloped, or "cookie cutter" in appearance; satellite holes may be present around the main entry site
    (1) A wad abrasion may be found near the primary entry hole. At ranges of 10 to 20 feet, the wad used in the ammunition to enclose the shot travels with the shot toward the target. Because of the distance, the wad does not have enough velocity to enter the body but, depending on the clothing present, may have enough velocity to cause an abrasion or laceration. At distances of less than 10 feet, the wadding may be found inside the body or partially embedded in the entry wound.
iv) Contact range
    (1) At very close ranges, the wounds (particularly to the head area) are devastating, and difficulties may arise in reconstructing the direction of fire and the entry wound.

(2) Large amounts of powder should be present along the wound track.
(3) A wad should be found inside the wound.

5) Classification of exit wounds
    a) It is a myth that the exit wound is always larger than the entrance wound.
    b) Distinguish exit from entrance wounds.
        i) Exit wounds do not show an abrasion collar.
        ii) Triangular skin tags or tears may be present at the exit hole.
        iii) No soot or stippling will be present.
        iv) Injuries to the bony structures indicate that bone chips are knocked inward (i.e., coning, beveling) on entrance and knocked outward on exit wounds.
    c) There may be problems in distinguishing entrance versus exit wounds
        i) Shored (supported) exit wound
            (1) Whenever is supported by an external object (e.g., sitting in a chair, leaning against a wall, wearing tight clothing), then the exit wound may produce a pseudomargin of abrasion. On close examination, these pseudomargins of abrasions may be distinguished from a true margin of abrasion because they are asymmetrical.
        ii) Bullet wipe
            (1) A gray ring caused by dirt, grease, and lead wiped from the bullet as it passes through clothing or skin is left around an entrance wound. It should not be mistaken for a margin of abrasion.

PRIMARY FOCUS OF INVESTIGATION

1) Was the wound produced by a handgun, rifle, or shotgun?

2) Is the weapon at the scene? If so, identify the type and caliber of weapon:
    a) Handgun
        i) Revolver
        ii) Semiautomatic pistol
        iii) Single shot
        iv) Derringer
    b) Rifle
    c) Shotgun
    d) NOTE: Machine guns use rifle ammunition; submachine guns fire pistol ammunition.

3) Identify number and location of wounds.

4) Identify entrance and exit wounds.

5) What was the approximate range of fire? Is the entrance wound a:
    a) Contact shot?
    b) Intermediate shot?
    c) Distant shot?

6) What is the trajectory of the bullet's path?

7) What is the number of injuries noted versus the number of shots fired, as developed through:
    a) Witness-supplied information

b) Examination of the wounds

c) Number of shell casings present at the scene or the number of expended casings still present in the revolver's cylinder

8) Is the shooting a homicide, a suicide, or an accident?

NOTIFICATION

1) A pathologist should be requested on all homicides or uncertain manner of death where the following details may be in question:

a) Time frame since death

b) Type of weapon causing the death

c) Possible activities associated with bloodletting

2) A pathologist should be requested on any case in which the manner of death is undetermined or confused, or the decedent or some other interested party appears to have attempted to alter the circumstances of the death.

3) If the body is badly decomposed or skeletonized, a forensic anthropologist may be desired at the scene.

SCENE PHOTOGRAPHS

1) Follow the death-scene photographic guidelines with regard to the particular situation of the case (e.g., outdoors, indoor, vehicle scenes). In addition, give particular attention to the following.

a) Photograph any resistance that was demonstrated by the decedent.

i) Torn clothing, including buttons ripped from clothing

ii) Defense injuries of hands, arms, legs, and feet

iii) Eyeglasses broken or thrown on the floor

iv) Rifled purse, wallet, dresser drawers, jewelry box, safe, pulled-out pockets from decedent's pants, etc.

v) Overturned furniture

b) Photograph any weapon present, including the following:

i) Relationship of weapon with location and position of body

ii) Area where the weapon may have originated

iii) A close-up photograph showing the gun with and without a ruler present

iv) Close-up photograph of any trace evidence observable on the suspected weapon.

c) Photograph the body of the decedent, including the following:

i) All areas of injuries involving the decedent

ii) All areas of blood on decedent; his clothing; and his feet, socks, or shoe (soles of feet or shoes)

iii) All areas of blood immediately adjacent to the body

iv) Body condition as it relates to time frame of death

v) Any inconsistencies with the time frame of death, as evidenced by the condition of the remains:

(1) Rigor mortis

(2) Lividity

vi) Any transfer evidence observable on the decedent

vii) Any indication of animal or insect activity involving the decedent's body

viii) Any apparent efforts made by rescue workers to resuscitate the decedent.
d) Photograph all evidence and items that may depict the circumstances of the incident.
    i) Directional evidence, including:
        (1) Blood spatter
        (2) Glass fractures
        (3) Footprints, tire tracks, etc.
    ii) Relational evidence or evidence that may relate to the incident, for example, a hat found on top of the kitchen counter not belonging to anyone who lives at the residence
    iii) Inferred evidence (evidence that is significant in its absence), for example, dust surrounding a clean area on top of a television set that may indicate a VCR has been taken.

SCENE INVESTIGATION

1)   Identify essential informants.
    a) Eyewitnesses
    b) People who found decedent or were first at the scene
    c) Doctor, nurse, or paramedic who gave emergency treatment

2)   Examine the scene of the shooting.
    a) Identify exact time when decedent was found.
    b) Identify when the decedent was last known to be alive.
    c) Describe the building, room, or place where the decedent was found.
    d) What reason did the decedent have to be at this place?
    e) Describe the exact position of the body.
    f) Describe how the decedent is dressed.
    g) Describe the exact position of the weapon.
    h) Detail all articles pertaining to the incident that are present at the scene, including:
        i) Cleaning apparatus
        ii) Stick or strings
        iii) Expended shell casings
        iv) Live ammunition rounds
        v) Written notes
    i) If he was alive when found, what did the decedent say?

3)   Examine the gun and ammunition.
    a) Describe the make, type, caliber, etc., of the weapon.
    b) Who is the owner of the weapon?
    c) Why did the decedent have this weapon?
    d) How many shells were found in the gun? Describe their position and whether they were live or expended rounds.
    e) Was the firearm in good working order?
    f) Was the firearm equipped with a safety catch? If yes, describe the operation of the mechanism. Was it operational?
    g) Is there any indication that the weapon may have been handled improperly or fired under unusual circumstances?
    h) Is there any blood noted in the muzzle of the weapon?
    i) Did the gun or nearby material (e.g., rags, oil, ramrod) give any evidence of the gun's having being cleaned?

j) Do the decedent's hands give any indication of having cleaned the weapon (e.g., grease marks, dirt, oil)?

k) How far is the trigger from the muzzle?

4) Describe the wound.

a) At what point did the bullet or pellets enter the body?

b) What course did the projectile take? Did it exit the body? If yes, at what point?

c) Are there powder burns evident on the clothing or skin? If yes, describe the appearance.

d) Was the shot through the clothing or uncovered portion of the body?

e) Is there any discernible powder on the decedent's hands or fingers?

f) Is any blood spatter present on the decedent's hands or fingers? If yes, describe.

5) Investigate the circumstance.

a) If there is a suggestion of hunting, what game was in season? Did the decedent have a hunting license?

b) When was the firearm last used and for what purpose?

c) Develop the decedent's height.

d) Develop whether the decedent was left- or right-handed.

e) Develop the decedent's experience at using firearms. Was he considered cautious or careless?

f) Describe the events preceding death. Detail any conversations or comments made by the decedent during the events leading up to his death.

BODY TRANSPORT FROM THE SCENE

1) If blood interpretation may be significant in this case, consider removing those items of clothing prior to transporting the remains (obtain approval from the on-call pathologist).

2) Check the remains for any possible trace evidence. If any of this evidence may be lost during transport, the evidence technician should collect it after photographing it.

3) Bag (paper) the decedent's hands.

PROCESSING AT THE MEO/MORGUE

1) If homicide or suicide is suspected, do the following:

a) Consider examining the body for latent or patent prints.

b) Collect any trace evidence that may be present.

c) Collect the bags used to cover the decedent's hands while traveling to the morgue.

d) Collect fingernail scrapings and clippings from the decedent.

e) Obtain pulled and combed hair standards from the decedent.

f) Collect a tube of blood for typing purposes.

g) Obtain major case prints.

h) Collect, air-dry, and separately pack any item of the decedent's clothing.

i) Perform a neutron-activation swabbing of the decedent's hands.

2) X-ray the gunshot wounds.

a) Always take X-rays determine if the projectile(s) is still present.

3) If a homicide is suspected, collect whatever evidence may be required based on the motive indicated (e.g., complete sexual swabbings if a sexual homicide is indicated).

4)   If the decedent's remains are skeletonized or badly decomposed, the pathologist may wish to consult a forensic anthropologist before conducting an autopsy.

FOLLOW-UP INVESTIGATION

1)   If a homicide is suspected, follow guidelines appropriate for the motive indicated.

2)   If suicide is suspected, follow the guidelines in Chapter 26. In addition, consider the following:
      a) Keep in mind that the great majority of suicide victims do not leave notes.
      b) The initial presumption of victims having suffered a contact gunshot wound will be a suicide rather than an accident or a homicide.
      c) In self-inflicted gunshot wounds involving long arms, look for the possibility of a trigger trip at the immediate scene of the body.
      d) A suicide victim may also use furniture or some architectural element to steady the long arm before pulling the trigger. Look for scuff marks created by the contact of the weapon with some nearby anchor-type item.
            i) For a victim of a rifle or shotgun wound to the chest or abdomen, check the trajectory of the wound to determine if suicide is likely or even possible. Consider the following:
                  (1) "With the weapon butt on the ground and the body hunched over it, the trajectory is downwards (not upwards). Reaching for the trigger with the right hand rotates the body so that the trajectory is right to left (vice versa if reaching with the left hand)" (Pounder, 1993).
      e) There will be suspicious suicides.
            i) The location of the gunshot wound may produce doubt about the self-inflicted nature of the death.
            ii) Suicide by multiple gunshot is uncommon but not rare. The incapacitating power of the victim's injuries will be critical in assessing whether a suicide is likely or even possible.

BODY-SELECTION TARGET FOR SUICIDE VICTIMS
(POUNDER, 1993)

HANDGUN		SHOTGUN		RIFLE	
Head	80%	Head	80%	Head	50%
Chest	15%	Chest	15%	Chest	35%
Abdomen	<5%	Abdomen	<5%	Abdomen	15%

MOST COMMON HEAD SELECTION SITES
(POUNDER, 1993)

	MOST COMMON	Temple Mouth
	LEAST COMMON	Underside of chin Forehead

f) It is not unusual to find that a second or third shot has been fired or test-fired by the victim prior to his firing the fatal round.

g) Whether the victim is left- or right-handed becomes less important when the weapon is held in an uncomfortable position. A weapon is made to be pointed away from the person holding it. For this reason, it is not unusual to find that the shooter steadied the weapon with his strong hand while pulling the trigger with his weak hand.

    i) If this is the case, high-velocity blood spatter may be observed on the back of the hand that was used to steady the muzzle as well as on the back of the hand that fired the weapon.

    ii) The steadying hand used to hold the muzzle may also show soot deposition on the radial margin of the forefinger, the adjacent surface of the thumb, and the radial half of the palm from the muzzle blast.

    iii) In cases where a revolver was used to effect the victim's own death, the cylinder gap may allow soot to be deposited on the ulnar side of the shooter's palm.

h) Examine contact wounds on clothing.

    i) Cotton and cotton blends

        (1) Contact wounds from medium- and large-caliber weapons usually produce crosslike tears in the fabric.

    ii) Synthetic materials

        (1) Contact areas on synthetic fabrics usually show burn holes with scalloped edges.

3) An accident may be indicated.

a) Reconstruct the events based on the evidence acquired and the statements made to the investigators.

b) Obtain complete background information on the decedent, including:

    i) Financial (include status of insurance policies)

    ii) Health (include any psychiatric or physical problem that may have contributed to the incident)

    iii) Domestic

c) Develop any previous accidents involving the decedent.

GUNSHOT WOUND MORTALITY RATE
(Wilber, 1977)

Organ	Mortality Rate
Liver	30%
Kidney	22%
Colon	18%
Stomach	18%
Bladder	12%
Small bowel	12%
Spleen	8%

This chart shows the probability of a fatal gunshot wound if the indicated organ is involved.

CHAPTER 43: APPARENT NATURAL DEATH

CONSIDERATIONS

1)   Natural deaths are caused by disease. The types of natural disease that can cause death are numerous; however, the death investigator will usually be involved in two situations in which a natural death has occurred.

      a) Sudden incapacitation or death of an individual considered being relatively functional. The causes of death are usually attributed to the following:

        i) Heart attack

          (1) If the blood supply to a portion of the heart is completely cut off by total blockage of a coronary artery, the result is a heart attack. This is usually caused by a sudden closure from a blood clot forming on top of a previous narrowing.

        ii) Arteriosclerotic heart disease, sometimes referred to as arteriosclerotic cardiovascular disease (ASCVD) or coronary heart disease (CHD)

          (1) Narrowing of the coronary arteries that feed the heart causes heart disease. Like any muscle, the heart needs a constant supply of oxygen and nutrients, which are carried to it by the blood in the coronary arteries. When the coronary arteries become narrowed or clogged by cholesterol and fat deposits—a process called atherosclerosis—and cannot supply enough blood to the heart, the result is CHD.

            (a) If too little oxygen-carrying blood reaches the heart, the person may experience chest pain, called angina.

          (2) Cholesterol is a waxy, fatlike substance that occurs naturally in all parts of the body. The body uses cholesterol to produce many hormones, vitamin D, and the bile acids that help to digest fat. It takes only a small amount of cholesterol in the

ARTERY CROSS SECTION

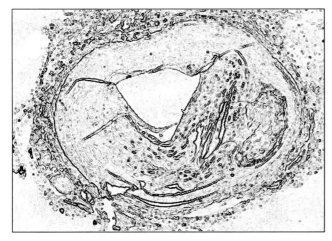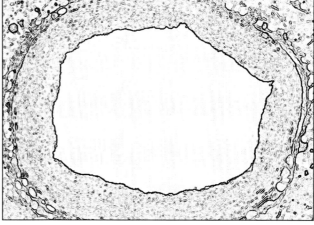

Examples of a cross section of an artery. The artery on the left is severely narrowed, while the artery on the right has only a small percentage of plaque collected on the inside of its wall. The artery section is collected at autopsy, and thin cross sections are cut. The specimen is stained and placed on a slide. Under a microscope, a pathologist can determine what percentage the artery was occluded or blocked. It is very similar to cross sectioning of a garden hose.

blood to meet these needs. If too much cholesterol is in a person's bloodstream, the excess is deposited in arteries, including the coronary arteries, where it contributes to the narrowing and blockages that cause the signs and symptoms of heart disease.

- (a) This depositing within the arteries feeding the heart causes the arteries to narrow.
- (b) Usually pathologists consider plaque as dangerous when it begins to occlude, or block, 70 percent of the cross-sectional area of an artery.
- (c) On occasion, the plaque breaks off and travels along an artery until the narrowing of a particular artery causes a clot (thrombus) to form. The clot interrupts the blood flow serving a particular area of the heart muscle, causing this area of muscle to die from lack of blood (infarct).
- (d) If an individual survives this attack, scarring of the heart muscle results. Previous infarcts are visible in an autopsy.
- (e) There is usually pain associated with a heart attack.
- (f) Smoking, poor diet, diabetes, hypertension, and genetic factors contribute to arteriosclerosis.

(3) In a heart where an infarct has occurred, the heart muscle's rhythm becomes unusual because one part of the heart muscle is receiving adequate blood and another part of the heart is not receiving blood. This can lead to abnormal electrical impulses (ventricularfibrillation). This ineffective rhythm (arrhythmia) interrupts the blood flow to the brain. Unconsciousness occurs within 10 seconds. Death of the brain follows within a few minutes.

(4) "Cessation of cardiac rhythm causes:
- (a) Unconsciousness in less than 15 seconds; usually instantaneous.
- (b) Paralysis of [the] respiratory center of the brain within a few minutes.
- (c) Irreversible cessation of brain function within 5 minutes.
  - (i) This is the window of opportunity allowing for the collapsed individual to be revived" (Irvine, 1995).

(5) These are common nonspecific signs and symptoms:
- (a) Fatigue
- (b) Loss of appetite
- (c) Nausea
- (d) Vomiting
- (e) Epigastric (heartburn) pain
- (f) Restlessness or anxiety

(6) These are common specific signs and symptoms:
- (a) Shortness of breath with even slight or no activity
- (b) "Cold" sweat
- (c) Chest pain (angina) may be brief, intermittent, or entirely absent (silent M.I.). In most cases, pain will be reported as radiating down the arm or back or into the jaw.

        (d) Dizziness, palpitations (skipping beats), unconsciousness

   (7) These are common activities engaged in before death:

        (a) Physical exertion (including sexual activity)

        (b) Emotional stress at home or at work, including a recent death or severe illness involving a family member or close friend

   (8) Decedent may have a history involving the following type of surgery:

        (a) Coronary bypass

        (b) Pacemaker implant

        (c) Valve replacement

        (d) Repair of congenital defect

        (e) Aortic aneurysm

   (9) These medications may be found at the scene:

        (a) Cardiac glycosides

        (b) Diuretics

        (c) Antihypertensive (high-blood-pressure) agents

        (d) Antianginal agents

        (e) Antiarrhythmias

        (f) Heart drugs

  (10) Scene indicators of a natural death may involve the following:

        (a) The body has a midline chest scar.

        (b) The decedent is found in the bathroom or seated on the toilet.

        (c) The decedent is propped up on pillows to sleep or breathe.

        (d) The incident occurred during the early-morning hours (3 to 6 A.M.).

        (e) The decedent has a history of recent exertion.

            (i) Environmental conditions may be hazardous because of smog, smoke, or extremely high outdoor temperatures.

        (f) The decedent used antacids.

iii) SIDS (see Chapter 34 on child deaths)

iv) Abnormal heart rhythm that becomes fatal

   (1) The heart is an electrical organ, which causes contraction of the heart in an effort to move blood through the body. If anything interferes with this conduction system (e.g., inefficient contraction, no rhythm, a rhythm that does not cause contraction, many muscles trying to take over at once), fibrillation may result.

   (2) This conduction system is very delicate. Its integrity can be challenged by the following:

        (a) Ischemia (lack of oxygen)

        (b) Cold

        (c) Drugs, including:

            (i) Alcohol, caffeine, diet pills, nasal decongestants, tobacco, cocaine, PCP, and amphetamines

        (d) Hypertrophic (enlarged) heart

            (i) Heart muscle enlarged because it has t do more work

               1. Hypertension may be a source of this extra work.

(e) Metabolic causes
  (i) Especially associated with an excess of potassium salts
(f) Stress
(g) Trauma to the nervous system, such as a blow to the chest or testicles.
(h) Disease of the conduction system itself
  (i) Age, scarring, calcium deposits, iron deposits, etc.
(i) Electrical shock
(j) Trauma

v) Other cardiac conditions
  (1) Cardiomyopathy
    (a) This is a disease of the heart muscle itself.
    (b) It is usually not sudden and follows a protracted course.
    (c) Sudden death usually involves asymmetric septal hypertrophy when a bulging of the dividing wall of the heart prevents flow out of the heart. This type of case is usually seen in the death of a young athlete, following a collapse, with no previous health problems.
  (2) Myocarditis
    (a) Inflammation of the heart
    (b) Maybe caused the death of a young person after an otherwise inconsequential viral infection
  (3) Undiagnosed birth defects
  (4) Calcified aortic valves
  (5) Endocarditis
    (a) Valve infection of the heart
    (b) Usually seen in IV drug abusers
  (6) Rheumatic heart disease
    (a) Usually involves scarring of the heart valves
  (7) Mitral valve prolapse
    (a) Floppy valves

vi) Pulmonary thromboembolism
  (1) This occurs when a blood clot forms in the deep veins, usually of the legs or pelvis, and then breaks off and travels through the body before it lodges in a vessel in the lung. Death results because the forward flow of the blood between the right side of the heart is now blocked.
  (2) Symptoms include:
    (a) Sudden shortness of breath
    (b) Chest pain
    (c) Coughing up blood
  (3) Scene indicators include:
    (a) Immobility of person before death
      (i) Bed rest
      (ii) Lengthy recovery from surgery
      (iii) Extended travel with limited movement before the clot is found
      (iv) A cast on the decedent's leg or arm

vii) Sudden death may also involve asthma, epilepsy, or spontaneous ruptures of diseased arteries.

        (1) Berry aneurysm
            (a) Causes rapid accumulation of blood into the confined spaces of the brain
                (i) This may be a result of high blood pressure or abuse of cocaine or stimulants.
                (ii) The subject may have complained about having "the worst headache of my life."
        (2) Epilepsy
            (a) An associated activity, such as drowning or a traffic accident, may cause death.
    viii) Aside from heart and lung problems, there are relatively few natural diseases that result in sudden death.
  b) Diseases eventually causing the death of individuals who refuses to visit a doctor, seek medical attention, or take care of themselves. These people tend to be antisocial, preferring to live alone. The death investigator usually encounters these types when they are discovered dead. The causes of death are usually attributed to the following:
    i) Alcoholism and its manifestations
        (1) Alcohol is a poison. The person who drinks is protected from the effects of the poison by the detoxification action of his liver.
        (2) Although all organs (e.g., liver, heart, brain, upper gastrointestinal tract) suffer as a result of chronic alcohol abuse, natural deaths usually involve the following:
            (a) Bleeding into the gastrointestinal tract from a peptic ulcer or bleeding tendencies
            (b) Esophageal varices (distended veins in the esophagus due to back pressure from a fibrosed liver)
            (c) Generally, an increased tendency to bleed more freely from injuries
            (d) Pancreatitis
            (e) Pneumonia
            (f) Cardiomyopathy
                (i) Enlarged heart from the toxic effect of alcohol
            (g) Fatty metamorphosis of the liver (FML), or cirrhosis
    ii) Cardiac rhythm disturbances (ventricular fibrillation) associated with problems of malnutrition
    iii) Diabetes
    iv) Infections such as pneumonia and sepsis
        (1) Sepsis is an infection spread by the blood. Vessels away from the heart and lungs dilate, and blood pools in the arms and legs, causing shock.
        (2) Toxins from the bacteria affect organs directly, causing the organs to begin to fail one by one.
    v) Necrotizing pancreatitis
    vi) Senility and its complications
    vii) Complications from pregnancy resulting in death of the mother
        (1) Ectopic pregnancy
            (a) The embryo lodges on the outside of the uterus, which can cause severe bleeding and the death of the mother.
        (2) Amniotic fluid embolism

(a) The fluid from around the fetus enters the large veins in the distended uterus and travels into the lungs.
(3) Uterine rupture
(a) This usually occurs after a previous cesarean section.
(4) Postpartum hemorrhage
(5) Pulmonary embolism
(6) Toxemia
(a) This is swelling, protein in the urine, and seizures.
(7) Placenta previa
(a) The placenta becomes implanted over the cervical opening.

2) What makes a death unexpected?
   a) There were no previous symptoms before collapse and death.
   b) Symptoms may have been present but were ignored, rationalized, or misinterpreted.

PRIMARY FOCUS OF INVESTIGATION

1) Eliminate any other manner of death.

2) Eliminate the possibility that the subject's death is the result of some other cause mimicking a natural death. Consider the possibility of environmental hazards causing the death, for examples:
   a) Poisonous gases. Consider these cases when more than one body is present at the scene, and it appears that the subjects succumbed to natural causes.
      i) Carbon monoxide
         (1) An odorless, colorless gas byproduct formed through the incomplete combustion of these:
            (a) Gasoline
            (b) Diesel fuel
            (c) Kerosene
            (d) Butane
            (e) Propane
            (f) Liquefied petroleum gas.
            (g) Wood
            (h) Charcoal
         (2) Carbon monoxide may be indicated as a possible cause of death through the discovery at the scene of a stove, happy heater, etc., which is set in the "on" position even though the fuel has been completely consumed.
      ii) Hydrogen sulfide
         (1) A deadly gas formed by the decomposition of organic material, it is usually associated with the collapse of an individual who may be working on a sewer line, digging a ditch, or doing something in a ship's hold. Rescuers may also become ill, collapse, or expire from their attempts to aid the involved party without understanding the cause of the original collapse.
   b) Electrocution
      i) This should be considered whenever there is an electrical appliance associated with the collapse of an individual.

NOTIFICATION

1) Pathologist is not required at the scene unless:
   a) The manner of death may be confused or the decedent or some other interested party appears to have attempted to alter the circumstances of death.
   b) The decedent's identification may be affected because of decomposition.

SCENE PHOTOGRAPHS

1) Photograph the entire area of the involved scene showing the condition of the premises.

2) Photograph any areas showing any movement or activity of the decedent immediately before his death.

3) Photograph any indications of security or absence of foul play that suggest that scene is most that of a natural death.

4) Photograph any items from or areas of the scene that may indicate the time frame involved with the subject's death.

5) If drugs, drug paraphernalia, or alcohol containers are found at the scene, photograph them.

6) Photograph the decedent's body relative to its position within the scene area.

7) Photograph the body to depict consistency or inconsistency of time frame changes on the decedent (e.g., rigor mortis, lividity, skin slippage, blistering).

8) Document the absence of injuries to the decedent's remains.
   a) If the decedent has injuries that may have resulted from his collapsing to the floor, photograph any item that the subject may have struck during his fall. Take close-up photographs of any injuries that may have resulted from the fall.

9) Take an identification photograph of the subject.

SCENE INVESTIGATION

1) Scene of the death
   a) Give a general description of the scene. Make a special note of the condition of the premises.
   b) Describe the decedent and any indication of previous movement by him within the scene.
   c) Describe any evidence that no foul play was involved with the demise of the decedent, for example:
      i) Describe the security of the residence.
         (1) How was entry gained?
         (2) Is there any indication that the site has been rifled?
         (3) Is there any indication that a VCR, television, stereo, or anything else has been taken?
      ii) Describe the security of the personal effects, including wallet, purse, jewelry, or checkbook of the decedent.

　　　d) Describe any medication found at the scene.
　　　　　i) Describe the medications observed and their position relative to the body.
　　　e) Describe any activity or item that might suggest the time frame of the subject's death
　　　　e.g., newspapers collecting on front porch, food preparation).

2)　　Circumstances of the death
　　　a) How was death discovered?
　　　b) When was the decedent last seen alive?
　　　c) Describe the activities of the decedent shortly before death.
　　　d) Describe the terminal episode.

3)　　History of the decedent
　　　a) Develop any complaints the decedent may have made before death.
　　　b) Develop the decedent's past medical history, including all physicians.
　　　c) Develop the decedent's social history, including drinking and drug habits.
　　　d) Develop any changes in the decedent's household, eating, sleeping, and work habits.
　　　e) Develop the decedent's prescriptive medication history.

4)　　Body examination
　　　a) Describe the position of decedent's body.
　　　b) Describe clothing worn by the decedent. Is the clothing appropriate under the circumstances of the incident?
　　　c) Describe the time frame factors associated with the examination of the decedent's remains (e.g., rigor mortis, lividity). Are these factors consistent with the information known concerning the subject's death?
　　　d) Describe any areas of injury observed on the decedent. Are there any items or conditions present that could have caused the injuries, or could the final activities of the decedent have caused the injuries (e.g., the decedent's collapsing from a standing position and striking his head on the floor or on a table)?

TRANSPORTING REMAINS

1)　　Collect all prescriptive medications associated with the decedent and transport them with the remains.

2)　　Secure all valuables.

PROCESSING AT MEO/MORGUE

1)　　Fingerprint the decedent.

FOLLOW-UP INVESTIGATION

1)　　If it appears there may be a problem in the identification of the decedent because of decomposition:
　　　a) Search the subject's residence for background information that may assist in the identification of the decedent. Look for these:
　　　　　i) Appointment books listing physicians and dentists
　　　　　ii) Personal telephone books listing doctors and dentists
　　　　　iii) Telephone book with handwritten telephone numbers on the front or back cover or in the section listing physicians or dentists
　　　　　iv) Canceled personal checks listing payments to doctors or dentists

2) If there may be a problem in locating the next of kin, search the decedent's residence to develop the following:

    a) Personal address book that may include the next of kin or people with similar last names, who may be related

    b) Christmas or birthday cards tht may have been sent by relatives

    c) Current or past employers, insurance papers, family Bible, or other items that may identify family members or friends of the decedent who may have knowledge of family members

    d) Personal computer examination

AVERAGE PULSE RATES*	
Subject's Age	**Average Beats Per Minute**
Unborn child	140–150
Newborn infant	130–140
Child (1st year)	110–130
Child (2nd year)	96–115
Child (3rd year)	86–105
7 to 14 years	76–90
14 to 21 years	76–85
21 to 60 years	70–75
60+ years	67–80

Information obtained from the U.S. Vitamin and Pharmaceutical Corporation.

AVERAGE RESPIRATION RATES*	
Subject's Age	**Number of Respirations Per Minute**
Child (1st year)	25–35
12 to 17 years	20–25
Adulthood	16–18

Information obtained from the U.S. Vitamin and Pharmaceutical Corporation

AVERAGE BLOOD PRESSURE RATES*

Subject's Age	Systolic	Diastolic
10	103	70
15	113	75
20	120	80
25	122	81
30	123	82
35	124	83
40	126	84
45	128	85
50	130	86
55	132	87
60	135	89

Systolic pressure is the force with which blood is pumped by the heart during heart contraction.
Diastolic pressure is the force with which blood is pumped by the heart during dilation or relaxation.

Information obtained from the U.S. Vitamin and Pharmaceutical Corporation.

CHAPTER 44: DEATH BY POISONING

CONSIDERATIONS

1)   Deaths by poisoning are much rarer as homicides than as suicides or accidents.

2)   Poisonings are difficult cases to work and run a substantial chance of being missed because poisonings mimic natural deaths. Investigators should become suspicious when the events or illness preceding the death is suspicious.
      a) Acute poisonings
         i) More than one person sharing similar activities becomes gravely ill (e.g., 15 people report that they ate a fish dish at the same restaurant earlier in the evening).
         ii) A person not in ill health suddenly becomes sick after eating food, drinking some substance, or taking some medication.
         iii) A person with no significant health history or complaints suddenly becomes ill and dies.
         iv) Individuals who suffer a sudden attack with vomiting, convulsions, and coma.
      b) Chronic poisoning
         i) A person suffering from chronic ill health and circumstances that include the following:
            (1) Medical examinations fail to find any reasons for the subject's continuous ill health.
            (2) The patient's health improves when he is away from home and suffers dramatically when he returns home.
            (3) The doctor's instructions for health care are ignored.

3)   Suspicion of poisoning may be brought to the investigator's attention by a relative, friend, or associate of the deceased.
      a) It is not unusual for families of decedents to voice their suspicions about a poisoning death, especially when the decedent had a relationship with an individual of whom the family does not approve. It is not unusual to learn that the estate of the decedent has been altered to favor the current relationship. Although there may be a legitimate suspicion associated with the death, most of these assertions are baseless and used to drag the investigative agency into the middle of an estate dispute.

4)   Types of poisons
      a) Inorganic
         i) Metals
            (1) Includes arsenic, mercury, lead, copper, thallium, beryllium, antimony, bismuth, zinc, cadmium, chromium, barium, nickel, silver, and manganese
         ii) Nonmetals
            (1) Cyanides, yellow phosphorus, fluoride, iodine, strong acids, and alkalis
            (2) Gases, including carbon monoxide, hydrogen sulfide, arsine, and phosgene

b) Organic
    i) Volatile substances
        (1) Ethyl alcohol
        (2) Other alcohol, including methyl or wood alcohol
        (3) Anilene
        (4) Phenol (carbolic acid)
        (5) Miscellaneous organic liquids that may be inhaled, including benzene, gasoline, acetone, ketones, aldehydes, carbon disulfides, carbon tetrachloride, ether, and chloroform
        (6) DDT
    ii) Nonvolatile materials (plant origin)
        (1) Alkaloids, including strychnine, morphine, cocaine, heroin, brucine, atropine, codeine
        (2) Barbiturates (sleep producing—the choice drugs for suicides), including phenobarbital, amytal, veronal, allonal, and seconal
        (3) Glycosides (related to sugar groups), including digitalis
        (4) Drugs and synthetics, including salicylates, antipyrine, pyramidone, and sulfonamides
        (5) Hashish
    iii) Miscellaneous, including ricin (from castor bean), botulinus toxin, snake venom, and curare

5) Another difficulty associated with working possible poison-related deaths is the presence of thousands of innocuous items that may contain poison in most homes. Most of the poisons indicated are not present in pure form but may be present within a household in the following:
    a) Cosmetics
    b) Ant poison
    c) Agriculture sprays
    d) Rat poison
    e) Paint solvents
    f) Industrial chemicals and cleaning supplies

PRIMARY FOCUS OF INVESTIGATION

1) Determine the manner of death.
    a) Accident, suicide, or homicide?

2) If homicide is suspected, the following must be developed:
    a) The suspect had access to the poison.
        i) Was it a common substance that was readily available?
        ii) Would the suspect have access to a particular type of poison through his job?
        iii) Was the substance purchased?
            (1) Is the substance a regulated product that has to be signed for before purchasing?
        iv) Can the suspect be physically linked to the poison?
            (1) Fingerprints on the item suspected of containing the poison
            (2) Fingerprints on packaging paper (if the poison was sent to decedent)
            (3) Handwriting comparison (if a sample was mailed to the victim)
    b) The suspect had access to the victim.
    c) The suspect intended to kill the victim and had knowledge of what the poison would do.

        i) Due to this premeditation, a homicidal poisoning is always a first-degree murder.

3)   Identify the particular poison.
        a) On many occasions the investigator will become aware of use of poison after the fact (the patient's admission to the hospital or during the autopsy examination). Get to the scene as quickly as possible and conduct a thorough search of the premises, not only looking for a poison container but other household items that may contain the poison or other items the victim might have come into contact with shortly before the onset of the symptoms. Consider partially eaten food, beverage containers, or medications that might have been altered. The search should include:
            i) Trash receptacles
            ii) Medicine closets
            iii) Insecticides
            iv) Cleaners

4)   Determine the circumstances surrounding the ingestion of the poison.

5)   Compile a detailed history leading up to the death, including the symptoms (in detail) and appearance of the decedent.
        a) It may indicate poison.
        b) It may assist in the development of a suspect.

6)   Obtain the prior medical history of the decedent.

NOTIFICATION

1)   A pathologist is not required at the scene unless:
        a) The manner of death may be confused, or the decedent or some other interested party appears to have attempted to alter the circumstances of death.
        b) The decedent's identification may be affected because of decomposition.

2)   Full notification and full lab and crime scene capabilities are required if the poisoning may involve an altered retail product.

3)   If poisoning is suspected, the forensic pathologist should be notified of the circumstances. He may wish to come to the scene to help locate the suspected poison.

SCENE PHOTOGRAPHS

1)   Photograph the entire area of the involved scene showing the condition of the premises.

2)   Photograph any areas containing indication of movement and activities of the decedent immediately before his death.

3)   Photograph any indications of the presence of security measures or the absence of foul play, which suggest that the scene is probably that of a natural death or a suicide.

4)   Photograph any items or areas of the scene that may indicate the time frame of the subject's death.

a) Newspapers collecting on front porch, food preparation, etc.

5) If alcohol containers, drugs, and drug paraphernalia are found at the scene, photograph them.

6) Photograph any items or containers suggesting that a poison may have been used.

7) If poison is suspected, photograph any containers, beverage glasses, and packages that may indicate what happened and what has been used.

8) Photograph the decedent's body relative to its position within the scene area.

9) Photograph the body to depict consistency or inconsistency of time frame changes on the decedent (e.g., rigor mortis, lividity, skin slippage, blistering).

10) Document the presence or absence of injuries to the decedent's remains.
    a) If the decedent has injuries that may have resulted when he collapsed to the floor, photograph any item he may have struck. Take close-up photographs of the injuries he may have incurred in the fall.
    b) Photograph any areas of discoloration around the decedent's mouth area.

11) Photograph any areas containing vomit material.

12) Take an identification photograph of the subject.

SCENE INVESTIGATION

1) Scene of the death
    a) Give a general description of the scene. Make special note of the condition of the premises.
    b) Describe the decedent and any indication of his previous movements within the scene. There may be multiple scenes associated with the decedent's demise, including the following:
        i) Location where the decedent is found
        ii) Areas where vomit is present
        iii) Area in which the poison was prepared
            (1) Tools
            (2) Utensils
            (3) Containers
            (4) Clothes
            (5) Gloves
            (6) Research material
        iv) Where poison may have been stored
            (1) Medicine bottles
            (2) Food or drink
            (3) Under kitchen counter
            (4) Garage/shed area.
        v) Where poison or poison container may have been disposed
            (1) Trash cans
            (2) Storage areas
            (3) Sink traps

    c) Describe any evidence that shows that there was no foul play associated with the demise of the decedent. For example:

        i) The security of the residence

            (1) How was entry gained?

            (2) Any indication that the site was rifled?

            (3) Any indication that the VCR, television, stereo, or any other item was taken?

        ii) The security of the personal effects, including wallet, purse, jewelry, or checkbook of the decedent

    d) Describe any medication found at the scene.

        i) Medications observed relative to the body

    e) Describe any packaging, containers, drinking glasses, etc., that suggest a poison may have been involved in the decedent's death.

    f) Describe any activity or item indicating the time frame of the subject's death (e.g., newspapers collecting on front porch, food preparation).

2)   Circumstances of the death

    a) How was the death discovered?

    b) When was the decedent last seen alive?

    c) Describe the decedent's activities shortly before the illness and then death.

    d) Describe the terminal episode.

3)   History of the decedent

    a) Develop any complaints the decedent may have made prior to his death.

    b) Develop the decedent's past medical history, including all physicians.

    c) Develop the decedent's social history, including drinking and drug habits.

    d) Develop any changes in the decedent's household, eating, sleeping, and work habits.

    e) Develop the decedent's prescriptive medication history.

4)   Body examination

    a) Describe the position of decedent's body.

    b) Describe the clothing worn by the decedent. Is the clothing appropriate under the circumstances of the incident?

    c) Describe the time frame factors associated with the examination of the decedent's remains (e.g., rigor mortis, lividity). Are these factors consistent with the information known about the subject's death?

    d) Describe any areas of injury observed on the decedent. Are there any items or conditions present that could have caused the injuries, or could the decedent's final activities have caused them (e.g., the decedent's collapsing from a standing position and striking his head on the floor or on a table)?

5)   If poisoning is suspected, and it is believed the poison may have been self-administered, the item responsible may be in the immediate vicinity of the remains. Look for any bottle or other container that could have contained the poison.

    a) Look for and collect beverage glasses.

6)   If someone killed the decedent, the scene should be searched extensively for any indication of the poison.

    a) Search all trash, including that found outside the house.

    b) Search tool sheds, garages, and other remote areas of the house.

    c) Search the grounds of the involved residence, as well as weeds or woods adjacent to it.

7)   If a container involving the suspected poison is not found and a suspect is known, consider widening the search to locations associated with this suspect, including his vehicle.

TRANSPORTING BODY

1)   No particular precautions are necessary in transporting the remains.

2)   If poisoning is suspected, the entire inventory of medicines, household cleaners, insecticides, and other substances that may poison should be boxed up and transported with the remains.

BODY AT THE MEO/MORGUE

1)   Fingerprint the decedent. Take major case prints if homicide is a possibility (partial palm prints may be found on the vial suspected of containing the poison).

FOLLOW-UP INVESTIGATION

1)   If suicide is involved, follow guidelines in Chapter 26 on suicidees.

2)   If homicide is indicated, work the case initially as a contract murder unless the circumstances of the death clearly indicate that the subject obtained the poison as a random act in which he was just the unlucky person who happened to purchase the altered item. If this is the case, work the case as a crime of opportunity.
   a) Determine, for example, if the item was altered at the factory, the store, or some other placed on the shelf at the store. Once this is developed, concentrate your activities in this direction. If the investigation reveals that the item was altered at an unknown location and brought into the store, work the case in an effort to develop a time frame in which the incident may have occurred. Develop witnesses to support this time frame. Consider the following sources of information:
      i) Employees who worked during this time, especially security personnel
      ii) Customers who were at the store during the time, who may be developed through the following:
         (1) Credit card receipts taken at the time
         (2) Prescriptions filled during this time period
         (3) Refunds or exchanges that may have occurred during the time
         (4) Employee discounts registered at the time

HOMICIDE BY POISON

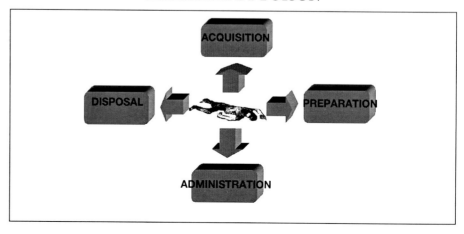

(5) Try to obtain videotapes from security cameras not only at the involved store but also adjacent stores.

iii) Activate full processing and lab capabilities to try to develop latent prints and trace the possible poison.

3)   Develop proof of a homicide.
        a) Poisoning must be the cause of death. This can be established through:
                i) Chemical analysis
                ii) Pathology examination
        b) The perpetrator gave the poison to the victim.
                i) The opportunity of the suspect to commit the crime must be developed.
                ii) It must be developed through the investigation that the suspect had access to or possession of the poison.
                iii) Rule out other people as the poisoner
        c) The suspect was aware of the lethality of the poison or the act.

4)   Determine where the poison was procured.
        a) Examine receipts.
        b) Check whether there is a poison register associated with the type of poison suspected.
        c) Could poison have been stolen?

5)   Were any special efforts made by the suspect to learn about the use and effects of poison?
        a) Library research
        b) Internet searches
        c) Media cases that may have influenced the suspect's actions
        d) Chemical catalogs
        e) Diaries or journals

6)   Consider product tampering.
        a) The Federal Anti-Tampering Act makes it a federal offense to tamper with food, drugs, devices, cosmetics, and other consumer products.
        b) Considerations for contamination access:
                i) During the manufacturing process by an employee
                ii) During product distribution, usually at the retail level
                iii) After purchase of the product
                        (1) This may be associated with a consumer attempting to get a product liability settlement from the manufacturer.

7)   Identify types of poisoners.
        a) The types of poisoners are classified based on the specificity of the victim and the degree of planning involving in the poisoning effort.

INVESTIGATIVE CONSIDERATIONS

POISONING DEATHS HOMICIDE CONSIDERATIONS			
Highly planned crime	**Specific Victim** Carefully planned crime with a carefully selected poison	**Camouflaged Victim** Carefully planned crime with a carefully selected poison camouflaged by poisoning others randomly; poison placed in location(s) where random victims would have access to the poison	**Random Victim** Slowly planned crime with carefully selected poison
Spontaneous crime	Quick decision, with a poison selected as a weapon of opportunity		

PROFILE OF THE TYPICAL POISONER		
Poisoner's age	Considerations based on individual circumstances of the incident.	
Poisoner's sex	**Specific Victim** The initial focus on a suspect involving a specific victim killed with a specific poison may involve a female	**Random Victim** Male or female
	Just as in other murders, the vast majority of murderers using poison as their weapon of choice will be men. Because of the nonconfrontational aspect of this type of crime, if a woman is going to commit murder, poison may be the weapon she chooses. If a man is the poisoner, expect him to have a nonconfrontational personality. That is, the poisoner will tend to be shy or cowardly. He should have the characteristics of an emotionally submissive male who will be equally uncomfortable with confrontation. This is a cowardly, predatory crime in which the poisoner's chosen course of action demonstrates his or her weakness.	
Race	Considerations are based on individual circumstances of the incident.	
Marital status adjustment	• Has/had an unfortunate married life • Has/had an abnormal life with spouse, children and/or home	
Intelligence	Has an absolute defiance of legal authority; refuses to accept any moral basis for life	
Scholastic achievement adjustment	Tends to require some intelligence and education for the planning and operation of the incident. Libraries and other references (Internet) may have been consulted to effect the crime.	
Lifestyle	Considerations are based on individual circumstances of the incident.	

Rearing environment	Specific Victim Childhood has usually been one of two categories: • Spoiled by parents. Poisoning is a childish act that turns the victim into an object with no feelings. • Reared in an unhappy home	Random Victim Considerations are based on individual circumstances of the incident.
Social adjustment	• Has a long line of personal failure throughout life, especially with opposite gender of own age and own intelligence level • The poisoner will have bouts of depression and long-standing feelings of despair. • Will have feelings of inadequacy, helplessness, and impotence. • Feels as though he is being unfairly maligned by those around him or by society in general.	• Depressed • Nocturnal loner • Depressed • Nocturnal loner
Personality characteristics	• Fairly narrow-minded; does not have any sympathy or imagination. • Childish personality. The poisoner possesses an immature desire to have his own way. He may have a dreamy, romantic disposition. • There is something in the poisoner's personality that keeps him permanently immature. He never seems to grow up. • The poisoner will try and make the world obey his will by cheating it in minor ways and thereby stealing what it refuses to give him.	
Demeanor	Considerations are based on individual circumstances of the incident.	
Appearance and grooming	Considerations are based on individual circumstances of the incident.	
Emotional adjustment	• Probably has failed to make any kind of impression on life. • Probably is a daydreamer and/or fantasist. • Very possibly has an "artistist temperament."	
Evidence of mental decompensation	Considerations based on individual circumstances of the incident.	
Pathological behavioral characteristics	• Vanity of the poisoner convinces him that he cannot be discovered. • The poisoner has carefully calculated the odds of committing the crime and believes he can get away with it.	

Employment history	• High proportion have connections with the medical world.
	  Physicians
	  Nurses	

	Pharmacists Dentists Other healthcare workers Laboratory workers familiar with chemicals • Will gravitate toward positions of authority or pseudo-authority. • A history of trouble holding a job.
Work habits	Considerations are based on individual circumstances of the incident.
Socioeconomic status	Considerations are based on individual circumstances of the incident.
Military experience	• May have military background, possibly U.S. Army or Marines • Expect to see some psychiatric treatment in ethe individual's service record book. • Expect to see some behavioral problems in the subject's military background.
Prior criminal arrest history	Considerations based on individual circumstances of the incident.

Motive	Specific Victim Kills for personal gain, either emotionally or materially.	Random Victim General rule of thumb: an organized offender will use the the random poisoning as an extortion attempt. He is strictly after the money. A disorganized offender will kill out of revenge or anger.

ASSOCIATED PHYSICAL MANIFESTATIONS OF SOME POISONS
(Fox, 1973)

Type of Poison	Symptoms or Evidence
Caustic poison (lye)	Characteristic burns around the lips and mouth of the victim
Carbon monoxide	Red or pink patches on the chest and thighs; unusually brighter red lividity
Sulfuric acid	Black vomit
Hydrochloric acid	Greenish-brown vomit
Nitric acid	Yellow vomit
Silver salts	White vomit turning dark upon exposure to daylight
Copper sulfate	Blue-green vomit

Phosphorous	Coffee brown vomit; onion or garlic odor
Cyanide	Burnt-almond odor
Ammonia, vinegar, lysol	Characteristic odors
Arsenic, mercury, lead salts	Pronounced diarrhea
Methyl (wood) alcohol, isopropyl (rubbing) alcohol	Nausea and vomiting, unconsciousness, possibly blindness

SOME COMMON POISONS USED IN SUICIDES AND HOMICIDES
(Trestrail, not dated)

ARSENIC

In homicides, administered doses may be small, but fatally cumulative in an effort to disguise the homicide. In a suicide, the amount of poison taken may be massive and acutely administered.

Color	Metal is steel gray; salts come in a white powder.
Odor	Basically odorless, although there is a faint garlicky odor to breath.
Solubility	Salts are water soluble.
Taste	Virtually tasteless
Sources	Pesticides, rodent poison, ant poison, homeopathic medication, weed killers, paints, ceramics, livestock feed
Lethal dose	200 milligrams
Methods of administering	Generally administered to the victim through food or drink
Onset of symptoms	Depends on dosage; can vary from hours to days
Acute symptoms	Bloody diarrhea, vomiting, severe abdominal pain, burning esophygeal pain, metallic taste in the mouth, death from circulatory failure
Chronic symptoms	Diahrrhea, abdominal pain, hyperpigmentation of palms of hands, and soles of feet, localized edema of face and ankles, sore throat, stomatitis (inflammation of the mucous membranes of the mouth), pruritis, cough, tearing, salivation, garlic odor, hair loss, Aldrich-Mees lines (horizontal white lines visible on the nail bed area that usually takes 5 to 6 weeks to appear), burning pain on the soles of the feet
Misdiagnosis	Gastroenteritis

Other considerations	Arsenic can be detected in hair, bones, fingernails, and, in some cases, in cremated remains, years after the poisoning.
Items for arsenic examination	Food, beverages, medications, blood, urine, gastric contents, hair, nails, autopsy organ specimens

CYANIDE

Cyanide is very rapid and lethal. Few poisons act as rapidly. Onset of symptoms can be anywhere from immediatelt to 30 seconds. Abrupt onset of profound symptoms after exposure is a hallmark of cyanide exposure.

Forms	Cyanide in liquid form is called prussic acid. Hydrogen cyanide in its purest form is a gas. Industrial cyanide comes in a large nugget form. It is referred to as cyanide eggs. Crystalline cyanide is found as sodium, potassium, or calcium cyanide salt.
Color	White
Odor	A percentage of the population is able to distinguish the "burnt-almond" smell of cyanide.
Solubility	Salts dissolve in aqueous liquids.
Taste	Cyanide salts have a bitter taste and may burn tissue.
Sources of cyanide	• Fumigants, insecticides, rodent poison, metal (silver) polish, electroplating solution, metallurgy extraction solutions, photographic processing solutions • Inside the pits and seeds of certain plants such as peach, cherry, bitter almond, cassava, and apricots (laetrile) • Can be produced through the burning of certain synthetics, such as polyurethane and polyacrylonitrile • Also produced through the sythesizing of phencylidine (PCP)
Lethal dose	• 270 ppm (air) • 50 milligrams (HCN) • 200-300 milligrams (NaCN or KCN)
Method of administering	In food or drink
Acute symptoms	Headache, nausea, breathing difficulties, confusion, seizures, coma, gasping respirations, cardiovascular collapse
Chronic symptoms	Weakness, headache, confusion, nausea, vomiting
Misdiagnosis	Heart attack; asthmatic attack

Specimens to collect for testing	Food, beverages, medications, blood, urine, gastric contents autopsy organ specimens
Toxic levels	Blood: 12.4 milligrams/liter; 0.1 milligram/liter
Other	Mouth-to-mouth resuscitation provided to the victim could prove harmful to the Good Samaritan.

SODIUM FLUOROACETATE

This is one of the most toxic substances known. As little as 1 milligram may be enough to cause death or serious illness. There is no known antidote. It is only sold to licensed pest control operators and others qualified by training and experience in rodent control.

Forms	• Sodium monofluoroacetate (SMFA) • Fratol (Furatol) • Ratbane 1080 (Compound 1080) • Fluorakil (Fussol) • Megarox (Yancock) • Compound 1081 (Giftblaar plant from South Africa)
Color	White, crystalline compound resembling flour or baking soda
Odor	No odor
Solubility	Very water soluble; less soluble in ethanol
Taste	May have a slight vineagar taste
Source	Pesticides, rodent poison, insect poison, coyote poison
Lethal levels	2 to 10 milligrams/kilogram
Methods of administering	Through food or drink; can be absorbed through broken skin
Acute symptoms	Nausea, vomiting, diarrhea, agitation, confusion, seizures, lethargy, coma, respiratory arrest, cardiac arrhythmias
Chronic symptoms	n/a
Misdiagnosis	Gastroenteritis, viral infection, heart attack
Specimens to collect for testing	Blood, urine, gastric contents
Toxic levels	• Urine 65 milligrams/liter • Gastric 12 milligrams/liter • Liver 58 milligrams/kilogram

STRYCHNINE

Strychnine causes seizure-like symptoms, with the victim maintaining consciousness. These "contractions" are extremely painful.

Forms	Strychnine is a plant compound obtained from the tree *Strychnos nux-vomica*. Pure strychnine comes in a powder.
Color	White
Odor	No odor
Taste	Extremely bitter. May be masked in bitter alcohol drinks.
Source	Rodent poison: distributed only to licensed exterminators.
Lethal levels	5 to 8 milligrams; oral ingestion: 30 to 100 milligrams
Methods of administering	Food, beverages, medications
Acute symptoms	Muscle stiffness, painful cramps followed by muscle contractions; opisthotonic convulsion (victim's body takes the form of an arch with only the head and heels touching the floor); sardonic grin or forced-smile muscle contraction; intermittent muscle convulsions triggered by emotional or physical stimuli; death due to respiratory arrest
Misdiagnosed as	Grand mal seizure, tetanus
Specimens to collect for testing	Food, beverages, medications, blood, urine, gastric contents, autopsy specimens
Toxic levels	• Blood: 21 micrograms/milliliter • Urine: 9.1 micrograms/milliliter • Gastric: 61 micrograms/milliliter

CHAPTER 45:
POLICE AND CORRECTIONAL CUSTODY DEATHS

CONSIDERATIONS

1) These include the following types of cases:
   a) Police shooting deaths where the police officer has shot and killed an individual
      i) May also include include the fairly recently recognized category sometimes referred to as "suicide by cop," or police-assisted suicide.
         (1) This involves an individual who cannot kill himself, so he places himself in a threatening posture, compelling a responding police officer to shoot the individual to protect himself, other officers, or bystanders.
   b) Deaths occurring as a result of the police attempting to subdue or place an individual under arrest
   c) A death occurring while a suspect is confined to a jail or prison cell

2) There are not many other cases that will attract the media as much and draw criticism about how the case was handled, regardless of the circumstances or the validity of the criticism. Expect problems from the following:
   a) The family of the decedent
      i) Regardless of the circumstances, losing a family member produces hostility and resentment, which are often aired by the media. The family finds it difficult to understand why deadly force was necessary to stop the actions of the family member involved. Criticism often recounts the number of times the individual was shot ("Why did they have to shoot him *nine* times?"); where the individual was shot ("Why couldn't they shoot him in the knee?"), and the fact that he was *murdered* by the police.
   b) Minority groups
      i) When a member of a minority is killed, minority groups (especially those not normally covered by the media) often take this unfortunate incident as an opportunity to raise issues not necessarily pertinent to this particular case. Almost without exception, when these minority groups speak to media representatives they rarely have reviewed all the available investigative information.
   c) Attorneys
      i) Given the litigious nature of our society, as well as the glut of attorneys we have, there are always attorneys out there who realize that these types of cases often come with a fairly tidy profit built in because the likelihood of a settlement is high, not necessarily because of any wrongdoing but because it is seen as the cost of doing business. That is, settlement may be less expensive than taking the case to court and risking a judgment, as well as all the bad publicity.
      ii) It is not unusual to find that the source of the seemingly never-ending news stories about the case is the attorney handling the case for the family. Look at this source in explaining leaks to the news media.
      iii) Most attorneys will take these cases on a contingency basis. That is, they do not get paid unless they arrange a settlement or win a judgment. The more

criticism and accusations they can bring to the case, the better the chances for obtaining a judgment.

    d) News media

        i) Controversy creates interest. The bigger the story, the more newspapers will be sold or the more people who will watch the news programs. This means advertising dollars for the media.

3)   The investigation in these types of cases must not only be thorough but expeditious.

    a) Assume every case of this nature is going to court.

    b) Rarely do these cases involve deliberate wrongdoing on the part of the law enforcement or correctional agency, although the news media will insinuate that this is the case. The investigative agency is unable to refute these allegations because the investigators cannot make public statements as they conduct the investigation. There is no such gag restrictions on those individuals who are not part of the investigation and have no accountability after the investigation for anything they said that was less than accurate. Keeping the findings of the investigation confidential or secret plays into the hands of these individuals. To counter the accusations, present the findings of the investigation in a public forum, if at all possible.

4)   The scene visit may require caution, especially if conditions exist for violent crowd behavior. This information should be related to all responding parties to expedite handling. The sight of the dead body lying in the street may further antagonize the community.

5)   A review of all of the information available on the case should involve the prosecuting attorney, crime lab personnel, medical examiner pathologist/coroner, and investigating detectives.

6)   Make a concerted effort to have all reports completed and photographs developed within 3 days of the incident. These reports should include the autopsy, toxicology, crime lab, and initial investigative reports.

7)   In a situation where a police officer is possibly involved in the death of an individual, two separate investigations will be conducted.

    a) Internal affairs

        i) Investigators are concerned with any violations involving policy and procedures.

        ii) During an internal investigation, the police officer is covered by the officer's bill of rights.

        iii) Under an internal investigation, the officer may be compelled to submit a statement.

    b) Criminal investigation

        i) Investigators are concerned with whether the officer violated the law.

        ii) The police officer is entitled to protection under the U.S. Constitution.

        iii) The police officer may elect not to give a statement, as provided under the Fifth Amendment right against self-incrimination.

8)   The internal probe and criminal investigation should be conducted by two separate investigators.

    a) The investigator conducting the criminal investigation should not have access to the information developed by internal affairs, but the investigator conducting the internal probe can be present as the criminal investigator is developing information. Under these circumstances, however, the internal affairs representative should not ask questions or inject his ideas into the investigation. His only purpose at this point in the investigation is to observe.

b) Past experience has demonstrated that it is much easier to coordinate the two investigations by delaying the start of the internal affairs investigation until the criminal probe has been completed.

9) The investigation should be assigned to the most senior detective available.

10) Media considerations include these:

a) Any media release should come from one source.

b) Be considerate of the media for the job they have to do; they face tight deadlines and fierce competition to obtain information. Understand that if law enforcement agencies supply no information to the press, they are forced to obtain alternative sources of information, which may or may not be accurate.

PRIMARY FOCUS OF INVESTIGATION

1) Preserve the scene.

2) Determine cause of death.

3) Determine the manner of death.

4) Develop witnesses to the incident.

5) Develop and collect evidence.

6) Reconstruct the event to determine whether statements are consistent or inconsistent with regard to participants and witnesses.

7) Set up media controls.

NOTIFICATION

1) Initiate a major case squad call-out, including:

a) Forensic pathologist

b) Prosecuting attorney

c) Full crime lab capabilities, if necessary, including but not limited to:

i) Blood-spatter expert

ii) Firearms examiner

iii) Scene analysis unit

iv) Footprint/tire tread examiner

d) Grief counselors

SCENE PHOTOGRAPHS

1) Photograph the overall scene, including:

a) Aerial photographs of the scene

b) Relationship of building or vehicle to other buildings, landmarks, and streets

c) Address location of incident

        d) Overall shots of the area containing the decedent
        e) If it is a night scene, the location of illuminating street lights.

2)   Gather evidence relating to the particular incident, including but not limited to:
        a) Tire impressions
        b) Foot or shoe impressions
        c) Discarded cigarettes or cigarette packs
        d) Discarded cans or cups
        e) Any articles left behind
        f) Any weapon, ammunition, shell casings, or fired projectiles
        g) Any bullet holes
        h) Articles of clothing
        i) Fingerprint areas
        j) Hair or fibers
        k) Tool marks

3)   Photograph any area that may indicate any movement of the involved parties, including:
        a) Blood spatter
        b) Overturned, broken, or obviously disturbed articles.
        c) Rifled drawers, jewelry boxes, purses, wallets, safes, etc.
        d) Broken window or glass
        e) Drag marks

4)   Photograph any item that may indicate a disruption in the participants' activities at the time of the incident.

5)   Take photographs of the decedent.
        a) Photograph decedent from all four sides.
        b) Photograph the body in relation to certain features or evidence in the area (e.g., possible weapon, prescription vials).
        c) Take overall and close-up photographs of all wounds and areas of injuries.
        d) Photograph blood spatter on the clothing of the decedent.
        e) Photograph any area of bloodletting around or adjacent to the decedent.
        f) Photograph any unusual signs of activities involving the decedent's body:
            i) Pockets turned inside out
            ii) Unusual placement of weapon
            iii) Inconsistent position of the decedent's body with regard to rigor mortis or lividity
        g) Photograph the decedent's hands and feet.
        h) Photograph any apparent signs of drug abuse.
        i) Photograph the area under the decedent's body once the body has been removed.
        j) Photograph any trace evidence on the body.

SCENE INVESTIGATION

1)   Immediately rope off and maintain the security and integrity of the involved scene. No one is to be allowed into the scene except for the following:
        a) Homicide detectives
        b) Crime lab personnel and evidence technicians
        c) Prosecuting attorney
        d) Forensic pathologist

2)   Describe the scene.

3)   Describe the decedent's location within the scene as well as thse of all other participants and witnesses.

4)   Determine what happened.
        a) Identify, accumulate, and separate all witnesses.
        b) If possible, arrange for separate reenactment of the witnesses and participants.
        c) Detail activities of the decedent shortly before his death.
        d) Describe the activities of the decedent at the time of his death.
        e) Develop a history of the decedent.
            i) Specific complaints leading up to the death
            ii) Past medical history
            iii) Social history, including alcohol and drug habits
            iv) Employment history

5)   Make an observation of the decedent.
        a) Describe the position of the decedent's body.
        b) Describe the clothing worn by the decedent (include any signs of a struggle).
        c) Describe the time frame of death characteristics of the body.
        d) Describe any injuries observed.

6)   Set up media controls.
        a) The initial media release can include the following information (if the criteria for notification have been met and potential testimony of witness(es) will not be influenced).
            i) Identify who was killed.
            ii) Identify the name of the officer involved with the death.
            iii) Identify the location of the incident.
            iv) Identify the time that the incident occurred.
        b) The next media release should not take place until after the third-day conference, which is attended by the forensic pathologist, prosecuting attorney, investigating officers, crime lab personnel, and crime-scene technicians.

7)   If the decedent expired at the hospital, obtain the following information from attending physicians, nurses, and rescue personnel:
        a) Develop the date and time of subject's arrival at the hospital and the date and time the decedent was pronounced dead.
        b) Obtain medical opinion about the cause of death.
            i) Detail all of the decedent's injuries.
        c) Determine if any evidence was removed from the subject (e.g., projectiles, coring of gunshot wound).
        d) Determine if urine or pretransfused blood had been collected from the subject. If yes, make arrangements to obtain a specimen and transfer it to the forensic pathologist responsible for conducting the autopsy on the subject.
        e) Develop and detail medical treatment received by the subject:
            i) At the hospital
            ii) During rescue efforts
        f) Develop a listing of all medications given to the subject during his treatment.
        g) Determine if any statements were made by the subject to rescue attendants, nurses, or physicians.
        h) Collect the subject's clothing and valuables.

8) Investigate the scene of beating or shooting death.
    a) Identify and secure evidence at the scene, including but not limited to the following (if pertinent):
        i) Locate and secure the guns of all suspected shooters, including live ammunition contained in the weapons.
        ii) Locate and secure casings.
        iii) Locate and secure projectiles.
        iv) Locate all bullet holes.
        v) If a struggle is involved or if the officer was wounded, secure all clothes, holsters, flashlights, night sticks, radios, handcuffs, and shoes.
        vi) Identify, process, and impound any motor vehicles involved in the incident.
        vii) Identify blood spatter present at the scene.
        viii) If the incident happened at night, identify all sources of light in the area.
        ix) Obtain all radio transmissions about the incident.

9) Investigation of the death involving a prisoner in custody should include the following:
    a) Obtain a complete medical and social history of the victim, including past injuries or previous suicide attempts.
    b) Develop the reason the decedent came into contact with the police or corrections officer.
    c) Develop the details on the subject's arrest and be especially concerned with any injuries or statements made by the subject before, during, or after the original arrest.
    d) Develop any medical treatment received by the subject after his arrest.
    e) Obtain details on any phone calls the subject made following his arrest.
    f) Obtain any videotape from surveillance cameras that recorded the subject at any time during his confinement.
    g) Develop any individuals who may have had occasion to visit with, talk to, or observe the subject, including but not limited to:
        i) Food servers
        ii) Jail nurse
        iii) Counselors
        iv) Mail distributors
        v) Medication distributors
        vi) Trustees
    h) How was the decedent found? Detail the circumstances surrounding the discovery of the decedent, including:
        i) Who found the decedent?
        ii) Where was the decedent found?
        iii) When did this occur?
    i) Obtain a list of all personnel on duty during the time frame of the incident.
    j) If the body was found hanging:
        i) Detail how and by whom the body was taken down.
        ii) Is there any possibility the body may have been injured during this process?
        iii) What was used as a ligature?
        iv) How was the ligature placed at the point of suspension, and how was the ligature placed about the neck?
        v) Did corrections officers violate any jail regulations by failing to take away potential ligatures from the decedent?
        vi) Detail any resuscitation efforts or medical treatment the subject may have received immediately after his body was discovered.
    k) Obtain a list of all prisoners in the lockup, cells, exercise yard, etc., since the admission

of the subject. Include those who have already been released. Obtain enough identifying information about these potential witnesses to find them at some later date and time. Keep in mind, some prisoners may not feel comfortable talking about the incident while confined to this particular facility.

l) Photocopy the prisoner's check, visitor, and telephone log.

BODY TRANSPORT FROM SCENE

1) Transport the ligature, clothing, and any medications belonging to the subject.

2) If blood spatter on clothing is deemed important and there is a risk of losing the pattern during transport or while decedent is lying on a tray waiting for an autopsy examination, contact the forensic pathologist handling the case. Through the scene visit and with the approval of the pathologist, the clothing can be photographed and then removed from the decedent prior to transporting the remains.

3) Bag the hands of the decedent for transport to the MEO.

PROCESSING AT MEO/MORGUE

1) If a shooting death is suspected, perform a neutron activation swabbing on the hands of the decedent.

2) Take fingernail scrapings and clippings.

3) Obtain major case prints from the decedent.

4) Obtain any loose hair or fibers from the decedent.

5) Collect hair standards from the decedent.

6) Collect, air-dry, and separately bag the decedent's clothing.

7) Obtain a tube of blood for typing purposes.

FOLLOW-UP INVESTIGATION

1) The decedent's next of kin should be notified immediately.

2) Obtain photographs taken of the decedent during his arrest, booking, and incarceration.

3) Obtain details on any phone calls the subject made following his arrest.
   a) Contact these individuals and obtain any information the subject may have related about his mistreatment.
   b) Did the subject make any statement about his mental condition?

4) Interview all personnel who were on duty at the time of the incident.

5) Interview any prisoner who may have knowledge about the incident or who may have been in contact with the subject during some period of his incarceration.

6) Obtain the decedent's criminal history.

7) Obtain the personnel file of the involved officer, including:
    a) Length of service
    b) Record of training
    c) Promotional status
    d) Internal review profile, including complaints, commendations, use of force, etc.

CHAPTER 46: SCUBA-RELATED DEATHS

CONSIDERATIONS

1) Since 1970 there have been more than 3,000 scuba-diving deaths. Out of that number, approximately 300 occurred as a result of cave diving.

2) Most scuba fatalities are as a result of extra-alveolar air syndrome (air embolism) or being lost in a cave.
    a) Air embolism
        i) The deeper the dive, the greater the pressure on the diver's body. Due to this pressure, the air in the lungs becomes compressed, and more air is required to function. As the diver ascends to the surface, the air in the lungs begins to expand as the water pressure decreases. If the diver ascends too quickly or vessels in the lungs may rupture. With the ruptures, air bubbles enter the bloodstream, which prevents normal circulation of blood to the brain. Paralysis, permanent brain damage, or death may result.

3) There is a huge difference between open-water and cave diving.
    a) Open-water diving
        i) There is a direct vertical ascent to the surface at all times.
        ii) The age of 35 appears to be a significant benchmark involving the cause of diving fatalities.
            (1) Of diving fatalities involving divers over the age of 35, 22 percent were associated with heart problems (Voboril, 1990). .
            (2) In diving fatalities where the decedent is less than 35, heart attacks are involved in 1/2 of 1 percent (Voboril, 1990).
        iii) Divers in open water die when they get swept away by currents, snagged in underwater wrecks, hit by boats, or break the two cardinal rules of open-water diving—never hold your breath, and ascend to the surface slowly.
    b) Cave diving
        i) Cave diving is extremely dangerous. Out of the approximately 300 scuba deaths involving cave dives, 22 of these involved certified cave-diving instructors.
        ii) Just as a driver's license does not qualify one to fly a plane, an open-water diving certification does not qualify one to scuba dive in a cave.
        iii) Dangers include the following:
            (1) Cave ceiling
                (a) This prevents the diver from making a free ascent to the surface should anything go wrong.
            (2) Currents
                (a) Strong currents within the cave area can result in overexertion involving the diver. This can lead to many problems, including unplanned overuse of the air supply.
            (3) Silt
                (a) A diver must swim differently in a cave than in open water to avoid a careless flick of a flipper causing a silt-out. Even though the diver may be extra careful in avoiding stirring up the bottom, some silt may accumulate on ledges and walls of

cave and could cause a silt-out situation for the unsuspecting diver.

(b) Types of silt include the following:

(i) Sand, which is not too dangerous because it is heavy and usually settles back down quickly.

(ii) Mud, which is usually found near the entrance of the caves and can cause serious problems

(iii) Red clay, which is is sometimes compared to a powder-puff effect. It is extremely dangerous because it almost instantly produces a total silt-out condition with a cloud-like effect. Visibility is nonexistent even with a flashlight because the light produced is reflected toward the diver. A silt-out can take several days to clear.

(c) A cavern dive can turn into a cave dive with a total silt-out situation.

(4) Safety line

(a) Many of the caves break into mazes, necessitating a guide line.

(b) A safety line is the only way out of a cave when a total silt-out condition has been created.

(c) The line should only be used for guidance, never for pulling.

(d) The line should be of a certain quality so that it will sink if broken or cut.

(e) A slack line becomes very dangerous because it can cause the equipment or diver to become entangled.

(f) The diver's gear should be adapted or worn in such a way that it will not have the "danglies." That is, the equipment should not be loose, hang down, or dangle, which invites the diver's becoming entangled in the guideline.

(g) A diver should never swim under the line; he should swim over the line. Equipment behind the diver may cause the diver to become entrapped in the line.

(5) Swimming techniques must be adapted for cave diving. While in caves, the swimmer keeps his feet higher than his head and never swims (as sometimes occurs with open-water diving) in an upright or near-upright position. Cave divers are never supposed to swim very fast or fan their flippers rapidly; this avoids causing the silt to be stirred.

iv) Recovery divers usually know where they will find the bodies before they ever begin the retrieval process. The errors these divers make are predictable. In fact 90 percent of cave-diving fatalities involve an infraction of one or more of the following five rules:

(1) Be properly trained in cave diving.

(a) Scuba-diving equipment should be adapted for cave diving. The diver should have two complete regulators, double tanks, and three flashlights, and his gear should be worn close to the body with no surfaces open to collect and possibly entangle him in cord. If the diver elects to carry a knife, for example, the space between the sheath and the knife handle could create a situation where a cord entangles him.

(2) A direct line must be maintained to the entrance.

    (a) A diver venturing into a cave should carry a continuous line and know how to use it properly. An improper line can be as hazardous as not having one at all. Recovered bodies have been found wrapped in hundreds of feet of cord.

    (b) A line is necessary because of the large number of tunnels and the problem of silt. A large deposit of silt is normally present because there is little water flow in these areas. A careless pass of a flipper can cause an almost immediate and total silt-out. Depending on the type of silt, the cave may be in a silt cloud for days. In total silt-outs, the diver is unable to distinguish up from down, let alone find the small access used to enter the cave system. The only possible way for the diver to return to the surface is following a line. As mentioned, lights do no good, and the only way for the diver to return to the surface is to follow a line.

(3) Save two-thirds of the air in the tank to return to the surface. Only one-third of the air should be used for exploring the cave. The extra air in the tank should be saved for an emergency involving the diver or his partner.

    (a) For example, if a diver enters a cave with 1,500 pounds of air per square inch (psi), under the rule of thirds, the diver should only use 500 pounds of air for his and save the remaining 1,000 pounds for the return trip to the surface.

(4) Do not dive too deep. For most divers, the maximum depth is 130 feet.

(5) Have proper lights. Since cave diving is done in total darkness, three lights are recommended for use and backup.

v) The typical cave-diving fatality involves the following:

(1) The fatality will occur in Florida, although fatalities have occurred in Texas, Missouri, Kansas, Rhode Island, and Hawaii.

(2) On average, there are seven cave-diving deaths each year.

(3) The average victim is 26 years old.

(4) Although most occur in Florida, 60 percent of the victims are not Florida residents.

(5) Many victims are in the military.

(6) Many victims are certified open-water divers.

vi) Why do divers like the caves?

(1) Crystal-clear water

(2) Interesting rock formations

(3) The challenge of going where few others have been. Many equate the feeling as being as close to floating above the lunar surface as you can get.

vii) What lures untrained divers into the caves?

(1) Ego

(2) Curiosity

(3) False confidence

PRIMARY FOCUS OF INVESTIGATION

1) Establishing whether the death was caused by any one or resulted from a combination of the following:
   - a) Environmental conditions, including but not limited to:
     - i) Water conditions
     - ii) Adverse currents
     - iii) Entrapment potential
     - iv) Silt
     - v) Damage inflicted by boats in the area
     - vi) Marine life
   - b) Equipment operation, including but not limited to:
     - i) Scuba gear, including:
       - (1) Operation, proper use, and proper maintenance
   - c) Diver considerations
     - i) Experience, including proper training and certification for the particular dive
     - ii) Psychological problems
     - iii) Chemical problems
       - (1) Alcohol
       - (2) Drugs
       - (3) Carbon monoxide
     - iv) Physical illness

NOTIFICATION

1) No special notification of a pathologist is required.

2) A diver's network is available for the recovery of scuba-related fatalities. Contact the nearest qualified diver through NCIC.

SCENE PHOTOGRAPHS

1) No shots are expected if the dive is a rescue, not a recovery effort.

2) Of course, the scene will be extremely limited to a photographer unless one of the recovery team brings along an underwater camera. Even then, based on the water depth and clarity and the natural light, overall shots of the area are significantly affected.

3) Take overall shots of the area in which the fatality occurred (unless completely within open waters).

4) Close-up shots of the diver at the recovery site (if possible) and on the surface should include:
   - a) Condition and status of equipment:
     - i) Is the regulator in the subject's mouth?
     - ii) Is the equipment entangled or stuck on an object?
     - iii) What is the condiion of the flashlights?
     - iv) What do the pressure and depth-gauge recordings indicate?
     - v) What is the condition of he face mask?
     - vi) What is the buoyancy compensator status?
     - vii) What is the status of the weight belt?

b) Photograph any injuries evident on the decedent.

c) Photograph the decedent's condition from the standpoint of time frame of death.

d) Take some identification shots of the decedent (on the surface).

SCENE INVESTIGATION

1) Deceased diver profile, including the following:
   a) Diver's age, height, and weight
   b) Diving certification
   c) Number of years of experience diving
   d) Total number of dives the decedent had made during his lifetime
   e) Number of dives the decedent had conducted in the past 12 months
   f) General experience level:
      i) Noncertified
      ii) Novice (0 to 5 dives)
      iii) Inexperienced (6 to 20 dives)
      iv) Intermediate (21 to 40 dives)
      v) Advanced (41 to 60 dives)
      vi) Experienced (61 or more dives)
   g) Experience level with the particular activity diver was engaged in at the time of the fatality:
      i) Noncertified
      ii) Novice (0 to 5 dives)
      iii) Inexperienced (6 to 20 dives)
      iv) Intermediate (21 to 40 dives)
      v) Advanced (41 to 60 dives)
      vi) Experienced (61 or more dives)

2) Dive conditions
   a) Identify the particular location involved in the fatality.
   b) Identify the type of water entry:
      i) Shore
      ii) Private boat
      iii) Charter boat
   c) Identify the altitude of the incident location:
      i) Sea level
      ii) Less than 1,000 feet
      iii) Between 1,000 and 3,000 feet
      iv) Greater than 3,000 feet
   d) Identify water type:
      i) Salt or fresh water?
   e) What is the water temperature?
   f) What is the water depth at this location?
   g) Describe seas:
      i) Calm
      ii) Moderate
      iii) Rough
   h) What is the visibility of the water (in feet)?
   i) Describe surge condition:
      i) None

        ii) Mild
        iii) Moderate
        iv) Strong
   j) Describe weather conditions
   k) Describe the type of bottom present.
   l) Was this the first time the diver was at this location?
   m) Describe the diver's exposure suit.
   n) Was a dive tender present?
   o) How many people were in the dive party?
   p) Was a dive buddy present?
        i) If yes, did buddy separation occur?
   q) Describe the dive activity.
   r) Was this a specialty dive?
        i) If yes, describe.
        ii) If yes, was the diver specialty certified?

3)   Diver health
   a) Did the diver panic?
   b) Was the diver physically fit?
   c) Describe predive health of the diver:
        i) Nausea/vomiting
        ii) Hangover
        iii) Alcohol
        iv) Diarrhea
        v) No problem
        vi) Other (describe)
   d) Describe the mental status of the decedent befire the fatal dive:
        i) No problem
        ii) Stressed
        iii) Anxious
        iv) Quiet
        v) Talkative
        vi) Agitated
        vii) Other (describe)
   e) Describe any previous dive accidents involving the decedent.
   f) Describe any previous major illnesses involving the decedent.
   g) Describe any undiagnosed health problems the decedent may have complained about but did not seek medical attention for.
   h) Describe any current health problems involving the decedent.
   i) Identify any prescription medications taken by the decedent.
   j) Identify any nonprescription medications taken by the decedent.
   k) During the time of the incident, did fatigue, alcohol, or recreational drugs influence the decedent?

4)   Other dive factors
   a) Describe any equipment problems.
   b) Describe any buoyancy problems.
   c) What is the weight of the weight belt used by the decedent?
        i) Was the weight belt-dropped?
   d) Was the decedent familiar with the equipment used?

e) Is there any indication of nitrogen narcosis? If yes, describe.

f) Is there a possibility of rapid ascent? If yes, describe.

g) Describe the air supply:

    i) Scuba

    ii) Surface supplied

    iii) Mixed gas

    iv) Breathhold diving

    v) Buddy breathing/sharing air

h) Was the diver:

    i) Lost

    ii) Trapped

    iii) Entangled

5) Dive profile

a) Was this a single dive or part of a series of dives?

    i) If multiple dives were involved, describe the following for each dive:

        (1) Depth of dive (in feet)

        (2) Bottom time (in minutes)

        (3) Surface interval (in minutes)

b) Was a dive computer in use? If yes, what does it indicate?

6) Recovery and first aid

a) Was the event witnessed?

b) Problem occurred at:

    i) Surface/predive

    ii) Descent

    iii) Bottom

    iv) Ascent

    v) Surface/postdive

c) How long into dive did problem occur?

d) At what depth did problem occur?

e) Were there any signs diver was in distress? If yes, detail.

f) How soon after the incident did a search commence to find diver?

g) Identify the amount of time that had elapsed from the dive to the recovery of the body.

h) Describe any life-saving measures attempted.

BODY TRANSPORT FROM SCENE

1) Recover and transport all of the diver's gear and equipment.

PROCESSING AT MEO/MORGUE

1) Fingerprint the decedent.

FOLLOW-UP INVESTIGATION

1) It is recommended that you contact a qualified and knowledgeable diver to conduct the following investigation:

a) Examine diver's equipment.

        i) Tanks containing compressed air
            (1) Examine for dirt in the filter.
            (2) Consider having oxygen content of the residual air measured by a Beckman oxygen analyzer.
            (3) Status of air (quantity) remaining in the tank. Please note: because of the differences in air pressure associated with scuba diving, some air may erroneously register as being in the tanks when they are examined after surfacing.
        ii) The regulator
            (1) This works on a demand principle. Air will only come out when the diver sucks on the mouthpiece. Examination should include checking the mechanism for proper functioning.
        iii) Pressure and depth gauges
            (1) Pressure gauges are used in monitoring the air supply in the tank.
            (2) Depth gauges are used in monitoring the depth and ascent of the diver because the chances of his suffering an air embolism or nitrogen narcosis increase as the depth of the dive increases.
        iv) Buoyancy compensator
            (1) This consists of an air bladder that can be inflated or deflated to enable the diver to obtain neutral buoyancy (he neither rises nor sinks). This is critical when using the compensator to control ascent to the surface and reduce the possibility of an air embolism.
        v) Weight belt
            (1) This is used to compensate for the natural buoyancy of the diver's weight. Improper weight employment will result in the diver using too much of his tank's air.
    b) Examine diver's gear in cave-diving deaths. This should give investigators a good idea as to whether the cave diver knew what he was doing. For example:
        i) Tanks should not have a J valve, which has been known to malfunction and is easy to knock down. Double tanks are recommended.
        ii) The diver should be equipped with a dual-regulator system. One of the regulators could be used as a backup if the primary regulator fails. In addition, the backup regulator should be equipped with a longer regulator hose to facilitate buddy breathing should this emergency arise.
        iii) A buoyancy compensator should be present. This provides the diver with enough lift to not stir up the silt along the bottom.
        iv) Check the number of flashlights, and note battery status and on-off position of each.
            (1) Note: The power of the batteries may have been exhausted since the death and recovery of the remains.

2)   Report all scuba diving deaths to:

Diver's Automated Network (DAN)
Box 3823
Duke University Medical Center
Durham, NC 27710

National Underwater Accident Data Center
University of Rhode Island
Kingston, Rhode Island 02881

CHAPTER 47: SHARP-FORCE INJURIES

CONSIDERATIONS

1) Sharp-force injuries involving the manner of death
    a) Cutting and stabbing injuries are the second leading cause of homicidal deaths in the United States (after firearms-related deaths).
    b) They are initially distinguishable as a homice as opposed to a suicide or accident because of the following:
        i) There are a multiplicity of injuries present.
        ii) The area of the injury precludes the possibility of self-infliction.

MANNER OF DEATH CONSIDERATIONS

The multiple wounds eliminate any consideration except homicide for the manner of death in this case.

        iii) Self-defense type injuries can appear on the hands, arms, feet, or legs of the decedent.
        iv) The nature of the injuries may offer investigators important clues about the death. For example:
            (1) An unusual number of wounds present, suggesting an overkill, may indicate the following:
                (a) The perpetrator was acting in a rage at the time of the incident, which may suggest that he knew the victim since the assailant appears to want to destroy, not just kill, the victim.

DEFENSE WOUNDS

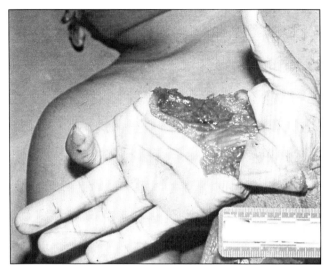
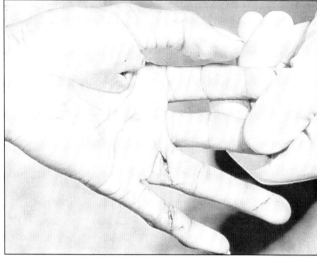

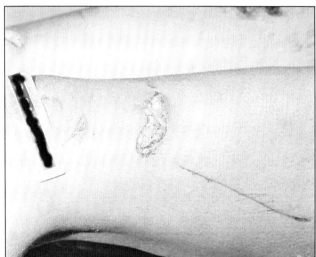

These photos demonstrate examples of defense wounds on stabbing victims. The injuries can occur from the victim's attempting to protect his body by blocking the action or grabbing the knife blade during the assaultive behavior. Defense wounds may also be present on the victim's legs. These usually occur as the victim is trying to keep the perpetrator away by kicking at him.

MULTIPLE STAB WOUNDS

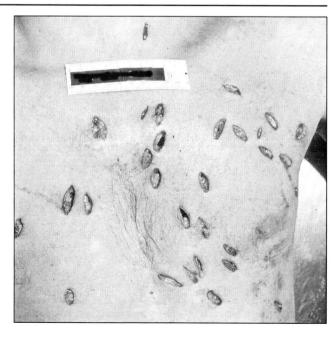

In a homicide case, multiple stab wounds on the victim may indicate to investigators that the perpetrator was angry with the decedent, the victim's death may have been sexually motivated, or the killer was inexperienced. In any multiple-stabbing scene, keep in mind that all the blood found at the scene may not belong to the victim.

(b) Multiple stab wounds should "red flag" the investigator to the possibility of a sexual motive for the case. In male victims, consider the possibility of a homosexual assailant.

(c) The perpetrator had difficulty killing the victim. This may indicate a lack of experience on the part of the perpetrator or a lack of planning for the homicide.

(2) Grouping of wounds in areas such as the breasts, vagina, penis, scrotum, or anus may indicate a sexual motivation for the homicide.

(a) Postmortem mutilation in these areas may indicate a psychotic personality, subject to criminal analysis profiling of the suspect.

HESITATION MARKS

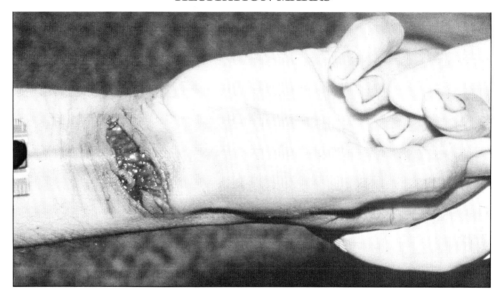

An example of a suicide by wrist slashing. The lethal wound is accompanied by many superficial cuts.

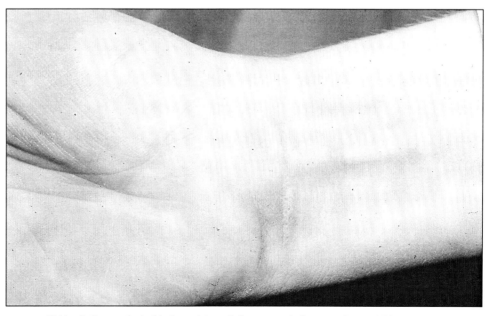

Old hesitation marks inside the wrists and elbows may indicate previous suicide attempts.

    c) Although not common, suicides by sharp-force injuries are not rare. Suicide by cutting is much more common than suicide by stabbing.

        i) Location of the wound is important.

            (1) The area involved must be accessible to the victim.

            (2) Vital parts of the body are generally picked to ensure a quick death. Favorite targets include throat, heart, or blood vessels of the wrist or at the bend of the arm inside the elbow.

        ii) Hesitation marks may be present at or near the site of the injury as the victim tests the sharpness of the weapon, the amount of pressure to apply, or the amount of pain associated with the attempt.

        iii) In most cases, the weapon should be found in close proximity to the decedent or by following a trail of blood. But death is not necessarily instantaneous, and recovery of the weapon may not be easy.

        iv) The victim of a suicide stabbing or cutting may open or remove clothing to gain direct access to the injured area.

        v) In anticipation of significant bloodletting, the victim will often complete the attempt in a bathtub or outdoors, or place protective covers over furniture or floors.

        vi) Associated injuries will be absent. The victim usually does not injure other areas of the body unless an alternative method has been tried and failed immediately prior to the fatal action.

        vii) Scars may be present indicating previous attempts. They will usually appear as clusters of parallel or crisscrossed thin scars. They are more commonly present on the wrist or neck.

        viii) The left- or right-handed nature of the wound should be noted, especially in those cases in which some dexterity may be indicated. Generally, a right-handed person inflicts wounds to the left side of the body, and a left-handed individual inflicts injuries to the right side of the body.

    d) Accidental (fatal) cuttings or stabbings are not very common.

        i) Most cases of accidental fatal cuttings or stabbings involve freak accidents such as plate glass shattering or boat propellers spinning out of control.

2)   Classification of sharp-force injuries

    a) Cut or incised wounds

        i) A wound longer than it is deep and made by a sharp edged instrument is classified as a cut or incised wound.

INCISED WOUND

An example of an incised wound. Sliding the sharp edge of the instrument across the involved area produces the wound.

(1) No bridging of tissue should be discernible inside the wound since the edges of the wound should be clean and the deep tissues divided cleanly and evenly. The cut should bleed freely.

DISTINGUISHING A LACERATION FROM AN INCISED WOUND

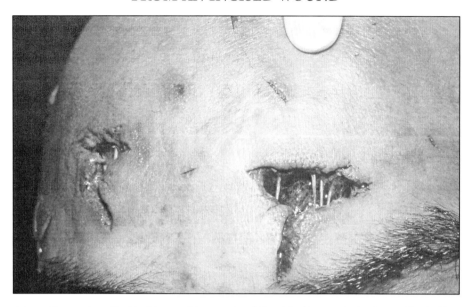

A laceration produced by blunt-trauma injury can be distinguished from an incised wound by looking down into the wound itself. Blunt trauma causes the skin to tear away from the force of the trauma, leaving behind tears of skin and bridging tissue. A sharp incision should not leave behind any traces of bridging tissue because that should have been cut through during the incision process.

(2) The wound is produced by a sliding action.
(3) The skin adjacent to the cut seldom shows any sign of bruising.
(4) The beginning of a cutting wound is usually deeper than the end of the wound.
(5) A cut wound made by a piece of glass, metal, or other object that has sharp edges may show some of the characteristics of a wound made with a cutting instrument. Some differences that may be noted in the incised wounds of this instrument compared with those made by a razor blade, scalpel, or sharp knife include:
    (a) Generally the former will have more ragged or irregular edges due to the skin being pulled into small folds in front of the advancing cutting edge.
    (b) The former may have bruises along the margin of the wound caused by the pressure of the object doing the cutting.
    (c) The former may have parts of the cutting object or foreign material in the wound.

STAB WOUND

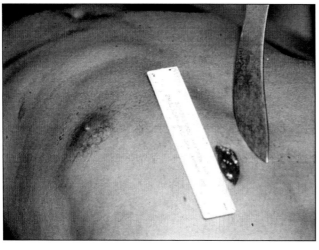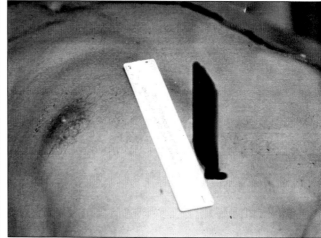

A thrusting motion is used to produce a stab wound. The second photo represents the knife handle with the blade embedded in the wound.

SHARP-FORCE INJURIES

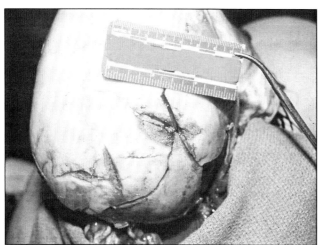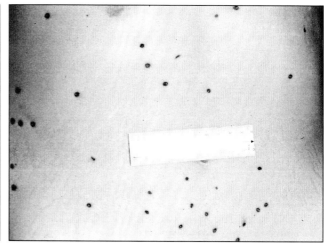

Example of a chopping wound involving an ax.
Example of multiple-puncture wounds produced by an ice pick.

b) Stab wounds
  i) A wound produced by a thrusting action. The wound is deeper than it is long.
c) Chopping wounds
  i) A wound produced by a heavy bladed instrument (e.g., ax, hatchet, machete, cleaver, sword) moving toward the object. Crush and sharp wounds appear together. The crushing force produces contusions.
  ii) If the cutting edge of a chopping weapon is dull, the tissues are contused and lacerated as well as incised.
d) Puncture wounds
  i) A wound produced by an instrument with a sharp point but without sharp edges (e.g., ice pick, screwdriver)
    (1) The wound may exhibit characteristics similar to those of a gunshot wound (i.e., a circular defect surrounded by a margin of abrasion).
    (2) Pairing of puncture wounds usually indicates an item with a set of prongs (e.g., barbecue fork, scissors).

3)   Determinations from the features of sharp-force injuries
        a) Width of the wound
                i) How the wound appears on the body is based on stress or tension lines involving the skin and referred to as "Langer's lines" or "lines of cleavage." The problem in estimating the width of the blade in comparison with the width of the wound lies in the cutting nature of a blade. In a stabbing action, the blade will rarely go straight in and be withdrawn sraight out. There is usually some cutting to adjacent areas during the insertion and withdrawal of the blade.

LANGER'S LINES OF CLEAVAGE

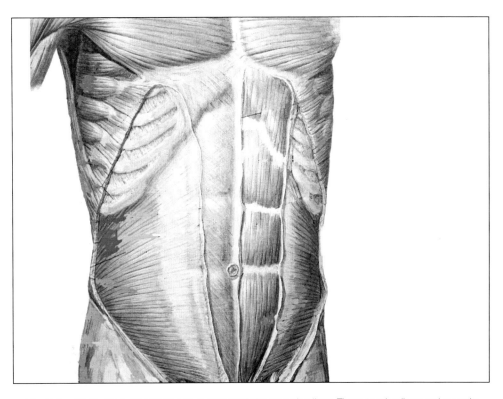

Like the grain in wood, human muscle is arranged along tension lines. These tension lines, or Langer's lines, influence the appearance of sharp-force injury.

                    (1) If an incised wound is made parallel to the skin and muscle fibers, the wound is long and narrow.
                    (2) If the muscle and tissue are cut across the grain or at an oblique angle, the wound will appear as a gaping injury with the muscles retracting and separating at the wound edge. The retraction causes eversion of the skin edges and may produce varying degrees of distortion of the shape of the wound.
                    (3) The stab wound may appear to be V-shaped or fishtailed. This tends to indicate that the knife blade was either twisted upon insertion or during the withdrawal phase of the stabbing.
        b) Depth of the wound
                i) The depth of the wound should be not used to gauge the length of the knife. The knife may have not been inserted to its full extent, or the elasticity of the tissue involved may have allowed the knife blade to travel much farther into

STAB WOUND APPEARANCE ON SKIN

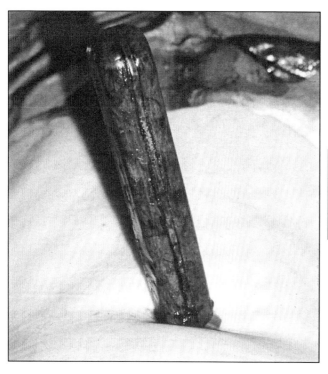

The varied appearance of stab wounds may make it seem that a second or third weapon was involved. In fact, the variety in appearance may be attributable to the location of the stab wound on the skin, as well as the muscle tension line involved.

V-SHAPED STAB WOUND

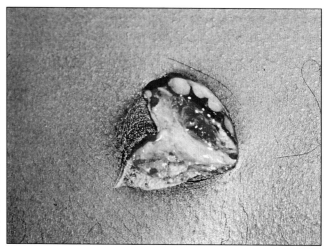

An example of a V-shaped stab wound indicates a twisting, stabbing thrust.

ELASTICITY OF STAB WOUND AREA

The depth of the wound is not particularly indicative of the length of the offending weapon. Where on the body the victim is stabbed is one of the considerations associated with this interpretation. The elasticity of the area stabbed, the force with which the person is stabbed, and the depth of the insertion are some of the variables a pathologist considers.

WOUNDS MADE BY A SINGLE- AND DOUBLE-EDGED KNIFE BLADE

An example of a wound made by a double-edged blade.

An example of a wound made by a single-edged blade.

SERRATED KNIFE BLADE

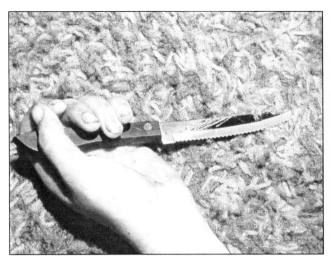 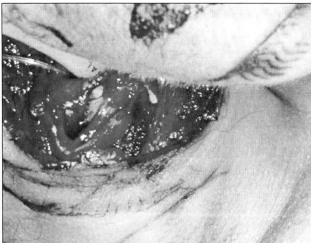

A serrated knife blade marks the injury site with small scratches accompanying the adjacent areas of major sharp-force injury.

the tissue as a result of the thrusting pressure associated with the insertion.

ii) The exception to gauging the length of the weapon by the depth of the wound is stab wounds to the side involving the rib cage. This is a fairly inflexible area and may indicate the length of the weapon.

iii) The character of the blade

    (1) Single-edged

        (a) The wound appears with a sharp edge on one end and a blunt, square back edge. Often, the blunt edge will show two small tears appearing as "rabbit ears."

        (b) The blade thickness may be discerned if the blade has passed through cartilage or bone.

    (2) Double-edged

        (a) Both edges have a sharp appearance.

    (3) Serrated

        (a) Usually single-edged, it isn't normally distinguishable from a single-edged unserrated blade unless there has been an effort, either deliberate or undeliberate to incise an area rather than stab. In these cases an interrupted pattern of abrasion may be present, leading to or away from the wound.

    (4) Hilt mark

        (a) A contusion around a stab wound may be caused by the hilt of the weapon if enough force was used to thrust the weapon into the body.

        (b) This contusion should be examined closely because a particular pattern may be present to align with the hilt of a particular weapon.

4)   Lethality of injuries

    a) People who are stabbed or cut die from hemorrhaging (exsanguination).

        i) The scene in which the stabbing or cutting occurs may or may not contain a significant amount of blood. Wounds may reseal due to tissue pressure, or the victim may fall in such a way that the skin surface wound is facing upward. Massive internal hemorrhaging may be occurring but will not be noticed unless the body is rolled over.

ii) Victims suffering injuries to their abdominal viscera, especially to the bowel area, may not die immediately from the hemorrhaging but rather from complications associated with peritonitis or sepsis.

iii) Stab or incised injuries are rarely immediately incapacitating, except in the following or similar cases:

(1) Severe chopping injuries of the head or stabbing of the head affecting the basal ganglia or brainstem

(2) Stab wound of the heart with a rapidly developing pericardial tamponade

(3) Stab wounds to the back where the spinal cord is penetrated

(4) A stab wound affecting the kidney so painful that it incapacitates the victim.

iv) A fatal injury may occur when an artery or vein is cut. An artery that is only partially severed will bleed much more than a completely severed artery. In a complete transection, the artery's ends will retract, causing a partial self-sealing to occur. This does not happen in a partial transection.

5)   Evidence considerations in sharp-force injuries

a) Trace evidence

i) Close physical contact had to have occurred between the victim and the assailant for the victim to sustain sharp-force injuries. The possibility of recovering such meaningful trace evidence as hair and fibers is excellent.

(1) Examine the decedent's hands and fingernails before bagging (paper) the hands and transporting the decedent to the morgue.

b) Clothing

i) The examination of clothing becomes critically important in a sharp-force injury death, especially in those cases where the victim does not die immediately (a delayed-fatal death). Not only is the potential for the recovery of trace evidence important, but the character and dimension of the offending weapon may be more discernible through examination of the clothing than in the examination of the wound.

ii) On those cases in which rescue personnel have been called to the scene and even
transported the victim to the hospital prior to his expiring, make a diligent effort to seek and recover any articles of clothing that may have been removed from the victim during lifesaving measures.

iii) Bloodletting involving the decedent usually allows for reconstruction of a preserved scene.

(1) Don't overlook the possibility that blood present at the scene belongs to the assailant. This may become obvious only after reconstructing the event.

(2) Because of the slippery nature of blood, the thrusting force necessary to effect a stabbing injury, the assumed lack of cooperation by the victim, and the gripping requirement of the weapon used by the assailant, the assailant's hand may slip onto the blade, causing an incised wound and producing blood spatter at the scene. It will usually be brought to the scene investigator's attention by the blood spatter's nonconformity with other blood present at the scene. This

STAB WOUNDS THROUGH CLOTHING

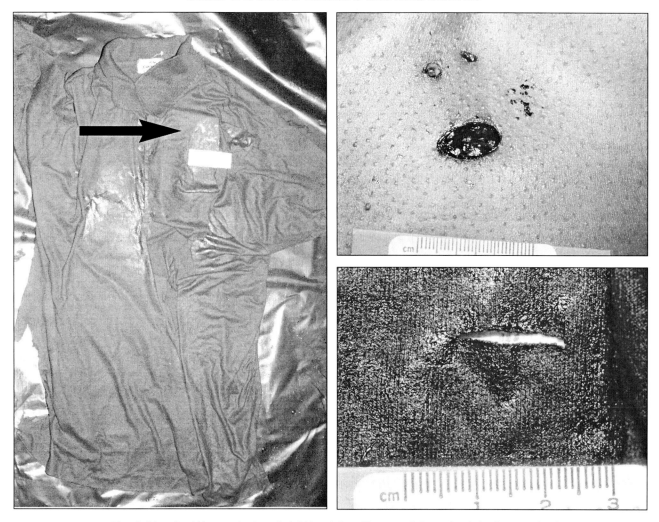

The clothing should be acquired on all stabbing victims. The wound site on the victim does not clearly indicate the type of blade that may have been used to bring about the decedent's death. The shirt of the victim clearly indicates the single-edged-blade nature of the offending weapon.

may be a distinct possibility in those scenes suggesting that a prolonged struggle may have occurred.

iv) Always X-ray the decedent. The possibility exists that the knife tip has broken off when striking bone and may still be in the body.

v) Tool mark identification is possible if the knife blade struck bone.

PRIMARY FOCUS OF INVESTIGATION

1) What is the cause and manner of death?

2) What type of instrument was used to cause the death?
    a) Did the particular weapon submitted as the fatal weapon cause the wounds?

3) How much time elapsed between the time the wound was inflicted and the death?

4) Were the injuries inflicted before or after death?

WEAPON DETERMINATION

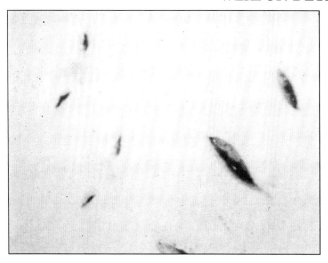

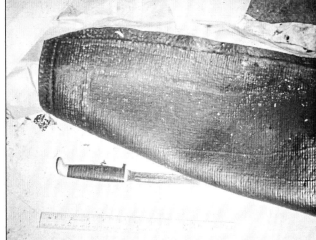

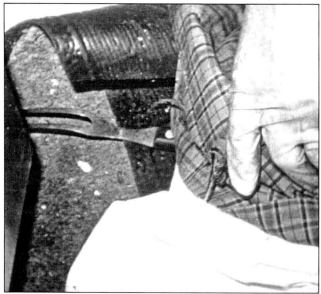

The victim suffered multiple stab wounds depicted in the top left photo. The original medical information indicated that the decedent's wounds were attributed to the knife recovered at the scene. In fact, a barbeque fork, recovered at the scene, made the smaller wounds. Determining how many weapons were used on the victim is incredibly important to homicide detectives because it may indicate how many perpetrators were involved in the homicide.

NOTIFICATION

1)   The pathologist should be requested on all homicides or deaths of uncertain manner where the following details may be in question:

   a) Time frame since death
   b) Type of weapon causing the death
   c) Possible activities associated with bloodletting

2)   The pathologist should be requested on any case in which the manner of death is undetermined or confused, or the decedent or some other interested party appears to have attempted to alter the circumstances of the death.

3)   If the body is badly decomposed or skeletonized, a forensic anthropologist may be desired at the scene.

FORENSIC ANTHROPOLOGY AND SHARP-FORCE INJURY

An example of why a forensic anthropologist should be used in all cases involving the recovery of skeletal remains, decomposed bodies, and fire-related deaths. The rib bone in this photograph shows the small incised area indicative of a sharp-force injury. A cause of death has now been established.

SCENE PHOTOGRAPHS

1) Follow the death scene photographic guidelines relating to the particular circumstances of the case (e.g., outdoor, indoor, vehicle scenes). In addition, give particular attention to the following:

    a) Photograph the resistance that may have been demonstrated by the decedent.

        i) Torn clothing, including buttons ripped from clothing

        ii) Defense injuries to hands, arms, legs, and feet

        iii) Eyeglasses broken or thrown on the floor

        iv) Rifled purse, wallet, dresser drawers, jewelry box, safe, pulled-out pockets from decedent's pants, etc.

        v) Overturned furniture

    b) Photograph any weapon present, including the following:

        i) Relationship of weapon with location and position of body

        ii) Area where weapon may have originated and any other matching utensils

demonstrating origination of cutting or stabbing tool (e.g., a meat-carving knife rack located in the residence where the decedent was found)
      iii) A close-up photograph showing the knife with and without a ruler present
      iv) Close-up photograph of any trace evidence observable on the suspected weapon
   c) Photograph the body of the decedent, including the following:
      i) All areas of injuries involving the decedent
      ii) All areas of blood on the decedent, his clothing, and his feet, socks,or shoes (soles of feet or shoes)
      iii) All areas of blood immediately adjacent to the body
      iv) The body condition as it relates to time frame of death
      v) Any inconsistencies with regard to the time frame of death as evidenced by the condition of the remains
         (1) Rigor mortis
         (2) Lividity
      vi) Photographs of any transfer evidence observable on the decedent
      vii) Photographs of any indication of animal or insect activity involving the decedent's body
      viii) Photographs of any apparent efforts by rescue workers to resuscitate the decedent.
   d) Photographs of all evidence or items that depict the circumstances of the incident.
      i) Directional evidence, including:
         (1) Blood spatter
         (2) Glass fractures
         (3) Footprints, tire tracks, etc.
      ii) Relational evidence or evidence present that may be related to the incident (for example, a hat found on top of the kitchen counter that may not belong to anyone who lives at the residence).
      iii) Inferred evidence, which is significant in its absence (for example, dust surrounding a clean area on top of a television set that may indicate a VCR has been taken).

SCENE INVESTIGATION

1)   Locate and develop information from the essential informants, including:
   a) Eyewitnesses
   b) Persons who found the body or were first at the scene
   c) Doctor, nurses, or EMTs who gave medical attention

2)   From the original scene of the incident develop the following information:
   a) Exact time of incident
   b) Exact time when the decedent was found
   c) Description of the building, room, or place where body was found
   d) Reason the decedent was at this this location
   e) Exact position of the body
   f) Clothing worn by the decedent
      i) Note any tears, missing buttons, blood stains, etc.
   g) The exact position of any knife or sharp bladed instrument found on the scene
   h) Any other (possible) weapon and its location
   i) Any other items of potential evidence, including blood spatter, overturned furniture,

ransacked drawers, suicide note, etc., and their locations
    j) If the decedent was alive when found, any comments he made

3)   Develop a weapon description.
    a) Describe any sharp instrument believed to be associated with the injuries incurred by the decedent:
        i) Include measurement of the utensil, type of utensil, and whether or not the item was brought to the scene or was from the scene originally.
        ii) Describe the type of edge visible on this item.
        iii) Who is the owner of this item?
    b) If the weapon is not inserted in the decedent when he is found, is there any blood or other trace evidence visible on it?

4)   Give wound description.
    a) Describe the areas of apparent injury to the decedent.
        i) Inspect the hands for defense marks.
        ii) Was the decedent stabbed through his clothing or was the clothing pulled away to effect the cutting or stabbing?

5)   Describe the circumstances.
    a) Describe what happened.
    b) If there is any suggestion that the decedent's death may be accidental, describe this in detail.
    c) What is the cutting instrument is normally used for what purpose? Where is item normally kept? Where was item prior to the stabbing or cutting?
    d) Is the decedent right- or left-handed?
    e) Describe the events preceding the death. Detail any comments made by the decedent during this period.

BODY TRANSPORT FROM SCENE

1)   If blood interpretation may be significant in this case, consider removing affected items of clothing before transporting the remains (obtain prior approval from the on-call pathologist).

2)   Check the remains for any possible trace evidence. If these items may be lost during transport, the evidence technician should collect them after photographing them.

3)   Bag (paper) the decedent's hands.

PROCESSING AT THE MEO

1)   If homicide involved or suspected or if suicide is not a certainty:
    a) Consider examining the body for latent or patent prints.
    b) Collect any trace evidence that may be present.
    c) Collect the bags used to cover the decedent's hands while in transit to the morgue.
    d) Collect fingernail scrapings and clippings from the decedent.
    e) Obtain pulled and combed hair standards from the decedent.
    f) Collect a tube of blood for typing purposes.
    g) Obtain major case prints.
    h) Collect, air-dry, and separately pack any item of clothing of the decedent.

2) If the case is a homicide, collect whatever evidence may be required based on the motive indicated. For example, complete sexual swabbings if sexual homicide is indicated.

3) If the decedent is skeletonized or badly decomposed, the pathologist may consult a forensic anthropologist prior to conducting an autopsy. The significance of finding knife marks on the bone under microscopic examination may be markedly reduced because of the use of a scalpel in the area by the pathologist during an autopsy examination.

FOLLOW-UP INVESTIGATION

1) If the case is a homicide, follow guidelines for the motive suggested by the homicide.

2) If the case is suicide, follow the guidelines listed in Chapter 26.

3) If an accident is indicated:
    a) Reconstruct the events based on the evidence acquired and statements made to the investigators.
    b) Obtain complete background information on the decedent, including:
        i) Financial (include status of insurance policies)
        ii) Health (include any psychiatric or physical problem that may have contributed to the incident)
        iii) Domestic
    c) Develop any previous accidents involving the decedent.

ACTIVITY OF VICTIM AFTER SHARP-FORCE INJURY

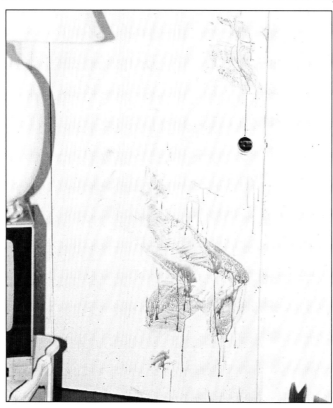

This person, suffering from sharp-force injuries, held the door shut while the killer was attempting to push it open. Her body outline, in blood, is seen against the door.

STAB WOUND SEQUENCE

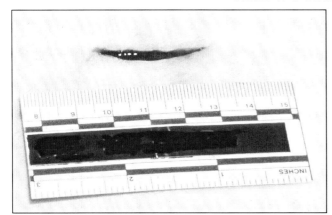
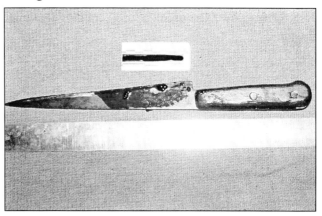

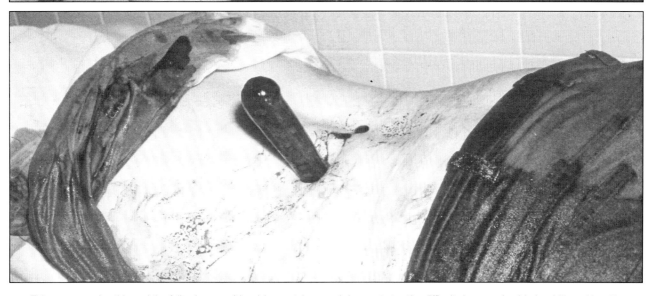

This sequence (on this and the following page) involving a stab wound demonstrates the difficulty in assessing blade width and length.
A knife may not be plunged directly into a struggling body, therefore causing a wound that is wider than the blade width.
Depending on where the person is stabbed and the force with which the knife is plunged into the body, the depth of the
wound may be much greater or much shorter than the length of the blade.

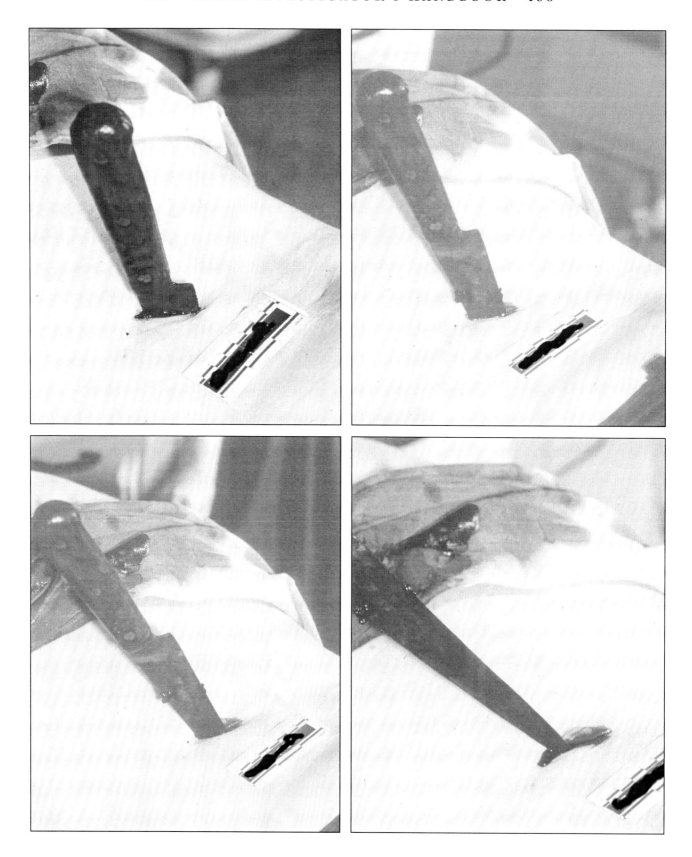

CHAPTER 48:
RAILROAD DEATH INVOLVING A PEDESTRIAN

CONSIDERATIONS

1) This includes deaths involving:
   a) Pedestrians versus trains
   b) Driver or passenger of a vehicle involved in a collision with a train.

PRIMARY FOCUS OF INVESTIGATION

1) Suicide versus accident versus homicide

2) Identification of the decedent

NOTIFICATION

1) No special notification is required unless the scene investigation begins to indicate that the body may have been dead when placed on the tracks. Notification to the on-call pathologist should then be made.

SCENE PHOTOGRAPHS

1) Overall scene, including any unusual features of the landscape that may have contributed to the cause of the incident (e.g., track curves, trestle, multiple tracks)

2) Point of impact at track site

3) Point of impact on the train

4) Final resting place of body

5) Path of the body from initial impact to the final recovery site

6) Any indications of alcohol or drug use or abuse

SCENE INVESTIGATION

1) Develop any eyewitnesses, including the engineer of the train.

2) Determine the speed of the train.

3) Is the track crossing smooth or rough at the impact site?

4) How many tracks is it necessary to cross? Which track was the involved train traveling on at the time of impact?

5) Were there any warning lights, barriers, or train whistles that could have alerted the subject?

6) Were there any visual obstructions (e.g., trees, shrubbery, houses, curves) at the approach? How far could the train be seen before reaching the point of impact?

7) Was the decedent familiar with this area of tracks? Did the decedent cross these tracks often or was he a stranger to this area?

8) Was the decedent familiar with the train schedule? Was the train involved in the incident a regularly scheduled train? Was the train on time?

9) What were the weather conditions (e.g., foggy, rainy, clear)?

10) What was the decedent doing at the time of the incident and immediately preceding the impact?

11) Was there any evidence of alcohol? Were alcohol containers found at the scene? Was the smell of alcohol noted on observing the decedent?

12) Did the decedent have a history of poor eyesight, impaired hearing, heart attacks, vertigo, or fainting spells? Did the decedent wear glasses? Were glasses found?

13) Where was the decedent heading? Was the decedent driving with a time limitation?

14) Obtain drug abuse and prescriptive history of the decedent.

TRANSPORTING REMAINS

1) No special handling required unless it is suspected that the decedent may be a homicide victim.

2) If homicide is suspected, it is possible that the decedent may have been carried to the impact location. A transfer of hair or fiber may have occurred.
   a) Wrap the decedent in a clean sheet for transporting to the MEO/morgue.

PROCESSING AT MEO/MORGUE

1) If this case is not a homicide, fingerprint the decedent.

2) If it is a homicide, collect the following:
   a) Transport sheet
   b) Separately bagged clothing
   c) Fingernail scrapings
   d) Head hair standards

3) Consider identification procedures, if warranted.

FOLLOW-UP INVESTIGATION

1) If suicide is possible, follow the guidelines in Chapter 26.

2) If homicide is indicated, follow the specific guidelines related to the suspected motive.

CHAPTER 49:
TRAFFIC FATALITY—VEHICLE VERSUS VEHICLE

CONSIDERATIONS

1) Occupant kinematics
- a) The study of the type of movements that the bodies of vehicle drivers and passengers are subjected to as a result of a traffic collision
- b) The study combines some basic laws of physics with the principles of human anatomy and physiology, thus allowing some predictions to be made regarding the likelihood of personal injuries from a given type of accident.
- c) Principal factors involving the vehicle versus another vehicle are the following:
  - i) The direction of travel
  - ii) The angle of the collision
  - iii) The state of health of the occupants and the presence of preexisting conditions
  - iv) The speeds at which the vehicles were traveling before the collision
    - (1) Fast-moving vehicles produce more damage than slower moving ones.
- d) Occupant kinematics becomes an integral part of the scene reconstruction and is critically important to the traffic homicide investigator and the medical examiner in understanding what may have happened.
- e) The mass or weight of the involved vehicles is critical.
  - i) Heavier vehicles are more destructive than lighter vehicles traveling at the same speed.
- f) Whether or not the restraints were used or properly adjusted (e.g., headrests, lap and shoulder harnesses) is important.
- g) What was the crashworthiness of the involved vehicle?
  - i) It is the energy not absorbed by the vehicle components during a collision that is transmitted and injures the occupants.
  - ii) Design engineers of vehicles consider it desirable that vehicles crush easily, thus absorbing most of the energy of the impact.
- h) What was the type of occupant-restraining system?
- i) What was the duration of the impact?
  - i) Shorter impacts are more dangerous because there is no time for the dissipation of the collision energy.

2) Mechanics of a vehicle crash with a stationary object

3) Types of crashes
- a) Head-on collision
  - i) Types of injuries
    - (1) Driver
      - (a) Face goes into the windshield.
        - (i) Facial lacerations
        - (ii) Possible skull fractures
      - (b) Head goes into the roof or steering wheel.
        - (i) Possible frontal skull fractures (racooning of eyes)
        - (ii) Possible subdural and subarachnoid hemorrhage
        - (iii) Possible frontal and temporal lobe contusions

COLLISION OF VEHICLE AT 30 MILES PER HOUR

0.00   Moving vehicle strikes a stationary object. Vehicle comes to an abrupt stop.

0.10   Moving driver or passenger strikes the now stationary vehicle.

0.12   Internal organs of the driver or passenger strikes the now stationary skeletal frame.

(c) Chest and abdomen slam into the steering wheel.
    (i) Possible cardiac contusion and laceration
    (ii) Possible aortic laceration
    (iii) Possible fractures of sternum and ribs
    (iv) Possible liver and spleen lacerations
    (v) Knees slam into dashboard.
        1. Possible fracture of femur, tibia, or pelvis
        2. Possible posterior dislocation of hip
        3. Possible dislocation of ankle

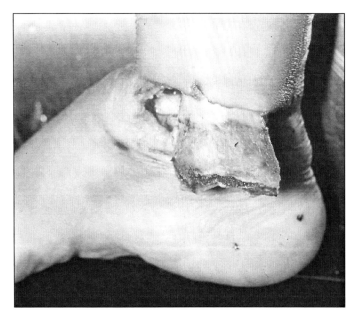

An example of a dislocated ankle injury incurred by a driver in a head-on crash. The sudden stopping of the vehicle, combined with the crushing of the occupant cabin toward the passengers, caused the fractured ankle.

        (2) Front passenger
              (a) Worst possible position in a crash, with twice the incidence of serious injury than that of the driver.
              (b) Head, chest, and abdomen will usually slam into the dashboard.
        (3) Rear passenger
              (a) Less severe injuries because the front seat acts as a restraint
              (b) The unrestrained passenger tends to hit his head on the roof, causing severe head injury.
              (c) The rear passenger wearing a seat belt (sash type)
                    (i) Possible lumbar spine fractures
                    (ii) Possible pelvic fracture
                    (iii) Possible rupture of duodenum or pancreatic contusions.
b) Side impact (T-bone, T-bar collisions)
    i) Occupants of the vehicle are subject to serious injuries because the vehicle is usually constructed to withstand head-on collisions. Penetration into the cabin area produces injuries.
        (1) Occupant will usually be injured as a result of:
              (a) Direct impact
              (b) Being thrown against the opposite side of the vehicle
              (c) Deceleration injuries
c) Rear impact to the vehicle
    i) The seat provides adequate protection unless the cabin is crushed.
d) Roll-over of vehicle
    i) Types of injuries
        (1) Collapse of the roof onto the occupant may result in traumatic asphyxia due to the compression of the chest.
              (a) Develop extrication details.

(2) Various type of injuries as the decedent may come into contact with various surfaces, including the road, during the roll-over process, including:
    (a) Skull fractures
    (b) Spinal fractures
    (c) Chest and abdominal injuries
    e) Ejection of occupant
        i) Unrestrained occupants, especially in roll-over and head-on collisions will suffer the following injuries:
            (1) Massive head injuries
            (2) Crush-type injuries to the chest
            (3) Multiple rib fractures
            (4) Deceleration (driving force) injuries including aortic laceration or cardiac contusions
            (5) Lacerations to the liver, spleen, or kidneys
            (6) Pelvic fractures
            (7) Long-bone fractures
            (8) Glass and road abrasions

4) Determination of who was driving the vehicle
    a) Just one occupant of vehicle
    b) Person wedged into driver's seat by instantaneous collapsing cabin
    c) Person found in driver's seat with seat belt clasped
    d) Injuries and bloodletting of decedent consistent with damage and blood spatter observed at the scene and in the vehicle
    e) Trace evidence (e.g., hair, fibers, blood) from a particular area of the vehicle consistent with the decedent's being the operator of the vehicle
    f) Brake or accelerator pedal impression on the shoe sole of the suspected driver
    g) Witness statements

PRIMARY FOCUS OF INVESTIGATION

1) Identify the decedent.

2) Establish the cause of death.

3) Establish the manner of death.
    a) Vehicular suicide
    b) Accident
    c) Homicide
    d) Natural cause

4) Who was the operator (driver) of the vehicle?
    a) What were the seating arrangements of the passengers?

5) What was the cause of the crash?
    a) Human error?
        i) What is the lethal injury?
        ii) Did natural disease contribute to the crash?
        iii) Was the driver's ability to operate the vehicle impaired by alcohol or drugs?

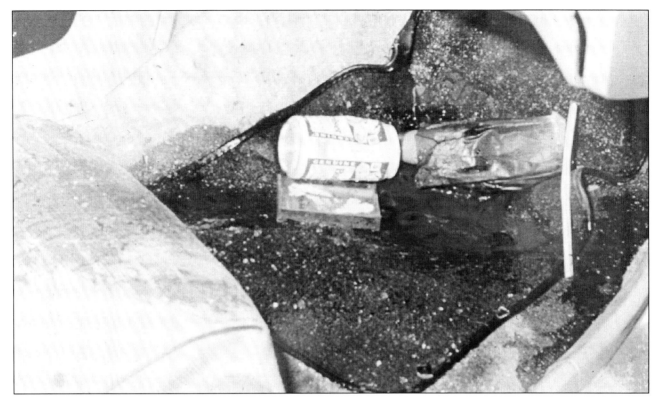

Suspicion of alcohol consumption should always be suspected in car crashes. Investigators should be alert for alcohol containers inside a vehicle or the smell of "stale" alcohol when handling the decedent.

            iv) Were seat belts in use?
            v) Was an infant car seat in use?
            vi) Did the driver fall asleep at the wheel?
            vii) Was the vehicle speeding?
      b) Vehicle malfunction?
            i) What role, if any, did the vehicle's mechanical operation play in the crash?
                  (1) Tires
                  (2) Brakes
                  (3) Seat belt
                  (4) Air bag deployment
                  (5) Other mechanical defaults? If yes, detail condition.
      c) Weather conditions
            i) Weather conditions that could have contributed to the cause of the accident
            ii) Rain, wet pavement, or standing water
            iii) Fog
            iv) Snowy or icy conditions
            v) High winds
      d) Roadway conditions
            i) Poor lighting
            ii) Roadway construction
            iii) Detour
            iv) Dangerous curve or other road hazard

6)   Reconstruct the incident.

NOTIFICATION

1)   No special notification is required unless the following conditions exist:
     a) There are multiple fatalities.
     b) Fire makes identification of occupants difficult.
     c) Reconstruction of the incident is particularly difficult.
     d) Circumstance indicate that the decedent did not die as a result of the accident and that the accident was staged to conceal a homicide.

SCENE PHOTOGRAPHS

PHOTOGRAPHING A CRASH VEHICLE: 14 POINTS

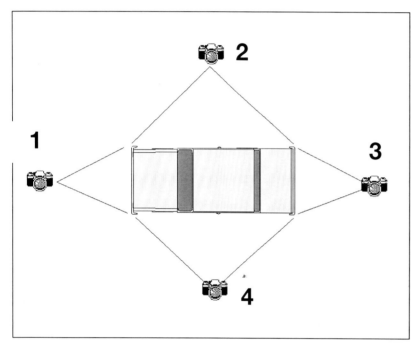

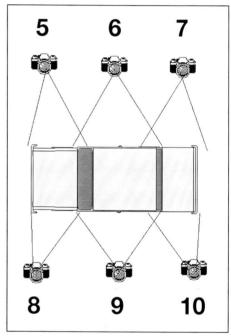

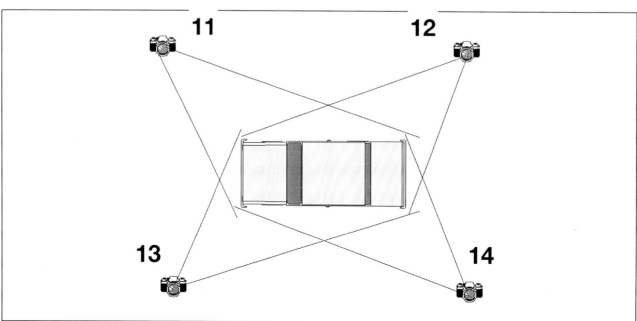

1) Photograph the following in relation to the overall area:
    a) Vehicle(s) involved
    b) Victim(s) thrown from vehicle
        i) Cloth, tissue, blood spatter on roadway surface
    c) Skid marks
    d) Vehicle debris, including:
        i) Broken glass, plastic, chrome, etc.
    e) Property damaged during the incident
    f) Any areas that may have acted as an obstruction
        i) Hills, curves in roadway, signs, bushes, etc.
    g) Any fluid spills
        i) Oil, coolant, battery acid, etc.

2) Determine the point of impact at the scene.

3) Determine the final resting place of vehicles in relation to the point-of-impact site.

4) Photograph decedent's vehicle and all other vehicles involved, including the following:
    a) Exterior of the vehicle, including:
        i) All four sides
        ii) Status of doors and locks
        iii) Status and condition of glass on all windows
        iv) Tires
            (1) Inflated versus deflated status
            (2) Blowouts versus bead breakdown
            (3) Tread wear
            (4) Cracked rims or other damage
        v) Status of headlamps, tail lamps, and brake lamps
        vi) Vehicle's tag and vehicle identification number
        vii) Vehicle damage
            (1) From crash
            (2) From extrication efforts
    b) Photograph interior of vehicle, including:
        i) Damage inside vehicle
            (1) Photograph points of occupant contact
                (a) Tissue, blood spatter, fabric, or hair in glass, metal, or dash areas
        ii) Alcohol containers, drugs, or drug paraphernalia
        iii) Status of safety equipment
            (1) Seat belt status
                (a) If the body transported or ejected:
                    (i) Photograph area of belt that was cut or torn
                    (ii) Photograph clasp area of belt
                    (iii) Photograph scoring or absence of scoring on area of belt where it would have been held by the D-ring.
                (b) If the body remains in the vehicle:
                    (i) Photograph status of belt use.
                    (ii) Photograph clasp area of the belt.
                    (iii) Photograph scoring or absence of scoring on area of it where belt would have been held by the D-ring.

(2) If the vehicle is equipped with a driver's-side air bag, photograph the steering wheel to document that the air bag did or did not deploy.

    iv) Any cargo that may have acted as a source of obstruction

    v) Clothing, shoes, or personal effects

c) Photograph the underbody of the vehicle, including:

    i) Condition of tie rods, exhaust system, or obvious damage to equipment

    ii) Damage to hoses and lines

    iii) Underbody debris or rust

d) Photograph the engine compartment for the following:

    i) Status of fluid levels in brake master cylinder, power steering reservoir, battery acid, and coolant

5)   Photograph the decedent.

    a) Interior impact patterns

    b) Dicing type of injuries

    c) Knee injuries

    d) Steering wheel injuries

    e) Windshield impacts

    f) Roadway abrasions

SCENE INVESTIGATION

1)   Describe the roadway.

    a) Number of lanes

    b) Interstate, highway, street, driveway, private road, etc.

    c) Section involved an intersection or uninterrupted road area?

        i) If it is an intersection, identify the following:

            (1) Traffic light or blinking warning light

            (2) Two-way or four-way stop sign

            (3) Intersection not controlled

            (4) Other

    d) Roadway area a straightaway or curved road area?

        i) If curved road area, describe:

            (1) Left-hand or right-hand curve

    e) Indication of whether a hill is present

        i) Incline or decline

    f) Composition of road surface (e.g., concrete, blacktop, dirt, brick).

    g) Description of center area of roadway

        i) Concrete barrier, median, or center stripe

            (1) If there is a center stripe, is it double-lined or single-lined?

            (2) Are there interrupted or uninterrupted lines?

    h) Is guardrail present?

        i) What is the posted speed limit?

    j) Condition of the roadway

        i) Dry, wet, snow, ice, mud, or standing water?

        ii) Roadway under construction?

        iii) Does involved stretch contain a detour section?

        iv) Describe lighting condition of roadway.

        v) Describe any other roadway hazards or obstructions.

2)   Describe weather conditions.
   a) Clear, cloudy, windy, freezing, etc.?
   b) Rain, snow, sleet, or hail?
   c) Fog?

3)   Describe the area.
   a) Rural, commercial, or residential?

4)   Describe the vehicles involved.
   a) The decedent's vehicle
      i) Passenger vehicle, pickup truck, truck (describe), jeep, van, bus, motorcycle, bicycle, all-terrain vehicle (ATV), or other?
         (1) Make, model, year, and whether two-door or four-door
   b) Estimated speed at impact
   c) Describe impact site.
      i) Front, rear, right side and/or left side of vehicle
   d) Describe any indication of vehicle malfunction.
      i) Describe the status of doors and locks.
      ii) Describe the condition of the glass in each window, including windshield, rear window, and side driver and passenger windows. Be specific.
      iii) Any problem detected with steering?
      iv) Any problem detected with the braking system of the vehicle?
      v) Any problem detected with the exhaust system of the involved vehicle?
      vi) Any indication of tire problems on the involved vehicles?
         (1) Status of each tire (inflated versus deflated)
         (2) Obvious damage (blowouts versus bead damage)
         (3) Tread wear
         (4) Rims cracked or broken
      vii) Develop the condition of head, tail, and brake lights at the time of the crash.
         (1) Is the light switch on or off?
         (2) Are head lamps, tail lamps, and brake lamps broken or intact?
   e) Describe the other vehicle involved.
      i) Passenger vehicle, pickup truck, truck (describe), jeep, van, bus, motorcycle, bicycle, ATV, or other?
         (1) Make, model, year, and whether two-door or four-door
   f) Describe impact site of other vehicle involved.
      i) Front, rear, right side and/or left side of vehicle
   g) Describe any indication of vehicle malfunction.
      i) Describe the status of doors and locks.
      ii) Describe the condition of the glass in each window, including windshield, rear window, side driver, and passenger windows. Be specific.
      iii) Was any problem detected with steering?
      iv) Was any problem detected with the braking system?
         (1) Status of fluid level in the master cylinder
         (2) Status of brake lines
      v) Was any problem detected with the exhaust system?
      vi) Was there any indication of tire problems on the involved vehicles?
         (1) Status of each tire (inflated versus deflated)
         (2) Obvious damage (blowouts versus bead damage)
         (3) Tread wear

    (4) Cracked or broken rims
   vii) Develop the condition of head, tail, and brake lights at the time of the crash.
    (1) Is light switch on or off?
    (2) Are head lamps, tail lamps, and brake lamps broken or intact?
  h) Was there any indication that the involved vehicle may have struck or tried to miss an animal crossing the roadway or some other object? Describe the incident.

5) Describe the collision.
  a) Identify the point of impact.
  b) Identify the point of final rest of all vehicles and bodies involved with the incident.
  c) Describe the actions of the involved vehicles from the time immediately before the crash to the conclusion of the incident.
   i) Identify the lanes and direction of all involved parties.
   ii) Describe any evasive action taken by the driver and where the action occurred in relation to the overall description of the incident.
    (1) Steering right or left, application of brakes, acceleration of vehicle.
  d) Describe any physical evidence observed that is most likely related to the crash.
   i) Skid marks
   ii) Debris
   iii) Scarring of roadway surface due to contact with metal surface
   iv) Damage to roadside objects

6) Driver's behavior, developed through observation at the scene and interviews of survivors and witnesses.
  a) Did the driver have the windows up on his vehicle?
  b) Did the driver have the radio playing? At what level?
  c) Was the vehicle's air conditioner or heater in the "on" position?
  d) Was there conversation between other parties in the vehicle at the time of the incident?
  e) Any other activities developed that may have diverted the driver's attention?
   i) Smoking, drinking, eating, adjusting radio, etc.
  f) Was alcohol found in the vehicle? If yes, describe.
  g) Where had the driver been?
  h) Where was the driver headed?
  i) How long had the driver been driving the vehicle during the time immediately before the crash?

BODY TRANSPORT FROM SCENE

1) No special requirements are necessary unless some confusion exists as to who may have been operating the vehicle. If driver is not positively established, wrap the decedent in a clean, white sheet to ensure that transfer evidence remains intact until collection is done at the MEO.

BODY PROCESSING AT THE MEO

1) Fingerprint the decedent.

2) If some question exists as to the decedent being a driver or passenger in the involved vehicle, follow the following procedures:
  a) Take head hair standards.

b) Take blood specimens or buccal swabbings.
c) Collect clothing of the decedent.
d) Collect debris found on the decedent's remains.

FOLLOW-UP INVESTIGATION

1) Continue efforts to complete the primary focus of the investigation.

AIR BAGS IN TRAFFIC FATALITIES

(The following information is obtained from a pamphlet put out by the U.S. Department of Transportation, National Highway Traffic Safety Administration.)

1) The operation of an air bag
    a) The air bag is designed to supplement the protective actions of a safety belt.
    b) In a frontal impact of sufficient severity, comparable to a collision into a wall at 10 to 14 mph, sensors in the vehicle detect the sudden deceleration and trigger the inflator module. This causes the solid chemical propellant sealed inside the inflator, principally sodium azide, to undergo a rapid chemical reaction. This reaction produces nitrogen gas, which inflates a woven nylon bag packed inside the steering wheel hub or the instrument panel for the front seat passenger.
    c) The bag inflates in less than 1/20th of a second, splitting open its protective cover and inflating in front of the occupant.
    d) As the occupant contacts the bag, the nitrogen gas is vented through openings in the back of the bag, thus cushioning forward movement.
    e) Once the air bag deploys, it begins to deflate. It will appear as a drooping bag coming out of the steering wheel hub or the instrument panel on the passenger side.
    f) The air bag is designed to deploy only in frontal or near-frontal collisions. An air bag will not deploy in crashes involving side, rear-end, or roll-over type of accidents.

2) Dangers associated with the air bag.
    a) Deployed air bag
      i) Deployed air bags are not dangerous to normal-sized adults. They have been fatally deployed in some cases involving infants, children, and small-sized adults.
        (1) Deployment may produce a dust associated with the packing and preservation of the air bag. This dust may cause minor skin or eye irritation, which can be avoided through the proper wearing of gloves and safety goggles.
        (2) After deployment, the air bag module and steering wheel hub will be hot for a short period. The module is relatively inaccessible and should pose no problems to investigators. The bag itself will not be hot.
      ii) Undeployed air bag
        (1) An undeployed air bag is unlikely to deploy after a crash. In those cases where a victim may be pinned directly behind an undeployed air bag, the following special procedures should be followed:
          (a) Disconnect or cut both battery cables.
          (b) Avoid positioning your body or objects against the air bag module or in the deployment path of the air bag.
          (c) Do not mechanically displace or cut through the steering column until the system has been fully deactivated.

(d) Do not cut or drill into the air bag module.
(e) Do not apply heat in the area of the steering wheel hub.
(2) Deactivation times for air bag backup power supply are depicted in table below.

MAKE	TIME
Acura	15 seconds
Audi	10 seconds
Bentley	30 minutes
BMW	20 minutes
Chrysler	2 minutes
Ford	various
GM	10 minutes
Isuzu	10 minutes
Lexus	20 seconds
Mazda	10 minutes
Mercedes	1 second
Mitsubishi	30 seconds
Nissan	10 minutes
Porsche	10 minutes
Rolls Royce	30 minutes
Saab	20 minutes
Toyota	20 seconds
Volkswagen Cabriolet	10 minutes
Volvo	10 seconds

NOTE: 1990 Jaguar coupes and convertibles cannot be deactivated in the field.

IDENTIFYING A CAR EQUIPPED WITH AN AIR BAG

The steering wheel hub is large and rectangular (approximately 6 by 9 inches). The large hub is covered with a scored, soft plastic material containing the words "Supplemental Inflatable Restraint" or "Air Bag" or the initials "S.I.R." or "SRS."

The vehicle identification number (VIN) is coded to indicate whether an air bag is present.

MOTORIST AND VEHICLE SERVICES AVAILABLE THROUGH THE INTERNET

Alabama
http://www.ador.state.al.us/motorvehicle/
Information on driver's licenses, vehicle registration, titles, and liability insurance

Alaska
http://www.state.ak.us/dmv/
Various services

Arizona
http://www.dot.state.az.us/MVD/mvd.htm
Vehicle registration, fleet registration, duplicate driver's licenses, and change of address

Arkansas
http://www.state.ar.us/dfa
Renew tags online and review other motor vehicle information

California
http://www.dmv.ca.gov
Vehicle registration, driver's licenses, and other services

Colorado
http://www.state.co.us/gov_dir/revenue_dir/MV_dir/mv.html
Driver's license and vehicle registration information

Connecticut
http://dmvct.org
Registration and titles, vehicle inspections, driver's licenses, customized plates

District of Columbia
http://dmv.washingtondc.gov/main.shtm
Online vehicle registration and "digitized driver's license"

Florida
http://www.hsmv.state.fl.us/index.html
Driver's license and vehicle registration information

Georgia
http://www.dmvs.ga.gov/
License plates, registration, titles, and more

Hawaii
http://www.co.honolulu.hi.us/mvl/index.htm
A link to the Hawaii Motor Vehicle Department and licensing information

Idaho
http://www2.state.id.us/itd/dmv/index.htm
Information on driver's licenses, vehicle registration, skills tests, violation points, and more

Illinois

http://www.sos.state.il.us/depts/drivers/mot_info.html
Motorist services and online address changes

Indiana

http://www.state.in.us/bmv
Driver's license and vehicle registration/title information

Iowa

http://www.dot.state.ia.us/mvd/index.htm
Driver and vehicle services

Kansas

http://www.ink.org/public/kdor/dmv
Information on vehicle registration, driver's license examination and control, the new teen driving law, and the OPT IN (opening driver's license records) program

Kentucky

http://www.kytc.state.ky.us/Traffic_Center/home.htm
Clearinghouse for Kentucky's maps, travel conditions, and construction reports

Louisiana

http://www.dps.state.la.us/omv/home.html
Online forms include accident reports, driver's license applications, personalized plate requests, and more

Maine

http://www.state.me.us/sos/bmv/bmv.htm
"Driver cross check," driving records search, registration records search, title records search, vanity plate availability check, and information on posted roads

Maryland

http://www.mva.state.md.us
Connection to the MVA office

Massachusetts

http://www.state.ma.us/rmv/
Online transactions include registration renewal, change of address, special plate ordering, traffic citation payment, and more.

Michigan

http://www.sos.state.mi.us
Lists holiday hours of motor vehicle services offices, gives guidance on required decals for mopeds and watercraft, plus a sample driver's license renewal test

Minnesota

http://www.dps.state.mn.us/dvs/index.html
Includes information on specialized license plates, a chart for title fees, getting a driver's license, and even bicycle registration

Mississippi

http://www.mmvc.state.ms.us
A link to the Mississippi Motor Vehicle Commission

Missouri

http://www.dor.state.mo.us/dmv
Includes state driving manuals in English and Spanish, and mail-in driver's license application forms.

Montana

http://www.doj.state.mt.us/mvd/index.htm
Features downloadable forms, information on obtaining and renewing license plates, and frequently asked questions (FAQs) page

Nebraska

http://www.nol.org/home/DMV
List of numbers to call for assistance at the DMV, answers to questions about getting a driver's license, and commercial driver-training school locations.

Nevada

http://www.state.nv.us/dmv_ps
Answers to FAQs about getting a driver's license and titling and registering a vehicle

New Hampshire

http://www.state.nh.us/dmv
Links to other state government services and agencies and information about organ donation

New Jersey

http://www.state.nj.us/mvs
Lists hours of operation and locations of driver-testing facilities. as well as the updated state driver`s manual

New Mexico

http://www.state.nm.us/tax/mvd/mvd_home.htm
License plates renewal, samples of the "vanity plates" offered, and motor vehicle division forms

New York

http://www.nydmv.state.ny.us/index.htm
Major credit cards and check cards accepted here for renewing license plates and car registration; also includes title and registration FAQs

North Carolina

http://www.dmv.dot.state.nc.us
Instructions for what to do if a driver's license is stolen or you are changing auto insurance companies

North Dakota

http://www.state.nd.us/dot/dnv.html
The "rules of the road," as well as driver's license requirements and the points schedule

Ohio

http://www.state.oh.us/odps/division/bmv/bmv.html
Forms for obtaining abstracts of driving records, as well as information about renewing driver's licenses

Oklahoma
http://www.dps.state.ok.us/dls
Driver's license services

Oregon
http://www.odot.state.or.us/dmv/index.htm
Downloadable accident report forms, instructions for what to do if an animal is hit on the road, driver's license renewal

Pennsylvania
http://www.dmv.state.pa.us
Downloadable forms and fact sheets, information about the young driver program

Rhode Island
http://www.dmv.state.ri.us
Driver's license service locations, hours of operation, and a link to the state's motor vehicle laws

South Carolina
http://www.state.sc.us/dps/dmv
Watercraft licensing, voter registration, and commercial driver licensing

South Dakota
http://www.state.sd.us/revenue/motorvcl.htm
Downloadable forms and instructions and information on how to obtain specialty and duplicate license plates and decals

Tennessee
http://www.state.tn.us/drive.html
State road construction areas and road conditions, state driver's manual, and information on the renewal of license plates

Texas
http://www.txdps.state.tx.us
Driver's license information

Texas
http://www.dot.state.tx.us
Information on specialty plates, motor vehicle registration and titling, and state road conditions

Utah
http://www.dmv-utah.com/
Auto buyer's survival guide and automobile and boat registrations

Vermont
http://www.aot.state.vt.us/dmv/dmvhp.htm
Information for school bus and commercial vehicle drivers, as well as driver's license and vehicle registration guidance

Virginia
http://www.dmv.state.va.us
State license plate designs and how to create personal messages for automobile tags

475 · TRAFFIC FATALITY—VEHICLE VERSUS VEHICLE · 475

Washington
http://www.wa.gov/dol
FAQs pages for vehicles, boats, and driver's licenses information, as well as information on a special 5-year license and a teen driver's license

West Virginia
http://www.wvdot.com/6_motorists/dmv/6G_dmv.htm
Regional offices and their hours, license and registration forms and applications, information about motorcycle safety

Wisconsin
http://www.dot.state.wi.us/dmv/dmv.html
How to obtain a "digital driver's license" and tips on selling a car

Wyoming
http://wydotweb.state.wy.us/Docs/Licenses/DriverServices.html
Mail-in driver's license renewal, accident procedures, fees for licenses, and other services

CHAPTER 50:
TRAFFIC FATALITY—VEHICLE VERSUS PEDESTRIAN

CONSIDERATIONS

1)   There are four different types of actions that may result from a vehicle striking a pedestrian.
     a) The classical impact involves the striking of an individual by a motor vehicle, causing that person to be thrown onto the hood of a car. Very seldom are people run over by a vehicle traveling faster than 25 mph.

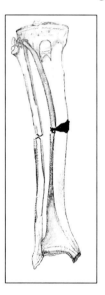

A pathologist can determine the direction of the impact by examining the fractured bone. A wedge-shaped V indicates the direction of the force. Point of impact can be discerned by identifying a pocket (hemorrhage) under the skin. The pocket will be found on the side of the body to which the impact occurred.

       i) The primary impact of the vehicle involves the bumper bar's striking the legs of the pedestrian, usually resulting in a fracture of the tibia. The primary impact point is the best indicator of the pedestrian's position at the time of the impact.
          (1) A vehicle usually must be going at least 20 mph to cause a fracture to the leg of a young adult. An older adult's leg will often be fractured by a vehicle traveling at a speed of 10 mph or more.
          (2) An important measurement involves the distance from the ground (measured as the heel of the pedestrian's foot) and the point of the leg where the injury exists. This will roughly correspond with the height of the bumper at the time of impact. This area may measure somewhat lower than the actual bumper if the brakes were applied, thereby causing the front of the vehicle to dip at the time of the impact.
      ii) The pedestrian's buttocks are struck by the hood of the vehicle.

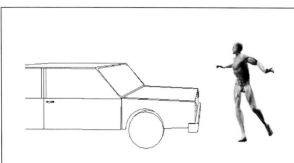

The size of the pedestrian and the speed of the vehicle will determine what happens when a pedestrian is struck by a vehicle.

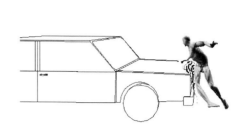

Unless the pedestrian is a small child or the vehicle is driving very slowly, the projection of the bumper will strike the pedestrian initially. The front hood of the vehicle then strikes the victim on the buttocks/hips.

The force of the vehicle causes the pedestrian to be thrown onto the hood of the vehicle.

Depending on the speed of the vehicle, the pedestrian may be thrown into the windshield or over the car entirely.

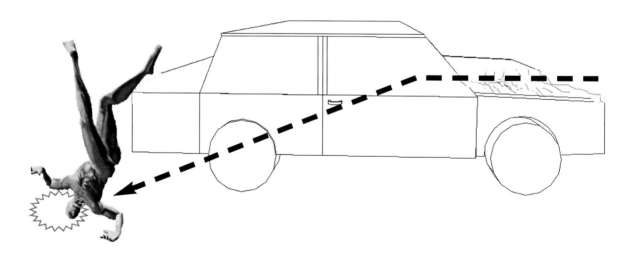

When thrown from the vehicle, the pedestrian may die from striking his head on the pavement.

iii) A secondary impact occurs after the pedestrian is thrown onto the hood. Most pedestrians die from the secondary injuries resulting from striking their heads, not from the primary impact.

    (1) If the vehicle is traveling more than 30 but and less than 60 mph, the pedestrian may miss the windshield altogether, instead striking the top or back of the vehicle.

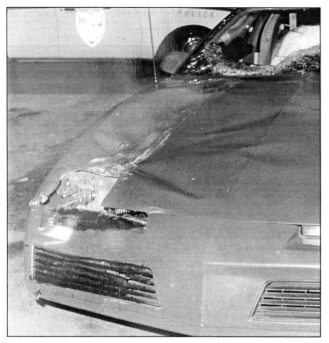

Typical damage occurring when a pedestrian is struck by a vehicle.

The protruding edge of the vehicle (usually the front bumper) will be the first surface to strike the pedestrian. It is important to obtain this measurement and compare it with the fractured height (heel to fractured center) on the leg of the victim. The fracture height may indicate that the vehicle was accelerating or braking at the time of impact.

    (2) In speeds in excess of 60 mph, the pedestrian may be thrown completely over the vehicle, incurring massive head or chest injuries with multiple abrasions and fractures of long bones and the pelvis.

b) Pedestrian versus a high vehicle (pickup trucks and larger vehicles): a bumper bar 24 inches or higher will usually result in the pedestrian's being pushed under the vehicle, not over the hood.

    i) The primary impact site is often higher than what is seen when a victim struck by an automobile. Patterned abrasions from the grill, headlight, and insignias (badges) of the involved vehicle may be present as patterned abrasions on the decedent.

    ii) The secondary impact may involve the following:

        (1) The victim is often run over by the vehicle.

        (2) Tire impression patterns may be present on the decedent.

        (3) Injuries of the head, chest, and abdomen may involve crushing.

        (4) Deep lacerations and depressed fractures involving the skull may be present on the decedent as a result of his coming into contact with protruding objects under the chassis of the vehicle. There may also be a good deal of grease from the undercarriage of the vehicle deposited onto the victim.

c) Vehicle versus child: because of their lower center of gravity, children tend to be pulled under the vehicle rather than being knocked over the hood. Children are often hit by slower moving vehicles that are backing up. The bumper strikes the knee of the child, causing it to become locked under the vehicle. Unable to free the leg, the child is pulled under and run over by the vehicle.

          i) The primary impact point involves the knee or thigh (femur) of the victim.

          ii) The secondary impact sites involve crush injuries of the head, chest, and abdomen. Tire abrasions may be present on the victim.

     d) Atypical actions involving vehicles versus pedestrians:

          i) No primary impact site is found on the calf of the decedent. Other injuries tend to indicate that the victim may have been in an unusual position when struck by the vehicle, such as:

              (1) Lying in the roadway may indicate that the victim was:

                   (a) Intoxicated

                   (b) Attempting suicide

                   (c) Hit previously by another vehicle

                   (d) Already dead and dumped in the roadway

                       (i) Overdose victim dumped in the roadway by others

                       (ii) An effort to conceal a homicide

              (2) The victim may have been kneeling or squatting in the roadway if the primary impact site is found on the arms or on the trunk of the body. Kneeling or squatting victims would have a low center of gravity, causing them to be pushed under the vehicle.

2)   Deliberate murder by using the vehicle as a weapon

     a) These are very rare.

     b) An autopsy may show indications of acceleration (higher primary impact fracture than the actual bumper of involved vehicle), with accompanying severe chest and abdominal injuries.

     c) Without eyewitness testimony, it may be very difficult to determine.

PRIMARY FOCUS OF INVESTIGATION

1)   Identifying the decedent

2)   Establishing the cause of the incident

     a) Driver error

          i) Was the driver's ability to operate the vehicle impaired by the effects of alcohol or drugs?

          ii) Was the driver's full attention focused or diverted from his driving responsibilities at the time of the incident?

          iii) Did the driver of the vehicle fall asleep at the wheel?

          iv) Was the driver speeding?

     b) Pedestrian error

          i) Did the effects of alcohol or drugs influence the pedestrian's action or inaction?

          ii) Did the pedestrian make an error in judgment?

          iii) Did the pedestrian's natural disease or physical handicap contribute to the incident?

     c) Vehicle malfunction

          i) What contribution, if any, did the vehicle's mechanical operation contribute to the cause of the incident?

              (1) Tires

              (2) Brakes

              (3) Possible other mechanical defaults

     d) Weather conditions

    i) Could the weather conditions have contributed to the cause of the accident?
      (1) Rain, wet pavement, or standing water
      (2) Fog
      (3) Snow or icy conditions
      (4) High winds
  e) Roadway conditions
    i) Could any of the following conditions at the roadway site have contributed to the accident?
      (1) Lighting
      (2) Roadway construction
      (3) Detour
      (4) Dangerous road curve or other road hazard

3) Identification of hit and run involved
    a) Collection of evidence on the roadway
    b) Collection of evidence from the body

4) Reconstruction of the incident

NOTIFICATION

1) No special notification is required unless the following conditions exist:
    a) Multiple fatalities
    b) Reconstruction of the incident is particularly difficult
    c) Circumstances indicate that the decedent did not die as a result of the accident and the accident may have been staged to conceal a homicide.

SCENE PHOTOGRAPHS

1) Photograph the scene.
    a) Photograph the overall scene showing the entire area involved.
      i) On night scenes, it may be particularly useful to use painting-with-light techniques.
    b) Photograph skid marks.
    c) Photograph vehicle debris, including:
      i) Broken glass, plastic, chrome, etc.
    d) Photograph property that was damaged during the incident.
    e) Photograph any areas that may have acted as an obstruction.
      i) Hills, curves in roadway, signs, bushes, etc.
    f) Photograph any fluid spills.
      i) Oil, coolant, battery acid, etc.
    g) Photograph the point of impact on the roadway.
    h) Photograph the final resting place of the vehicle in relation to the point of impact and the final resting place of the body.

2) Photograph the vehicle (if present at the scene).
    a) Photograph the exterior of the vehicle.
    b) Photograph the damaged area of the vehicle.
      i) Place a ruler next to the damaged area of the vehicle. One end of the ruler should be flush with the ground. Photograph the damage to the bumper with the indicated height from the ground represented by the ruler.

  ii) Repeat this process with the ruler showing the damage to the front hood of the vehicle with the height of the damage from the ground indicated by the ruler.
  iii) Photograph any damaged areas involving the grill, badges (car insignia), or headlight frames that may have caused patterned areas in the decedent's body.
c) If the decedent has been run over by a vehicle, photograph the underside of the vehicle, particularly documenting any areas of the underside of the carriage that may jut out and have caused injuries to the victim.
d) Photograph any areas of the vehicle where transfer of tissue or fabric may have been left during the accident.
e) Photograph the status and condition of all glass on the vehicle.
f) Photograph the tires of the vehicle.
  i) Inflated versus deflated status
  ii) Blowouts versus bead breakdown
  iii) Tread wear
    (1) Place ruler across the treads. Photograph the tread pattern.
  iv) Cracked rims or other damage
  v) Status of headlamps
  vi) Vehicle's tag and VIN
  vii) Photograph interior of vehicle, including:
    (1) Alcohol containers, drugs, or drug paraphernalia
    (2) Any cargo that may have acted as a source of obstruction

3) Photograph the decedent.
  a) Impact injuries
  b) Dicing-type injuries
  c) Roadway abrasions
  d) Pieces of glass in the decedent's hair or clothing
  e) Decedent's clothing

SCENE INVESTIGATION

1) Describe the roadway.
  a) Number of lanes?
  b) Interstate, highway, street, driveway, private road?
  c) Is the road area involved an intersection or uninterrupted road section?
    i) If it is an intersection, identify the following:
      (1) Traffic light or blinking warning light
      (2) Two-way or four-way stop sign
      (3) Intersection not controlled
      (4) Other
  d) Is roadway area a straightaway or curved road area?
    i) If it is a curved road area, describe:
      (1) Left-hand or right-hand curve?
  e) Identify whether a hill is present.
    i) Incline or decline?
  f) Describe the composition of the road surface (e.g., concrete, blacktop, dirt, brick)
  g) Describe the center area of the roadway.
    i) Concrete barrier, median, or center stripe?
      (1) If there is a center stripe, is it double- or single-lined?

(2) Interrupted or uninterrupted lines?
h) Is guardrail present?
i) What is the posted speed limit?
j) What was condition of the roadway?
   i) Dry, wet, snow, ice, mud, or standing water?
   ii) Roadway under construction?
   iii) Involved roadway contains a detour section?
   iv) Describe lighting condition of roadway.
   v) Describe any other roadway hazards or obstructions.

2) Describe weather conditions.
   a) Clear, cloudy, windy, freezing, etc.?
   b) Rain, snow, sleet, or hail?
   c) Fog?

3) Describe the area.
   a) Rural, commercial, or residential?

4) Describe the vehicles involved.
   a) The vehicle that struck the pedestrian
      i) Passenger vehicle, pickup truck, truck (describe), jeep, van, bus, motorcycle, bicycle, ATV, or other?
         (1) Identify the make, model, year, and whether it was two-door or four-door model.
      ii) What was the estimated speed at impact?
      iii) Describe the impact site.
         (1) Front, rear, right side or left side of vehicle?
      iv) Describe any indication of vehicle malfunction.
         (1) The status of doors and locks.
         (2) The condition of the glass in each window, including windshield, rear window, and side driver and passenger windows. Be specific.
         (3) Any problem detected with the steering?
         (4) Any problem detected with the braking system?
         (5) Any problem detected with the exhaust system?
         (6) Any indication of tire problems?
            (a) Status of each tire (inflated versus deflated)
            (b) Obvious damage (blowouts versus bead damage)
            (c) Tread wear
            (d) Cracked or broken rims
         (7) Develop the condition of head, tail, and brake lights at the time of the crash.
            (a) Is the light switch on or off?
            (b) Are head lamps, tail lamps, and brake lamps broken or intact?
      v) Describe any other vehicles involved.
         (1) Passenger vehicle, pickup truck, truck (describe), jeep, van, bus, motorcycle, bicycle, ATV, or other?
            (a) Identify make, model, year, and whether it was a four-door or two-door model.
      vi) Describe any impact damage.
      vii) Is there any indication that the involved vehicle may have struck or attempted

to avoid striking an animal crossing the roadway or some other object? Describe the incident.

5)   Describe the collision.
a) Identify the point of impact.
b) Identify the point of final rest of all vehicles and bodies.
c) Describe the actions of the involved vehicles from the time immediately preceding the crash to the conclusion of the incident.
i) Identify the lanes and direction of all involved parties.
ii) Describe any evasive action taken by the driver and where the action occurred in regard to the overall description of the incident.
(1) Steering right or left, application of brakes, accelerating of vehicle, etc.
iii) Establish the position of the pedestrian at the time of the impact.
(1) Was the decedent lying, standing, or sitting at the time of the initial impact?
(2) Describe the direction of the impact.
iv) Describe the possible involvement of any other vehicles that may have run over the decedent after the initial collision.
d) Describe any physical evidence observed that is most likely related to the crash.
i) Skid marks
ii) Debris
iii) Scarring of roadway surface due to contact with metal surface
iv) Damage to roadside objects
v) Blood, tissue, body fragments, etc.
vi) Measure chassis width if the decedent run over by the vehicle

6)   Describe driver behavior (develop through observations at the scene and interviews of survivors and witnesses).
a) Did the driver have the windows up on his vehicle?
b) Did the driver have the radio playing? At what level?
c) Was the vehicle's air conditioner or heater in the on position?
d) Was there conversation between other parties in the vehicle at the time of the incident?
e) Any other activities developed that may have diverted the driver's attention?
f) Smoking, drinking, eating, adjusting radio?
g) Was alcohol found in the vehicle? If yes, describe.
h) Where had the driver been?
i) Where was the driver headed?
j) How long had the driver been driving the vehicle during the time immediately before the crash?

BODY TRANSPORT FROM SCENE

1)   No special requirements are necessary unless the decedent is:
a) A hit-and-run victim
i) Cross transfer of evidence is critical in identifying the vehicle. This physical evidence may involve the following:
(1) Paint from the vehicle
(2) Grease from the vehicle
(3) Plastic, glass, or other parts that may be fractured match the involved vehicle.
ii) The decedent's hair, blood, or tissue may have been left in the suspect's vehicle.

In addition, the fabric impression involving the decedent's clothing may be imbedded in the paint of the suspect vehicle.

    iii) Wrap decedent in a clean, white sheet. Transport to the MEO or morgue facility.

b) On a suspected homicide, place the decedent in a clean, white sheet. Transport to the MEO or morgue facility.

BODY PROCESSING AT THE MEO/MORGUE

1)   Fingerprint the decedent.

2)   If the case is a hit and run or suspected homicide, collect the following:
    a) Head hair standards
    b) Blood specimens
    c) Clothing of the decedent (separately bag each piece)
    d) Debris found on the decedent's remains
    e) Sheet used in transporting the remains

FOLLOW-UP INVESTIGATION

1)   Reconstruct the accident. Determine if the findings are consistent with information received.

2)   If this is a hit-and-run case, attempt to identify the suspect vehicle.
    a) Follow all leads concerning the identification of the vehicle.
        i) Bumper/hood height
        ii) Chassis width
        iii) Tire tread
        iv) Vehicle fragments, including glass, plastic, and badges
        v) Paint composition
        vi) Patterned impression on the decedent
    b) Use the media to assist in locating the suspect vehicle and additional witnesses.
    c) Consider proactive canvassing of the area to locate witnesses who were in the area at the time the incident was believed to have occurred.

3)   If homicide is involved, develop the motive. Proceed in the investigation based on the motive indicated for this homicide.

CHAPTER 51: MASS-DISASTER INVESTIGATION

CONSIDERATIONS

1) A mass disaster is an incident involving multiple deaths in which the particular community involved will be significantly taxed in coping with the situation. No set number of deaths is required before a mass disaster can be said to have occurred.

The Pentagon after the bombing on September 11, 2001.

2) There are two types of mass disaster:
    a) Natural
        i) These are usually the most difficult to work because the area involved may be large, and disruption may have occurred to communication, transportation, equipment, fuel sources, food supplies, and personnel.
            (1) Examples of natural disasters include hurricanes, earthquakes, tornadoes, and floods.
    b) Man-made
        i) These types of disasters are usually more localized to a particular area but less disruptive from an equipment, accessibility, and personnel standpoint.
            (1) Examples of man-made disasters include airplane crashes, shipwrecks, bus accidents, train collisions/derailments, mining accidents, fires, explosions, and mass suicides/murders.

3) The disaster will usually involve many agencies' having to work together. Planning and coordination between agencies must be considered prior to any incident.
    a) Law enforcement and medical examiner/coroner

i) As a general rule, the major burden for handling the disaster rests with law enforcement agencies. However, examination and collection of the deceased normally are the responsibility of the medical examiner/coroner.

b) Rescue and fire engine units

i) Injured individuals may also be part of the scenario. Their treatment, safe removal from the scene, and transportation to medical facilities must also be considered.

c) Auxiliary agencies

i) Units from the armed forces, National Guard, and state police agencies may be called upon to assist in the securing or processing of the scene.

ii) Representatives from American Red Cross, Civil Defense, Salvation Army, and various ministerial associations can also be used to assist in various duties associated with the disaster.

d) Specialized personnel

i) Consideration should be given to utilizing expertise from other agencies and professional groups, including:

(1) Fingerprint specialists used for obtaining fingerprints from the decedents and comparison analysis for establishing identification

(2) Forensic odontologists used in charting postmortem dentition, obtaining antemortem dental records, and establishing the identity of the decedents through comparison analysis

(3) Scene technicians/photographers to assist in the processing and photographing of the scene, evidence, valuables, and bodies

(4) Forensic anthropologists to assist in scenes involving dismembered or burned bodies

(5) Radiologists to assist in the acquisition and interpretation of antemortem X-rays, as well as the taking of postmortem X-rays and comparison analysis for establishing identification

(6) Various specialists whose particular areas of expertise may provide a better understanding of the cause and effect of the mechanism involving the disaster or may improve rescue or recovery efforts and techniques

(7) Grief counselors used to coordinate and assist in the exchange of information between the involved agencies and the decedents' next of kin. In addition, the counselors can be used to monitor the performance and mental health of the recovery and processing teams

4) As a general rule, the successful processing of a mass disaster site is contingent on the following requirements:

a) There must be cooperation and a spirit to get along among the various agencies sharing responsibility for the processing of the scene.

b) The morale of the workers must be an important consideration. Every member monitors one another for signs of stress.

c) The scene workers must be given frequent breaks. Vary assignments, if possible.

d) The collection of evidence and recovery of bodies should be a joint area with each representative aware of the specialized handling required.

e) The command post must be established as an area in which the true exchange of information is occurring. It should not be used as a site to drink coffee and eat doughnuts.

f) Take time to evaluate the entire scene. The supervisory personnel charged with the overall responsibility for processing the scene should attempt to visualize their entire task by traveling over the area in a helicopter initially and then throughout the area on foot. The work force should then be addressed collectively and each member advised of the goals, responsibilities, and the overall situation. Brief all beforehand. Be truthful.

g) Mandatory group debriefings, recognition, and commendations of all persons assisting in the disaster are essential. Allow members the opportunity for expression.

h) Provide humor and music.

5) Specialized equipment is required:
a) Refrigerated trucks retard decomposition of the remains.
i) For hygiene purposes, the floor of the refrigerated truck must have a metal floor, not a wooden one.
ii) Refrigerated trucks are usually be borrowed or rented. If the commercial company is identified on the outside of the refrigerated trailer, paper should be used to cover the name of the company.
b) Helicopters
c) Bulldozers
d) Boats and dredges
e) Gas-powered chain saws
f) Gas-powered electric generators
g) Four-wheel-drive vehicles

6) Decomposing bodies represent a health hazard. The recommended immunizations for disaster team members are as follows:
a) Smallpox
b) Typhoid
c) Polio
d) Tetanus
e) Cholera
f) Yellow fever
g) Diphtheria
h) Typhus
i) Hepatitis

7) Establish good media relations.
a) Release factual information only.
b) Refrain from any speculation, including the cause of the accident.
c) There is no such thing as an "off-the-record" conversation.
d) On-site news briefings should be handled with caution. It is not unheard of for media representatives to wander through the facility if given the opportunity.
e) Be cautious of audio recording capabilities, which can cover great distances, especially in those situations in which the national media become involved. The competition is fierce, and a parabolic microphone may be part of the equipment sent to the scene.
f) One person should be designated as the press information officer, and all information released to the media should come through him.
g) No information should be released regarding the identification of any decedent until the next of kin have been notified.
h) Treat the press fairly, but local reporters should take precedence because they are

the ones who will get the local information out to the local constituents. Be cognizant of their deadlines. Release information to the entire group. Keep in mind that the press serves an important function: informing the community about the way the situation is being handled and the progress toward the restoration of normal conditions. Negative reporting may occur and should be a cause for concern. For example, if the media sensationalize a few incidents of looting in a hurricane-damaged area, individuals who had left their homes in the wake of the advancing storm may begin returning prematurely to their homes because they are concerned about their homes being looted. As they return to the area, they exacerbate the traffic and security problems.

8)   A temporary morgue facility must be established.
        a) If the particular jurisdiction does not have the capacity to process large numbers of bodies, consider creating a temporary morgue facility. Gymnasiums, auditoriums, armories, airplane hangars, meatpacking plants, and refrigerated trucks are all potential sites. Consider the following factors when looking for a temporary facility:
            i) Space
                (1) This should allow for a comfortable working condition, and movement of the remains should be minimal and easy. Areas containing steps or an elevated platform should be avoided.
            ii) Security
                (1) Use employees trained in the difficult task of identification for tasks related to identification. Do not task specially trained personnel with the responsibility for maintaining physical security. Law enforcement patrol personnel, private security contractors, or volunteers are suitable for restricting access to the facility to authorized personnel only. An identification badge specifically designed for this case will greatly facilitate this important function.
                    (a) Morgue security should also include securing valuables and night security for the facility if the identification process will not be continuous.
            iii) Communications
                (1) Depending on the type of disaster and the area affected, regular communication efforts may no longer exist. Telephone lines and microwave and radio towers may be the first areas affected in a severe storm. You may have to contact ham radio operations or the military (satellite communication) for assistance.
            iv) Electrical provisions
                (1) Lighting, electrical outlets, and cooling capabilities are considerations.
            v) Accessibility to the disaster site
            vi) Assembly point
                (1) An area away from the scene and the area in which the bodies are being examined should be selected for receiving and working with families and friends of the decedents.
                (2) This area should have individual interview rooms for interviewing and counseling families and for them to view articles possibly belonging to the decedents.

8)   The morgue facility must be secure.
        a) Security must be of immediate and primary importance.
            i) The facility will be inundated with curiosity seekers, bereaved relatives, and

media. Setting up an identification pass system and creating a perimeter with security should be the first priorities. These will assist in alleviating the initial onslaught.

b) The telephone system is the second area of greatest concern.

i) Existing phone lines will be overloaded, and the orderly processing of the deceased will become quite difficult in an already stress-producing situation. Some people will have to be assigned to answer the flood of inquiries. They should be instructed to answer the calls as briefly as possible.

ii) It is helpful to designate regular times and locations for updating the media. Media callers can then be supplied with this information.

iii) Possible relatives of the decedents can be referred to the antemortem information-gathering team.

iv) All other callers can be handled on a "take a message" basis, with the messages being checked periodically and either referred to the antemortem team or the grief counselors, or handled as time permits.

v) Additional telephone lines will have to be employed if the antemortem information-gathering team is to work on-site. These lines should only be used to collect information for developing a manifest of potential victims or for identifying decedents.

c) Once a member of the antemortem team has made contact with a relative of a suspected victim, the former should be the only individual who contacts the relative.

PRIMARY FOCUS OF THE INVESTIGATION

1) Direct and coordinate the recovery of the dead.

2) Collect and safeguard the personal effects.

3) Identify the deceased and oversee the notification of the next of kin.

a) Identification is important for humanitarian and other reasons, specifically:

i) The natural inclination of people is to give a proper burial to their loved ones.

ii) It is a legal requirement for the settlement of estates, validation of wills, and proof of death for insurance purposes.

iii) The ability of survivors to remarry and carry on with their lives is affected by the identification of the decedents.

iv) It allows for adjustments of partnerships and businesses to occur.

4) Process the dead and issue death certificates.

5) Coordinate media announcements relative to the identity of the dead and the situation as it exists at the scene.

NOTIFICATION

1) Full notification of all involved agencies and supervisory personnel should be instituted immediately. Initial information should be directed toward the safety of responding to the involved site.

2) The following information should be given upon notification of members of the mass-disaster response team:

a) Type of incident
b) Approximate number of victims
c) Any known hazards to scene workers
d) Exact location of the incident
e) Best route access
f) Time of occurrence
g) Whether or not anything else may affect the response

SCENE PHOTOGRAPHS

1) As a general rule, one photographer should be assigned to each team at the scene. The actual needs will be determined by the nature of the disaster and the degree of mutilation. For example, an air crash involving several hundred bodies and parts of bodies would require a photographer to be deployed constantly with each team, whereas after a hurricane when bodies may be uncovered from debris over a long period. In this type of situation, one photographer may be available to service several teams at one time.

2) A photographer should be assigned to the staging area for photographing personal effects.

3) The number assigned to each body, body part, or item recovered should be included in every photograph taken.

4) Photograph the scene as follows:
   a) Take aerial photographs of the involved area.
      i) Shoot the area to show the path of the destructive force (e.g., airplane, tornado, high wind, high wave), if applicable.
   b) Photograph each disaster victim as found at the scene, showing the relationship of each item to each body
      i) Include detailed photographs depicting clothing.
      ii) Include detailed photographs of all jewelry observed on the body.
      iii) Photograph the full face of each victim (if possible) and any other view that may be useful in establishing identity.
   c) Photograph any item of evidentiary value that may be useful in understanding the cause of the disaster or the specific cause of each death.

SCENE INVESTIGATION

1) Secure the area.
   a) Determine the perimeter of the scene and secure this area immediately.
      i) The scene will attract media representatives, curiosity seekers, and thieves.
      ii) The scene may be unsafe, and creating and maintaining a perimeter may add to the fatality and injury totals.
   b) Establish staging areas.

2) Process the scene.
   a) The individual responsible for coordinating the processing of the scene should fly over the area in a helicopter if possible and walk through the area for assessment purposes. This individual should then meet with all involved parties responsible for the processing to discuss the situation and procedures for working the scene.
   b) The coordinator should make certain that scene personnel are wearing appropriate

The author helping to identify remains at the Pentagon
site after the September 11, 2001, attack.

Pentagon site.

safety gear to protect them from injury during the recovery process. A determination
should be made as to the type and number of equipment and materials necessary to
process the scene.

   c) The disaster area may be divided into quadrants and given alphabetical listings.

3) Recovery teams should be created. Ideally, each team should consist of a team leader, a
photographer, and a recorder. Two body recovery members may also be included with this
group.

   a) Keep accurate records of members working for each team.

   b) Provide relief to the teams as needed, keeping in mind that fatigue causes errors.
Constantly monitor the members of the team for stress.

4) Set areas of responsibility for each recovery team.

5) Establish the system of gridding. Decide if natural boundaries or rope is to be used to establish
the recovery area for each team.

6) Recovery of the remains and articles from the scene.

   a) Each area where a separate item of body, body part, clothing, jewelry, or other artifact
associated with the incident should be tagged, photographed, diagrammed, and
collected. The location of the remains or articles in relation to a wrecked aircraft, train,
building, or structure involved in causing the death may have a direct bearing on the
identity of the victim or the cause of the mishap. For this reason, it is extremely
important that the identification procedure begin at the scene before the bodies are
moved from the position in which they are found.

      i) A simple chronological numbering system can be instituted assigning a number
to each item, body part, or body. A letter representing the specific grid area
team in which the body was recovered or the particular recovery team involved
should be included with the body number. For example, Body B3 means the
grid location was area B and the decedent is the third item recovered from the
B sector.

      ii) Develop a diagram showing the approximate location, distances from known points, etc. (NOTE: This may not be possible because of the conditions at the disaster site.

b) The body will not be identified at the recovery site.

BODY TRANSPORT FROM THE SCENE

1) No body will be moved until the transport system and receiving area, including cooling arrangements, have been completed.

2) Body parts attached loosely by tendons or other tissue must be handled with caution. The specimen must be kept intact. Carelessness in removing the bodies may cause this portion of the body to separate and become lost.

   a) Be especially careful in handling skin peeling away from fingers, toes, hands, and feet. Take whatever precautions are necessary to prevent the skin in these areas from disassociating.

   b) Parts of bodies are assigned numerical identification in the same manner; however, no attempt should be made to associate parts of bodies to bodies at the disaster site.

   c) Scraps of clothing or whole articles of clothing still clinging to the decedent should be secured with the remains of the decedent.

   d) In tagging the remains, use a tag or ink (permanent) that will not be affected by moisture.

      i) Tagging should include the body and the bag that will carry the remains. Tag the decedent's foot or toe if feasible.

   e) A record of each item removed should be maintained. This may assist during later efforts to identify the decedents or their body parts.

   f) Before removing the remains, mark the location with a durable stake. The stake should contain the same number placed on the body, body part, or item being removed. The markings on the stake should be large enough to be easily visible during wide-angle camera shots of the overall scene.

   g) Never remove any clothing, jewelry, wallet, or other possession from the decedent or his clothes! The clothes should be searched and any objects removed at the morgue facility.

BODY PROCESSING AT THE MEO/MORGUE

1) In a mass disaster that requires facilities to handle a great many casualties in a short period, the autopsy examination for establishing cause of death is much less of a priority than establishing the identity of the remains. Many mass-disaster victims will have died in a similar fashion. Initial examination is directed at establishing postmortem descriptions of the remains for later comparison with the information being simultaneously collected by the antemortem investigators. This process is called *reconciliation*. Ideally, a database computer software program (e.g., CAPMI, WinID) can assist in comparing antemortem versus postmortem identifying characteristics.

   a) Work with the easiest cases first. The idea is to bring the facility back to normal as quickly as possible. The more quickly the numbers of unknowns can be reduced, the more quickly the facility is dealing with a smaller group of remains. Identification of the more difficult cases is reduced to a smaller number of possibilities.

   b) After arriving at the morgue, the bodies should be placed in a cooler-type of facility. The bodies are retrieved one by one. Each body will then be processed as follows:

      i) Photograph the victim before any examination or cleaning of the remains.

495 · MASS-DIASTER INVESTIGATION · 495

(1) Take an overall shot of the body and a close-up shot of the face.
(2) Once the body has been cleaned, take another close-up of the face.
(3) Photograph all jewelry prior to removing.
(4) Photograph all clothing prior to removal.
(5) Photograph all areas of possible identifying characteristics, such as scars, tattoos, medical appliances, etc.

ii) X-ray the remains.
iii) Fingerprint the remains.

(1) Note any amputations and whether or not the amputations occurred prior to the incident.
(2) Footprint all children.

iv) The pathologist will examine the remains. The autopsy protocol is as follows:

(1) Describe any personal effects, including jewelry, wallet, ticket/seat allocation, or passport.
(2) Clothing description should include garment, type, color, size, label, and laundry marks.
(3) The autopsy will include these:

(a) Identifying characteristics, including age, race, sex, height, weight, eye color, hair color, facial hair, tattoos, surgical/other scars, circumcision, anomalies, and birthmarks
(b) Description by diagnosis of external trauma by body region
(c) Description by diagnosis of internal trauma
(d) Distribution of fractures, blunt force trauma, internal hemorrhage, airway (e.g., trauma, soot, drowning) description
(e) Identity previous surgeries, such as removal of gallbladder, appendix, or uterus.
(f) List anatomic findings
(g) Toxicology, including blood, urine, stomach contents, lung, liver, kidney, and brain

2) Prepare a folder with the corresponding body number assigned. The regular medical examiner or coroner number for new cases will not be assigned until the body has been identified. The folder should include the following:

a) Fingerprint, palm prints, or footprint card
b) Postmortem body chart indicating the description of the decedent, including:

i) Sex, race, approximate age, height, weight, hair color, eye color, facial hair description, scars, tattoos, circumcision, and birthmarks
ii) Clothing worn
iii) Jewelry and other valuables found on the decedent

(1) The exact location of the jewelry must be accurately recorded (e.g., left ring finger).

iv) Medical appliances

c) Postmortem dental chart of the decedent
d) Postmortem photograph of the decedent

FOLLOW-UP INVESTIGATION

1) Postmortem team may be required to follow up efforts at identification by assisting in the following areas:

   a) Jewelry
      i) Charred, blackened jewelry may be restored to an identifiable condition with the use of a small brush, carbon tetrachloride, or water. Dates, initials, and other useful information are sometimes inscribed in rings, watches, lockets, pens, and bracelets.
      ii) Once examined, the jewelry is to be placed in a plastic bag, sealed with evidence tape, labeled with the body number, and secured in a locked area.
   b) Clothing labels
      i) Record size, manufacture, fabric type, color, and any other information present on the label of clothing articles recovered.
   c) Locating known prints
      i) Fingerprints of a suspected decedent may be available from local/state law enforcement agencies, the FBI, some state driver's license bureaus, armed forces identification cards, hospital birth records (e.g., baby's foot, mother's finger), and private employer's records.
      ii) On those cases where fingerprints for a decedent cannot be located, it may become necessary to dust known personal items belonging to him for latent finger and palm prints to compare with the postmortem prints obtained. Items from the suspected decedent's home (e.g., toothpaste tube, deodorant can, shaving cream can, letters, checks) should be processed. At the suspected decedent's business, his desk, filing cabinet, etc., can be dusted for prints.

2) The antemortem team should be made up of individuals who have some experience in dealing with people going through the initial stages of grief. Do not disregard professionals in the victims' advocacy field. It is imperative that a thorough, time-consuming interview be conducted and important information elicited at the worst possible time in the family's life. Please do not refer to the source of your inquiry as the decedent or victim in dealing with the family until positive identification has been completed. Extreme care must be taken when making initial inquiries. Make no assumption that the list of names present on a passenger manifest is true and correct.
   a) The antemortem team has two purposes:
      i) Obtain or develop a manifest or a list of potential victims. This may be as easy as being handed a passenger list from an airline representative or as difficult as checking through missing persons records for an extended period.
         (1) Please keep in mind that infants are not always carried on an airline's manifest. An infant younger than 24 months can be carried by his parent. The manifest may or may not have "inf" after a parent's name.
      ii) Obtain and develop identifying information on suspected disaster victims, specifically:
         (1) Full name of victim
         (2) Any other names used by victim, including maiden, from previous marriages, aliases, etc.
         (3) Race and sex
         (4) Date of birth, place of birth
         (5) Marital status, date of marriage, full name of spouse
         (6) Has subject ever been fingerprinted for any reason (e.g., applicant, alien, criminal, military service, merchant marine, driver's license, personnel records)? If so, for what reason, with what organization, and on what date?
         (7) What is the subject's Social Security number?
         (8) Was the subject ever in the military? If yes, what branch? What is his military number? When did the subject serve?

(9) What is the subject's home address?

(10) What is the subject's business address?

(11) What is he subject's occupation?

(12) Describe the subject, including:

        (a) Height, weight, and build

        (b) Color, style, and length of hair; wig or toupee worn

        (c) Eye color

        (d) Glasses or contact lenses worn

        (e) Facial hair, if any

        (f) Any scars, birthmarks, anomalies, or tattoos

(13) What is the nationality of the subject?

(14) Did the subject smoke? If yes, what brand of tobacco

(15) Describe in detail the clothing the subject was wearing, including the color, type of fabric, label/brand, where purchased, size, and any other descriptive factors (e.g., laundry or dry cleaning marks). Consider the following items:

        (a) Overcoat

        (b) Suit or dress

        (c) Jacket

        (d) Sweater

        (e) Trousers or slacks

        (f) Shirt or blouse

        (g) Vest

        (h) Tie or scarf

        (i) Socks or hose

        (j) Gloves

        (k) Shoes

        (l) Girdle

        (m) Belt

        (n) Panties, shorts, or briefs

        (o) Undershirt or bra

        (p) Slip

        (q) Hat

        (r) Any other items worn?

(16) Was nail polish worn on hands or feet?

(17) Describe any jewelry (get detailed description, including color of metal, color andnumber of stones, engravings, brand names of watches, and where the item was worn). Include the following:

        (a) Watch

        (b) Ring(s)

        (c) Bracelet

        (d) Earrings

        (e) Necklace(s)

        (f) Tie clip

        (g) Money clip or wallet

        (h) Ankle bracelet

        (i) Belt buckle

        (j) Good luck charm, coin, or currency

        (k) Medals

        (l) Association pin

        (m) Knife

       (n) Any other item

       (o) Was subject wearing anyone else's jewelry?

       (p) Did the subject conceal valuables and or money in the lining of his clothing?

       (q) Are ears pierced?

(18) Had subject ever been hospitalized where X-rays may have been taken? If yes, describe hospital and date of admission. If the subject had ever suffered any fracture, describe.

(19) Has the subject ever had any plastic surgery? If yes, describe.

(20) Does the subject have any foreign object lodged in his body, such as a steel plate, metal screws, pins, bullet, shrapnel, artificial hip, etc.?

(21) What is the name, address, city and state, and telephone number of the subject's dentist?

(22) Is blood type available? If yes, where?

(23) Was the subject on medication? If yes, identify the medication. If yes, did the subject carry the medicine with him?

(24) Identify the source of this information:

       (a) Name

       (b) Address

       (c) Phone

       (d) Relationship

(25) Is there some other person who may have additional information on this subject? If yes, identify this person by name and telephone number.

3)   A comparison or reconciliation of information should be made between the data collected by the antemortem team and the data accumulated by the postmortem team. Specifically, the comparison should be made on the following details:

     a) Teeth (dental)

     b) Fingerprints

     c) DNA

     d) Other considerations:

         i) Race and sex

         ii) Age

         iii) Height and weight

         iv) Hair color

         v) Eye color

         vi) Previous fractures

         vii) Scars

         viii) Tattoos

         ix) Anomalies and or prostheses

         x) Jewelry

         xi) Clothing

         xii) Facial hair

         xiii) Circumcision

4)   Basis for degree of certainty in identification:

     a) Positive

     b) Consistent with

     c) Unidentified

CHAPTER 52: VICTIM IDENTIFICATION

When a dead body is discovered, one of the following positive identification techniques or several of the tentative techniques should be undertaken to effect identification.

Body recovery starts the identification process.

POSITIVE IDENTIFICATION TECHNIQUES

1) Visual identification by relatives or friends
    a) Requirements:
        i) Visual identification is the easiest and most accepted method of identification, providing the decedent is visibly identifiable and there are no reasons to suspect the identification. This form of identification has the greatest potential for producing a misidentification.

2) Fingerprint comparisons
    a) Requirements:
        i) Body must be suitable for obtaining postmortem prints. Antemortem prints must be available.

VISUAL IDENTIFICATION

FINGERPRINTS IN HUMAN IDENTIFICATION

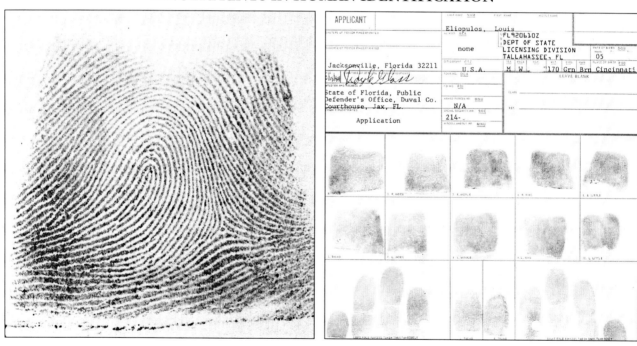

Fingerprints in human identification.

3)   Dental comparisons
    a) Requirements:
        i) Antemortem dental records must be obtained. Dental X-rays are preferred but should be accompanied by dental charts and any models made of the teeth or jaw.
    b) Caution:
        i) Be sure to consider the possibility that the decedent may have been seen by a particular dentist and using someone else's insurance.

FINGERPRINT IDENTIFICATION

Even with the devastating effects of fire, the flash effect can often leave protected parts of the body unburned. In this particular case, a partial print from the decedent was obtained within the curled fingers protecting the pads of the fingers. The severely burned corpse was still identified through fingerprints.

X-RAY COMPARISON IN IDENTIFICATION

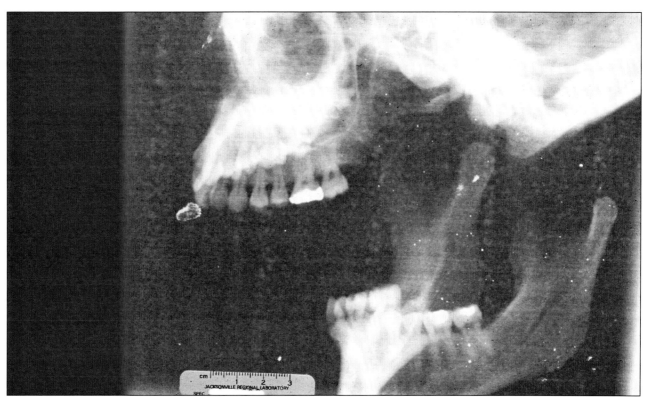

X-rays can be examined by a radiologist where individual characteristics of identifiable features can be discerned.

4)   X-ray comparisons
            a) Requirements:
                   i) Antemortem X-rays must be located and obtained.

5)   DNA comparison
            a) Requirements:
                   i) Antemortem specimens must be obtained or specimens can be taken from the
                      parents of the suspected decedent. Postmortem remains must be suitable for
                      obtaining specimens.
            b) Caution:
                   i) Paternity issues may be misrepresented by the suspected parents of the
                      decedent. Be sure to allow the mother of the suspected decedent ample time
                      and opportunity with the investigator for her to reveal any private revelations
                      concerning the natural father of the decedent.

MITOCHONDRIAL CHART

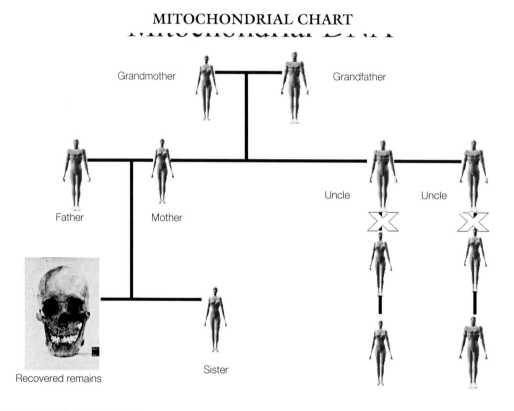

TENTATIVE IDENTIFICATION TECHNIQUES

1)   Anthropologic characteristics
            a) Requirements:
                   i) Remains should be submitted to a forensic anthropologist for development of
                      characteristics, including race, sex, age, height, build, any unusual infirmities or
                      disease, whether left or right handed, any unusual characteristics, and time
                      since death. This information can then be compared to the characteristics of a
                      suspected missing person.

SUPERIMPOSITION IDENTIFICATION

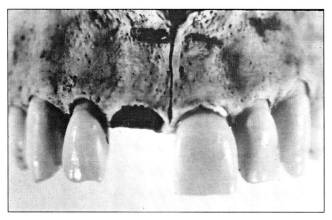

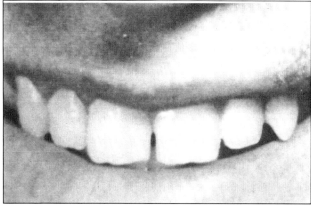

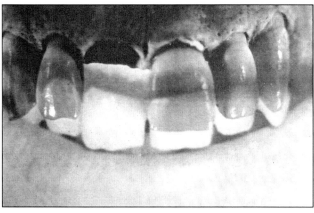

In superimposition, the recovered skull is photographed with similar camera equipment, including lens, or a video camera is used to duplicate the position, angle, and distance of the antemortem photograph. The two images are then superimposed with one another in an effort to determine similarities and discrepancies.

2)   Superimposition photography or videotaping

a) Requirements:
i) The skull of the decedent is necessary, along with a clear antemortem photograph of the suspected missing person. This antemortem photograph should be a smiling shot of the subject with the teeth clearly displayed.

3)   Serologic analysis(not including DNA) or hair comparisons
a) Requirements:
i) Antemortem and postmortem specimens must be available.

4)   Clothing, documents, and jewelry found on or around the body
a) Requirements:
i) These are used in conjunction with exclusion. There should be no suspicion of of any intention to mislead investigators. A friend or relative must be located who would be able to identify items of jewelry and clothing belonging to the decedent.

5)   Exclusion
a) Requirements:
i) This is used to compare facts about the decedent with those of the suspected missing individual.

CHAPTER 53:
UNIDENTIFIED REMAINS PROTOCOL

1)   The protocol for processing of unidentified remains in cases where it appears identification may be a difficult challenge.
   a) At the scene, take photos of the decedent's head from straight on and in profile, including:
      i) Close-up of hairline
      ii) Close-up of ears
      iii) Close-up of face
   b) Determine the race, sex, and approximate age of the individual.
   c) Obtain an approximation of how long the decedent may have been dead.
   d) Note the clothing found with the remains.
   e) Note any identifiable characteristics, including:
      i) Hair color, style, and length
      ii) Facial hair description
      iii) Tattoos

2)   At the medical examiner's office, do the following:
   a) If possible, take three full sets of fingerprints.
      i) Submit one set of prints to the identification bureau of the local police.
      ii) Submit a second set of prints to the identification bureau of the state police.
      iii) Submit one set of prints to the FBI's Identification Section in Washington, D.C.
   b) If prints are not available or did not "hit" (identify) the subject locally, continue handling by:
      i) Record the style, color, and size of all clothing. Examine clothing for laundry marks or names.
      ii) Check missing persons for possible candidates.
      iii) Jaws should be removed and charted by a forensic odontologist.
      iv) Collect DNA specimens.
      v) Consult a forensic artist about having a drawing completed on the decedent.
      vi) Complete an NCIC Unidentified Person Packet and submit to NCIC.
      vii) Prepare a media release.

3)   On possible candidates or on leads developed, obtain the following information:
   a) Race, sex, age, and name of individual
   b) How long has this person been missing?
   c) What are the circumstances of this person's going missing?
   d) Was this person ever fingerprinted?
   e) Was this person ever hospitalized? Were X-rays taken?
   f) Identify the subject's dentist.
   g) Develop next-of-kin information.

CHAPTER 54: FORENSIC ART IN IDENTIFICATION

CONSIDERATIONS

1) *Forensic art* is a catchall term used to describe the work produced by an artist through his association with criminal justice agencies in criminal matters.

2) In the past, the artist was usually contracted or volunteered his services to the involved agency. Recently, progressive agencies have recognized the importance and potential of this field.

3) Basically, a forensic artist can assist in the following areas:
   a) Identification of an unknown, including:
      i) Three-dimensional reconstruction (sculpture) of what a person might have resembled from an unidentified skull for identification purpose
      ii) Two-dimensional drawings of what a person may have resembled from a unidentified skull for identification purposes
      iii) Drawing of unknown decedents for identification purposes with injuries removed and their eyes opened for a presentable release to the public
      iv) Drawings of unidentified decomposed remains with the decomposition features removed

4) Other uses
   a) Updated drawings of missing persons or at-large suspects from photographs in older cases
   b) Composite drawings of suspects
   c) Demonstrative displays for court or investigative purposes

PRIMARY FOCUS

1) Of primary importance to the forensic death investigator are the benefits available through identification techniques. The cases referred for this technique should be cases where the normal identification procedures have not resulted in an identification.

2) The ultimate use of this information is a release to the public asking for leads that may help identify the unknown person.

INVESTIGATION

1) All cases involving skeletal remains should have been referred to the forensic anthropologist by the time this case is submitted to a forensic artist.

2) Upon submission to a forensic artist, the investigator should have the following information about the decedent:
   a) Race
   b) Sex
   c) Best estimate of age
   d) Best possible estimate of the length of time he has been dead
   e) Description of hair (from that found at the scene), including:
      i) Color
      ii) Texture (e.g., curly, wavy, straight)

        iii) Length (include placement on head where length was noted)
        iv) Style (if possible)
    f) All facial characteristics noted by the forensic anthropologist
    g) Any facial characteristics noted by a forensic odontologist
    h) Whether the subject was emaciated, normal, or obese immediately before death
    i) A copy available of all photographs involving the decedent, including those taken at the scene.
    j) Have the skull available to the artist

PHOTOGRAPHING OF DECEDENT FOR FORENSIC ART PURPOSES

1) With the exception of skulls (whose condition does not worsen with time), photographing the decedent for submission to the forensic artist must be anticipated. Since the recovery of the body, and by the time the investigator has reached the stage where an artist rendering may assist in the identification, the decedent's appearance may have been significantly altered due to the effects of decomposition. Therefore, these photographic requirements should be made mandatory on all unidentified remains.

    a) Unidentified decedents (nonskeletal) including fresh, decomposed, and mummified remains.
        i) Roughly align the head along the Frankfort plane.
            (1) Photograph the head from straightaway and in profile.
            (2) Photograph the head from straightaway and in profile with the eyes opened.
            (3) Take a close-up photo of the nose from straightaway and in profile.
            (4) Take a close-up of the mouth area from straightaway and in profile.
            (5) Take a close-up of the mouth area from straightaway and in profile with the teeth showing.
        ii) Photograph the hairline of the decedent.
        iii) Photograph the head showing the hair style and hair texture, if possible.
        iv) Photograph of the side the head, showing the ears of the decedent.
        v) Take a close-up photographs of the ears of the decedent.
    b) Photographing the skull
        i) Align the skull along the Frankfort plane and take a photograph from the front and profile of the skull.
            (1) Use a contrasting background to clearly delineate the outline features of the skull.
            (2) Have a ruler present running laterally and longitudinally along the skull. Markings along the ruler should be large and clearly visible; these will be used to make photographic prints of the skull on a one-to-one basis.
            (3) Lighting for photographs should be directed at an obtuse angle to facilitate identification of various features on the skull's surface.

DISPERSAL OF THE FINISHED PROJECT

1) Prepare a press release, including the following information:
    a) Have a disclaimer make it clear that the public is not looking at a drawing of what the person looked like. They are seeing a drawing of what the person may have looked like. Certain features may be entirely incorrect.

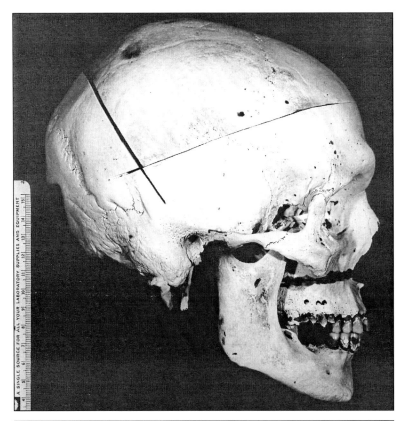

LATERAL VIEW

Photographing the skull along the Frankfort plane.

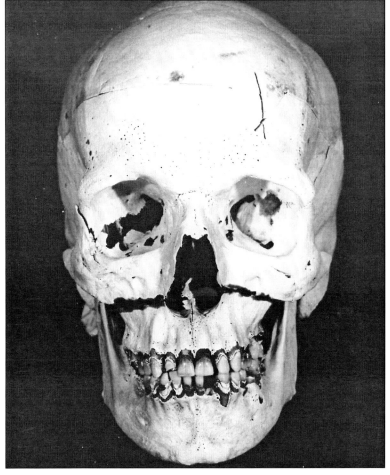

FRONTAL VIEW

Proper photography of a skull to be used in a drawing by a forensic artist. The skull is aligned along the Frankfort plane.

　　　　b) Describe the decedent, including:
　　　　　　i) Race and sex
　　　　　　ii) Age approximation
　　　　　　iii) Height and weight
　　　　　　iv) Hair and eye color, if known
　　　　　　v) General descrition of any scars or tattoos. Leave specific details for the caller to describe.
　　　　c) Description of the time frame involved in the death
　　　　　　　i) Indicate when the body was found and how long the body may have been dead.

2)　　Perform a general dispersal.
　　　　a) Release the drawing with the above information to the media. Give a specific time and telephone number for callers with information.

3)　　Perform a targeted dispersal.
　　　　a) Prepare a flyer on the subject. Include the drawing of the subject, disclaimer for the drawing, description of the decedent, and time frame involved in his death. Give a particular person, at a particular telephone number for an interested party to call.
　　　　b) Saturate a particular area or type of store, bar, fish camp, etc., in which information has been developed that indicates the decedent may have been associated with or known by the people in these areas during his life.

4)　　Prepare for a response.
　　　　a) Arrange for telephone inquiries to come in while you are working and able to handle the calls or the supervision of the calls.
　　　　b) All calls, or the results of all calls, should go through one delegated person. This representative should be the person who knows the most about the case.
　　　　c) Let anyone who may deliberately or inadvertently answer the telephone calls to be aware of what is happening. Give them specific instructions as to what they should do if they do answer one of these phone calls.
　　　　d) Establish who will be responsible for receiving incoming calls.
　　　　e) Prepare a call-in sheet of questions to ask each caller. Include the following:
　　　　　　i) Who they believe the caller may be
　　　　　　ii) Description of who they believe decedent may be
　　　　　　　　(1) Include height, weight, date of birth, identifying marks, or tattoos.
　　　　　　　　(2) Was this person ever arrested, or does the caller know of any fingerprints this person may have on file? Did this person serve time in any institution?
　　　　　　　　(3) Does the caller know of any dentist who may have treated this person?
　　　　　　　　(4) Does the caller know of any hospitalizations or other associations with medical facilities that may have resulted in X-rays?
　　　　　　　　(5) Does the caller have a photograph, preferably one showing a close-up of the head and some of the teeth of the person who the drawing may resemble?
　　　　　　iii) When was the subject last seen alive?
　　　　　　iv) Identify the next of kin and contact information for next of kin of the person the caller believes the drawing to be.
　　　　　　v) Why does the caller believe the person he is calling about may be the person depicted in the drawing?

vi) Does the caller know of anyone else who may have more information about this subject?

vii) Obtain the name, address, and telephone number of the caller. (NOTE: Save the identification of the caller for the end of the conversation. Callers are somewhat reluctant to get involved. Not asking for their name initially may help in getting information. By the end of your conversation, the caller should be somewhat more at ease in his conversation with the representative.)

viii) Arrange for callers to be assisted should you be absent.

f) Work all leads!

CHAPTER 55: HANDLING NEXT OF KIN

NOTIFICATION OF NEXT OF KIN

1) The legal hierarchy of the next-of-kin relationship to the decedent is as follows:
   - a) Spouse
   - b) Child of legal age
   - c) Parent
   - d) Brother or sister
   - e) Other relative
   - f) Friend

2) The highest level of hierarchy possible is necessary for notification.

3) Notification of next of kin is required to be made as soon as possible after the identification of the decedent has been established by the investigating agency.

4) The investigating agency should allow sufficient time for other family members to be notified (by other family members) prior to releasing the identification information to the news media. Under no circumstances should a preliminary identification of the decedent be released to the news media prior to a definite identification of the decedent.

SPECIFIC PROCEDURES IN HANDLING THE NOTIFICATION

1) Never make the notification by telephone. Without exception, a personal visit should be made.

2) If notification involves another jurisdiction, a teletype, fax, or telephone call should be placed to the law enforcement agency having jurisdiction. Upon notification, a telephone number should be supplied to the family along with the name of the officer or investigator assigned the case. This will allow the family the opportunity to call the investigative agency to seek additional details of the incident. In addition, the investigator will be able to further advise the family of time tables involving the release of the remains for final disposition.

3) Be honest and open with the decedent's family. Tell the family that if they may not wish to hear the details involving the death, not to ask the question. Being less than candid with the family in trying to spare their feelings may create a situation where it appears the investigating agency is covering up information.

4) Upon notification, the family will normally be in some state of shock. Subsequent contact by the family will usually produce more in-depth questions; however, upon initial contact, the family will normally ask the following questions:
   - a) What happened?
   - b) How do you know it is their family member (how was identification made)?
   - c) How did decedent die specifically?
   - d) Did he suffer?
   - e) What should they do now (disposition of remains)?

5) Never say any of the following to the family:
   - a) "It's God's will."

514 · DEATH INVESTIGATOR'S HANDBOOK · 514

b) "You're so strong, I know you can handle this."

    c) "Tell me what I can do."

    d) "I understand."

    e) "It was a blessing that . . ."

    f) "He's with God now and at peace."

    g) "I know how you feel."

    h) "You'll get over this."

    i) "Remember to be strong for the children."

    j) "Just be thankful that . . ."

    k) "You're lucky that . . ."

    l) "He probably didn't know what hit him."

6)   Proper address can involve the following statements to the bereaved family:

    a) "I'm sorry that this has happened."

    b) "I can't imagine how difficult this must be for you. I'd like to be with you for a while, if you don't mind."

    c) "It's not your fault."

THE BEREAVED FAMILY

1)   Handling the bereaved family of a decedent is critically important and often overlooked as a potential source of information. One of the first stages of the grief process involves anger. During the initial period following the notification, this anger is often not directed at the person most responsible for the death. It does not take much prompting for the anger to be directed at the officer conducting the investigation, especially if that investigator does not take time to speak with the family, ignores the case, or makes excuses for why the case will never be solved. What the investigator has succeeded in doing is giving that family a focus for their anger and a purpose for their involvement and new activity stemming from their original sense of helplessness in the death of their family member. Avoid these problems at all costs by using the following:

    a) If your area has grief counselors, get them involved in the process.

    b) Make yourself available to answer the questions and take suggestions from the family.

    c) Keep the family apprised of the progress of the investigation. Regardless of the absurdity, incorporate into your own investigation the suggestions of the family for handling the case. Remember, the more involved the family is made to feel, the more the family will respect and trust your handling of the case and the less they will feel they have to help you solve the case.

THE GRIEF PROCESS

1)   Don't draw conclusions about how someone grieves or doesn't grieve. People go through the grieving process in different ways.

    a) Some people don't need to cry.

    b) Some people will release their emotions at some other place and time.

2)   The process family and friends will go through involves the following:

3)   The grief process involves what is known as the "SIGH" process.

    a) **S**—Somatic

        i) Shock is the most common feature. The individual becomes "zombie-like" and automatic in his activities. There is a tremendous despair and depression associated with great fatigue and loss of appetite.

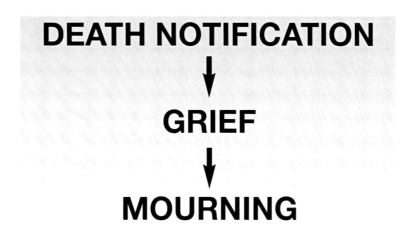

b) **I**—Imagery
    i) The grieving family will have dreams in which the decedent will appear and make specific comments about their status in the afterlife. The bereaved may also hear the decedent's voice in specific circumstances.

c) **G**—Guilty
    i) Depending on the circumstances of the death, the bereaved will feel some sense of guilt for actions and inactions on their part. The family members may feel as though they did not do enough for the decedent. This is especially obvious in cases of sudden, unexpected death and especially prevalent with suicides. This is one of the major reasons the family has the most difficulty in accepting suicide as the manner of death.

d) **H**—Hostility
    i) There is a deep-seated anger over the loss of the loved one. Their immediate reaction is to question why this person was taken from them.
    ii) The anger may be useful. It may indicate that the bereaved is coming out of his depression. It is very important to remember that when this anger is directed toward you, do not fight back!

4) With the mourning process comes the reality that the bereaved never really recovers. The actual recovery process involves the bereaved coming to a new level of being able to deal with or cope with the loss.

THE ABNORMAL GRIEF PROCESS

1) Signs of abnormal grief reaction involve the following:
    a) Overactivity
    b) Acquired symptoms
    c) Medical illness
    d) Altered relationships with others

GETTING THROUGH GRIEF

1) For the individual to get through the grief process, the bereaved will have to take the following action:
    a) Face reality.
    b) Accept death.
    c) Give up on the physical person.

CHAPTER 56: MEDIA MANAGEMENT

CONSIDERATIONS

1) A criminal justice agency will never control the media, nor will it never win a battle with the media. What remains is the only possible compromise: media management.

2) As the investigation of a death scene is being carried out, the actions and considerations of the media are normally on the bottom of the investigator's priority list. However, the management of the media should be a critical consideration, on an even par with any of the assignments and responsibilities given to the investigative team, on this particular case. It is here that the public will first learn of the deaths. The media will get the story out to the public regardless of the investigator's input. Refusing to speak or release any information to the media will serve no purpose to the investigation other than having the media release incorrect, incomplete, or harmful information. At the very least, some control over what is released to the public can result through the cooperation of the investigative principles and the media.

3) Never speculate about the case for the media's benefit.

4) Members of the media despise information officers and attempt to circumvent them whenever they can. They see the major responsibility of this person as a stone wall to keep the media from the actual information and the people who are actually working on that information. On the other hand, the investigators assigned to the case are extremely busy working the case and following leads, especially during the first critical 48 hours. Periodic briefings by an investigator supervisor in conjunction with an information officer may be a compromise solution.

5) Before any media release, careful consideration should be given to the work product of assisting agencies. Police conducting the death investigation should be careful not to release information concerning the cause or method of death, nor should legal considerations be released to the media without consultation and input from the medical examiner/coroner or prosecuting attorney. If any disagreements cannot be resolved about the information that should or should not be released, the final decision will ultimately rest with the prosecuting attorney.

6) The decision as to whether or not specific information is released should be the same on all cases.
   a) For example, in a police-involved shooting case, when it appears a "good" shooting has occurred (i.e., it appears the officer was legally justified in firing his weapon at an individual), all the information developed by the investigative team is placed at the disposal of the media. However, if a police shooting appears to be in a "gray" area (i.e., the police shooting is somewhat questionable), media representatives are told that no information will be released because the case is under active investigation.
      i) If the agency ever wants to "red flag" a case to the media, handling a case differently than other cases will immediately put the media on notice that something is amiss.

7)   The media does provide a useful function. There is a need and justification for sharing information with the media. The media is part of the same community in which the criminal justice agency is called upon to serve and protect. The media provides one way the agency has to talk with the community. More often than not, the more the community knows, the more the community will understand what is occurring.

8)   Understand the difference between an incident of local importance and an incident of national significance. Media behavior will be completely different because national media representatives do not have to be concerned with creating a long-lasting working relationship. They do not care if they "burn their bridges." The competition for news stories, angles on news stories, and deadlines brings out the worst in their character.
    a) Local reporters should take precedence because they are the ones who get the local information out to local constituents.
    b) Competition among the media will eventually result in a loss of ethics and irresponsible behavior. Be cautious and make plans for the following:
        i) Directional microphones
            (1) Used by the media to pick up sounds at long distance. Conversations investigators normally have at the scene concerning the case are subject to being picked up by listening devices from a distance.
        ii) Telephoto lenses
            (1) Media reps are able to set up their cameras from far away from a scene that the investigator may feel is secure.
        iii) Police radios as a form of communication
            (1) Private conversations should not take place. Digital scanners are available to the general public that enable the user to immediately program any particular frequency he may wish to monitor.
        iv) Cellular portable phones
            (1) These are subject to monitoring with inexpensive equipment available at electronic retail stores.
        v) Media briefing sites
            (1) Schedule any conferences away from the site at which the investigators are working. Reporters will wander around the building and snoop in areas containing reports, photographs, and charts.
            (2) The media tends to take over and disrupt areas where they collect. They tend to mob lobbies and can interfere with or even curtail the normal business of the agency.
            (3) Notify the telephone company of a potential gridlock at least 15 minutes before releasing information. Immediately after each briefing, the media will search for telephones to call in their stories.
        vi) Security of information
            (1) Some members of the media may offer a great deal of money (up to a year's salary in some cases) to members and associates of the investigative team, as well as security and janitorial personnel, for reports, pictures, and other information relating to the incident. The media may offer up to 1 year's salary to any agency employee to turn over information concerning the incident. For example, morgue security may be breached during early morning hours to provide access to a media photographer. Secure all aspects of the investigation.

Don't assume that the investigation is secure because it sits in the investigator's desk overnight.

9) Never lie to the media. If the investigator or spokesperson lies to the media, he is lying to the community.

10) Never place a time frame on when the public can expect the case to be solved. This places undue pressure on the involved agency and the people responsible for solving the case.

11) Be careful about what information is released.
   a) Criminals read newspaper accounts and watch electronic media news stories of their exploits. They will alter their activities as they learn through media accounts of the progress the investigation is making.
      i) For example, the killer may begin dumping bodies in the river as opposed to on interstate highways because the media reported that the police have had a breakthrough in the case by finding carpet fibers on the bodies of interstate highway dumpings.
   b) Do not release details of the incident.
      i) Investigators will not be able to evaluate those individuals who come forward with information about the crime.
      ii) One of the first actions a competent defense attorney will act on during his representation of his client charged with murder, who has confessed to police, is to determine if that confession contains any details only the murderer could know. Once this is accomplished, the defense attorney will then examine whether those details had been previously released to the media and, subsequently, published or broadcast.
   c) Be cautious in speaking of the brutality of the particular incident or the condition of the remains. Keep in mind that the families of the victim will be watching and reading accounts of the death. Choose words carefully.
      i) Do not refer to the body as "it."
      ii) Be cautious in speaking in terms of sexual assault or sexual mutilation.

12) Monitor and collect media reports, especially from the print media.
   a) The media may come up with witnesses the investigators have not developed during the course of the investigation.
   b) This allows the investigators to understand what information is public when suspects come forward or are developed.

ESTABLISHING A PERIMETER FOR THE SCENE

1) In some cases, a natural perimeter already exists that allows investigators and other associates of the scene to work unimpeded and with little concern for the media. In most cases, a perimeter will have to be established. Follow these general guidelines.
   a) Establish where the outer fringes of an incident are likely to be. Items such as shell casings; bullet fragments; food and beverages; overturned, broken, or disordered articles; and blood spatters should be identified as part of the scene.
   b) Once the outermost area or perimeter containing evidence is identified, add 50 percent more area to this location to establish a sufficient perimeter.
   c) Work quickly. The media is monitoring the police radio and will often beat the detective to the scene.

2)   Consider establishing a secondary area inside the cordoned-off area for the media. They may appreciate this gesture of having a little closer viewing area than the general public. They may also appreciate being separated from the general public during their efforts to film the scene.

3)   Don't attempt to assume responsibility for what the media may videotape by attempting to stop this activity. If a good-faith effort has been made to keep the media away from the immediate scene, nothing else can be done. Media personnel assume responsibility for what they ultimately place on the air. They do not operate in a vacuum.

RELEASING INFORMATION

1)   Consider these four areas that may be affected by the release of information:
        a) Witness(es)
            i) Witnesses who have been developed during the processing of the scene should be protected, especially if the suspect is still at large.
            ii) The witness should never be identified by name, employment, or home address.
            iii) On cases where admitting to the media that there is a witness would be tantamount to identifying that witness, make no statement either acknowledging or denying this information.
            iv) The context of what the witness has told investigators should not be released.
        b) Victim
            i) Never release information concerning the following:
                (1) The number of times a victim was shot, stabbed, or struck by an object, etc.
                (2) A specific description of the weapon involved. For example, state that the weapon was "a firearm," not a ".25-caliber semiautomatic handgun." "A blunt instrument" is sufficient to explain a baseball bat, brick, or other item that caused blunt trauma.
                (3) Strangulation-type deaths should never be distinguished as a manual or ligature strangulation.
            ii) What appears on the death certificate should be enough to explain the cause of death. The police and prosecutor should be consulted prior to the release of any cause of death by the pathologist assigned to the case.
            iii) Do not release the identification of the decedent until proper notification has been made to the next of kin and there has been enough time for other family members to be notified.
            iv) Do not release information concerning the possible motive of the crime.
            v) The time frame of death is an investigative consideration. It is not subject for release to the media.
        c) Suspect
            i) No information should be released concerning the modus operandi of the event, including (but not limited to):
                (1) How entry was gained
                (2) Weapon used
                (3) Activities at the scene
                (4) Interaction with the victim
                (5) Anything that may have taken from the scene
                (6) Any evidence
                (7) Whether or not the investigators are looking at any similar cases

ii) Prior to the arrest of the suspect, certain information may be released to the media to seek the public's assistance in apprehending the suspect.

(1) Be cautious in preparing the release. Remember, the presumption for this suspect is innocent until proven guilty.

iii) After the arrest of the suspect, the following information is subject for release:

(1) Suspect's name, age, last known address, and other background information (check applicable federal, state, or local law for release of criminal history). Criminal records are a matter of public record in most jurisdictions. Release of a mug shot is also possible if it serves a a purpose. Certainly if the suspect is at large, a photograph may assist law enforcement in apprehending him.

(2) The particular charge for which the suspect was arrested

(3) The place where the suspect was arrested and the identification of the arresting agency

(4) A description of the circumstances involving the arrest of the suspect

iv) No information should be released concerning whether or not the suspect participated in an electronic test to validate truthfulness (a "lie-detector test") and, if the suspect did take the test, what the results may have shown.

v) No information should be released concerning the contents of a confession.

vi) Photographing, videotaping, or the jail "walk-over" of the suspect should never be arranged for the convenience of the media. However, no attempt should be made to prevent the media from covering this unless the suspect may be needed for lineups or identification purposes in other cases.

d) Releasable information concerning the incident

i) Victim information, including name (providing that the next of kin have been notified), age, sex, marital status, and address (list the "hundred" block for the numerical; do not list the exact address).

ii) The address location of the incident and a description of the premises

iii) The time the decedent was discovered

iv) How the decedent was recovered

v) The manner of death (homicide, suicide, accident, natural, undetermined, or under investigation)

vi) Cause of death (after completion of autopsy and approval of the pathologist, prosecuting attorney, and lead investigator).

CASES IN WHICH THE MEDIA MAY HELP THE INVESTIGATION

1) Identification of unknown decedents

2) Locating of potential witnesses in cases involving stranger-to-stranger murders

3) Generating interest in older cases that may bring new information forward

CHAPTER 57:
INVESTIGATION RESOURCES FOR CONDUCTING LOCATION AND BACKGROUND INVESTIGATIONS

COMMON SOURCES OF INFORMATION

1) Directory search
   a) Check directories to develop employment, occupations, names of other family members, other addresses, etc.
   b) Check telephone directory and telephone information.

2) Residence address(es)
   a) The last known address is usually the most logical to begin the investigation. Relatives should be contacted to develop current address. Consider landlord or rental agency.

3) Employer(s)
   a) Start with most recent employer. Develop any information from a prospective employer. Where was withholding tax statement (Form W2) sent? Any relatives or references listed in file, etc.?

4) Post office
   a) Request change-of-address search from the post office.

5) Schools
   a) If subject had children, check at appropriate school. Does school have record where the children transferred?

6) Local union office
   a) If the subject was a union member, contact the local office.

7) Clubs, associations, or hobbies
   a) Develop any clubs or associations the subject may have belonged to in the area.

8) Public utilities
   a) Gas, electric, or water services for new cut-ins

9) Marriage records
   a) Check marriage records for possible change of name due to marriage. Check neighbors, church, or marriage record for name of spouse and other leads.

10) Voter registration records

11) Tax or property records

12) Licensing records
   a) Certain types of business or occupations (e.g., cab drivers, bartenders, food handlers) must be licensed in some areas.

13)   Criminal and traffic records
            a) Check for any recent violations and the new address.

14)   Financial statements
            a) Develop names of finance companies, banks, etc., that may have the subject's new
               address.

15)   Motor vehicle record
            a) Develop automobile registration and driver's license records with new address.

16)   Birth and death records
            a) If there was a recent birth or death in family, develop for leads.

SOCIAL SECURITY NUMBERS

The following numbers are codes used by the Social Security Administration for the first three numbers identifying the state where the SSN was issued. This can be helpful in checking records in states where it appears the subject may have originated.

001–003	New Hampshire	400–407	Kentucky
004–007	Maine	408–415	Tennessee
008–009	Vermont	416–424	Alabama
010–034	Massachusetts	425–428	Mississippi
035–039	Rhode Island	429–432	Arkansas
040–049	Connecticut	433–439	Louisiana
050–134	New York	440–448	Oklahoma
135–158	New Jersey	449–467	Texas
159–211	Pennsylvania	468–477	Minnesota
212–220	Maryland	478–485	Iowa
221–222	Delaware	486–500	Missouri
223–231	Virginia	501–502	North Dakota
232–236	West Virginia	503–504	South Dakota
237–246	North Carolina	505–508	Nebraska
247–251	South Carolina	509–515	Kansas
252–260	Georgia	516–517	Montana
261–267	Florida	518–519	Idaho
268–302	Ohio	520	Wyoming
303–317	Indiana	521–524	Colorado
318–361	Illinois	525	New Mexico
362–386	Michigan	526–527	Arizona
387–399	Wisconsin	528–529	Utah

530	Nevada	575–576	Hawaii
531–539	Washington	577–579	Washington, D.C.
540–544	Oregon	580	Virgin Islands
545–573	California	581–582	Puerto Rico
574	Alaska		

PUBLIC RECORDS

The following list contains some examples for using public records to develop information about an individual or business. Many of these records exist at various levels in state, county, and local agencies, although the particular department containing these records may vary from state to state. Most of the employees of the courthouses are more than happy to assist an individual in locating the particular department that handles the item the investigator is seeking.

Court Clerk Offices

Adoptions (normally confidential records)
Arrest warrants
Child support
Civil law equity

Alimony
Bonds
Change of name
Civil records division
  • Associate businesses.
  • Condition of businesses.
  • Depositions in which the complete background has been supplied concerning an individual or business
  • Medical history on the subject

Code violations
Criminal felony records
  • Depositions
  • Psychiatric examination reports
  • Letters from defendants
  • Fingerprints
  • Bond information identifying employer, relatives, and associates

Conservatorships
Criminal misdemeanor record division will include:
  • Bond information including employer, relatives, and associates
  • Traffic misdemeanor offenses will include
    —Association with the owner of the vehicle if different from the driver
    —Association with the owner of the vehicle, if different from the driver
    —Description of vehicle driven by the subject
Traffic enforcement division records will:
  • Place a subject in a particular area at a particular time
  • Place the subject with associates
  • Place subject in a particular car and describe the vehicle, including the color

Delinquency proceedings

Dissolution of marriage

Dispositions of all felonies, misdemeanors, traffic, municipal ordinances, and civil suits
Divorce records
  • Describe and document threats involving the subject
  • Identify attorney who may have background information
  • Identify next of kin, other relative, friends, or associates of a particular individual

- May identify potential sources for background information purposes by identifying previous addresses for a subject
- May identify potential sources who may be able to identify the subject's current whereabouts

Exhibits from trials

Foreclosure actions
Indictments
Jury lists
Juvenile court
Liens
Mental health information
- Includes voluntary and involuntary admissions, substance abuse admissions, etc.
- Identifies next of kin of the subject
- Provides background information on the subject.
Paternity actions
Preliminary complaints

Satisfaction of judgments
Small claims court
- Records may assist in identifying:
—Financial condition of the subject
—A possible source for development of subject's associates who may be able to provide additional information on the subject if interviewed, including present location
Support payments
Termination of parental rights
Traffic violations
Trial information
Victim restitution
Warrants of commitments
Worker's compensation payments to minors
Writ of certiorari
Writ of mandamus
Writ of replevin

Fictitious names
- Identifies individuals who own businesses
- Fidelity and surety certificates of authority.
Guardianships
Injunctions
Jury verdicts
Landlord attachments
Mechanic's liens
Order of discharge

Postconviction actions
Probate estates, guardianships, conservatorships, trusts, wills.
- Listed under decedent's name. Documents the last will and testament, businesses, finances, insurance, and those who benefited in the subject's death.
Search warrants and returns
Subpoenas

Surety company certificates
Titles, title changes
Transcripts of official proceedings and dispositions
Trust fund information
Warrants of arrests
Wills
Writ of attachment

Writ of habeus corpus
Writ of possession

County Offices

Agriculture land

Annual summary of occupational illnesses and injuries

Boat registrations

Campaign finance disclosure reports

Dog licenses

Fee book

Liquor sales licenses/beer sales permits

Motor home registrations

Motor vehicle titles
* Identifies previous owner of vehicle

Personal property tax list

Precinct lists

Real estate files

Revenue-sharing allocations

Special election requests

Tax sales register

Title transfer books

Voter registration records

Annual financial information

Audit information

Bond register

Delinquent tax list

Election registers

Hunting licenses

Marriage records division
* Identifies spouse, including maiden name if applicable
* Indicates previous marriage
* Identifies witnesses to ceremony who may be associates
* Give date of marriage and place where marriage occurred

Motor vehicle registrations
* Covers all automobiles, trucks, mobile homes, and boats
* Identifies date registered, vehicle identification number, title and tag number
* Gives lien holder and address of lien holder
* Provides a current source for last known address for a particular subject, as it is necessary to register a vehicle on an annual basis
* Identifies the subject's vehicles
* Supplies a date of birth for the subject

Occupational licenses
* Lists the date business began operation
* Provides address listing of the business
* Identifies the owner of the business
* Identifies whether the business is incorporated
* Describes the type of business

Plat books

Proposed budgets

Real estate tax sales book

Road books

Tax list

Tax statements

Veterans' affairs

Voucher payments

County or Property Assessor's Office

Assessments

Application for homestead and tax exemptions

Declarations of value

Homestead tax credit application

Aerial photographs of the county

Claims for tax exemptions

Exempt property reports

Military service tax exemptions

Plats

Identifies owner of the property

Protests of assessments

Real estate index

Property records for agricultural, commercial, industrial, residential property

Lists value of the property

Real estate assessment rolls

Real estate values

State/County Engineering Department

Accident reports on particular areas

Bridge inspections

Entrance permits

Road construction programs

Sign inventory

Traffic engineering studies

Acquisition of right-of-ways

Construction permits

Equipment maintenance records

Road equipment inventory

Snow reports

Planning and Zoning Offices

Appeals

Building permits

Zoning violations

Building permit applications

Minutes of the county zoning board

County/State Board of Health

Air pollution control permits, applications and violations

Hotel licenses

Reports of infectious and contagious diseases

Restaurant licenses

Condemnation procedures

Immunization summaries

Restaurant inspections

County Medical Examiner/Coroner

Autopsy reports and investigations

Fingerprints of decedents

Insurance claim inquiry

Paternity specimens

Cremation certificates

Identifying information on decedent

Next-of-kin information

Photographs of decedents

Local, County, and State Police Agencies

Accident reports

Complaints and commendations involving police personnel

Criminal records of individuals

Incident reports

Jail inspection reports

Permits to acquire firearms

Radio transmission recordings of specific incidents

Booking data

Criminal investigations

Impounded vehicles reports

Internal affairs investigations

Officer's daily report

Permits to carry concealed weapons

Official Records Clerk or the County Recorder

Affidavits

Antenupital agreements

Articles of dissolution

Articles of incorporation

Articles of merger or consolidation

Assignment of contract for security purposes

Assignment of real estate

Assignment of mortgage or deed of trust

Assignment of rents and leases

Bill of sale

Boat registration certificates

Building restrictions

Cemetery deeds

Certificate of limited partnership

Change of title

Condemnation proceedings

Corporation warranty deeds

Declaration of covenant

Declaration of value

Deed of trust

Deed without warranty

Drainage agreements

Easements

Escrow for deed

Farm leases

Farm names

Federal tax liens and releases

Fence agreements

Final judgments

Fishing, hunting, and trapping licenses

Home improvement liens

Homestead agreements

Leases

Military discharge

Mortgages

Notice of forfeiture

Notice of lien

Oil and gas leases

Options to buy

Ordinances

Patent deeds

Partial releases of mortgages

Personal tax liens and releases

Power of attorney

Promissory notes

Purchase agreements

Quitclaim deeds

Real estate contracts

Releases for real estate mortgages

Revocations for power of attorneys

Right-of-way permits

Security agreements

Snowmobile registration certificates

Special warranty deeds

State tax liens and releases

Tax liens

- Records of tax liens on a particular subject identifying subject, his business, or his property

Tax sale deeds

Tax stamp table

Termination of leases

Trade names

Uniform commercial credit (UCC) filings

Termination statements

Warranty deeds

Electric and Water Company

Provides a current address for the subject

Provides financial information on the subject

May provide the name of subject's spouse

Alcoholic Beverages and Tobacco Division

Alcohol license application may provide an extensive background on the subject detailing former addresses, criminal history, employment history, and associates

May give disciplinary information

Secretary of State

Provides corporate information on businesses, including the officers of the corporation, original stock subscribers, amount of authorized stock, current standing with the state, nature of the business, date of incorporation, address of the corporation, and resident agent for the business.

Motor Vehicle Records

Information available through motor vehicle records (MVR) includes:
• Address at time of issue
• Race, sex, and height
• Violations and accidents for the past seven years

Prison and Parole Records

Covers anyone who has served a sentence in the state prison system or has been paroled through the state parole or probation system

Source for fingerprints, X-rays, dental records, and next of kin for subjects with a criminal history

State Employment Records

Employment licensing records may exist in some states for the following professional associations:
• Architects
• Barbers
• Contractors
• Insurance agents
• Optometrists
• Physicians
• State employees
• Teachers
• Attorneys
• Beauticians
• Funeral directors
• Massage parlors
• Pharmacists
• Police officers
• Stock or security brokers

FEDERAL SOURCES OF INFORMATION

The following list represents other sources of information that may be available to investigators conducting background investigations, searches for next of kin and other types of inquiries. The sources may be accessed through public records availability (Freedom of Information Act, FOIA), with written authorizations, or through the issuance of investigative subpoenas. Records include the following:

Alien Registration

Available through the Commissioner of Immigration and Naturalization, Washington, D.C.
All aliens must register every year in January.

Aviation Deaths

The National Transportation Safety Board (NTSB) of the Federal Aviation Administration (FAA) makes a thorough investigation of each accident involving an airplane in the United States. Branch offices have limited information about an accident, and the official report is available only through the Washington, D.C., headquarters. Information needed includes the following:

- Date and exact location of the airplane accident
- Name(s) of pilot(s) involved
- Whether or not a fatality was involved
- The "N" number of the aircraft, if available

Bankruptcy Courts

Regional locations cover specific areas involving Federal Bankruptcy Court. An extensive amount of information concerning an individual's background and financial data is available to the general public. Regional offices include:

Alabama
- Anniston
- Birmingham,
- Decatur,
- Mobile,
- Montgomery,
- Tuscaloosa.

Alaska
- Anchorage

Arizona
- Phoenix
- Tucson

Arkansas
- Little Rock

California
- Ceres
- Eureka
- Fresno
- Los Angeles
- Oakland
- Sacramento
- San Bernardino
- San Diego
- San Francisco
- San Jose
- Santa Ana

Colorado
- Denver

Connecticut
- Bridgeport
- Hartford

Delaware
- Wilmington

District of Columbia
- District of Columbia

Florida
- Jacksonville
- Miami
- Tallahassee
- Tampa

Georgia
- Atlanta
- Columbus
- Macon
- Savannah

Hawaii
- Honolulu

Idaho
- Boise

Illinois
- Chicago
- Danville,
- East St. Louis
- Peoria
- Rockford
- Springfield

Indiana
- Evansville
- Gary
- Indianapolis
- South Bend

Iowa
- Cedar Rapids
- Des Moines

Kansas
- Kansas City
- Topeka
- Wichita

Kentucky
- Lexington
- Louisville

Louisiana
- Baton Rouge
- New Orleans
- Opelousas
- Shreveport

Maine
- Bangor
- Portland

Maryland
- Baltimore
- Hyattsville

Massachusetts:
- Boston
- Worcester

Michigan
- Bay City
- Detroit
- Flint
- Grand Rapids
- Marquette

Minnesota
- Duluth
- Minneapolis
- St. Paul

Mississippi
- Greenville
- Jackson

Missouri
- Kansas City
- St. Louis

Montana
- Butte
- Great Falls

Nebraska
- Omaha

Nevada
- Las Vegas
- Reno

New Hampshire
- Manchester

New Jersey
- Camden
- Newark
- Trenton

New Mexico
- Albuquerque

New York
- Albany

- Brooklyn
- Buffalo
- New York
- Poughkeepsie
- Rochester
- Utica
- Westbury
- White Plains

North Carolina
- Charlotte
- Greensboro
- Wilson

North Dakota
- Fargo

Ohio
- Akron
- Canton
- Cincinnati
- Cleveland
- Columbus
- Dayton
- Toledo
- Youngstown

Oklahoma
- Oklahoma City
- Okmulgee
- Tulsa

Oregon
- Eugene
- Portland

Pennsylvania
- Erie
- Harrisburg
- Philadelphia
- Pittsburgh
- Reading
- Wilkes-Barre

Puerto Rico
- Hato Rey

Rhode Island
- Providence

South Carolina
- Columbia

South Dakota
- Sioux Falls

Tennessee
- Chattanooga
- Knoxville
- Memphis
- Nashville

Texas
- Dallas
- Ft. Worth
- Houston

- Lubbock
- San Antonio
- Tyler

Utah
- Salt Lake City

Vermont
- Rutland

Virginia
- Alexandria
- Harrisonburg
- Lynchburg
- Norfolk
- Roanoke
- Richmond

Washington
- Seattle
- Spokane
- Tacoma

West Virginia
- Charleston
- Wheeling

Wisconsin
- Eau Claire
- Madison
- Milwaukee

Wyoming
- Cheyenne

Census Records
These are maintained by the U.S. Department of Commerce.

Federal Communications Commission
The FCC maintains details on all radio and television stations under the stations' call letters. This includes detailed financial and ownership information, licensing, etc.

Federal Government Employment Records
Present employees:
- Personnel record information is available in the departments where they are employed.

Ex-employees:
- Personnel records of ex-employees of all departments and agencies (except the FBI) are stored at the National Personnel Records Center in St. Louis. Medical information may be contained in the file.
- Records are ordinarily sent to the record center 30 days after the termination date of the employee. It is essential that the full name and physical location of the place of employment be supplied. Include date of birth, SSN, and maiden name of married women.

Disabled federal employees:
- The Office of Personnel Management, Department of Labor, 1900 E. St., Washington, D.C., acts as a worker's compensation carrier for civilian employees of all branches of the federal government.
- If an employee is injured or killed while performing work duties, this bureau makes a complete investigation, including compiling complete medical information.

The Office of Personnel Management maintains 12 regional offices. Listed here are the regional headquarters and the states under their purview:
- Boston—* Massachusetts, Maine, Connecticut, New Hampshire, Vermont, Rhode Island
- New York City—New York, New Jersey, Puerto Rico, Virgin Islands
- Jacksonville—Florida, Mississippi, Alabama, Georgia, South Carolina, North Carolina, Tennessee, Kentucky
- New Orleans—Louisiana, Arkansas, Oklahoma, Texas, New Mexico
- Cleveland—Ohio, Michigan, Indiana
- Chicago—Illinois, Wisconsin, Minnesota
- Kansas City—Missouri, Iowa, Nebraska, Kansas
- Denver—Colorado, Utah, Wyoming, Montana, North Dakota, South Dakota
- San Francisco—California, Nevada, Arizona
- Seattle—Washington, Idaho, Oregon, Alaska
- Honolulu—Hawaii
- Washington—Washington, D.C., Pennsylvania, West Virginia, Maryland, Delaware, Virginia

Retired employees:
- Retired employees who have retired because of disability or age are maintained by the Retirement Division, Civil Service Commission, Washington, D.C.

Immigration and Naturalization
Central records are in Washington, D.C. covering the time from September 27, 1906, to April 1, 1956. Records since April 1, 1956, are maintained in four regional offices of the Immigration and Naturalization Service, and are also duplicated in various district offices in most major cities. The regional offices are as follows:
- Federal Building, Burlington, Vermont—Covers New England states, New York, and New Jersey
- Federal Building, Fort Snelling, Twin Cities, Minnesota—Covers areas roughly bordered by Michigan, Indiana, Kansas north to North Dakota, then westerly to include Oregon, Washington, and Alaska
- Federal Building, Richmond, Virginia—Covers area from Pennsylvania and Ohio, southwesterly to include Louisiana and Arkansas
- Terminal Island, San Pedro, California—Covers Texas and Oklahoma, westerly to California, including Colorado, Wyoming, and Utah

Internal Revenue Service
It is very difficult to receive any information from this agency.

Interstate Commerce Commission
This agency maintains financial information, including information on all trucks and trailers operated by motor carriers and trucking companies dealing in interstate commerce or shipping.

Library of Congress
The library contains old city directories and other references, such as old *American Medical Directories* and *Who's Who in America*.

Merchant Marine Personnel
The U.S. Coast Guard in Washington, D.C., maintains employment records of seamen. The records include dates signed on and off each vessel, last address, and name of next of kin.

Motor Vehicle Records
These records can be very important in developing accidents, violations, and their locations. They

include subject's address, restrictions on driver's license, title registration, lien holder information of motor vehicles, and license tag information.

Passports

Passports are available through the Department of State, Washington, D.C., which has a complete record of all passports issued to individuals.

Pilots and Aircraft Records

Other than records of accidents and violations (which are in Washington, D.C.) all information pertaining to pilots and aircraft are maintained by the Federal Aviation Agency in Oklahoma City, Oklahoma.

Pilots:
- Type of airmen's certificate held (private, commercial, student)
- Rating (e.g., single-engine land, flight instructor)
- Certificate number
- Issue date
- Class of medical certificate (e.g., 1st, 2nd)
- Limitations, if any
- Date issued
- Total hours flown on date of last medical
- Total hours flown in past 6 months
- Results of medical examinations

Aircraft:
- Need make and model, serial number and registration number (the "N" number)
- Title, registration information, history of the aircraft from manufacture to present
- Liens or encumbrances on the aircraft
- Major repair and alteration
- Aircraft use and inspection
- Aircraft air worthiness
- Inspection report

Postal Service

- Postmasters will usually provide general directions to a rural patron's address or location when the information is requested in person.
- This does not apply to general delivery or for individuals who receive their mail through post office boxes.
- If the P.O. box is used for business purposes, postal service personnel are obliged to provide the actual address, telephone number, and name of the owner of the business.
- Local postmasters are authorized to furnish the change of address record for an individual under the Freedom of Information Act. Local offices usually maintain this change of address record for a year.

Prisons (Bureau of)

Located in Washington, D.C., the bureau maintains records on all past and present inmates of federal institutions.

Railway Retirement Board

Located in Chicago, Illinois, this board maintains up-to-date addresses only for individuals receiving pensions or other benefits.

School Census Records

Many states have been making annual censuses since the year 1920. These records are usually available at the department of education at the state capital. In most instances, the records are set up alphabetically by counties.

Securities and Exchange Commission

The SEC has financial information on corporations that sell stock as regulated by this commission.

Service Deaths

These are in the official records of U.S. Air Force, Army, Coast Guard, Navy, or Marine Corps deaths. See Military Records section below.

Social Security Records

These records are in Baltimore, Maryland. The Social Security Administration may forward a letter to the party sought. Records may give date of registration, city of registration, and parent's names.

State Census Records

Old state census records are available in a few states (e.g., New York and Iowa). Contact each state to see if old records exist.

State Highway Patrol

State highway patrols handle automobile accidents outside of local jurisdictions. Local patrols may have conducted traffic homicide investigations

Unemployment Benefits

Usually the unemployment office requires the claimant to appear, in person, at a certain time of the month. This is an excellent opportunity to locate a subject.

U.S. Air Force

See military records.

U.S. Army

See military records.

U.S. Coast Guard

For current and ex-employees of the Coast Guard, check military records. The Coast Guard maintains records of Merchant Marine seamen, as well as records involving missing ships, accidents, and any resulting deaths along the Atlantic Ocean, Pacific Ocean, Gulf of Mexico, most of the Mississippi River, and the Great Lakes. Search and rescue records are maintained in the following district offices:

- Boston, Massachusetts
- Cleveland, Ohio
- Long Beach, California
- Miami, Florida
- New Orleans, Louisiana
- New York City, New York
- Portsmouth, Virginia
- San Francisco, California
- Seattle, Washington
- St. Louis, Missouri

Marine casualty investigations records are maintained at the following Marine Inspection Offices:
- Baltimore, Maryland
- Boston, Massachusetts
- Buffalo, New York
- Chicago, Illinois
- Duluth, Minnesota
- Houston, Texas
- Miami, Florida
- Mobile, Alabama
- New Orleans, Louisiana
- Philadelphia, Pennsylvania
- Port Arthur, Texas
- Portland, Maine

The Coast Guard requires requests for reports be made in person or in writing. Generally, the Coast Guard requires the following information:
- Subject matter or title of record
- Date of incident
- Place of incident
- The particular Coast Guard unit that conducted the investigation

U.S. Marine Corps

See military records.

U.S. Marine Hospitals

See U.S. Public Health Service Hospitals

U.S. Navy

See military records.

U.S. Public Health Service Hospitals

These records contain medical history, beneficiaries, etc., involving veterans.

Veterans Administration Hospital

- These records include the medical history, beneficiaries, etc., of veterans.
- The SSN of the subject is necessary to access records.
- When a VA patient changes or moves his treatment from one VA facility to another, the patient's entire treatment record is also transferred to the current or most recent point of treatment. The only record remaining at the former place of treatment will be the location of where the record was sent.
- The headquarters of the Veteran's Administration is in Washington, D.C. Central inactive records are maintained in St. Louis. In addition, every state has a regional office.
  —Alabama: Montgomery
  —Alaska: Juneau
  —Arizona: Phoenix
  —Arkansas: Little Rock
  —California: Los Angeles, San Francisco
  —Colorado: Denver
  —Connecticut: Hartford
  —Delaware: Wilmington
  —District of Columbia

—Florida: St. Petersburg
—Georgia: Atlanta
—Hawaii: Honolulu
—Idaho: Boise
—Illinois: Chicago
—Indiana: Indianapolis
—Iowa: Des Moines
—Kansas: Wichita
—Kentucky: Louisville
—Louisiana: New Orleans, Shreveport
—Maine: Togus
—Maryland: Baltimore
—Massachusetts: Boston
—Michigan: Detroit
—Minnesota: St. Paul
—Mississippi: Jackson
—Missouri: Kansas City, St. Louis
—Montana: Fort Harrison
—Nebraska: Lincoln
—Nevada: Reno
—New Hampshire: Manchester
—New Jersey: Newark
—New Mexico: Albuquerque
—New York: Albany, Brooklyn, Buffalo, New York City, Syracuse
—North Carolina: Winston-Salem
—North Dakota: Fargo
—Ohio: Cleveland
—Oklahoma: Muskogee
—Oregon: Portland
—Pennsylvania: Philadelphia, Pittsburgh, Wilkes-Barre
—Philippines: Manila
—Puerto Rico: San Juan
—Rhode Island: Providence
—South Carolina: Columbia
—South Dakota: Sioux Falls
—Tennessee: Nashville
—Texas: Dallas, Houston, Lubbock, San Antonio, Waco
—Utah: Salt Lake City
—Vermont: White River Junction
—Virginia, Roanoke
—Virgin Islands: San Juan (Puerto Rico)
—Washington: Seattle
—West Virginia: Huntington
—Wisconsin: Milwaukee
—Wyoming: Cheyenne

Vital Statistics, Federal Bureau of

No information is available through this federal agency in Washington, D.C. It receives copies of birth and death certificates from all states, but uses them only for computing statistics. Names of individuals are disregarded in their filing.

Weather Records

- The records and statistics of temperature, rainfall, and other weather conditions recorded by all official U.S. Weather Bureaus are stored at the National Climatic Records Center, Federal Building, Asheville, North Carolina. All manuscript and microfilm records of all stations throughout the United States are preserved at this location.
- There is a lag in some instances of from 30 to 60 days in receiving these reports
- The Weather Bureau will furnish a copy of the weather record for any specific day.

NONTRADITIONAL METHODS FOR LOCATING OR CONDUCTING A BACKGROUND INVESTIGATION OF A SUBJECT

1)   Determining domestic and overseas activities involving a subject who may not wish to be found by law enforcement or civil authorities:

       a) Attempting to identify whether an individual has activities, business dealings, associates or foreign assets in a country outside the United States (foreign asset identification investigations)

       b) Attempting to document the foreign travel of an individual to a foreign country

          i) The U.S. Customs Service, El Paso Intelligence Center (EPIC), may document travel to a foreign country.

          ii) EPIC operates a database system based on the Customs card filled out by travelers as they reenter the United States.

             (1) This is especially useful in the investigation of the following:

                (a) Drug smuggling

                (b) Money laundering

                (c) Banking infractions or irregularities

          iii) EPIC reports this information to the Financial Crimes Enforcement Network (FinCEN), located in the Washington, D.C., area and maintained by several agencies. FinCEN will provide this and other financial information to law enforcement and regulatory agencies responsible for conducting investigations involving drug, financial, regulatory, or organized crime issues.

          iv) FinCEN's original mission was to provide a government-wide, multisource intelligence and analytical network to support the detection, investigation, and prosecution of domestic and international money-laundering and other financial crimes. In May 1994, its mission was broadened to include regulatory responsibilities.

             (1) Today, FinCEN is one of the Treasury Department's primary agencies to oversee and implement policies to prevent and detect money laundering. This is accomplished in two ways.

                (a) First, FinCEN uses counter–money laundering laws (such as the Bank Secrecy Act, BSA) to require reporting and record keeping by banks and other financial institutions. This record keeping preserves a financial trail for investigators to follow as they track criminals and their assets. The BSA also requires reporting suspicious currency transactions that could trigger investigations. FinCEN establishes these policies and regulations to deter and detect money laundering in partnership with the financial community.

                (b) FinCEN provides intelligence and analytical support to law enforcement. FinCEN's work is concentrated on combining information reported under the BSA with other government and public information. This information is then disclosed to FinCEN's customers in the law enforcement community in the form of intelligence reports. These reports help them build investigations and plan new strategies to combat money laundering

   v) Passports

      (1) Examination of passports should include passport stamps and visa information identifying foreign ports of call.

c) Determine the subject's activities in a foreign country.

   i) Receipts of purchases

   ii) Credit card accounts

      (1) These may provide investigators with a detailed account of the subject's airline travels, hotel accommodations, and purchases made by an individual in a foreign country.

      (2) A traveler may rely on his credit card in paying for hotel rooms to escape the added work in exchanging foreign currency. Using a credit card to pay for a hotel room eliminates the exchange since the conversion is done through the card.

         (a) Credit card records will identify the hotel. Once the hotel is identified, telephone calls charged to the room can be tracked, thereby identifying persons and businesses contacted by the subject while in a foreign country.

         (b) A review of the security film shot within the hotel may serve as confirmation of the subject's association.

   iii) Overnight package delivery records

   iv) Personal and business computers

   v) Telephone records

d) Identify the location of bank accounts and the individual's business relationships in a foreign country.

   i) Subject's telephone records, including cellular

      (1) These may be obtainable, or may have been obtained, through subpoena in a criminal or civil investigation

      (2) May identify a bank, an attorney, or a business agent the subject may be working with in setting-up a business or foreign financial relationship.

   ii) Money wire transfers

   iii) Traveler's check identification, as well as the purchase of money orders

      (1) Money orders and traveler checks may be traced to a location where they were cashed.

         (a) May identify the attorney, financial institution, or business associate of the subject in a foreign country.

   iv) Personal or business computer records, including e-mail traffic

e) Identify and interview individuals who may have knowledge of the subject's activities, business dealings, assets, and associates in a foreign country.

   i) If unable to locate foreign accounts or foreign activities of the subject by tracing transactions, the investigation should continue through the locating and interviewing people who may know of the subject's personal and business activities. They can include, but are not limited to, the following:

      (1) Enemies

        (a) Check courthouse lawsuit indexes for former employees, customers or associates who may have had a problem with the subject.

    (2) Friends

    (3) Former employers or employees

        (a) Secretaries may have been used to make travel plans for the subject. They may be used to identify travel agents, airlines, etc., that may be subject to further inquiry.

            (i) Former secretaries may be identified by examining the incorporated documents of a business. These may be filed in the state where the business is incorporated and are usually a matter of public record. The secretary may have been the individual who notarized the documents.

            (ii) Former secretaries of the suspect should be located and questioned about whether they may have the following:

                1. "A personal diary that details the employer's travel and business activities

                2. A personal Rolodex of numbers frequently called for the employer.

                3. A notary log that records the documents that the secretary notarized.

                4. Telephone directories the secretary may have kept to remember the employer's key contacts.

                5. Copies of documents made because of the secretary's personal concerns about the employer's ethics or business activities." (Pankan, 1992).

    (4) Ex-spouses

    (5) Travel agent

        (a) The agent may be identified through the subject's cellular phone records, personal Rolodex, address book, computer, etc. The agent may be in the same office building as the subject.

        (b) The travel agent should have at least a 3-year record of activity of the subject.

        (c) Airline Reporting Corporation (ARC) and International Air Transport Corporation (IATC)

            (i) ARC is the clearinghouse for all tickets sold by travel agents involving all of the major airlines in the United States. The IATC is its sister corporation responsible for collating the records of foreign travel for many of the world's airlines. Each time an agent issues a ticket or electronic transaction, the name of a validating carrier is designated on the transaction. ARC's processing centers can then identify the airline or travel agent to receive funds or commission for that ticket. ARC compiles and collates those tickets. Identification of the travel agent may result in developing travel information on the subject.

      ii) Trash pulls
          (1) The garbage thrown away by the subject may be used in an effort to gain information concerning the subject. They include, but are not limited to, the following:
              (a) Envelopes
                  (i) Return addresses found in the trash may identify associates, businesses, or family of the subject
                    1. Addresses of foreign banks
              (b) Confirmation and receipts for overnight mail
              (c) Bank statements
                  (i) These included routing and account numbers.
              (d) Credit card statements
              (e) Phone records
          (2) Certain days of the year, especially holidays and birthdays, should be scheduled for trash pulls. On these occasions, telephone calls and cards may find their way to and from the subject. Records of these encounters may ultimately find their way into the trash. They include the following:
              (a) Valentines Day
                  (i) Return addresses may have been thrown into the trash from the subject's mother, lover, or special friend. Trash may also contain receipts for gifts purchased and sent to a close associate of the subject.
              (b) Mother's and Father's Day
                  (i) A subject running from law enforcement may attempt to contact his mother on Mother's Day, his father on Father's Day, or the parent on the parent's birthday. Phone records involving that time period and cards may have been thrown out in the trash.
              (c) Thanksgiving and Christmas
                  (i) These are traditional times in which a person tempting to avoid law enforcement may attempt to make contact with his family. Criminals know that law enforcement is not fully staffed during these holidays.
                  (ii) Christmas is a good time to make trash pulls for credit card purchases, receipts for packages mailed, and return addresses on discarded envelopes from the subject's associates.

INTERNATIONAL CRIMINAL POLICE ORGANIZATION (INTERPOL)

1)   Worldwide cooperation of law enforcement
      a) Formed in 1923, this international criminal police organization was created to have police agencies from around the world join in a voluntary exchange of information about crimes that transcend national boundaries and the criminals who perpetrate such crimes.
      b) Today, INTERPOL membership includes nearly 175 nations.
      c) INTERPOL does not maintain a force of international police officers or agents. Instead, INTERPOL serves as a conduit for a cooperative exchange of criminal information to help detect and combat international crime. Criminal investigations

in one country that involve the citizens of another country or have investigative leads to another country are routed through INTERPOL for coordination.

2) How the network functions
    a) Each participating country sets up a National Central Bureau (NCB), which serves as the country's point of contact with the international law enforcement community.
        i) Each country operates its NCB within the parameters of its own national laws and policies.
    b) In the United States, authority for the INTERPOL function rests by law with the attorney general, and the U.S. National Central Bureau (USNCB) is an office under the control and direction of the Departments of Justice and Treasury, staffed by personnel from those and other federal and state law enforcement agencies.
    c) Law enforcement agencies represented at the USNCB, including:
        i) Bureau of Alcohol, Tobacco and Firearms (ATF)
        ii) Bureau of Diplomatic Security, U.S. State Department
        iii) Criminal Division, U.S. Department of Justice
        iv) Department of Agriculture's Office of the Inspector General
        v) Drug Enforcement Administration (DEA)
        vi) Federal Bureau of Investigation (FBI)
        vii) Federal Law Enforcement Training Center (FLETC)
        viii) Financial Crimes Enforcement Network (FinCEN)
        ix) Immigration and Naturalization Service (INS)
        x) Internal Revenue Service (IRS)
        xi) Massachusetts State Police
        xii) Naval Criminal Investigative Service
        xiii) Office of the Comptroller of the Currency
        xiv) U.S. Customs Service
        xv) U.S. Marshals Service
        xvi) U.S. Postal Inspection Service
        xvii) U.S. Secret Service
    d) Structure and activities of the USNCB include:
        i) Alien/fugitive enforcement
        ii) Financial fraud
        iii) Criminal investigations
        iv) Drugs
        v) State liaison

3) Liaison with state and local police
    a) The USNCB has invited each of the 50 states to set up a point of contact within their own police system to serve as the focal point of all requests involving international matters.
        i) Requests for investigative assistance from abroad that require action by the police of a particular state are forwarded by the USNCB to the liaison office in that state, which then directs the request to the appropriate state entity.
        ii) All 50 states participate in the program.

4) Contacting the USNCB
    a) The USNCB is accessible 24 hours a day. Contact may be made in the following ways:
        i) NLETS: DCINTEROO

543 · LOCATION AND BACKGROUND INVESTIGATIONS · 543

ii) Telephone: 202-616-9000
iii) State liaison: 202-616-1051
iv) Facsimile: 202-616-8400
v) Mailing address: INTERPOL—U.S. National Central Bureau
         U.S. Department of Justice
         Washington, D.C. 20530

5) INTERPOL member countries

- Albania
- Algeria
- American Samoa
- Andorra
- Angola
- Anguilla
- Antigua and Barbuda
- Argentina
- Armenia
- Aruba
- Australia
- Austria
- Azerbaijan
- Bahamas
- Bahrain
- Bangladesh
- Barbados
- Belarus
- Belgium
- Belize
- Benin
- Bermuda
- Bolivia
- Bosnia-Herzegovina
- Botswana
- Brazil
- British Virgin Islands
- Brunei
- Bulgaria
- Burkina Faso
- Burundi
- Cambodia
- Cameroon
- Canada
- Cape Verde
- Cayman Islands
- Central African Republic
- Chad
- Chile

- China
- Colombia
- Commonwealth of Northern Marianas Islands
- Congo, Republic of the
- Costa Rica
- Cote d'Ivoire
- Croatia
- Cuba
- Cyprus
- Czech Republic
- Denmark
- Dijbouti
- Dominica
- Dominican Republic
- Ecuador
- Egypt
- El Salvador
- Equatorial Guinea
- Estonia
- Ethiopia
- Fiji
- Finland
- France
- Gabon
- Gambia
- Germany
- Georgia
- Ghana
- Gibraltar
- Granada
- Greece
- Guam
- Guatemala
- Guinea
- Guinea-Bissau
- Guyana
- Haiti
- Honduras
- Hong Kong

- Hungary
- Iceland
- India
- Indonesia
- Iran
- Iraq
- Ireland
- Israel
- Italy
- Jamaica
- Japan
- Jordan
- Kazakhstan
- Kenya
- Kiribati
- Korea (Republic of)
- Kuwait
- Laos
- Latvia
- Lebanon
- Lesotho
- Liberia
- Libya
- Liechtenstein
- Lithuania
- Luxembourg
- Macao
- Macedonia
- Madagascar
- Malawi
- Malaysia
- Maldives
- Mali
- Malta
- Marshall Islands
- Mauritania
- Mauritius
- Mexico
- Monaco
- Mongolia
- Montserrat

- Morocco
- Mozambique
- Myanmar
- Namibia
- Nauru
- Nepal
- Netherlands
- Netherlands Antilles
- New Zealand
- Nicaragua
- Niger
- Nigeria
- Norway
- Oman
- Pakistan
- Panama
- Papua New Guinea
- Paraguay
- Peru
- Philippines
- Poland
- Portugal
- Puerto Rico
- Qatar
- Romania
- Russia
- Rwanda
- São Tomé and Príncipe
- Saudi Arabia
- Senegal

- Seychelles
- Sierra Leone
- Singapore
- Slovakia
- Slovenia
- Somalia
- South Africa
- Spain
- Sri Lanka
- St. Kitts and Nevis
- St Vincent and the Grenadines
- Sudan
- Suriname
- Swaziland
- Sweden
- Switzerland
- Syria
- Tanzania
- Thailand
- Togo
- Tonga
- Trinidad and Tobago
- Tunisia
- Turkey
- Turks and Caicos
- Uganda
- Ukraine
- United Arab Emirates
- United States
- United Kingdom

- Uruguay
- Venezuela
- Vietnam
- Yemen
- Yugoslavia
- Zaire
- Zambia
- Zimbabwe

United Kingdom Sub-Bureaus
- Anguilla
- Bermuda
- British Virgin Islands
- Cayman Islands
- Gibraltar
- Hong Kong
- Montserrat
- Turks and Caicos

U.S. Sub-Bureaus
- American Samoa
- Commonwealth of Northern Mariana Islands
- Guam
- Puerto Rico

Portugal Sub-Bureau
- Macao

MILITARY INFORMATION SOURCES

Military Discharge Records

A high percentage of returning veterans registered a copy of their discharge papers at the county courthouse.

Military Personnel and Medical Records
A request for information should include the following:
- Full name
- SSN (if discharged before 1969, requires service number)
- Branch of service
- Dates of service (show all periods of military service even though information from one period may be all that is needed)
- Reserve status (give full information, branch of service, dates, etc.)
- Last known address
- Date and place of birth
- Grade or rank

Military Dependents

Medical records of dependents of military personnel are retained at the point of treatment for 2 years after the treatment. After 2 years, the medical records are forwarded to the National Personnel Record Center in St. Louis. Include the following information to obtain records:
* The dependent's full name
* Date of birth
* SSN
* The name of the installation where the treatment was rendered
* The date or dates of such treatment and whether the patient was confined or treated on an out-patient basis.

Military Records

Military personnel and medical records are kept at varying locations, depending on the branch of service and whether or not the subject was on active duty.

Army
* Enlisted personnel on active duty, 2 or 3 months after discharge, and deceased while on active duty or retired:
  —Enlisted Personnel Records Center, Ft. Benjamin Harrison, IN
* All officers on active duty (and for 3 to6 months after discharge), deceased while on active duty, retired, and all retired general officers:
  —Adjutant General, Department of the Army, Washington, D.C.
* Discharged, deceased while on active duty, or retired (except retired general officers) for 2 to 6 months or more, plus all reservists and those on temporary disability retired list:
  —Military Personnel Records, 9700 Page Blvd., St. Louis, MO 63132

Air Force
* All active-duty personnel (and for 2 to 3 months after discharge, deceased while on active duty, or retired), general officers retired with pay, and those on Temporary Disability Retired (TDR) list
  —Air Force Personnel Center, Randolph Air Force Base, Texas
* Reservists not on active duty and all retired reservists in a nonpay status:
  —Air Reserve Personnel Center, Denver, CO
* Discharged, deceased while on active duty, or retired (other than general officers retired with pay) for 2 to 3 months or more
  —Military Personnel Records, 9700 Page Boulevard, St. Louis, MO 63132

Coast Guard
* All active-duty personnel (and for 3 to 6 months after discharge, deceased while on active duty, or retired) and all reserve members and those on TDR list:
  —U.S. Coast Guard, Washington, D.C.
* Those discharged, deceased while on active duty, or retired for 3 to 6 months or more:
  —Military Personnel Records, 9700 Page Boulevard, St. Louis, MO 63132

Marine Corps
* All those on active duty (and for 3 to 6 months after discharge, deceased while on active duty or retired), active reserve members, and those on TDR list:
  —U.S. Marine Corps, Washington, D.C.
* Inactive reservists:
  —Marine Corps Reserves, Kansas City, MO

- Discharged, deceased while on active duty, or retired for 3 to 6 months or more:
  —Military Personnel Records, 9700 Page Boulevard, St. Louis, MO 63132

Navy

- All active-duty personnel and those discharged, deceased while on active duty, or retired since June 1976 (personnel record only):
  —Department of the Navy, Washington, D.C.
- Reservists and those on TDR list, those discharged, those deceased while on active duty, or retired since June 1976 (medical records only):
  —Department of the Navy, 4400 Dauphin Street, New Orleans, LA
- Discharged, deceased while on active duty, or retired prior to June, 1976:
  —Military Personnel Records, 9700 Page Boulevard., St. Louis, MO 63132

Investigative Liaisons for Law Enforcement Agencies

Army

Headquarters, 3D Military Group (CID)
Commander
3D Military Police Group CID USACIDC
4699 N. 41st Street
Forest Park, GA 30197-5119
Telephone: (404) 362-7001
Fax: (404) 362-3351

Resident Agencies

ALABAMA
Fort Rucker Resident Agency
Special Agent in Charge
3D Military Police Group CID USACIDC
Building 5430
Fort Rucker, AL 36362-5351
Telephone: (334) 255-3070
Fax: (334) 255-9287

Redstone Resident Agency
Special Agent in Charge
3D Military Police Group CID USACIDC
Building 3421
Redstone Arsenal, AL 35898-7240
Telephone: (256) 876-2037
Fax: (256) 876-1369

ALASKA
Fort Richardson Resident in Charge
Special Agent in Charge
HHD P.O. Box 5309, Building 58
Chilhook Avenue
Fort Richardson, AK 99505
Telephone: (907) 384-3981
Fax: (907) 384-7825

Fort Wainwright Resident Agency
Special Agent in Charge
P.O. Box 36065, Building 1051
Gaffney Road
Fort Wainwright, AK 99703
Telephone: (317) 353-6210
Fax: (317) 353-6340

CALIFORNIA
Fort Irwin Resident Agency
Special Agent in Charge
Building T402, Langford Lake Road
Fort Irwin, CA 92310
Telephone: (760) 386-5882
Fax: (760) 386-4968

GEORGIA
Fort Benning Resident Agency
Special Agent in Charge
3D Military Police Group CID USACIDC
Building 1698
Fort Benning, GA 31905-6200
Telephone: (706) 545-3984
Fax: (706) 545-5271

Fort McPherson Resident Agency
Special Agent in Charge
3D Military Police Group CID USACIDC
1626 Lewis Circle SW.
Fort McPherson, GA 30330-1052
Telephone: (404) 464-2712
Fax: (404) 464-3255

Fort Stewart Resident Agency
Special Agent in Charge
3D Military Police Group CID USACIDC
Building 105, 460 Bultman Avenue
Fort Stewart, GA 31314-4004
Telephone: (912) 767-4611
Fax: (912) 767-3766

ILLINOIS
Rock Island Resident Agency
Special Agent in Charge
3D Military Police Group CID USACIDC
110 Rodman Avenue
Rock Island Arsenal, IL 61299-7570
Telephone: (309) 782-1163
Fax: (309) 782-8399

KANSAS
Fort Leavenworth Resident Agency
Special Agent in Charge
6th Military Police Group USACIDC
801 McClellan Avenue
Fort Leavenworth, KS 66027
Telephone: (913) 684-5695
Fax: (913) 684-3085

Fort Riley Resident Agency
Special Agent in Charge
6th Military Police Group USACIDC
Building 406, Pershing Circle
Fort Riley, KS 66442
Telephone: (913) 239-3931
Fax: (913) 239-6388

KENTUCKY
Fort Campbell Resident Agency
Special Agent in Charge
31st MD DEF CID DGE Air Assault
2745 Kentucky Avenue
Fort Campbell, KY 42223-5638
Telephone: (270) 798-6127
Fax: (270) 798-3213

Fort Knox Resident Agency
Special Agent in Charge
280th MP DET CID CASE
3D Military Police Group CID USACIDC
488 Old Ironsides Avenue
Fort Knox, KY 40121-5580
Telephone: (502) 624-3199
Fax: (502) 624-2192

LOUISIANA
Fort Polk Resident Agency
Special Agent in Charge
P.O. Box 3920
Fort Polk, LA 71459
Telephone: (318) 531-7184
Fax: (318) 531-7845

MARYLAND
Aberdeen Proving Ground Resident Agency
Special Agent in Charge
3D Military Police Group CID USACIDC
2210 Aberdeen Boulevard
Aberdeen Proving Ground, MD 21005-5001
Telephone: (410) 278-5261
Fax: (410) 278-5092

Fort Meade Resident Agency
Special Agent in Charge
3D Military Police Group CID USACIDC
2835 Ernie Pyle Street
Fort Meade, MD 29755-5345
Telephone: (301) 677-6872
Fax: (301) 677-7147

MISSOURI
Fort Leonard Wood Resident Agency
Special Agent in Charge
6th Military Police Group USACIDC
Building 1907
Fort Leonard Wood, MO 65473
Telephone: (314) 596-8025
Fax: (314) 596-0272

NEW JERSEY
Fort Monmouth Resident Agency
Special Agent in Charge
3D Military Police Group CID USACIDC
Building 917
Fort Monmouth, NJ 17703-5606
Telephone: (732) 532-4844
Fax: (732) 532-7087

NEW YORK
Fort Drum Resident Agency
Special Agent in Charge
62D MP DET CID DSE
3D Military Police Group CID USACIDC
4871 Netherly Street
Fort Drum, NY 13602-5013

Telephone: (315) 772-5418
Fax: (315) 772-6126

West Point Resident Agency
Special Agent in Charge
3D Military Police Group CID USACIDC
Building 616
West Point, NY 10996-1584
Telephone: (914) 938-4289
Fax: (914) 938-4289

NORTH CAROLINA
Fort Bragg Resident Agency
Special Agent in Charge
87th MP DET ABN CID
3D Military Police Group CID USACIDC
Building 8, 1221 Randolph Street
Fort Bragg, NC 28307-5000
Telephone: (910) 396-8777
Fax: (910) 396-8595

OKLAHOMA
Fort Sill Resident Agency
Special Agent in Charge
6th Military Police Group USACIDC
Fort Sill, OK 73503
Telephone: (405) 442-2856
Fax: (405) 442-7094

SOUTH CAROLINA
Fort Carson Resident Agency
Special Agent in Charge
6th Military Police Group USACIDC
48th MP DET (CID)
Fort Carson, SC 80913
Telephone: (719) 526-3991
Fax: (719) 526-4258

Fort Jackson Resident Agency
Special Agent in Charge
37th MP DET CID CASE
3D Military Police Group CID USACIDC
Building 5483, Marion Street
Fort Jackson, SC 29207-6045
Telephone: (803) 751-1506
Fax: (803) 751-7867

TEXAS
Fort Bliss Resident Agency
Special Agent in Charge

P.O. Box 6350
Building 13, USACIDC
Fort Bliss, TX 79906
Telephone: (915) 568-1360
Fax: (915) 568-1634

Fort Hood Resident Agency
Special Agent in Charge
P.O. Box V
Building 2200, Support Avenue
Fort Hood, TX 76544
Telephone: (254) 287-6312
Fax: (254) 287-3307

Fort Sam Houston Resident Agency
Special Agent in Charge
6th Military Police Group USACIDC
Building 268, 1490 Wilson Street
Fort Sam Houston, TX 78234
Telephone: (210) 221-0050
Fax: (210) 221-0728

VIRGINIA
Fort Belvoir Resident Agency
Special Agent in Charge
75th Military Police Detachment
3D Military Police Group CID USACIDC
6104 3D Street
Fort Belvoir, VA 22060-5592
Telephone: (703) 806-3306
Fax: (703) 806-3800

Fort Eustis Resident Agency
Special Agent in Charge
12th MP DET CID PASE
3D Military Police Group CID USACIDC
Building 2733
Fort Eustis, VA 23604-5534
Telephone: (757) 878-4811
Fax: (757) 878-0058

Fort Gordon Resident Agency
Special Agent in Charge
3D Military Police Group CID USACIDC
3800 A Avenue
Fort Lee, VA 23801-6090
Telephone: (804) 734-1234
Fax: (804) 734-1447

Washington Resident Agency
Special Agent in Charge
3D Military Police Group CID USACIDC
105 Fenton Circle
Fort Myer, VA 22211-1101
Telephone: (703) 696-3501
Fax: (703) 696-6270

WASHINGTON
Fort Lewis Resident Agency
Special Agent in Charge
44 th MP DET (CID)
Building 5183, N. Division Drive
Fort Lewis, WA 98433
Telephone: (253) 967-3151
Fax: (253) 967-7825

Navy and Marine Corps
Naval Criminal Investigative Service
Headquarters
Washington Navy Yard
Code 0023B
716 Sicard Street SE., Suite 2000
Washington, DC 20388-5380
Telephone: (202) 433-9234
Fax: (202) 433-4922

Naval Criminal Investigative
Service Field Offices
AREA: CALIFORNIA (CENTRAL), COLORADO,
NEVADA, UTAH, AND WYOMING
Naval Criminal Investigative Service Field Office
1317 West Foothill Boulevard, Suite 120
Upland, CA 91786
Telephone: (908) 985-2264
Fax: (908) 985-9763

AREA: ARIZONA, CALIFORNIA (SOUTHERN),
NEW MEXICO, AND TEXAS (WEST)
Naval Criminal Investigative Service Field Office
Box 368130
3405 Welles Street, Suite 1
San Diego, CA 92136-5050
Telephone: (619) 556-1364
Fax: (619) 556-3262

AREA: HAWAII AND PACIFIC ISLANDS
Naval Criminal Investigative Service Field Office
449 South Avenue
Pearl Harbor, HI 96860-4988

Telephone: (808) 474-1218
Fax: (808) 474-1210

AREA: DELAWARE, MARYLAND, VIRGINIA
(NORTHERN), WASHINGTON, D.C., AND WEST
VIRGINIA
Naval Criminal Investigative Service Field Office
1014 N Street S.E., Suite 102
Washington, D.C. 20374-5008
Telephone: (202) 433-6700
Fax: (202) 233-6045

AREA: VIRGINIA (TIDEWATER)
Naval Criminal Investigative Service Field Office
1329 Bellinger Boulevard
Norfolk, VA 23511-2395
Telephone: (804) 444-7327
Fax: (804) 444-3139

AREA: NORTH CAROLINA
Naval Criminal Investigative Service Field Office
H-32 Julian C. Smith Boulevard
Camp LeJeune, N.C. 28547-1603
Telephone: (910) 451-8071
Fax: (910) 451-8206

AREA: ALASKA, IDAHO, MONTANA, OREGON,
WASHINGTON, AND THE CANADIAN PROVINCES
Naval Criminal Investigative Service Field Office
Land Title Professional Building
9657 Levin Road NW., Suite L20
Silverdale, WA 98383
Telephone: (360) 396-4660
Fax: (360) 396-7009

AREA: NEW ENGLAND, NEW YORK,
PENNSYLVANIA, BERMUDA, AND CANADA
Naval Criminal Investigative Service Field Office
Naval Station Newport
344 Meyerkord Avenue, # 3
Newport, RI 02841-1607
Telephone: (401) 841-2241
Fax: (401) 841-4056

AREA: FLORIDA (WEST), ILLINOIS, INDIANA,
IOWA, KANSAS, LOUISIANA, MICHIGAN,
MINNESOTA, MISSISSIPPI, NEBRASKA, NORTH
DAKOTA, OHIO, OKLAHOMA, SOUTH DAKOTA,
TEXAS, AND WISCONSIN
Naval Criminal Investigative Service Field Office

341 Saufley Street
Pensacola, FL 32508-5133
Telephone: (904) 452-3835
Fax: (904) 452-2194

AREA: SOUTHEASTERN U.S., CUBA, PUERTO RICO, CENTRAL AMERICA, AND SOUTH AMERICA
Naval Criminal Investigative Service Field Office
Naval Station
P.O. Box 280076
Mayport, FL 32228-0076
Telephone: (904) 270-5361
Fax: (904) 270-6065

Air Force
HQ Air Force Office of Special Investigations/XOGV
Andrews Air Force Base
Camp Springs, MD 20331
Telephone: (240) 857-1703 (during normal working hours)
Fax: (240) 857-0967

MILITARY GRADE AND RANK

ENLISTED PERSONNEL

Pay Grade	Air Force	Navy/ Coast Guard	Army	Marines
E1	Airman Basic	Seaman Recruit	Private	Private
E2	Airman	Seaman Apprentice	Private	Private 1st Class
E3	Airman 1st Class	Seaman	Private 1st Class	Lance Corporal
E4	Sergeant/Senior Airman	Petty Officer 3rd Class	Corporal or Specialist	Corporal
E5	Staff Sergeant	Petty Officer 2nd Class	Sergeant	Sergeant
E6	Technical Sergeant	Petty Officer 1st Class	Staff Sergeant	Staff Sergeant
E7	Master Sergeant	Chief Petty Officer	Sergeant 1st Class	Gunnery Sergeant
E8	Senior Master Sergeant	Senior Chief Petty Officer	1st Sergeant Master Sergeant	1st Sergeant

E9	Chief Master Sergeant	Master Chief Petty Officer	Command Sergeant Major/ Sergeant Major	Sergeant Major/Master Sergeant Major/ Master Gunnery Sergeant
E10	Chief Master Sergeant of the Air Force	Master Chief Petty Officer of the Navy	Sergeant Major of the Army	Sergeant Major of the Marines

WARRANT OFFICERS

W1		Warrant Officer	Warrant Officer	Warrant Officer
W2,3,4		Chief Warrant Officer	Chief Warrant Officer	Chief Warrant Officer
W5		Master Warrant Officer	Master Warrant Officer	Master Warrant Officer

OFFICERS

O1	2nd Lieutenant	Ensign	2nd Lieutenant	2nd Lieutenant
O2	1st Lieutenant	Lieutenant Junior Grade	1st Lieutenant	1st Lieutenant
O3	Captain	Lieutenant	Captain	Captain
O4	Major	Lieutenant Commander	Major	Major
O5	Lieutenant Colonel	Commander	Lieutenant Colonel	Lieutenant Colonel
O6	Colonel	Captain	Colonel	Colonel
O7	Brigadier General	Rear Admiral (lower half)	Brigadier General	Brigadier General
O8	★★ Major General	★★ Rear Admiral (upper half)	★★ Major General	★★ Major General
O9	★★★ Lieutenant General	★★★ Vice Admiral	★★★ Lieutenant General	★★★ Lieutenant General
O10	★★★★ General	★★★★ Admiral	★★★★ General	General
	★★★★★ General of the Air Force	★★★★★ Fleet Admiral	★★★★★ General of the Army	

CHAPTER 58:
THE INTERNET LAW ENFORCEMENT SITES

ASSOCIATIONS

- American Bar Association
  http://www.abanet.org/
  The home page of the American Bar Association.

- Association of Federal Defense Attorneys
  http://www.afda.org/
  This site contains an extensive research section, including databases of case law summaries, a library for downloading documents, and links to key Web sites in federal law.

- Bar Associations
  http://dir.yahoo.com/Government/Law/Organizations/Bar_Associations
  Links to bar associations across the country.

- FBA Online
  http://www.fedbar.org/
  The home page of the Federal Bar Association. This site contains a wealth of constantly updated information for law students, new practitioners, experienced attorneys, and judges from all over the country.

- Mothers Against Drunk Drivers
  http://www.madd.org

- National Lawyers Association
  http://www.nla.org/

AUTO THEFT

- Auto Directory
  http://www.highstreetcentral.com/gocar.htm

- Auto Insurance
  http://www.insure.com/auto/index.html

- Auto insurance guide and links
  CPIC Stolen Car Search
  http://www.nps.ca/English/index
  Searches the entire national database of stolen cars.

- How Auto Theft Inv. Work
  http://www.insure.com/auto/thefts/experts.html
  An article on how auto theft investigators work.

- International Association of Auto Theft Investigators
  http://www.iaati.org/

- License Plate Search
  http://www.licenseplate.net/
  Searches license plate and vehicle ownership.

- National Highway Transportation Investigation Safety Board
  http://www.nhtsa.dot.gov/cars/problems/defect/investmmy1.cfm
  National Highway Transportation Safety Board: Office of Defects

- Stolen Car Recovery
  http://stolencar.com/

- Trackem
  http://www.toolcity.net/~richreen/trackem.html
  Allows the tracking of individuals.

- Stolen Property Search
  http://www.cpic-cipc.ca/English/index.cfm
  Allows for the search the national database of stolen properties.

- Vehicle History Report
  http://www.vehiclehistory.com/cgi-bin/vhr_home.cgi
  Links to many sites about automobiles.

- Western States Auto Theft Association
  http://www.wsati.org/investlinks.html
  This organization's goal is to reduce vehicle theft.

AVIATION

- Federal Aviation Administration
  http://www.faa.gov
  Home page for Federal Aviation Administration.

BANKRUPTCY

- Bankruptcy Court Directory
  http://212.179.36.21/easybkdocs/courts.asp
  Links to bankruptcy courts throughout the United States.

- Directory of Judges and Staff for U.S.
  http://www.abiworld.org/chambers/courtdirs.html
  Links to each state's bankruptcy court and the directory of judges and staff for the bankruptcy courts.

CENSUS USE

- How Far Is It?
  http://www.indo.com/distance/
  This service uses data from the U.S. Census and a supplementary list of cities around the world to find the latitude and longitude of two places, and then calculates the distance between them (as the crow flies)

CHILD CRIME AND SAFETY ISSUES

- American Professional Society on the Abuse of Children
  http://www.apsac.org/

- Child Abuse Prevention Network
  http://child.cornell.edu

- Child Quest International
  http://www.childquest.org
  A nonprofit corporation dedicated to the protection and recovery of missing, abused, and exploited children.

- Children's Institute International (CII)
  http://www.childrensinstitute.org
  CII is a private, nonprofit organization specializing in the treatment and prevention of child abuse and neglect.

- National Center for Missing Children
  http://www.missingkids.org

- National Clearinghouse on Child Abuse and Neglect Information
  http://www.calib.com/nccanch

- Parents of Murdered Children (POMC)
  http://www.pomc.com
  Provides emotional support plus assistance with the criminal justice system.

- Steps to Take if Your Child Is Missing
  http://www.pollyklaas.org/yourchild/index.htm
  Provides information about missing, abused, and exploited children.

- The Ohio Missing Children Clearinghouse
  http://www.mcc.ag.state.oh.us/

COMMERCIAL DATABASE PROVIDERS

- Autotrak
  http://atxp.dbt-online.com/
  Searches billions of records from your desktop computer with AutoTrackXPSM.

- CDB Infotek—The Public Records Information Company
  http://www.cdb.com/public/
  CDB Infotek provides government and businesses with access to critical county, state, and federal public records information, including UCC filings and other corporate documents. Tools and search engines are available for locating people and verifying business information and assets.

- Courtlink
  http://www.courtlink.com/welcome.html
  Courtlink is a research tool for professionals and allows researchers to access the most current court records. Primary uses include litigation history, discovery, case management, and background checks.

- Fulltext Search Online
  http://www.bibliodata.com/
  BiblioData publishes books and newsletters that support the online researcher.

- KnowX.com—Public Records Now
  http://www.knowx.com
  KnowX.com provides real-time access to billions of public records.

- Lexis-Nexis
  http://www.lexis-nexis.com/lncc/
  Offers credible, in-depth information in such areas as legal, business, government, and academic areas. A search engine is available to find exactly what you need.

- Superior Information Services
  http://www.cji.com/
  This site has a link to Superior Information Services, which is a public records information company affiliated with Charles Jones, LLC. The site allows instant, online searches of public records data.

COMMUNICATIONS

- Federal Communications Commission
  http://www.fcc.gov

COURTS

- Courts.net
  http://www.courts.net/
  This site has been developed to provide directory listings for courts across the United States.

- State Court Web Sites
  http://www.ncsconline.org/D_KIS/info_court_web_sites.html#State
  Links to court Web sites by state and links to federal and international court Web sites.

- U.S. District Bankruptcy Courts
  http://www.looksmart.com/eus1/eus317836/eus317916/
  eus53716/eus62703/eus53462/eus551901/eus551904/r_l&/
  Links to U.S. Federal Bankruptcy Courts by state via LookSmart.com

- U.S. District Judicial Districts
  http://www.looksmart.com/eus1/eus317836/eus317916/
  eus53716/eus62703/eus53462/eus551901/eus551905/r_l&/
  Links to U.S. Federal Judicial District Courts by state via LookSmart.com

- U.S. Marshals Service
  http://www.looksmart.com/eus1/eus317836/eus317916/
  eus53716/eus62703/eus53462/eus551227/r_l&/
  Links to U.S. Marshals Service via LookSmart.com

CRIME PREVENTION

- Elder Abuse Prevention
  http://www.oaktrees.org/elder
  Information and research.

- Executive Protection Institute
  http://www.personalprotection.com
  Training for personal protection.

- Gang Prevention, Inc.
  http://www.gangpreventioninc.com
  Provides training, consulting services and expert testimony to the law enforcement etc.

- Indiana Prevention Resource Center
  http://www.drugs.indiana.edu/drug_stats/home.html
  Use and the consequences of use of alcohol, tobacco, and other drugs.

- Indiana Prevention Resource Center
  http://www.drugs.indiana.edu/slang/home.html
  This online dictionary contains more than 3,000 street drug slang terms from the Indiana Prevention Resource Center files, with more than 1,200 additions from the National Drug and Crime Clearinghouse slang term list.

- National Crime Prevention Council
  http://www.weprevent.org
  McGruff the Crime Dog crime prevention site

- National Crime Prevention Council (NCPC)
  http://www.ncpc.org
  National Crime Prevention Council online resources.

- Preventing Crime: What Works; What Doesn't; What's Promising ((The Sherman Report)
  http://www.ncjrs.org/works/index.htm
  An insightful report about emerging issues in criminology and criminal justice.

- Safety Net Domestic Violence—The Resources
  http://home.cybergrrl.com/dv
  Domestic violence resources.

- Victim Assistance Online
http://www.vaonline.org
Victim-Assistance Online is an information, research, and networking resource for victims.

CRIMINAL JUSTICE INFORMATION

- American Board of Criminalists
http://www.criminalistics.com/ABC
Composed of regional and national organizations that represent forensic scientists.

- American Society of Criminology (ASC)
http://www.asc41.com
Multidisciplinary forum fostering criminology study, research, and education.

- America's Most Wanted Criminals
http://cpcug.org/user/jlacombe/wanted.html
Law enforcement (federal and state) listing of most wanted criminals.

- California Association of Criminalists
http://www.criminalistics.com/CAC
Professional membership organization of forensic scientists.

- California Criminalistics Institute (CCI)
http://www.ns.net/cci
Provides specialized training to personnel who are practitioners in the field of forensic science.

- Cecil Greek's Criminal Justice Page
http://www.criminology.fsu.edu/cj.html
Multi-listing of forensic resources.

- ChoicePoint Online for the Government
http://www.cpgov.com
CPS provides nationwide public record information, document retrieval, and related ($ fee) services using its proprietary databases and information obtained from third parties.

- Crime and Punishment
http://crime.about.com/culture/crime
Links to articles regarding alcohol/drugs, campus crime, capital punishment, crime scenes, death row, and many other subjects.

- Crime Scene Evidence Files
http://www.crimescene.com
Allows participation in actual crime cases.

- Crime Scene Investigation (CSI)
http://police2.ucr.edu/csi.htm
Crime-scene response guidelines, collection, and preservation of evidence. Information, CSI articles, CSI training, CSI resources and links.

- Criminology and Criminal Justice
  http://www.soc.umn.edu/~overall/crime.htm
  Criminology and criminal justice resources on the Internet.
- Domestic Violence Information Center
  http://www.feminist.org/other/dv/dvhome.html
  Domestic violence information.

- Dr. Cecil Greek's Criminal Justice Page
  http://www.fsu.edu/~crimdo/greek.html
  Excellent site for law enforcement and forensic links.

- Florida State University's (FSU) Criminal Criminal Justice
  http://www.fsu.edu/~crimdo/cj.html
  One of the oldest criminal justice resources on the Web, this site consists mostly of justice links to other sites.

- FSU School of Criminology and Criminal Justice Page
  http://www.fsu.edu/~crimdo/police.html

- Gang Information
  http://members.aol.com/ggarner539/index.html
  This site offers links, photos, and book reviews related to gangs, organized crime, law enforcement, and corrections.

- General Victims Assistance Information
  http://www.ncjrs.org/victhome.htm
  General information on victims' assistance.

- High Technology Crime Investigation Association
  http://htcia.org

- Illinois Criminal Justice Information Authority
  http://www.icjia.state.il.us

- Jane's Intelligence Watch Report and Terrorism Watch Report
  http://intelweb.janes.com/
  These reports track and monitor international terrorists groups and insurgency movements, and intelligence community, economic espionage and computer security issues.

- Justice Information Center: National Criminal Justice Reference Service (NCJRS)
  http://www.ncjrs.org/ncjhome.htm

- Michigan State University's School of Criminal Justice
  http://www.ssc.msu.edu:80/~cj

- National Association of Attorneys General
  http://www.naag.org
  Promotes cooperation and communication among the states' chief legal officers.

- National Center for Victims of Crime
  http://www.ncvc.org

- Stanford Computer Crime Page
  http://cse.stanford.edu/class/cs201/projects-98-99/computer-crime

- The Academy of Criminal Justice Sciences (ACJS)
      http://www.nku.edu/~acjs
  The Academy of Criminal Justice Sciences is an international organization established in 1963 to foster professional and scholarly activities in the field of criminal justice.

- The American Bar Association, Criminal Justice Section
  http://www.abanet.org/crimjust

- The Coroner's Report
  http://gangwar.com
  Information and resources on gang intervention and prevention.

- The Wall on the Web
  http://grunt.space.swri.edu/thewall/thewallm.html
  Listing of names from the Vietnam War Memorial in Washington, D.C.

- U.S. Department of Justice
  http://www.usdoj.gov/
  U.S. Department of Justice home page. Contains links and information, publications and documents, fugitives and missing persons, press releases, and more.

- U.S. Department of Justice Criminal Office of International Affairs Fugitive Unit
  http://www.usdoj.gov/criminal/oiafug
  Interagency international fugitive lookout division

- United Nations Crime and Justice Information Network
  http://www.ifs.univie.ac.at/~uncjin/uncjin.html
  Center for international crime prevention

- U.S. Department of Justice, Office of the Inspector General
  http://www.usdoj.gov/oig

- U.S, Marshals Service
  http://www.usdoj.gov/marshals

- Vermont Criminal Justice Services
  http://170.222.24.9/cjs/index.html

- Western (U.S.) Society of Criminology
  http://www.sonoma.edu/cja/wsc/wscmain.html
  Devoted to the scientific study of crime.

- World Factbook of Criminal Justice Systems
  http://www.ojp.usdoj.gov/bjs/abstract/wfcj.htm

DIRECTORIES

- 555-1212
  http://www.555-1212.com/
  Area codes, country codes, e-mail addresses, telephone numbers and Web sites searchable by area code.

- BigYellow—The Biggest Online Yellow Pages
  http://www.bigyellow.com/
  Telephone and e-mail address directory.

- BizWeb Business Guide to the Web
  http://www.bizweb.com/
  A Web business guide to more than 43,000 companies listed in more than 190 categories.

- ComFind Internet Business Directory
  http://www.comfind.com/
  The Internet's largest global business directory.

- HandiLinks
  http://www.ahandyguide.com/
  A directory of other directories and guides.

- InfoSpace Reverse Search
  http://www.infospace.com/info/reverse.htm

- Internet 800 Directory—Directory of free toll free
  http://inter800.com/search.htm
  The only toll-free directory on the Web that lists 800 or 888 numbers free, regardless of the long-distance carrier.

- MediaJump
  http://www.owt.com/dircon/mediajum.htm
  Direct Contact Publishing's comprehensive media guide to more than 3,000 magazines, professional journals, and trade and consumer publications.

- Switchboard White Pages, Yellow Pages—Find
  http://www.switchboard.com/
  Find people, businesses, e-mail addresses, and Web sites.

- The Ultimate Guide—InfoSpace
  http://www.infospace.com/
  A guide to finding people, places, and things.

- Welcome to WhoWhere!
  http://www.whowhere.com/
  A guide to finding people, addresses, phone numbers, e-mail addresses, and other information on the Web.

- World Directories
  http://www.globalyp.com/world.htm
  The Global Yellow Pages is a collection of phone directories from around the world.

- WORLDPAGES—Find Anything. Anyone. Anywhere.
  http://www.worldpages.com/
  Find people or business addresses and telephone numbers.

GENERAL

- Ancestry.com
  http://www.ancestry.com
  Free access to the master Social Security death index. Anyone with a SSN who has died since 1948 is listed.

- Dogpile
  http://www.dogpile.com
  A multi-engine search tool that searches with the best search engines, merges the results, and removes the redundancies.

- Echotech Geophysical
  http://www.echotech.com/index.html
  Echotech Geophysical specializes in environmental problems that can be solved using ground-penetrating radar (GPR), electromagnetic (EM), electrical resistivity, and magnetic (MAG) methods.

- FedEx/Tracking
  http://www.fedex.com/us/tracking/
  FedEx package tracking.

- For News Junkies
  http://www.pointcast.com
  Delivers news alerts.

- Travlang
  http://www.travlang.com/money/
  Currency exchange rates.

- Unclaimed Property
  http://www.unclaimed.org
  Links to state agencies throughout the country that keep track of unclaimed property.

GENERAL NEWS

- ABC NEWS
  http://www.abcnews.com/
  News site for ABC News.

- AJRNewsLink
  http://www.newslink.org/
  Extensive offering of general news sources compiled by the *American Journalism Review*.

- BBC News
  http://news.bbc.co.uk/BBC
  British Broadcasting Corporation news online resource.

- CNN Interactive
  http://www.cnn.com/
  Extensive news and customized news offering from Cable News Network (CNN).

- Fox News
  http://www.foxnews.com/
  News site from Fox News.

- Maps
  http://mapquest.com/
  MapQuest offers customizable road maps on the Internet.

- MSNBC
  http://www.msnbc.com/
  Extensive news offering from NBC and Microsoft.

- NAA(r) Hotlinks to Newspapers Online
  http://www.naa.org/hotlinks/index.asp
  The Newspaper Association of America offers extensive links to U.S. dailies, Canadian newspapers, selected international papers, weeklies, business papers, and alternative press publications.

- News Index
  http://www.newsindex.com/
  A comprehensive, up-to-the-minute news search engine for locating articles from newspapers from around the world.

- NewsHub—Summary of today's newest news every 15 minutes.
  http://www.newshub.com/
  NewsHub integrates and reports headlines from the world's premiere news sources.

- PR Newswire Home Page
  http://prnewswire.com/PR
  Newswire is one of the leading sources of immediate news from around the world

- Reuters Home Page
  http://www.reuters.com/
  Reuters' home page for worldwide news and financial information.

- *USA Today*
  http://www.usatoday.com/
  USA Today's online newspaper.

GOVERNMENT

- Bureau of Engraving and Printing
  http://www.bep.treas.gov

- Canadian Security Intelligence
  http://www.csis-scrs.gc.ca/

- CapWeb—The Internet Guide to the U.S. Congress
  http://www.capweb.net/classic/index.morph
  This is a guide to the U.S. Congress.

- Carroll's Government Directories
  http://www.carrollpub.com/
  This government personnel chart and directory site from Carroll's Directories provides and charts an accurate and up-to-date way for you to track and contact key decision makers in all levels of government.

- Congressional Directory
  http://www.access.gpo.gov/congress/cong016.html
  This is a congressional directory site sponsored by the U.S. House of Representatives and Senate.

- Constitution for the United States
  http://Constitution.by.net/uSA/Constitution.html
  U.S. and state constitutions, Bill of Rights, and additional amendments on the Internet.

- DefenseLINK—Official Web Site of U.S.
  http://www.defenselink.mil/
  An impressive collection of defense-related links to the Secretary of Defense, Joint Department of Defense Chiefs of Staff, National Guard, and U.S. Army, Navy, Air Force, and Marine Corps.

- Department of the Solicitor General
  http://www.sgc.gc.ca/
  The Solicitor General Portfolio is responsible for protecting Canadians.

- Department of the Treasury
  http://www.ustreas.gov

- Department of Transportation (DOT)
  http://www.dot.gov
  DOT news, safety, dockets, jobs, and other information.

- Department of Veterans Affairs (VA)
  http://www.va.gov

- Directories—Government
  http://www.wellesley.edu/Internet/GovDocs/govdir2.html
  Links to federal, state, local, and foreign government directories.

- Factbook on Intelligence
  http://www.odci.gov/cia/publications/facttell/index.html

- FBI Home Page
  http://www.fbi.gov
  FBI information, news, library, most wanted, etc.

- Federal Bureau of Prisons (FBP) Home Page
  http://www.bop.gov
  Information about inmates, jobs, etc.

- Federal Communications Commission (FCC)
  http://www.fcc.gov/
  FCC news, meetings, events, auctions, and handbook.

- FedLaw
  http://www.legal.gsa.gov/
  Provides legal research on federal statutes, judiciary, legislation, arbitration, state and territorial laws, and professional organizations.

- FedWorld Information Network
  http://www.fedworld.gov/
  Offers various search engines to find information about U.S. government reports and databases.

- Financial Crimes Enforcement Network (FinCEN)
  http://www.ustreas.gov/fincen/

- General Services Administration (GSA)
  http://www.gsa.gov/
  Official Web page of the GSA includes links to news, staff offices, and services and has a searchable database.

- Government
  http://www.einet.net/galaxy/Government.html
  This site has a collection of links to government agencies, publications, and directories.

- Government on the Web
  http://www.ipcress.com/writer/gov.html
  Links to federal, state, local, and international agencies.

- Government Printing Office
  http://www.gpo.gov

- Government Records
  http://www.governmentrecords.com/

- Governments on the WWW
  http://www.gksoft.com/govt/
  This site offers a comprehensive database of governmental institutions on the World Wide Web, including parliaments, ministries, law courts, embassies, city councils, central banks, and more.

- Governors
  http://www.looksmart.com/eus1/eus317836/eus64407/eus53476/eus270341/r-l&
  This site provides links to the governor's office for individual states.

- GovSpot Law
  http://www.govspot.com/categories/law.htm

This site is a resource guide of government information specifically relating to the court system and law resources.

- Govt. Information Xchange
  http://www.info.gov/
  The Government Information Exchange site has a search engine and links to federal directories, foreign and international embassies, and state and local government sites.

- GPO Access
  http://www.access.gpo.gov/su_docs/aces/aaces002.html
  Access to Government Printing Office databases and specialized search pages.

- Hamrick Software–U.S. Surname Distribution
  http://www.hamrick.com/names
  Maps of the distribution of people with a particular surname.

- Internal Revenue Service IIRS)
  http://www.irs.treas.gov

- LSU Federal Government Links
  http://www.lib.lsu.edu/gov/fedgov.html
  Louisiana State University libraries present the *U.S. Federal Government Agencies Directory*, a comprehensive list of federal agencies on the Internet.

- National Infrastructure Protection Center (NIPC)
  http://www.nipc.gov
  NIPC serves as the U.S. government's focal point for threat assessment, warnings, etc.

- National Institute of Justice (NIJ)
  http://www.ojp.usdoj.gov/nij

- National Security Website
  http://www.nationalsecurity.org/
  Provides information and policy analyses about national security issues.

- Office of International Affairs Fugitive
  http://www.usdoj.gov/criminal/oiafug/fugitives.htm

- Office of the Director of Central Intelligence Agency (CIA)
  http://www.odci.gov/
  The home page of the CIA.

- OIG Database
  http://www.hhs.gov/oig/
  OIG Database includes individuals and entities that are excluded from participation in Medicare, Medicaid, and other federal health care programs. Searches may be based on the legal bases for exclusion, the types and entities excluded, the states where individuals reside and entities do business, or individual/entity name.

- SAMHSA's Treatment Improvement
  http://text.nlm.nih.gov/ftrs/dbaccess/tip
  Center for substance abuse treatment articles and information protocols.

- SEC Enforcement Actions
  http://www.sec.gov/enforce.htm
  Resources for enforcement actions, trading suspensions, Internet enforcement, etc.

- Sites of the Legislatures
  http://www.ncsl.org/public/sitesleg.htm#sites
  Links to the state legislatures (nationwide).

- Social Security Online
  http://www.ssa.gov/
  The official Web site of the Social Security Administration.

- State and Local Government on the Net
  http://www.piperinfo.com/state/states.html
  Links to all state and local governments on the Net. Includes links by state, multistage sites, federal resources, and national organizations.

- Government of British Columbia
  http://www.gov.bc.ca/

- Government of Nova Scotia
  http://www.gov.ns.ca/

- Immigration and Naturalization Home Page
  http://www.ins.usdoj.gov

- Library of Congress
  http://lcweb.loc.gov/homepage/lchp.html
  Access to the Library of Congress catalog , copyright office, and other resources.

- U.S. Bureau of the Census
  http://www.census.gov
  Access to census reports, facts, estimates, projections, etc.

- U.S. Bureau of Transportation Statistics
  http://www.bts.gov/
  Transportation information including airline, international transportation, and jobs.

- U.S. Customs Service
  http://www.customs.treas.gov
  This site contains importing and exporting, enforcement, and travel information.

- U.S. Department of Commerce
  http://www.doc.gov/
  Extensive links to economic, governmental, and trade-related sites.

- U.S. Department of State Official Web Site
  http://www.state.gov/index.html
  The U.S. Department of State home page includes U.S. policy topics and news, geographic background notes, and worldwide governmental policy issues and developments.

- U.S. DOJ Interpol—U.S. National Central Bureau
  http://www.usdoj.gov/usncb
  U.S. Department of Justice point of contact for international law enforcement

- U.S. Government Links
  http://iridium.nttc.edu/gov_res.html
  The WWW virtual library of U.S. government information sources.

- U.S. Government Printing Office Government Information Locator Service
  http://www.access.gpo.gov/su_docs/gils/gils.html

- U.S. Marshals Service
  http://www.usdoj.gov/marshals/

- U.S. Postal Inspection Service
  http://www.usps.gov/websites/depart/inspect/jurisdic.htm

- U.S. Postal Inspection Service: Wanted Posters
  http://www.usps.gov/websites/depart/inspect/wantmenu.htm

- U.S. Postal Service Zip +4 Code Lookup
  http://www.usps.gov/ncsc/lookups/lookup_zip+4.html

- U.S. Postal Service
  http://www.usps.gov/
  Official site of the U.S. Postal Service includes information on post office locations, rates, and forms, as well as a searchable database.

- U.S. Secret Service
  http://www.ustreas.gov/usss
  Site contains information about the history, protection, investigations, etc., of the Secret Service.

- U.S. Small Business Administration (SBA)
  http://www.sbaonline.sba.gov/
  SBA home page with many links to resources from the SBA, as well as a searchable database.

- U.S. State Department Travel Warnings and Consular Information Sheets
  http://travel.state.gov/travel_warnings.html

- U.S. State Home Pages
  http://www.globalcomputing.com/states.html
  This page links to the home pages of all 50 U.S. states.

- U.S. Vital Records Information
  http://www.vitalrec.com/index.html
  Accessible records include birth, death, marriage, divorce, and U.S. maps.

- United State Government Links to Enviro Info
  http://www.bara.com/info/govlinks/usfederal.html
  Provides extensive links to U.S. federal government agencies.

- United States Coast Guard
  http://www.uscg.mil

- United States Intelligence Community
  http://www.odci.gov/ic
  A group of 13 agencies and organizations that carry out intelligence activities.

- Vietnam POW/MIA Database
  http://lcweb2.loc.gov/pow/powhome.html
  This database has government documents pertaining to U.S. military personnel killed or missing in Vietnam.

- Vital Records Information—U.S. States
  http://www.vitalrec.com/index.html
  This site contains exhaustive links to sources of state, territory, and county vital records information.

- Washington Post—The Federal
  http://www.washingtonpost.com/wp-srv/politics/govt/fedguide/fedguide.htm
  Federal Internet guide hosted by the *Washington Post.*

- Web-Law United States Government
  http://www.web-law.com/resources/usgov.html
  This site provides legal resources pertaining to the U.S. government, including links to official government agencies and departments.

- White House
  http://www.whitehouse.gov/
  Official Web page for the White House contains information on tours, State of the Union addresses, the president and vice president, news briefings, handbooks and the White House help des.

- Yahoo! Additional Government Links
  http://www.yahoo.com/Government/tree.htl
  Provides exhaustive list of government sites by category, local, state, national, and international, as well as foreign embassies for almost every nation.

- Yahoo! Government Links
  http://www.yahoo.com/Government/
  Links to government-related categories.

- Yahoo! Index of Governments by Country
  http://www.yahoo.com/Government/Countries
  Index of governments by country.

HEALTH CARE FRAUD RESOURCES

- Champus/Tricare (health care fraud)
  http://www.tricare.osd.mil
  U.S. Department of Defense Military Health System site.

- FDA Backgrounder: Top Health Frauds
  http://www.fda.gov/opacom/backgrounders/tophealt.html
  Current information from FDA on health fraud.

- Your Guide to Health Care Fraud
  http://www.quackwatch.com
  A guide to health care fraud, quackery, and intelligent decisions.

HEALTH CARE

- Academy of General Dentistry
  http://www.agd.org/

- AIM DocFinder
  http://www.fraudtools.com
  This site offers a professional licensing database provided by Administrators in Medicine (AIM) and its participating boards.

- AMA Physician Select
  http://www.ama-assn.org/aps/amahg.htm
  Search engine for physicians.

- American Dental Association (ADA)
  http://www.ada.org/
  The premier source for oral health information.

- American Medical Association (AMA)
  http://www.ama-assn.org
  Online site for the American Medical Association

- American Psychiatric Association (APA)
  http://www.psych.org

- American Psychological Association
  http://www.apa.org

- Centers for Disease Control and Prevention (CDC)
  http://www.cdc.gov/

- Champus/Tricare
  http://www.tricare.osd.mil/tricaremanuals
  Source for manuals essential for investigating health care frauds involving Champus/Tricare.

- Columbia Education
  http://cpmcnet.columbia.edu/texts/guide
  Complete home medical guide from Columbia University.

- Department of Health and Human Services (DHHS)
  http://www.os.dhhs.gov
  Online site for U.S. Department of Health and Human Services

- Drug Database
  http://www.personalmd.com/drugdatabase.shtml
  Home page of the Drug Database. Covering more than 98.5 percent of all retail prescriptions, this database is a comprehensive source of very useful information.

- Drug Index
  http://www.rxlist.com
  Prescription list of drugs.

- Food and Drug Administration (FDA)
  http://www.fda.gov/

- Genetic Technologies, Inc.
  http://www.genetictechnologies.com
  DNA, forensics, and paternity testing.

- MdNets
  http://www.mednets.com/
  Contains proprietary search engines for every medical specialty.

- Medical Dictionary
  http://www.personalmd.com/medicaldictionary.shtml
  This page provides a search engine of the online *Merriam Webster Medical Dictionary*.

- Medical Matrix
  http://www.medmatrix.org/
  Medical Matrix is a free directory of selected medical sites on the Internet.

- Medical NBC Online Information Service
  http://www.nbc-med.org
  Terrorism involving weapons of mass destruction.

- Medical Reference Desk
  http://www.fraudtools.com/medical.cfm/
  This page provides a listing of medical references

- National Committee on the Future of DNA (and related articles, publications, and links)
  http://www.ojp.usdoj.gov/nij/dna

- National Institutes of Health (NIH)
  http://www.nih.gov/
  NIH today is one of the world's foremost biomedical research centers and the federal focal point for biomedical research in the United States.

- National Institute of Justice on DNA Evidence
  http://www.cdc.gov/nchs/default.htm
  Online site for National Center for Health Statistics

- Pharmaceutical Information Network
  http://www.pharminfo.com/pin_hp.html
  PharmInfoNet maintains a drug database, searchable by generic and proprietary names.

- Psych Guides
  http://www.psychguides.com/
  Psychiatric treatment guidelines from experts.

- Quack Watch
  http://www.quackwatch.com/
  Guide to health fraud, quackery, and intelligent decisions.

- Radiology Resource
  http://www.radiologyresource.org/
  Online site for Radiological Society of North America.

- Reuters Health Information
  http://www.reutershealth.com
  Health resources for consumers and industry professionals.

- The Merck Manual of Diagnosis and Therapy
  http://www.merck.com/pubs/mmanual/ Merck

- U.S. FDA's Drug Information
  http://www.fda.gov/cder/drug.htm
  FDA site for the Center for Drug Evaluation and Research.

INFORMATIONAL HIGH-TECH CRIME SITES

- High-Tech Crime Consortium
  http://www.hightechcrimecops.org
  Provide high-technology crime investigation education and training in detecting, investigating, and analyzing crime cases where computers are used as (1) a tool to facilitate or enable an illegal activity, (2) a target of criminal activity, or (3) incidentally to a criminal offense to law enforcement agency personnel.

- Computer Crimes/Technical Services Links
  http://www.co.gloucester.nj.us/pros/tech.htm
  Listing of computer crimes and technical services links.

- Computer/High-Tech Crime and Related Sites
  http://members.aol.com/_ht_a/crimejust/hightech.html
  Listing of computer/high-tech crime sites

- Officer.com
  http://www.officer.com/special_ops/c_crimes.htm
  One of the most comprehensive law enforcement resources sites in the world.

INSURANCE

- Car Safety
  http://www.carsafety.org
  Online site for Insurance Institute for Highway Safety.

- FEMA—Home Page
  http://www.fema.gov/index.htm
  Online site for Federal Emergency Management Agency.

- Fraud Indicators
  http://www.finder.com/insinvsp/fraudind.html
  Providing services as insurance investigation specialists.

- Glossary of Coverages
  http://www.lcgroup.com/resource/
  Insurance and Planning Resource Center site providing insurance definitions and explanations of coverage.

- Insurance Adjusters Resource Center
  http://www.adjust-it.com/
  Online source for claim-related services.

- Insurance Information Institute
  http://www.iii.org/home.html
  Online site for Insurance Information Institute.

- Insurance Institute
  http://www.iii.org/inside.pl5?media=issues=/media/issues/autotheft.html
  Insurance Information Institute information on auto theft.

- Insurance Institute of Highway Safety
  http://www.hwysafety.org/
  Online site for Insurance Institute of Highway Safety.

- National Insurance Crime Bureau
  http://www.nicb.com/
  Online site for National Insurance Crime Bureau.

INTERNATIONAL BUSINESS

- Banks of the world
  http://www.gwdg.de/~ifbg/ifbghome.html
  This page contains links to banks worldwide, sorted by continent.

- Department of State
  http://www.state.gov/
  Home page of the U.S. State Department.

- Embassy Links
  http://www.embpage.org/
  This Web site provides links to embassy Web sites around the world.

- International Court of Justice (ICJ)
  http://www.icj-cij.org/
  Home page of the International Court of Justice, principal judicial organ of the United Nations.

- NATO
  http://www.nato.int/
  Home page of the North Atlantic Treaty Organization.

- Telephone Directories on the Web
  http://www.teldir.com/eng/
  This Web site is a search engine of international white and yellow pages for more than 150 countries around the world.

- U.S. Information Agency (USIA)
  http://usinfo.state.gov/
  Home page of the USIA.

- Yelloweb Europe Directory
  http://www.yweb.com/
  This Web site has a search engine for Europe's yellow pages.

INTERNATIONAL LAW ENFORCEMENT WEB SITES

- Australian Federal Police
  http://www.afp.gov.au/

- Bavarian State Police
  http://www.polizei.bayern.de/
  Online site for Bavaria's police (Germany).

- Buenos Aires—Policia Bonaerense
  http://www.pol.gba.gov.ar/
  Online site for Buenos Aires police force (Argentina).

- Canada Criminal Intelligence Service
  http://www.cisc.gc.ca/
  Criminal intelligence services for Canada.

- Canadian Criminal Justice Resource Page
  http://members.tripod.com/~BlueThingy/index.html
  Provides links to Canadian criminal justice resources.

- Financial Action Task Force on Money Laundering
  http://www.oecd.org/fatf/
  Develops policies combating money laundering.

- Finnish National Police
  http://www.poliisi.fi/
  Online site for Finland's national police.

- International Constitutional Law
  http://www.uni-wuerzburg.de/law/index.html
  International constitutional law details of various countries.

- Ireland's Police Service
  http://www.garda.ie/
  Online site for Ireland's national police.

- Japanese National Police Agency
  http://www.npa.go.jp
  Online site for Japan's national police agency.

- Metropolitan Police—The New Scotland Yard
  http://www.met.police.uk/
  Online site for London's Metropolitan Police.

- New South Wales Police
  http://www.police.nsw.gov.au/
  Online site for New South Wales police force (Australia).

- Royal Canadian Mounted Police—Main Page
  http://www.rcmp-grc.gc.ca/index_e.htm
  Online site for Royal Canadian Mounted Police.

- South African Police Service
  http://www.SAPS.org.za/
  Online site for South African Police Service.

- Sweden National Police
  http://www.police.se/
  Online site for Sweden's national police.

- United Nations Crime and Justice Information Network
  http://www.uncjin.org/
  Electronic clearinghouse of criminal justice information.

- Webhideout
  http://www.jibc.org/
  Web hideout search engine for Internet resources.

- World's Most Wanted Rewards
  http://www.mostwanted.org/Rewards.html
  Provides information to capture fugitives.

INTERNATIONAL NEWS

- ABCNEWS.com
  http://www.abcnews.com/sections/world
  This Web page provides ABC's international news articles. This site has a search engine and links to associated pages.

- CNN-WORLD News
  http://www.cnn.com/WORLD/
  Home page of CNN world news headlines. Provides a search engine to access archived news, as well as a reference section.

- *International Herald Tribune*
  http://www.iht.com/
  Home page of the *International Herald Tribune* newspaper has a search engine to find archived newspaper articles.

- MedicalNFO Links-Search Page
  http://www.mediainfo.com/emedia/
  This site is a search engine for media information links.

- The Largest Newspaper Index on the Web!
  http://www.concentric.net/~Stevewt/
  This Web page has links to more than 3,000 newspapers from more than 80 countries. You will find all the big newspapers here, including the *New York Times* and *Washington Post.*

- The Ultimate Collection of News Links
  http://pppp.net/links/news/
  This Web site contains a large collection of links to newspapers from around the world.

- Yahoo!—World Summary
  http://www.yahoo.com/text/headlines/international/
  Search engine with searchable world news headlines.

INTERNET AND HIGH TECHNOLOGY

- American Society of Industrial Security
  http://www.securitymanagement.com
  Provides information and links for security professionals.

- Cookie Central
  http://www.cookiecentral.com/
  A Web site dedicated to providing full information about Internet cookies.

- Cyber411 Parallel Search Engine
  http://helios.unive.it/~franz/cyber.html
  A meta search engine, allowing the user to enter a keyword, phrase, or question.

- Directory of Internet Service Providers
  http://www.boardwatch.com/isp/
  Resources and links for Internet service providers.
- DOWNLOAD.COM
  http://download.cnet.com/
  Web site that provides freeware and shareware downloads.

- Internet Fraud Complaint Center
  http://www.ifccfbi.gov/
  A partnership between the FBI and the National White Collar Crime Center, this site provides current statistics and trends involving Internet fraud.

- Introduction to Net Scams and Hoaxes
  v1.0http://www.locus.halcyon.com/gspam/netscams.html
  Information about Net scams and hoaxes.

- National Center for Missing and Exploited Children Cyber Tipline
  http://www.missingkids.org/cybertip
  The Cyber Tipline handles leads from individuals reporting the sexual exploitation of children.

INTERNET FRAUD RESOURCES

- Fraud on the Internet
  http://www.emich.edu/public/coe/nice/fraudrl.html
  Lists resources related to Internet fraud.

- FTC Consumer Alert
  http://www.ftc.gov/bcp/conline/pubs/alerts/netalrt.htm
  Warnings about fraudulent Internet business opportunities.

- Internet Fraud Watch
  http://www.fraud.org/internet/intset.htm
  Helps consumers identify Internet fraud.

INVESTIGATIVE SOURCES

- American Academy of Forensic Sciences
  http://www.aafs.org
  Forensic references and resources.

- American Board of Medical Specialists
  http://www.certifacts.org
  Medical specialist search page.

- American College of Forensic Examiners
  http://www.acfe.com
  Online site for American College of Forensic Examiners.

- America's Most Wanted
  http://www.amw.com
  Program on apprehension of fugitives

- AmeriCom's Area Decoder
  http://decoder.AmeriCom.com
  Enables searches for area, city, or country phone codes.

- Ancestry's Social Security Death Index Online Search
  http://www.ancestry.com/ssdi/advanced.htm
  Contains information provided by the Social Security Administration.

- California Peace Officer Standards and Training (POST)
  http://www.post.ca.gov
  Information is available on POST's background, legal authority, and significant programs and projects.

- Carpenter's Forensic Science Resources
  http://www.tncrimlaw.com/forensic/
  Forensic site and links.

- ChoicePoint Online for Companies
  http://www.choicepointinc.com
  Conducts credential verification for businesses.

- ChoicePoint Online for the Government
  http://www.choicepoint.net
  Provides credential-verification services.

- Cop Seek
  http://www.copseek.com
  Directory of law enforcement–related sites.

- Copnet (Police List of Resources)
  http://police.sas.ab.ca/homepage.html
  Community resource for links to law enforcement sites.

- Credientials Online Educational Degree Verification
  http://www.degreechk.com/
  Source for degree-verification services.

- Crime Mapping Research Center
  http://www.nlectc.org/cmrc/
  Crime mapping and analysis site.

- Expert Witness International Directory
  http://www.expertwitness.com/
  Directory for expert witnesses.

- Federal Bureau of Investigation's Fugitive Publicity
  http://www.fbi.gov/mostwant/fugitive/fpphome.htm
  Lists fugitives wanted by the FBI.

- Forensic Science Society
  http://www.forensic-science-society.org.uk/
  Links to forensic science resources

- Forensic Technology, Inc.
  http://www.fti-ibis.com
  Forensic Technology, Inc., is a company whose mission is to enable the forensic sciences to achieve increased effectiveness through the application of automation technology.

- Granite Island Group—Technical Surveillance Countermeasures
  http://www.tscm.com
  Granite Island Group is an internationally recognized leader in the field of technical surveillance countermeasures, signals intelligence, electronic surveillance technology, telecommunications, communications security, counterintelligence, training, and technical security consulting.

- Handwriting and Signature Examinations
  http://www.questioneddocuments.com/sigexam.html
  Information about documents in question.

- High Technology Crime Investigation Association
  http://htcia.org/index.html
  Allows interchange of data on high-tech investigations.

- Informus
  http://www.informus.com/mvrrpt.html
  Motor vehicle registration.

- Informus
  http://www.informus.com/adrrpt.html
  Name search by previous address.

- Informus
  http://www.informus.com/crmrpt.html
  Criminal records.

- Informus
  http://www.informus.com/edurpt.html
  Education verification.

- Informus
  http://www.informus.com/wrkrpt.html
  Worker compensation.

- Informus
  http://www.informus.com/ssnrpt.html
  SSN search.

- Informus
  http://www.informus.com/ssnlkup.html
  Find out if a SSN is valid and where it was issued.
- Informus
  http://www.informus.com/pevrpt.html
  Previous employment verification.

- Intelligence/Counter Intelligence Web Sites
  http://www.kimsoft.com/kim-spy.htm
  Information and links on intelligence/counterintelligence sites

- International Association of Arson Investigators
  http://www.firearson.com/
  Links and resources for arson awareness.

- International Association of Auto Theft Investigators
  http://www.iaati.org
  Provides communication among auto theft investigators.

- International Association of Computer Investigative Specialists
  http://www.cops.org/
  Nonprofit organization dedicated to forensic computer science education.

- International Association of Financial Crimes Investigators
  http://www.iafci.org
  Provides interchange for fraud investigators.

- International Association of Special Investigation Units (IASIU)
  http://www.iasiu.com
  Insurance fraud awareness and training site.

- Introduction to Forensic Entomology
  http://www.uio.no/~mostarke/forens_ent/introduction.shtml
  A guide to forensic entomology.

- Investigative Resources International
  http://www.factfind.com
  A professional investigation firm.

- Investigative Solutions
  http://www.pimall.com/nais/home.html
  Free investigative resource centers.

- Justice Research and Statistics and Association
  http://www.jrsainfo.org
  Site of criminal justice statistics and research.

- L.S.I. SCAN
  http://www.lsiscan.com
  Training for Scientific Content Analysis (SCAN)

- LEXIS-NEXIS
  http://www.lexis-nexis.com/
  Searchable research site for wide range of information
- Martindale Hubble
  http://www.martindale.com/xp/Martindale/home.xml
  Searchable index for lawyer listings.

- Merlin Data ($-fee)
  http://www.merlindata.org
  This site contains court records, business license records and marriage records.

- MoreLaw Legal Information Publishing Web Site
  http://www.morelaw.com/
  Information on online verdicts, experts, and reporters.

- National Archives and Records Administration (NARA)
  http://www.nara.gov
  Searchable records system from the National Archives.

- National Association of Legal Investigators
  http://www.nali.com/
  Conducts investigations related to litigation.

- National Directory of Expert Witnesses
  http://www.claims.com/
  Online site for National Directory of Expert Witnesses.

- National Insurance Crime Bureau
  http://www.nicb.com
  Nonprofit organization for facilitating the prosecution of insurance criminals.

- National Personnel Records Center
  http://www.nara.gov/regional/mpr.html
  The MPR houses military personnel and medical records, as well as the medical records for dependents and former members of the U.S. Navy and Marine Corps. The CPR stores IRS records, U.S. Postal money orders, Treasury checks, and the records of local federal agencies within the metropolitan areas, in addition to civilian personnel and medical records.

- National Registry of Experts
  http://www.expert-registry.com/
  Provides recognition of expert witnesses.

- Net Detective People Search Engine Software
  http://net-detective.capex.net/
  Provides resources for conducting investigations on the Internet.

- Network Solutions Domain Lookup
  http://www.networksolutions.com/cgi-bin/whois/whois
  Searchable index for Internet domain names.

- Offshore Business News and Research
  http://www.offshorebusiness.com/
  Newsletters, databases, and documents on offshore businesses.

- Organized Crime—A Crime Statistics Site
  http://www.crime.org
  Information on the use and application of crime statistics.

- Public Record Sources
  http://www.publicrecordsources.com/
  Links to public record resources

- Semaphore Corporation
  http://www.semaphorecorp.com
  This link allows interactive neighborhood browsing around any address in a country. It also searches by name or address; people who have moved and changed their name, phone numbers, and e-mail accounts; URL changes; and more.

- Sex Offender.Com
  http://www.sexoffender.com
  Database registry identifying sex offenders.

- Shortcut to Cryptography
  http://www.subject.com/crypto/
  Resources and links for cryptography

- The World E-Mail Directory
  http://worldemail.com
  Searchable index of e-mail addresses worldwide.

- The World's Most Wanted
  http://www.MostWanted.org/
  Information about fugitives and unsolved crimes.

- U.S. Data Search
  http://www.007seek.com/index.html
  Public records site for conducting background checks.

- UPIN (Unique Physician Identifier Number) Database
  http://www.cpg.mcw.edu/www/upin.html
  Searchable index by UPIN for physicians.

- VA State Police: Sex Offender and Crimes
  http://sex-offender.vsp.state.va.us/cool-ICE
  Registry program for Virginia state sex offenders.

- Webgator—Investigative Resources on the Web
  http://www.inil.com/users/dguss/wgator.htm
  Provides links to investigative resources online.

- Zeno's Forensic Site
  http://forensic.to/forensic.html
  Link to resources for forensic investigations in varying fields.

- A Prisoner's Dictionary
  http://www.wco.com/~aerick/lingo.htm
  This list contains words dealing with sex or violence, matters that are part of prison culture. Many of the terms relate to specific California procedures, such as "602s." However, since the list was first compiled, it has grown to contain words and phrases from prisons in various states.

- Airborne Law Enforcement Association
  http://www.alea.org
  Online site for Airborne Law Enforcement Association.

- American Probation and Parole Association (APPA)
  http://www.appa-net.org
  APPA is an international association composed of individuals from the United States, its territories, and Canada who are actively involved with probation, parole and community-based corrections, in

both adult and juvenile sectors, including all levels of governmental (local, state/provincial, and federal) agencies.

- American Society of Law Enforcement Trainers (ASLET)
  http://www.aslet.org
  Home page for the American Society of Law Enforcement Trainers.

- American Society of Questioned Document Examiners
  http://www.asqde.org
  Provides updated information on the ASQDE.

- Association of Firearms and Toolmarks Examiners
  http://www.povn.com/~4n6/afte.htm
  Firearm and tool mark information.

- Blue Line Learning Group, Inc.
  http://members.aol.com/copsmart
  Law enforcement training.

- Bureau of Alcohol, Tobacco, and Firearms (BATF)
  http://www.atf.treas.gov
  Contains information related to alcohol, tobacco, and firearms.

- California Highway Patrol (CHP)
  http://www.chp.ca.gov/
  Home page for the CHP.

- Canadian Police Research Centre (CCRC)
  http://www.cprc.org/cgi-bin/main.cfm
  The Canadian equivalent of the International Association of Chiefs of Police, CCRC evaluates police equipment and offers information and technology sources.

- Careers in Law Enforcement
  http://www.lejobs.com
  Information about agencies that are currently hiring for law enforcement.

- Concerns of Police Survivors (COPS)
  http://www.nationalcops.org
  Reaches out to the families of U.S. law enforcement officers killed in the line of duty.

- CopNet
  http://police.sas.ab.ca
  Offers CopNet directory, Justice directory, public services, COPNET Radio, CopMall, CopSource, and CopNet chronicles.

- Copnet Agency List
  http://www.copnet.org/local/index.html
  Home page for agencies around the world.

- CopsOnLine
  http://www.copsonline.com
  CopsOnLine is an informative, interactive police Web site that seeks to provide information and an exchange of ideas for officers and members of the public.

- C-Squad
  http://www.egroups.com/group/C-Squad
  Discusses computers and the Internet, as they pertain to the law enforcement.

- Defense Criminal Investigative Service
  http://www.dodig.osd.mil/dcis/index.html
  The OAIG for investigations includes the DCIS and the CIPO.

- Defense Technical Information Center
  http://www.dtic.mil
  Provides access to, and facilitates the exchange of, scientific and technical information.

- Department of Defense (DOD)
  http://www.defenselink.mil
  Official Web site of the DOD.

- Drug Enforcement Administration (DEA)
  http://www.usdoj.gov/dea/index.htm
  Home page for the DEA.

- Etak Guide
  http://www.etakguide.com
  Etak will find a location anywhere in United States.

- FATF—Financial Action Task Force on Money Laundering
  http://www.oecd.org/fatf/index.htm
  Home page of FATF, includes information about FATF and news releases.

- Federal Bureau of Prisons
  http://www.bop.gov/bopmain.html

- Federal Emergency Management Agency (FEMA)
  http://www.fema.gov
  Federal source for disaster preparation information.

- Federal Law Enforcement Training Center
  http://www.treas.gov/fletc
  Official Web site of the training center. Many of the center's documents are available for downloading in the FOIA area.

- Federal Protective Service
  http://r2.gsa.gov/html/fedprot.htm
  Law enforcement arm of the General Services Administration.

- Financial Crimes Enforcement Network (FinCEN)
  http://www.ustreas.gov/fincen
  Home page for FinCEN.

- Fraternal Order of Police (FOP) Network
  http://www.fop.net
  Home page for the FOP.

- High-Tech Crime Network
  http://www.htcn.org
  Unites the law enforcement and private sector in the fight against high-tech crimes.

- Institute of Police Technology and Management
  http://www.unf.edu/iptm
  Training for law enforcement, military, and the civilian communities. The course calendar is updated weekly to provide the latest information on the courses offered.

- International Association of Campus Law Administrators Enforcement Administrators (IACLEA)
  http://www.iaclea.org
  Home page for IACLEA.

- International Association of Chiefs of Police
  http://www.theiacp.org
  Home page for International Association of Chiefs of Police.

- International Association of Chiefs of Police Technology Clearinghouse
  http://www.IACPtechnology.org
  The source for law enforcement information technology.

- International Association of Law Enforcement Intelligence Analysts (IALEIA)
  http://www.ialeia.org
  Home page for IALEIA.

- International Association of Law Enforcement Planners
  http://www.ialep.org
  Serves as a forum to exchange ideas, programs, techniques, and policies.

- International Association of Women Police
  http://www.iawp.org
  Home page for the International Association of Women Police.

- International Fellowship of Police Chaplains
  http://www.ifoc.org/ifpc.htm
  Home page for police chaplains.

- International Narcotics Interdiction Association (INIA)
  http://www.inia.org
  Web site with the latest information and trends in targeting narcotics traffickers.

- International Police Association (IPA) American Section
  http://www.ipa-usa.org
  Worldwide FOP officers, active or retired.

- Ira Wilsker's Law Enforcement Sites
  http://www.ih2000.net/ira
  Extensive collection of links to law enforcement sites.

- Just for Cops
  http://www.cgclaw.com/Just4Cops.htm
  The Internet supersite for busy law enforcement professionals.

- Justice for All
  http://www2.jfa.net/jfa
  Criminal justice reform and victims' rights association.

- *Law and Order* Magazine
  http://www.lawandordermag.com
  Online magazine for police professionals.

- Law and Society Association Home Page
  http://www.lawandsociety.org

- Law Enforcement Agency Listings
  http://www.officer.com/agencies.htm
  Law enforcement resource site.

- Law Enforcement Analysts (LEANALYST) Home Page
  http://www.inteltec.com/leanalyst
  Home page for the LEANALYST

- Law Enforcement Careers
  http://www.policeemployment.com
  Employment, testing, and interviewing guides to federal and state police careers.

- Law enforcement Employment Pages
  http://www.cop-spot.com/employment/
  Free employment-listing information.

- Law Enforcement Internet Intelligence Report
  http://www.lawintelrpt.com
  A monthly online newsletter that presents in digest form the latest, most useful information for all law enforcement personnel.

- Law Enforcement Links
  http://www.leolinks.com
  A law enforcement guide to the World Wide Web.

- Law Enforcement Links
  http://www.av.qnet.com/~harv/law.htm
  This site has several services related to firearms or law enforcement.

- Law Enforcement Memorial
  http://www.policememorial.com
  Online law enforcement memorial.

- Law Enforcement Online
  http://www.pima.edu/dps/muni.htm
  This is a registered for sworn law enforcement personnel only. It promotes professional association among agencies through the sharing of reference material.

- Law Enforcement Product News
  http://www.law-enforcement.com
  Source for product information and what's new.

- Law Enforcement Product News Events Schedules
  http://www.law-enforcement.com/trade/conferences
  Expositions, conferences, and seminars for law enforcement, corrections, dispatch, and security personnel.

- Law Enforcement Search Engine
  http://www.cops.dk
  Law enforcement search engine with links to everything law enforcement related.

- Law Enforcement Sites—Current Events, Law and Net Links
  http://www.law.about.com/msub6.htm
  Annotated links to different sites on the Web.

- Law Enforcement Targets
  http://www.letargets.com
  Catalog for firearms training targets and additional shooting supplies to law enforcement and the shooting public.

- LEXIS-NEXIS Law Enforcement Information Services ($ fee)
  http://www.lexis-nexis.com/lawenf
  Allows you to verify addresses and telephone numbers, track down elusive parties, etc.

- Links to Justice Department, Courts,
  http://www.rmwest.com/resource/usgov.htm
  U.S. government resources on the Internet

- Lock's Law Enforcement
  http://www.fortunecity.com/campus/auburn/279/
  Home page for Lock's Law Enforcement

- National Drug Enforcement Officers Association
  http://www.ndeoa.org
  Promotes the cooperation, education, and exchange of information among all law enforcement agencies.

- National Law Enforcement Officers' Memorial
  http://www.nleomf.com
  Home page for the National Law Enforcement Officers' Memorial.• National Rifle Association

- National Rifle Association (NRA) of America
  http://www.nra.org

- National Security Agency (NSA)
  http://www.nsa.gov:8080

- National Sheriffs Association
  http://www.sheriffs.org

- National Tactical Officers Association
  http://ntoa.org
  A tactical information and educational resource.

- National Terrorism Preparedness Institute
  http://terrorism.spjc.cc.fl.us
  News and resources for terrorism preparedness.

- National White Collar Crime Center Internet (NW3C)
  http://www.nw3c.org
  Features a spotlight on insurance fraud, reader survey, and research on fraud.

- Nuclear Regulatory Commission (NRC)
  http://www.nrc.gov

- Office of Justice Programs—U.S.
  http://www.ojp.usdoj.gov
  Funding, training, programs, statistics, and research about the justice system, DOJ law enforcement, etc.

- Officer Down Memorial Page
  http://www.odmp.org
  Web site devoted to honoring fallen law enforcement officers.

- Other Side of the Wall
  http://www.wco.com/~aerick
  Discusses prison news, the death penalty, criminal justice, death row writings, prisons and prisoners, and more.

- Police Career
  http://www.policecareer.com
  Law enforcement pre-employment and promotional test preparation, career books and résumé services.

- Police Departments by State and Country
  http://www.cityofmyrtlebeach.com/police/links.html
  A large list, courtesy of the Myrtle Beach, South Carolina, Police Department.

- Police Guide—Directory of Police Memorial Web Pages
  http://www.policeguide.com/memorial.htm

- *Police* Magazine
  http://www.policemag.com
  Online version of *Police* magazine.

- Police One
  http://www.policeone.com
  Resource for Law Enforcement

- Police Stress
  http://stressline.com
  Focuses on the issue of police stress.

- Police Supervisors' Association
  http://www.policesupervisors.org
  News, information, and resources for police supervisors.

- Post Trauma Resources
  http://www.posttrauma.com

- Resources for Law Enforcement
  http://www.hrlef.exis.net/resource.htm
  Comprehensive law enforcement research and resource Web featuring a menu of law enforcement sites to search.

- Sarge's Police Directory
  http://www.cswnet.com/~bhiaumet/directory.html
  Includes law enforcement sites worldwide, as well as law enforcement sites throughout the United States and Canada.

- *Soldier Of Fortune* Magazine
  http://www.sofmag.com/
  Fact-finding magazine covering military and law enforcement.

- State, County, and Municipal Agencies Online
  http://www.pima.edu/dps/muni.htm

- Street Slang—Drugs
  http://www.drugs.indiana.edu/slang/
  Dictionary of street drug slang.

- The Corrections Connection
  http://www.corrections.com
  Provides links to almost any correctional organization in the country and to all kinds of corrections information.

- The Death Penalty Information Center
  http://www.essential.org/dpic

- The HIT Law Enforcement Links
  http://www.officer.com
  Thousands of police, law enforcement, and criminal justice links arranged in an easy-to-browse format.

- The Info Source-Law Enforcement Links
  http://info-s.com/police.html 67,738

- The National Institute of Corrections (NIC)
  http://www.nicic.org/inst.
  The NIC is an agency under the U.S. Department of Justice that provides assistance to federal, state, and local correction agencies working with adult offenders.

- The New York City Police Department (NYPD)
  http://161.185.203.7/html/nypd/finest.html
  Official Web site of one of the largest police agencies in the world.

- The Police Guide
  http://www.policeguide.com

- *The Police Marksman* Magazine
  http://www.policemarksman.com
  Online version of *The Police Marksman.*

- The Spy Page
  http://www.charweb.org/government/spy.html
  A collection of resources about intelligence gathering and the art of spying.

- The Terrorism Research Center
  http://www.terrorism.com
  Features essays and thought pieces on current issues, terrorism documents, and resources.

- The World's Most Wanted: Fugitives and Unsolved Crimes
  http://mostwanted.org
  Resource site for apprehension of fugitives.

- Universal Police Links
  http://www.spinet.gov.sg/pollink/index.html
  Includes many international agencies.

- Unsolved Crimes
  http://www.unsolvedcrimes.com/index.html
  Home page for unsolved crimes.

- Urban Legends Reference Pages
  http://www.snopes.com
  Search for urban legends.

- Cornell University—U.S. Code
  http://www.law.cornell.edu/uscode
  Legal Information Institute.

- Findlaw Cyberspace Law
  http://cyber.findlaw.com/criminal

- Law Guru
  http://www.lawguru.com
  Legal questions, answers, and research online.

- Law News Network
  http://www.lawnewsnetwork.com
  Most current and complete source for legal news anywhere.

- Rominger Legal
  http://www.romingerlegal.com
  Federal links, legal resources, and professional directories.

- U.S. Court of Appeals Federal Circuit
  http://www.law.emory.edu/fedcircuit
  Home page for the U.S. Court of Appeals Federal Circuit.

- University of Chicago Law School Library
  http://www.law.uchicago.edu/library/index.html

- Federal Judiciary Home Page
  http://www.uscourts.gov/alllinks.html#7th
  Links to federal district courts and courts of appeals.

- FedLaw—General Service Administration
  http://fedlaw.gsa.gov
  References for federal legal research.

- National Criminal Justice Referral System
  http://www.ncjrs.org/courwww.htm
  Criminal justice reference service.

- State Laws and Cases (Alternative Source)
  http://www.law.cornell.edu/states/listing.html
  Guide to state legal sites and statutes listed by jurisdiction.

- State Laws Cases and Codes
  http://www.findlaw.com/casecode/state.html
  Guide to state legal sites and statutes.

- U.S. Supreme Court Decisions
  http://supreme.findlaw.com/Supreme_Court/decisions.html
  Searchable guide to U.S. Supreme Court cases after 1893.

- U.S. Supreme Court Multimedia Database
  http://oyez.nwu.edu/
  U.S. Supreme Court multimedia database.

LITIGATION SUPPORT SERVICES

- CourtTV Lawyer Check
  http://www.courttv.com/legalhelp/check.html
  Attorney background checks for the United States.

592 · DEATH INVESTIGATOR'S HANDBOOK · 592

- Exhibit and Document Preparation
  http://www.expertlaw.com/experts/Exhibit/index.shtml
  ExpertLaw Web page on exhibit and document preparation, including links to document management, mapping, and presentation.

- Expert Witness Network
  http://www.witness.net/
  Expert Witness Network is a link to attorneys and expert witnesses via the WWW by using online technology. It reduces the time and costs of locating the best expert for a case.

- ExpertsRegistry
  http://www.experts.com/
  This is a worldwide resource for a rich variety of authors, consultants, specialists, and experienced expert witnesses.

- Find a PI
  http://www.findapi.com/
  A worldwide private investigator location service, this site also provides information on fraud news, fraud reports, fraud alerts, and more.

- Law Info.Com—Expert Witnesses
  http://www.lawinfo.com/biz/expertwitness.html
  Provides a searchable database of expert witnesses as well as other interesting tools.

- Westlaw
  http://www.westlaw.com/
  Legal and business research tool.

LOCAL/STATE LAW ENFORCEMENT WEB SITES

- COPNET: Police Resource List
  http://www.copnet.org

- High-Technology Crime Investigation
  http://www.htcia.org

- Law Enforcement Online
  http://www.pima.edu/DPS/organiz.htm
  Links to criminal justice organizations.

- Law Enforcement Sites on the Web
  http://www.ih2000.net/ira/ira.htm
  One of the largest and most award-winning law enforcement sites on the Internet.

- Police Departments in New England
  http://www.neilem.com/nepolice.html
  Includes most departments in Maine, Massachusetts, New Hampshire, Rhode Island, and Vermont.

- Southwestern Law Enforcement Institute
  http://www.slei.org

The Southwestern Law Enforcement Institute, located in Dallas, is a national leader in the areas of law enforcement management and ethics and training.

MAPS

- National Geographic Maps
  http://www.nationalgeographic.com/resources/ngo/maps
  National Geographic resource for maps, geography, and flags.

- Xerox Map Search
  http://pubweb.parc.xerox.com/
  Resource for maps.

MILITARY SITES

- Military City
  http://www.militarycity.com
  Locate a person or a military base.

- Military Network
  http://www.military-network.com
  The site includes links to the Internet with a military or military-related theme. All database records are searchable and may be selected individually and by various categories and subcategories.

- Military USA
  http://www.militaryusa.com
  Vietnam, Korean, Desert Storm casualties and military records. Includes a listing of more than 2.7 million Vietnam veterans, includes name, rank, branch of service, and MOS. Also has 680,000+ names of veterans who served in Desert Storm.

- U.S. Department of Veterans Affairs (VA)
  http://www.va.gov/

MISCELLANEOUS FEDERAL AND STATE CODES, STATUTES, AND LEGISLATION

- Federal Rules of Evidence
  http://www.law.cornell.edu/rules/fre/overview.html
  These rules govern the introduction of evidence in proceedings, both civil and criminal, in federal courts.

MISCELLANEOUS LEGAL

- ExpertLaw.com
  http://www.expertlaw.com/
  Allows attorneys to locate expert witnesses in a wide variety of fields and provides free information to assist experts, attorneys, and the general public on legal issues. Also provides information of interest to expert witnesses and litigation attorneys.

- ExpertPages.com
  http://www.expertpages.com/

Includes links to finding expert witnesses, experts, consultants; articles by experts; and federal rules of evidence.

- FindLaw-LawCrawler
  http://www.lawcrawler.com/
  A searchable legal database.

- Internet Legal Resources Guide
  http://www.ilrg.com/
  A categorized index of more than 4,000 selected Web sites and downloadable files, this site was established to serve as a comprehensive resource of the information available on the Internet concerning law and the legal profession, with an emphasis on the United States.

- Law Dictionary
  http://www.duhaime.org/diction.htm

- Duhaime's alphalink directory of legal information researched and written by lawyer Lloyd Duhaime Law Research.
  http://www.lawresearch.com/home.htm
  Contains more than 20,000 links to legal resources, including search engines, legal indexes, and links to facts and data.

- Law Schools
  http://dir.yahoo.com/Government/Law/Law_Schools/
  Links to law schools.

- Legal Links
  http://www.law.co.il/~ravia/dictio.htm
  Links to online legal directories and other legal links based on practice areas by Haim Ravia law offices.

- The Police Officer's Internet Directory
  http://www.officer.com/
  Contains links to agencies, associations, most wanted, investigations, supplies, and criminal justice.

NEWS

- APB News
  http://www.apbnews.com
  Source for news, information, and data on crime, justice, and safety.

- Newspapers On-line
  http://www.newspapers.com
  U.S., International, college, and business news.

- PBS Online
  http://www.pbs.org
  Contains 450 PBS television programs and specials.

- *USA Today Nation*
  http://www.usatoday.com/news/digest/nd1.htm
  Online version of the *USA Today Nation*

- *USA Today World*
  http://www.usatoday.com/news/world/nw1.htm
  Online version of the *USA Today World*.

NEWSPAPERS

- *Atlanta Journal-Constitution*
  http://www.accessatlanta.com/ajc/

- *Boston Globe*
  http://www.boston.com

- *Chicago Tribune*
  http://www.chicagotribune.com

- *Chicago Sun-Times*
  http://www.suntimes.com/

- *Dallas Daily News*
  http://www.dallasnews.com

- *Los Angeles Times*
  http://www.latimes.com

- *San Francisco Examiner*
  http://www.examiner.com

- *Daily Telegraph*
  http://www.telegraph.co.uk

- *Nando Times*
  http://www.nando.net
- *New York Times on the Web*
  http://www.nytimes.com

- *WashingtonPost.com*
  http://www.washingtonpost.com

- *USA Today*
  http://www.usatoday.com

OTHER NEWS SOURCES

- Google Groups
  http://groups.google.com/
  Google groups on a variety of topics.

- MSNBC News Index
  http://www.msnbc.com/news/contents.asp

- News Place for News and Sources
  http://www.niu.edu/newsplace
  Contains a wide variety of news and research resources.

PRIVATE INVESTIGATOR

- Home Study for Investigators
  http://www.advsearch.com/lionacademy.htm
  Lion Investigations Academy—how education relates to law enforcement, investigations, and security.

- Links to Private Investigation
  http://www.sover.net/~tmartin/Private.htm Acrecona

- National Search Locator
  http://www.nation-search.com/index.html
  People locator: national search and discovery

- Private Investigations Mall
  http://www.pimall.com/

- Private Missing Person Search
  http://www.aaronspi.com/search.htm
  Aaron's Private Investigation's Web site specialists search for information about subjects of interest.

- Spy Software
- http://www.spyheadquarters.com/main2GOTO.html
  OnlineDetective.com-online investigative tool.

PUBLICATIONS

- *Electronic Legal Journal*
  http://www.legaljournal.net
  Comprehensive collection of easy-to-use resources for lawyers, legal professionals, law students, business people, and consumers.

- Hieros Gamos: The Comprehensive Law and Government Portal
  http://www.hg.org/journals.html
  Index and links to law journals, newsletters, and bulletins, as well as links to Lexis-Nexis and Westlaw.

- National Registry of Magazines
  http://www.mediafinder.com
  Mediafinder.com—the most comprehensive database of print media in the United States and Canada.

- *Detroit Free Press*
  http://www.freep.com/

- *Detroit News*
  http://www.detnews.com/

- *U.S. News Online*
  http://www.usnews.com/usnews/main.htm

REFERENCES

- 164 Currency Converter by Oanda
  http://oanda.com/converter/classic

- Fingerprint Generator
  http://www.copscgi.com/fpc/fpcexample.shtml
  Generates examples of different fingerprint patterns.

- PCL Map Collection
  http://www.lib.utexas.edu/Libs/PCL/Map_collection/ Map_collection.html
  View maps of the world at this Web site.

- Price's List of Lists
  http://gwis2.circ.gwu.edu/~gprice/listof.htm
  Provides links to more than 1,000 searchable/interactive tools that cover materials not often accessible by general search tools.

- Web of Online Dictionaries
  http://www.facstaff.bucknell.edu/rbeard/diction.html
  Index of dictionaries for 218 languages.

- *Webster's Dictionary*
  http://www.m-w.com/netdict.htm
- Yahoo! Reference
  http://www.yahoo.com/reference/
  Yahoo! links to various reference sites.

SEARCH ENGINES/TOOLS

- 411 Locate
  http://www.411locate.com
  Searches for people by name and state and provides a map with driving directions.

- 555-1212
  http://www.555-1212.com
  Residential, business, and e-mail listings; area and country codes; reverse residential.

- Accufax
  http://www.accufax-us.com/
  Screening background checks.

- Advanced Research, Inc.
  http://www.advsearch.com
  People locates, asset searches, phone number traces, lie detection services, and investigations.

- All in One Search
  http://www.allonesearch.com/
  More than 500 of the Internet's best search engines, databases, indexes, and directories in a single site.

- All Search Engines.com
  http://www.vcilp.org/Fed-Agency/fedweb.exec.html#dod
  Listing of search engines by topics.

- All the Web
  http://www.alltheweb.com/
  All the Web, All the Time search engine.

- Alta Vista
  http://www.altavista.com
  One of the largest and most comprehensive search engines, it searches the entire HTML file for search terms.

- Alumni & Alumnae
  http://www.halcyon.com/investor/alumni.htm
  A homepage for finding fellow alumni and alumnae of a variety of institutions.

- American Library Association
  http://www.ala.org

- Anywho
  http://www.anywho.com
  Telephone number, e-mail, home page URL, fax, toll free, and address locator.

- Area Code Listing by Number
  http://www-cse.ucsd.edu/users/bsy/area.html
  Various area code listings by number.

- Arin: Whois
  http://www.arin.net/whois/index.html
  A search database that provides information on network names, network numbers, autonomous system numbers (ASNs), and host information, as well as the names, addresses, telephone numbers, and e-mail addresses for points of contact when you enter the server IP address. A great tool for tracing e-mails.

- Ask an Expert
  http://www.askanexpert.com/askanexpert
  Research information.

- Ask Jeeves
  http://www.askjeeves.com
  An Internet service that allows the user to ask a question and "Ask Jeeves" will locate the site for the answer.

- Bigfoot
  http://www.bigfoot.com
  Bigfoot.com search engine

- Biographical Dictionary
  http://s9.com/biography
  Biographical dictionary containing biographical information on more than 18,000 notable people.

- *Britannica Online*
  http://www.eb.com
  Online Encyclopedia Britannica

- City Search
  http://www.citysearch.com

- CNet Search Engines
  http://search.cnet.com
  Lists almost all available search engines on the Web.

- DirectSearch.net
  http://www.directsearch.net
  Lists search engines.

- Dogpile, the Friendly Multiengine
  http://www.dogpile.com/
  Search engine.

- Electronic Embassy (Worldwide)
  http://www.embassy.org
  Information on all the foreign embassies in Washington, D.C., forms the core of the electronic embassy.

- Excite
  http://www.excite.com
  Offers concept searching, useful for narrowing the scope of the search.

- FACSNET—Directory of Database
  http://www.facsnet.org/report_tools/CAR/cardirec.htm
  An information site for investigative journalists, this lists useful investigative data-services bases.

- FinderSeeker
  http://www.hamrad.com/search.html
  The search engine for search engines, a list of more than 300 links to Internet search engines.

- Go Network
  http://www.go.com
  Web site and search engine.

- Google
  http://www.google.com
  Search engine.

- Google Advanced Search
  http://www.google.com/advanced_search
  Advanced search engine.

- Highway 61
  http://www.highway61.com
  Submits your query to the six largest search engines simultaneously.

- Hot Sheet
  http://www.tstimpreso.com/hotsheet
  Search engine.

- Hotmail Web Site
  http://www.hotmail.com
  E-mail account Web site.

- Inference Find
  http://www.inference.com
  Web searcher.

- Infolaw
  http://www.infolaw.co.uk
  An extensive directory of legal resources in the United Kingdom, including government agencies,
  law schools, legal associations, and law publishers.

- Information Please Search Engine
  http://www.infoplease.com
  Search engine.

- Infoseek or Go
  http://www.go.com
  Most accurate engine on the Web, it pays close attention to all search terms.

- Info Space
  http://www.infospace.com
  Allows for the immediate location of individuals through name, phone number, and address.

- InfoUSA
  http://www.infoUsa.com
  People finder including reverse lookup.

- Internet Search Tools, Library of Congress
  http://lcweb.loc.gov/global/search.html
  Search engine that provides links to Web sites.

- Investigative Resource Center Databases
  http://www.lainet.com/factfind/database.htm
  Searchable databases and links for investigative professionals.

- *Investigator's Guide to Sources of Information* (1997)
  http://www.gao.gov/special.pubs/soi.htm

- Investigator's Tool Box
  http://www.pimall.com/nais/in.menu.html
  Sources of information.

- iTools Find it!
  http://www.iTools.com/find-it/
  Searches the Web, software libraries (for shareware), usernet groups, and for people.

- Korean War Project
  http://www.onramp.net/~hbarker
  Online database tool for Korean War casualties. Also has an area called Looking For, which allows inquiries for vets to be references to a page for units and reunions.

- Librarian's Index to the Internet
  http://sunsite.berkeley.edu/InternetIndex
  Contains annotated subject directory of 7,500+ useful Internet resources.

- Library of Congress Employee Directory
  http://lcweb.loc.gov/cgi-bin/phf/

- Look Up a Person
  http://www.theultimates.com
  Business, people, and e-mail directory searches are available.

- Lycos
  http://www.lycos.com
  One of the first search tools on the Internet, this search engine is keeping up to date with a variety of options available to display the results.

- Mamma
  http://www.mamma.com
  A parallel search engine.

- MegaWeb
  http://stoat.shef.ac.uk:8080/megaweb
  Allows you to choose from specific categories of search tool. A multilingual interface is available.

- MetaCrawler
  http://www.metacrawler.com/
  Search engine.

- Northern Light
  http://www.northernlight.com
  The most recent engine with good extensive content and a feature for classifying search results into user-defined custom search folders.

- Old Farmers Almanac
  http://www.almanac.com

- PageNet
  http://www.pagenet.net/pagenet/page_lnp.htm
  Sends alphanumeric pager messages.

- People Finder
  http://www.peoplesite.com
  Searches for individuals, even those not on the Internet

- Philatelic Web Sites in the United States
  http://www.si.edu/postal/development/postalmuseums.html
  Links to philatelic (postal) Web sites in the United States and around the world and around the world.

- Reference Research—My Virtual Reference Desk
  http://www.refdesk.com/ Search engine

- Reunion Hall
  http://www.xscom.com/reunion
  Brings together former classmates from around the world into one location with a mission to relink former classmates and create and information service surrounding the graduating class, the school, and its geographic region.

- Search Engine Watch
  http://www.searchenginewatch.com
  List of search engines.

- Starting Point
  http://www.stpt.com/
  Provides news, business resources, career, and education information, as well as a search function.

- Superhighway Web Site
  http://www.superhighway.is/

- Switchboard
  http://www.switchboard.com
  Comprehensive people locator.

- Telephone Directories on the Web
  http://www.contractjobs.com/tel
  National and international listings.

- The World E-Mail Directory
  http://www.worldemail.com
  More than 18 million e-mail addresses at your fingertips.

- The World Wide Web "Finger" Gateway
  http://www.cs.indiana.edu:800/finger/gateway
  "Finger" was an old command used on text-based systems to find someone's identity on the Web.

- TotalNEWS, all the news, on the Net.
  http://totalnews.com/
  TotalNEWS is a search engine and directory of domestic news sites.

- U.S. West Yellow Pages
  http://yp.uswest.com
  More than 22 million business listings and 70 million residential listings from across the country, searchable by name, business category, address, ZIP code, phone number, or combination searches.

- Virtual Reference Desk-Search Engines
  http://www.refdesk.com/newsrch.html
  Search engine resources

- Web Crawler
  http://webcrawler.com

- What's New Too
  http://nu2.com
  A comprehensive list of new Web sites.

- World Pages
  http://www.worldpages.com
  Business and people search.

- Zip2
  http://www.zip2.com
  Find a business or person, or get directions or maps.

- Zipcode.com
  http://www.zipcode.com
  Online ZIP code searches.

SEARCH FOR PEOPLE/BUSINESSES

- Frameset 7-International Telephone Directory
  http://www.infobel.be/infobel/infobelworld.html
  Yellow pages search engine.

- Telephone Directories on the Web
  http://www.teldir.com
  Search engine

- The Skip Trace and Locating Missing Persons Pages
  http://www.pimall.com/nais/missingm.html
  Resource center.

- The Ultimate White Pages
  http://www.theultimates.com/white
  Search engine.

- U.S. Surname Distribution
  http://www.hamrick.com/names/index.html

SENIOR-CITIZEN RELATED

- National Center on Elder Abuse
  http://www.gwjapan.com/NCEA/
  Site contains many resources to help you find the assistance, publications, data, etc.

INTERNET SOURCES BY STATE

Alabama

- Alabama Official Web Site
  http://alaweb.asc.edu

- Alabama Secretary of State
  http://sos.state.al.us/

- Alabama Department of Corrections Home Page
  http://www.agencies.state.al.us/doc

- Missing Persons, Sex Offenders, and Felony Fugitives
  http://www.gsiweb.net/

- Inmate Search
  http://agencies.state.al.us/doc/inmsearch.asp

- Missing and Exploited Children
  http://www.gsiweb.net/abiweb/missing_frame.html

- Most Wanted
  http://www.jeffcointouch.com/crimestoppers/criminallist.asp

- Sex Offender Searches
  http://www.gsiweb.net/so_doc/so_index_new.html

Alaska

- Alaska Official Web Site
  http://www.state.ak.us/

- Alaska Secretary of State
  http://www.gov.state.ak.us/

- Alaska Department of Corrections
  http://www.correct.state.ak.us

- Missing Persons
  http://www.dps.state.ak.us/ast/cib/Bulletins.htm
- Sex Offenders
  http://www.dps.state.ak.us/nSorcr/asp/

Arizona

- Arizona Official Web Site
  http://www.state.az.us/

- Arizona Secretary of State
  http://www.sosaz.com/business_services.htm

- Arizona Department of Corrections Home Page
  http://www.adc.state.az.us:81/

- Arizona Inmates on Death Row
  http://www.adc.state.az.us/DeathRow/DeathRow.htm

- Inmate Data Search
  http://www.adc.state.az.us/ISearch.htm

- Most Wanted
  http://www.adc.state.az.us/aztop10.htm

- Sex Offenders
  http://www.azsexoffender.com/

Arkansas

- Arkansas Official Web Site
  http://www.state.ar.us/

- Arkansas Secretary of State
  http://www.sosweb.state.ar.us/corp.html

- Escapee List
  http://www.state.ar.us/doc/escapee.html

- Inmate Searches
  http://www.state.ar.us/doc/inmate_info/

- Inmates on Death Row
  http://www.state.ar.us/doc/deathrow.html

- Missing Children
  http://leonardo.aristotle.net/acic/missing/missing-search.html

- Sex Offender Registry
  http://www.acic.org/registration/index.html

California

- California Official Web Site
  http://www.state.ca.us/

- California State Law and Other Information
  http://www.leginfo.ca.gov

- California Department of Corrections Home Page
  http://www.cdc.state.ca.us

- Death Row
  http://www.cdc.state.ca.us/Issues/Capital/PDF/Death_Row.pdf

- California Law Enforcement Basic Academies
  http://www.clew.org/CLEW/Trn/TrnCtrs/BasicAcad.html

- California Law Enforcement on the Web (CLEW)
  http://www.clew.org

- Missing Persons
  http://justice.hdcdojnet.state.ca.us/missingpersons/html/

- Most Wanted
  http://justice.hdcdojnet.state.ca.us/wanted/wanted.taf?function=form

- The Los Angeles Police Department (LAPD)
  http://www.lapdonline.org

- Unsolved Homicides in Los Angeles County
  http://www.unsolvedcrimes.com

Colorado

- Colorado Official Web Site
  http://www.state.co.us/

- Colorado Secretary of State
  http://www.sos.state.co.us/

- Escapees
  http://www.doc.state.co.us/Escapes/escapes.htm

- Most Wanted
  http://cbi.state.co.us/20_most_wanted.asp

- Sex Offenders Required Posting
  http://sor.state.co.us/off2/off2.listing.asp

- Sex Offenders Unregistered
  http://sor.state.co.us/off2/off3.listing.asp

Connecticut

- Connecticut Official Web Site
  http://www.state.ct.us/

- Connecticut Secretary of State
  http://www.state.ct.us/sots/

- Most Wanted
  http://www.state.ct.us/dps/BCI/MostWanted.htm

- Connecticut Department of Corrections
  http://www.state.ct.us/doc

- Sex Offenders Registry
  http://www.state.ct.us/dps/Sor.htm

Delaware

- Delaware Official Web Site
  http://www.state.de.us/

- Delaware Secretary of State
  http://www.state.de.us/sos/

- Delaware Department of Corrections
  http://www.state.de.us/correct

- Most Wanted
  http://www.state.de.us/dsp/wanted.htm

- Inmates on Death Row
  http://www.state.de.us/correct/Data/Death_Row.htm

- Department of State
  http://www.state.gov

- Sex Offender Registry
  http://www.state.de.us/dsp/sexoff/search.htm

Florida

- Florida Official Web Site
  http://www.state.fl.us/

- Florida Secretary of State
  http://www.dos.state.fl.us/

- Florida Department of Law Enforcement
  http://www.fdle.state.fl.us

- Florida Department of Corrections
  http://www.dc.state.fl.us

- Inmate Search
  http://www.dc.state.fl.us/ActiveInmates/search.asp

- Escaped Inmates
  http://www.dc.state.fl.us/EscapedInmates/search.asp

- Missing Children
  http://www.fdle.state.fl.us/missing_children/search_form.asp

- Missing Persons
  http://pas.fdle.state.fl.us/mpersons_search.asp

- Most Wanted
  http://www.fdle.state.fl.us/most_wanted/

- Sexual Predators
  http://www.fdle.state.fl.us/Sexual_Predators/index.asp

- Sheriffs
  http://flsheriffs.org/meet.htm

- Florida State Fire College
  http://www.fsfc.ufl.edu

- Wanted Persons
  http://pas.fdle.state.fl.us/wpersons_search.asp

Georgia

- Georgia Official Web Site
  http://www.state.ga.us/

- Georgia Secretary of State
  http://www.sos.state.ga.us/

- Georgia Department of Corrections
  http://www.dcor.state.ga.us

- Inmate Searches (includes photos)
  http://www.dcor.state.ga.us/OffenderQuery/asp/OffenderQueryForm.asp

- Sex Offender Registry
  http://www.state.ga.us/gbi/disclaim.html

Hawaii

- Hawaii Secretary of State
  http://www.hawaii.gov/

- Sex Offenders
  http://www.ehawaiigov.org/HI_SOR/

Idaho

- Idaho Official Web Site
  http://www.state.id.us/

- Idaho Secretary of State
  http://www.idsos.state.id.us/

- Idaho Department of Corrections
  http://www.corr.state.id.us

Illinois

- Illinois Official Web Site
  http://www.state.il.us

- Illinois Secretary of State
  http://www.sos.state.il.us/

- Wanted Persons
  http://www.isp.state.il.us/

- Unsolved Crimes
  http://www.isp.state.il.us/

- Illinois Department of Corrections
  http://www.idoc.state.il.us

- Inmates
  http://www.idoc.state.il.us/

- Inmate Search
  http://www.idoc.state.il.us/inmates/search.htm

- Sex Offenders
  http://www.samnet.isp.state.il.us/ispso2/sex_offenders/index.asp

Indiana

- Indiana Official Web Site
  http://www.state.in.us/

- Indiana Secretary of State
  http://www.state.in.us/sos/

- Indiana Department of Corrections
  http://www.ai.org/indcorrection

  Inmate Search
  http://www.in.gov/serv/indcorrection_ofs

- Sex Offenders
  http://www.state.in.us/serv/cji_sor

Iowa

- Iowa Official Web Site
  http://www.state.ia.us/

- Iowa Secretary of State
  http://www.sos.state.ia.us/

- Most Wanted
  http://www.state.ia.us/government/dps/wanted/

- Sex Offender Registry
  http://www.state.ia.us/government/dps/dci/isor/index.htm

Kansas

- Kansas Official Web Site
  http://www.state.ks.us/

- Kansas Secretary of State
  http://www.kssos.org/

- Kansas Department of Corrections
  http://www.ink.org/public/kdoc

- Escapees
  http://docnet.dc.state.ks.us/escapees/index.htm

- Offender Releases
  http://docnet.dc.state.ks.us/offenders/Offenders/releases.htm

- Parole Supervision
  http://www.docnet.dc.state.ks.us/offenders/county/20list.htm

- Registered Offender Search
  https://www.accesskansas.org/apps/kbi.search

Kentucky

- Kentucky Official Web Site
  http://www.state.ky.us/

- Kentucky Secretary of State
  http://www.sos.state.ky.us/

- Kentucky Vital Records Index
  http://www.ukcc.uky.edu:80/~vitalrec
  Searchable database of Kentucky vital statistics.

- Death Index 1911–1986
  http://ukcc.uky.edu/~vitalrec/

- Death Index 1987–1992
  http://ukcc.uky.edu/~vitalrec/

- Death Records 1911–2000
  http://userdb.rootsweb.com/ky/death/search.cgi

- Inmate Search
  http://www.cor.state.ky.us/~KOOL/

- Sex Offenders
  http://kspsor.state.ky.us/

Louisiana

- Louisiana Official Web Site
  http://www.state.la.us/

- Louisiana Secretary of State
  http://www.sec.state.la.us/

Maine

- Maine Official Web Site
  http://www.state.me.us

- Maine Secretary of State
  http://www.state.me.us/sos/

- Maine Department of Corrections
  http://janus.state.me.us/corrections/homepage.htm

- Death Index
  http://thor.ddp.state.me.us/archives/plsql/archdev.death_archive.search_form

Maryland

- Maryland Official Web Site
  http://www.mec.state.md.us/

- Maryland Secretary of State
  http://www.sos.state.md.us/

Massachusetts

- Massachusetts Secretary of State
  http://www.state.ma.us/

- Most Wanted
  http://www.state.ma.us/doc/wanted/index.html

- Locate an Inmate
  http://www.state.ma.us/doc/locate.html

- Massachusetts Department of Corrections
  http://www.magnet.state.ma.us/doc

Michigan

- Michigan Official Web Site
  http://www.state.mi.us/migov/MichiganGovernor.htm
- Michigan Secretary of State
  http://www.sos.state.mi.us/

- Michigan Crime Victim Rights
  http://www.gop.senate.state.mi.us/cvr

- Michigan Department of Corrections
  http://www.state.mi.us/mdoc

- Inmate Search
  http://www.state.mi.us/mdoc/asp/otis2.html

- Most Wanted
  http://www.msp.state.mi.us/wanted/fugitiv.htm

- Sex Offender Registry
  http://www.mipsor.state.mi.us/

Minnesota

- Minnesota Official Web Site
  http://www.state.mn.us/

- Minnesota Secretary of State
  http://www.sos.state.mn.us/search.html

- Inmate Search
  http://info.doc.state.mn.us/PublicViewer/main.asp

- Minnesota Department of Corrections
  http://www.corr.state.mn.us

- Sex Offenders
  http://www.corr.state.mn.us/level3/level3.asp

- Most Wanted
  http://info.doc.state.mn.us/Fugitive/main.asp

Mississippi

- Mississippi Official Web Site
  http://www.state.ms.us/

- Mississippi Secretary of State
  http://www.sos.state.ms.us/

- Mississippi Department of Corrections
  http://www.mdoc.state.ms.us

Missouri

- Missouri Official Web Site
  http://www.ecodev.state.mo.us

- Missouri Secretary of State
  http://mosl.sos.state.mo.us/

- Death Row
  http://www.missourinet.com/CapitalPunishment/inmates.htm

- Missing Children
  http://www.missingkids.com/precreate/MO.html

- Most Wanted
  http://www.ago.state.mo.us/wanted.htm

Montana

- Montana Official Web Site
  http://www.mt.gov/

- Montana Secretary of State
  http://www.state.mt.us/sos/

- Montana Department of Corrections
  http://www.state.mt.us/cor

- Parole Violators
  http://www2.state.mt.us/bopp/parole_violators_at_large.htm

Nebraska

- Nebraska Official Web Site
  http://www.state.ne.us

- Nebraska Secretary of State
  http://www.nol.org/home/SOS/

- Sex Offender Registry
  http://www.nsp.state.ne.us/sor/find.cfm

- Nebraska Department of Correctional Services
  http://www.corrections.state.ne.us

Nevada

- Nevada Official Web Site
  http://www.state.nv.us/

- Nevada Secretary of State
  http://sos.state.nv.us/

- Inmate Search
  http://www.ndoc.state.nv.us/ncis/lookup.php?btnReset=TRUE

New Hampshire

- New Hampshire Official Web Site
  http://www.state.nh.us/

- New Hampshire Secretary of State
  http://webster.state.nh.us/sos/

New Jersey

- New Jersey Official Web Site
  http://www.state.nj.us/

- New Jersey Secretary of State
  http://www.state.nj.us/state/

- New Jersey State Department of Corrections
  http://www.state.nj.us/corrections

- Parole Eligibility Notice
  http://www.state.nj.us/paroleeligreport.shtml

New Mexico

- New Mexico Official Web Site
  http://www.state.nm.us/

- New Mexico Secretary of State
  http://www.sos.state.nm.us/

- Sex Offenders
  http://www.nmsexoffender.dps.state.nm.us/servlet/fstate_serv.class

- New Mexico Department of Corrections
  http://www.state.nm.us/corrections

New York

- New York Official Web Site
  http://www.state.ny.us/

- New York State Department of State Home Page
  http://www.dos.state.ny.us/

- New York City Department of Corrections
  http://www.ci.nyc.ny.us/html/doc

- New York State Department of Correctional Services
  http://www.docs.state.ny.us

- Inmate Locator
  http://www.pac-info.com/location.php?lid=2226

- Most Wanted
  http://www.troopers.state.ny.us/WntdMiss/WntdMissindex.html

North Carolina

- North Carolina Office of the Attorney General
  http://www.jus.state.nc.us
  Includes the State Bureau of Investigation (SBI).

- North Carolina Official Web Site
  http://www.state.nc.us

- North Carolina Secretary of State
  http://www.secstate.state.nc.us/

- North Carolina Department of Corrections
  http://www.doc.state.nc.us

- Inmate Escapes
  http://webapps.doc.state.nc.us/escape/

- Inmate Releases
  http://webapps.doc.state.nc.us/release/

- Inmate Searches
  http://webapps.doc.state.nc.us/apps/offender_servlets/search1

- Sex Offenders
  http://sbi.jus.state.nc.us/SOR_20/Default.htm

North Dakota

- North Dakota Official Web Site
  http://www.state.nd.us/

- North Dakota Secretary of State
  http://www.state.nd.us/sec/

- Sex Offenders
  http://www.pac-info.com/location.php?lid=6481

Ohio

- Ohio Official Web Site
  http://www.state.oh.us/

- Ohio Secretary of State
  http://www.state.oh.us/sos/

- Inmate Searches (includes photos)
  http://www.drc.state.oh.us/cfdocs/inmate/search.htm

- Parole Violators
  http://www.drc.state.oh.us/web/fugitive.html

- Ohio Law Enforcement Training Center
  http://www.firms.findlaw.com/OLETC/contact.htm

Oklahoma

- Oklahoma Official Web Site
  http://www.state.ok.us

- Oklahoma Secretary of State
  http://www.state.ok.us/~sos/

- Fugitives
  http://www.doc.state.ok.us/Fugitives/all_fugitives.htm

- Inmates
  http://www.pac-info.com/location.php?lid=2453

- Most Wanted
  http://www.doc.state.ok.us/Fugitives/most_wanted.htm

- Oklahoma Department of Corrections
  http://www.doc.state.ok.us

Oregon

- Oregon Official Web Site
  http://www.state.or.us/

- Oregon Secretary of State
  http://www.sos.state.or.us/

- District Attorneys
  http://www.sos.state.or.us/elections/other.info/da.pdf

- Oregon Department of Corrections
  http://www.doc.state.or.us

Pennsylvania

- Pennsylvania Official Web Site
  http://www.state.pa.us/

- Pennsylvania Secretary of State
  http://www.dos.state.pa.us/

- Fugitives at Large
  http://www.pacrimestoppers.org/csindex.htm

- Inmate Searches
  http://www.cor.state.pa.us/locator.htm

- Most Wanted
  http://sites.state.pa.us/PA_Exec/State_Police/mwanted/ten.htm

- Pennsylvania Department of Corrections
  http://www.cor.state.pa.us

Rhode Island

- Rhode Island Secretary of State
  http://www.state.ri.us/

- Rhode Island Department of Corrections
  http://www.doc.state.ri.us

South Carolina

- South Carolina Official Web Site
  http://www.state.sc.us/

- South Carolina Secretary of State
  http://www.scsos.com/

- South Carolina Department of Corrections
  http://www.state.sc.us/scdc

South Dakota

- South Dakota Official Web Site
  http://www.state.sd.us/

- South Dakota Secretary of State
  http://www.state.sd.us/sos/sos.htm

- South Dakota Department of Corrections
  http://www.state.sd.us/state/executive/corrections/ corrections.html

- Fugitives
  http://www.state.sc.us/scdc/fugitive.htm

- Sex Offender Registry
  http://www.sled.state.sc.us/SLED/default.asp?Category=SCSO&Service=SCSO_01

- Escapees
  http://www.state.sd.us/corrections/wanted.htm

Tennessee

- Tennessee Official Web Site
  http://www.state.tn.us/

- Tennessee Secretary of State
  http://www.state.tn.us/sos/soshmpg.htm

- Missing Children
  http://www.ticic.state.tn.us/Missing_Children/miss_child_new.htm

- Most Wanted
  http://www.tbi.state.tn.us/Fugitives/TBI_MWD4.HTM

- Metro Nashville Police Department
  http://www.Nashville.Net/~police/risk
  "Rate Your Own Risk Threat" assessment is a means for you to calmly evaluate your risks.

- Probation and Parole
  http://www.ticic.state.tn.us/Database/ISC_search_oct.htm

- Sexual Offender Registry
  http://www.ticic.state.tn.us/SEX_ofndr/search_short.asp

- Tennessee Department of Corrections
  http://www.state.tn.us/correction

Texas

- Texas Department of Corrections
  http://www.tdcj.state.tx.us

- Texas Official Web Site
  http://www.state.tx.us/

- Texans for Equal Justice
  http://www.tej.lawandorder.com/index.htm
  Statewide crime victims advocacy organization in Texas.

- Texas Secretary of State
  http://www.sos.state.tx.us/

- Escapees
  http://people.txucom.net/tdcj-iad/

- Missing Persons
  http://www.txdps.state.tx.us/mpch/

- Most Wanted
  http://www.txdps.state.tx.us/wanted/

- Death Records
  http://userdb.rootsweb.com/tx/death/search.cgi

- Sex Offender Database
  http://records.txdps.state.tx.us/soSearch/default.cfm

Utah

- Utah Secretary of State
  http://www.state.ut.us/

- Utah Department of Corrections
  http://www.cr.ex.state.ut.us/home.htm

- Burial Database
  http://utstcess.dced.state.ut.us/NEWBURIALS/SilverStream/Pages/pgStandardSearch.html

- Cemetery Database
  <http://utstcess.dced.state.ut.us/NEWBURIALS/SilverStream/Pages/pgCemeterySearch.html;jsessionid=%40447e3a%3aebc3bc8d31>

- Death Certificate Inquiry
  http://hlunix.hl.state.ut.us/hda/mortality/

- Escapees
  http://corrections.utah.gov/offenders/mostwanted/

- Most Wanted
  http://www.udc.state.ut.us/offenders/mostwanted/

- Sex Offender Search
  http://www.udc.state.ut.us/asp-bin/sexoffendersearchform.asp

Vermont

- Vermont Official Web Site
  http://www.state.vt.us/

- Vermont Secretary of State
  http://www.sec.state.vt.us/

Virginia

- Virginia Official Web Site
  http://www.state.va.us/

- Virginia Secretary of State
  http://www.soc.state.va.us/

- Virginia Department of Corrections
  http://www.cns.state.va.us/doc

- Death Records Index
  http://eagle.vsla.edu/drip/

- Most Wanted Fugitives
  http://www.vadoc.state.va.us/fugitives/fugitives1.htm

- Inmates
  https://www.vipnet.org/cgi-bin/vadoc/doc.cgi

- Sex Offender Registry
  http://sex-offender.vsp.state.va.us/Static/Search.htm

Washington

- Washington Official Web Site
  http://access.wa.gov

- Washington Secretary of State
  http://www.secstate.wa.gov/

West Virginia

- West Virginia Secretary of State
  http://www.state.wv.us/

- West Virginia Division of Corrections
  http://www.state.wv.us/wvdoc/default.htm

- Missing and Exploited Children
  http://www.wvstatepolice.com/children/

- Most Wanted
  http://www.wvstatepolice.com/wanted/

- Sex Offender Registry
  http://www.wvstatepolice.com/sexoff/

Wisconsin

- Wisconsin Department of Corrections
  http://www.wi-doc.com

- Wisconsin Official Web Site
  http://www.state.wi.us

- Wisconsin Secretary of State
  http://badger.state.wi.us/agencies/sos/

Wyoming

- Wyoming Official Web Site
  http://www.state.wy.us/

- Wyoming Secretary of State
  http://soswy.state.wy.us/corporat/corporat.htm

- Wyoming Department of Corrections
  http://www.state.wy.us/~corr/corrections.html

- Wyoming Secretary of State Corporation Search
  http://soswy.state.wy.us/corps1.htm
  Public access to corporations in Wyoming.

- Sex Offender Registry
  http://attorneygeneral.state.wy.us/dci/so/so_registration.html

U.S. AND U.S. TERRITORIES

- U.S. State Department Bureau of Diplomatic Security
  http://www.heroes.net/content.html

Guam

- Sex Offenders
  http://jisweb.justice.gov.gu/sor/index.html

VIOLENCE RELATED

- Gang Colors
  http://www.gangcolors.com
  Web page chronicling gang actions.

- Gangs in Los Angeles County
  http://www.streetgangs.com

- National Coalition Against Domestic Violence
  http://www.ncadv.org

- National Coalition of Homicide Survivors
  http://www.mivictims.org/nchs
  Links to nationwide victim service agencies, support hotlines, court case updates.

WEATHER

- ABCNews.com Weather
  http://webapp.abcnews.com/cgi/news/asps/weather/w_intro.asp
  Weather service provides up-to-the-minute forecasts for U.S. and international cities.

- CNN—Weather
  http://www.cnn.com/WEATHER/
  Weather, news, and four-day forecasts for 6,100 cities worldwide.

- The Weather Channel—Home Page
  http://www.weather.com/homepage.html
  Forecasts for U.S. and international cities.

- Yahoo Weather Forecast
  http://weather.yahoo.com/
  Weather maps and news.

CHAPTER 59: INFORMATION AVAILABLE THROUGH VITAL STATISTICS

UNITED STATES

The following agencies maintain official records about births and deaths occurring in the various states. In some cases, the agency in charge of vital statistics may also have records about marriages and divorces. Keep in mind that these are state agency records. Vital statistics involving counties or cities may also be maintained at a local level.

Release of this information may be subject to various restrictions, charges, and authorizations or subpoena. When contacting the individual sources of information, you must supply the following information, although dates may have to be the subject of a search:

1) Full and complete name of the person whose record is involved
2) Race, sex, and date of birth, if known
3) Parents' names, including mother's maiden name, if known
4) Month, day, and year of searchable event
5) Location where event occurred
6) Reason the information is being sought

U.S. STATES	Birth	Death	Marriage	Divorce
Alabama Bureau of Vital Statistics State Department of Public Health Montgomery, AL 36104 • Records from 1908 • Fairly complete since 1919	X	X	X	X
Alaska Bureau of Vital Statistics Department of Health and Welfare Juneau, AL 99801 • Few birth records from before 1913 • Records complete from 1913	X	X	X	X
Arizona Division of Vital Records State Department of Health Phoenix, AZ 85030 • Records since 1887 • Complete since 1909	X	X		

	Birth	Death	Marriage	Divorce
Arkansas Division of Vital Records State Department of Health Little Rock, AR 72201 • Births recorded from 1914 • For pre–1914 records, contact city clerk in city where birth or death occurred	X	X	X	X
California Vital Statistics Section State Department of Public Health Sacramento, CA 95814 • Birth records from 1905 • Records very incomplete but go back as far as 1852 for individual cities and counties • No records in San Francisco before April 1906 (destroyed by fire)	X	X	X	X
Colorado Records and Statistics Department of Health 4210 East 11th Avenue Denver, CO 80220 • Marriage and divorce available at county level • Birth records date back to 1900 • Complete birth records since 1907 • Colorado Springs births since 1890 • Denver births since 1892 • Pueblo births since 1886	X	X		
Connecticut Public Health Statistics Section State Department of Health Hartford, CT 06115 • Births registered since 1897 • Divorce available at county level	X	X	X	
Delaware Bureau of Vital Statistics State Department of Health and Social Services Dover, DE 19901 • Births since 1881 • Divorce available at county level	X	X	X	

	Birth	Death	Marriage	Divorce
District of Columbia Vital Records Division District of Columbia Department of Public Health 615 Pennsylvania Avenue, N.W. Washington, D.C. 20001 • Births complete since 1897 • Incomplete births prior to 1874 • Marriage and divorce records available through clerk of the Superior Court	X	X		
Florida Bureau of Vital Statistics State Department of Health and Rehab. Services P.O. Box 210 Jacksonville, FL 32201 • Complete records since 1917 • Incomplete records since 1865 • Marriage and divorce records available at county level	X	X		
Georgia Vital Records Unit State Department of Human Resources 47 Trinity Avenue, S.W. Atlanta, GA 30334. • Births since 1919 • Marriage and divorce records available at county level • Incomplete birth records available at individual cities such as: —Atlanta since 1896 —Macon since 1891 —Savannah since 1890	X	X		
Hawaii Research and Statistics Office State Department of Health Honolulu, HI 96801 • Complete birth records since 1909 • Incomplete birth records since 1865 available at county level	X	X	X	X
Idaho Bureau of Vital Statistics State Department of Health and Welfare Boise, ID 83720 • Birth records since 1911	X	X	X	X

	Birth	Death	Marriage	Divorce
Illinois Vital Records State Department of Public Health Springfield, IL 62761 • Birth records since 1921 Marriage and divorce records available at county level	X	X		
Indiana Division of Vital Records State Board of Health 1330 West Michigan Street Indianapolis, IN 46206 • Births registered to 1907 • Birth records for certain cities and individual counties since 1880	X	X		
Iowa Division of Records and Statistics State Department of Health Des Moines, IA 50319 • Births registered since 1880	X	X	X	X
Kansas Bureau of Registration and Health Statistics Topeka, KS 66620 • Births registered since 1911	X	X	X	X
Kentucky Office of Vital Statistics State Department of Health 275 East Main Street Frankfort, KY 40601 • Births registered since 1911 • Birth records for Louisville available at city level since 1898	X	X	X	X
Louisiana Office of Vital Records State Department of Health State Office Building 415 Loyola Avenue New Orleans, LA 70160 • Does not include New Orleans • Birth records since 1914 • Some parishes have records going back much further • Marriage and divorce records available at parish (county) level	X	X		

	Birth	Death	Marriage	Divorce
Maine Office of Vital Records State Department of Health and Welfare Augusta, ME 04330 • Births recorded since 1892	X	X	X	X

Maryland
Division of Vital Records
State Department of Health
Baltimore, MD 21203
• Birth records since 1898
• Marriage and divorce records at county level, only;
   Does not include Baltimore prior to 1973
• Baltimore has incomplete birth records to 1875;
   Complete birth records from 1910 through 1972:
    Baltimore City
    Bureau of Vital Records
    City Health Department
    Baltimore, MD 21201
	X	X		

Massachusetts
Registrar of Vital Statistics
McCormick Building
Boston, MA 02108
• Births registered since 1849
• Divorce available at county level
• Boston birth records:
    City Registrar
    Health Department
    City Hall Square
    Boston, MA 02108.
	X	X	X	

Michigan Department of Public Health Office of Vital and Health Statistics 3500 N. Logan Lansing, MI 48909 • Births records since 1867 • Complete birth records since 1906 • Marriage and divorce records available at county level	X	X		

	Birth	Death	Marriage	Divorce

Minnesota
Vital Statistics
Minnesota Department of Health
717 Delaware Street, S.E.
Minneapolis, MN 55414
• Birth records since 1890
• Complete birth records since 1900 except for the following exceptions:
  —For Minneapolis, St. Paul, and Duluth, contact the health departments in the individual cities prior to 1913.
  —Prior to 1908 in other cities in the state, apply to the clerk of the district court in the county of birth. Some birth records go back to 1870.
• Marriage and death records available at county level
	X	X		

Mississippi Vital Records Unit State Board of Health State Capitol Jackson, MS 39205 • Birth records registered from November 1912 • Birth records not maintained at county levels • Divorce records available at county level	X	X	X	X

Missouri
Bureau of Vital Records
State Department of Public Health and Welfare
Jefferson City, MO 65101
• Births recorded since 1910
• Incomplete birth records available at the following cities:
  —Kansas City since 1874
  —St. Joseph since 1896
  —St. Louis since 1870
• Marriage and divorce records available at county level only
	X	X		

Montana Bureau of Records and Statistics State Department of Health Helena, MT 59601 • Birth records since 1907 • Individual counties have incomplete birth records going back to 1890.	X	X		

	Birth	Death	Marriage	Divorce
Nebraska Bureau of Vital Statistics State Department of Health Box 95007 Lincoln, NE 68509 • Birth records since 1905 • Some incomplete birth records registered at the county level going back to 1900	X	X	X	X
Nevada Division of Health Section of Vital Statistics State Department of Human Resources Carson City, NV 89710 • Births registered since 1911 • Marriage records available since 1968; prior to 1968, available at county level	X	X	X	
New Hampshire Department of Health and Welfare Bureau of Vital Statistics Concord, NH 03301 • Births registered back to 1800 • Divorce records available at county level	X	X	X	

New Jersey
State Department of Health
Bureau of Vital Statistics
Trenton, NJ 08265
• Birth records go back to May 1, 1848. Records are fairly complete except records for Trenton from 1876–1877 and for Newark from 1860–1861 are missing.
• Divorce records available from:
   Superior Court
   Chancery Division
   Trenton, NJ 08625
		X	X	X

New Mexico Vital Statistics Bureau State Health Services Division Santa Fe, NM 87503 • Births recorded since 1910 • Incomplete birth records available at county level • Marriage and divorce records available at county level	X	X		

	Birth	Death	Marriage	Divorce
New York (not including New York City) Bureau of Vital Records State Department of Health Albany, NY 12237	X	X	X	X

- From 1880–1913 inclusive for the state, exclusive of Albany, Buffalo, Yonkers, and New York City, which maintained their own records for this period
- Complete records (except NYC) from 1914
- Marriage records since 1907
- Divorce records since 1963; before 1963 available at county level

	Birth	Death	Marriage	Divorce
New York City Department of Health Bureau of Records 125 Worth Street New York, NY 10013	X	X		

- Birth and death certificate filed alphabetically by year
- Records prior to 1898 for Queens County and Richmond County (Staten Island) on file with the state office

	Birth	Death	Marriage	Divorce
North Carolina Vital Records Branch Department of Human Resources Raleigh, NC 27602	X	X	X	X

- Births registered from 1914

	Birth	Death	Marriage	Divorce
North Dakota Division of Vital Statistics State Department of Health Bismarck, ND 58505		X	X	

- Births registered back to 1893
- Birth records incomplete (approximately 50 percent) from 1907–1924; complete since 1925
- Marriage and divorce records indexed at the state level, available at the county level

	Birth	Death	Marriage	Divorce
Ohio Division of Vital Statistics State Department of Health Columbus, OH 43215	X	X		

- Births registered since 1909
- Births recorded with the clerk of the probate court 1867 to 1909
- Marriage and divorce records available at the county level, indexed at the state level

	Birth	Death	Marriage	Divorce
Oklahoma Vital Records Section State Department of Health Oklahoma City, OK 73105 • Births registered to 1908, complete since 1917 • Marriage and divorce available at county level	X	X		
Oregon Vital Statistics Section State Health Division Department of Human Resources Box 116 Portland, OR 97207 • Births registered back to 1903 • Counties have incomplete records going back to 1877	X	X	X	X
Pennsylvania Bureau of Vital Statistics State Department of Health New Castle, PA 16103 • Birth records back to 1906 • Marriage and divorce records indexed at state level but available at county level • Most cities have birth records dating back to 1893	X	X		
Puerto Rico Division of Demographic Registry and Vital Statistics Department of Health San Juan, PR 00908 • Birth records back to 1931; earlier records available from local registrar (*registrador demografico*) • Divorce records available at county level	X	X	X	
Rhode Island Division of Vital Statistics State Department of Health Providence, RI 02908 • Births registered to 1852 • Divorce records available at local county level	X	X	X	
South Carolina Division of Vital Records Department of Health Columbia, SC 29201 • Births have been registered since 1915 • Earlier records dating to 1877 available for Charleston	X	X	X	X

	Birth	Death	Marriage	Divorce
South Dakota Division of Public Health Statistics State Department of Health Pierre, SD 57501 • Births registered since July 1905	X	X	X	X
Tennessee Division of Vital Statistics State Department of Public Health Nashville, TN 37219 • Births registered since 1914; earlier birth records available at individual cities and counties • Records for Memphis back to 1874 (scant in early years)	X	X	X	X
Texas Bureau of Vital Statistics State Department of Health Resources Austin, TX 78701 • Birth records available since 1903, complete since 1925 • Marriage and divorce records at county level, indexed at state level	X	X		
Utah Division of Vital Statistics Health Department State of Utah 150 N. West Temple Salt Lake City, UT 84111 • Births registered since 1905 • Counties have incomplete records since 1890 • Marriage and divorce records available at county level only	X	X		
Vermont Secretary of State Vital Records Department Montpelier, VT 05602 • Fairly complete records going back to 1800 • Records available through clerk at town or city where birth or death occurred	X	X	X	X
Virginia Bureau of Vital Records and Health Statistics State Department of Health Richmond, VA 23208 • Birth records complete since June 1912, incomplete 1853–1896	X	X	X	X

	Birth	Death	Marriage	Divorce
Washington Bureau of Vital Statistics State Department of Social and Health Services Olympia, WA 98504 • Births registered from June 1907 • Seattle, Spokane, and Tacoma omitted from state records prior to 1934 —Seattle birth records from 1890 —Spokane birth records from 1891 —Tacoma birth records from 1887	X	X	X	X
West Virginia Vital Statistics Division State Health Department Charleston, WV 25305 • Death records available from 1917 • Marriage and divorce available at county level only	X	X		
Wisconsin Bureau of Health Statistics State Division of Health Madison, WI 53701 • Records complete from 1907 • Some records back to 1870 • Many counties have birth records preceding state records	X	X	X	X
Wyoming Vital Records Services Division of Health and Medical Services Cheyenne, WY 82002 • Births registered since 1909	X	X	X	X

CANADA

	Birth	Death	Marriage	Divorce
Alberta Registrar General Division of Vital Statistics Department of Health and Social Development Edmonton, AB T5J OA6 • Incomplete records from 1883 • Complete records since 1905	X	X	X	
British Columbia Director of Vital Statistics Department of Health Victoria, BC V8V 1X4 • Records began in 1872; Earlier records incomplete	X	X	X	

	Birth	Death	Marriage	Divorce
Manitoba Resources Division Department of Health and Social Development Winnipeg, MB R3C 0V8 • Birth and death records since 1827 • Have acquired baptismal records from churches going back to 1827	X	X	X	X
New Brunswick Vital Statistics Department of Health Fredericton, NB • 1888 to 1919 (inclusive) must know the county in which the event occurred; Records incomplete • 1920 to present, records complete	X	X	X	
Newfoundland Registrar of Vital Statistics Department of Provincial Affairs and Environment St. John's, NF • Records since 1891 • Records from local cathedrals of the Roman Catholic Church and the Church of England back 120 years	X	X	X	
Nova Scotia Director of Registration Department of Public Health Halifax, NS B3J 2M9 • Records available from 1864 to 1876 • Records from 1877 to October 1908 destroyed by fire • Records complete since November 1908	X	X	X	
Ontario Office of Registrar General Vital Statistics Toronto, ON M7A 1Y5 • Incomplete registration of births since July 1869 • Complete records from 1884	X	X	X	X
Prince Edward Island Registrar General Vital Statistics Branch Department of Public Health Charlottetown, PE C1A 7N8 • Records from 1907	X	X	X	

	Birth	Death	Marriage	Divorce
Quebec Vital Statistics Department of Social Affairs Quebec City, QC • Birth records since 1926 • Marriage records kept by the Minister of Justice, Quebec City	X	X		
Saskatchewan Division of Vital Statistics Department of Public Health Regina, SK S4S 0D3 • Incomplete records from 1854 • Complete records from 1895	X	X	X	X

CHAPTER 60:
DEATH PENALTY IN THE UNITED STATES

Jurisdiction	Statute	Primary Method
Alabama	15-18-82(a)	Electrocution Lethal injection
Arizona	13-704	If committed before 11-23-92, inmate may select lethal injection or lethal gas.
Arkansas	5-4-617(a)(1)	Lethal injection
California	3604	Lethal injection or gas Inmate may select lethal injection or lethal gas.
Colorado	16-11-401	Lethal injection
Connecticut	54-100	Lethal injection
Delaware	4209	Lethal injection If lethal injection is held unconstitutional, then hanging.
Florida	922.105	Lethal injection or electrocution Lethal injection unless inmate elects electrocution. If lethal injection is held unconstitutional, then any legal method.
Georgia	17-10-38	Lethal injection If committed after 5-01-2000, lethal injection.; if before, electrocution. If electrocution is held unconstitutional, then lethal injection.
Idaho	19-2716	Lethal injection If lethal injection is impractical due to lack of "technical assistance," then firing squad
Illinois	C. 20 - 5/119-5(a)	Lethal injection If lethal injection is held unconstitutional, then electrocution
Indiana	35-38-6-1	Lethal injection
Kansas	22-4001	Lethal injection

Kentucky	431.220	Lethal injection Lethal injection, unless inmate was sentenced before 03-31-98 and chooses electrocution
Louisiana	569	Lethal injection
Maryland	27-627	Lethal injection
Missouri	546.720	Lethal injection or gas
Montana	49-19-103(3)	Lethal injection
Nebraska	29-2543	Electrocution
Nevada	176.355	Lethal injection
New Hampshire	630:5 (XIII)	Lethal injection If lethal injection is "impractical," then hanging
New Jersey	2C:49-2	Lethal injection
New Mexico	31-14-11	Lethal injection
New York	C. 43 - Art.22-B,658	Lethal injection
North Carolina	15-187	Lethal injection
Ohio	2949.22	Electrocution or lethal injection Electrocution, unless inmate selects lethal injection. If lethal injection is held unconstitutional, then electrocution.
Oklahoma	1014	Lethal injection If lethal injection is held unconstitutional, then electrocution. If electrocution is held unconstitutional, then firing squad.
Oregon	137.473	Lethal injection
Pennsylvania	3004	Lethal injection
South Carolina	24-3-530	Lethal injection or electrocution Lethal injection, unless inmate elects electrocution.
South Dakota	23A-27A-32	Lethal injection

Tennessee	40-23-114	Lethal injection On or after 01-01-99, then lethal injection. Before 01-01-99, then electrocution, unless inmate selects lethal injection. If lethal injection is held unconstitutional, then electrocution.
Texas	TCCP, Art. 43.14	Lethal injection
Utah	77-18-5.5	Firing squad or lethal injection Lethal injection, unless inmate selects firing squad.
Virginia	53.1-233	Lethal injection or electrocution Lethal injection, unless inmate selects electrocution.
Washington	10.95.180	Hanging or lethal injection Lethal injection, unless inmate selects hanging.
Wyoming	7-13-904	Lethal injection If lethal injection is held unconstitutional, then lethal gas.
Federal Government, U.S. Military	28 CFR 26.3 18 USC 3596	Lethal injection or state method Lethal injection is general method pursuant to 28 CFR, Part 26. However, under the Violent Crime Control Act of 1994, the method is that of the state in which the conviction took place, pursuant to 18 U.S.C. 3596.

LETHAL INJECTION

1) Procedure
    a) State statutes typically provide that "the punishment of death must be inflicted by continuous intravenous administration of a lethal quantity of an ultrashort-acting barbiturate in combination with a chemical paralytic agent until death is pronounced by a licensed physician according to accepted standards of medical practice."
    b) The execution protocol for most jurisdictions authorizes the use of a combination of three drugs:
        i) The first, sodium thiopental or sodium pentothal, is a barbiturate that renders the prisoner unconscious.
        ii) The second, pancuronium bromide, is a muscle relaxant that paralyzes the diaphragm and lungs.
        iii) The third, potassium chloride, causes cardiac arrest.
    c) Each chemical is lethal in the amounts administered.

d) The inmate is escorted into the execution chamber and is strapped onto a gurney with ankle and wrist restraints. The inmate is connected to a cardiac monitor, which is connected to a printer outside the execution chamber.

e) An IV is started in two usable veins, one in each arm, and a flow of normal saline solution is administered at a slow rate. One line is held in reserve in case of a blockage or malfunction in the other.

f) At the warden's signal, 5.0 grams of sodium pentothal (in 20cc of diluent) is administered, and then the line is flushed with sterile normal saline solution. This is followed by 50cc of pancuronium bromide, a saline flush, and finally 50cc of potassium chloride.

2) The most common problems encountered are collapsing veins and the inability to properly insert the IV. Some states allow for a Thorazine or sedative injection to facilitate IV insertion.

3) History
   a) In 1977, Oklahoma became the first state to adopt lethal injection.
   b) Texas performed the first execution by lethal injection in 1982, with the execution of Charlie Brooks.

4) Current application
   a) Currently 18 states and the federal government authorize lethal injection as the sole method of execution.
   b) An additional 18 states provide for lethal injection as the primary method of execution but provide alternative methods depending on the choice of the inmate, the date of the execution or sentence, or the possibility of the method's being held unconstitutional.

ELECTROCUTION

1) Procedure
   a) State statutes typically provide that "the sentence shall be executed by causing to pass through the body of the convict a current of electricity of sufficient intensity to cause death, and the application and continuance of such current through the body of such convict shall continue until such convict is dead."
   b) The execution protocol for most jurisdictions authorizes the use of a wooden chair with restraints and connections to an electric current.
   c) The offender enters the execution chamber and is placed in the electric chair.
      i) The chair is constructed of oak and is set on a rubber matting and bolted to a concrete floor.
   d) Lap, chest, arm, and forearm straps are secured.
   e) A leg piece (anklet) is laced to the offender's right calf, and a sponge and electrode are attached.
   f) The headgear consists of a metal headpiece covered with a leather hood that conceals the offender's face. The metal part of the headpiece consists of a copper wire mesh screen to which the electrode is brazened. A wet sponge is placed between the electrode and the offender's scalp.
   g) The automatic cycle begins with the programmed 2,300 volts (9.5 amps) for 8 seconds, followed by 1,000 volts (4 amps) for 22 seconds, followed by 2,300 volts (9.5 amps) for 8 seconds. When the cycle is complete, the equipment is disconnected and the manual circuit behind the chair is disengaged. If the offender is not pronounced dead, the execution cycle is then repeated.

h) The most common problems encountered include burning of parts of the body to varying degrees and a failure of the procedures to cause death without repeated shocks. Witness accounts of many botched executions over the years have caused electrocution to be replaced with lethal injection as the most common method of execution.

2) History
   a) From 1930 to 1980 it was clearly the most common method of execution in the United States.

3) Current application
   a) Only two states, Alabama and Nebraska, currently use electrocution as the sole method of execution. Eight other states provide for electrocution as an alternative method, depending on the choice of the inmate, the date of the execution or sentence, or the possibility of the method's being held unconstitutional.
   b) Of the countries outside the United States that impose capital punishment, none prescribes execution by electrocution.

LETHAL GAS

1) Procedure: state statutes typically and simply provide that "the punishment of death must be inflicted by the administration of a lethal gas."
   a) The execution protocol for most jurisdictions authorizes the use of a steel, airtight execution chamber, equipped with a chair and attached restraints.
   b) The inmate is restrained at his chest, waist, arms, and ankles, and wears a mask during the execution.
   c) The chair is equipped with a metal container beneath the seat. Cyanide pellets are placed in this container. A metal canister is on the floor under the container filled with a sulfuric acid solution.
   d) There are three executioners, and each turns one key. When the three keys are turned, an electric switch causes the bottom of the cyanide container to open, allowing the cyanide to fall into the sulfuric acid solution, producing a lethal gas.
   e) Unconsciousness can occur within a few seconds if the prisoner takes a deep breath. However, if he holds his breath death can take much longer, and the prisoner usually goes into wild convulsions.
   f) A heart monitor attached to the inmate is read in the control room, and after the warden pronounces the inmate dead, ammonia is pumped into the execution chamber to neutralize the gas. Exhaust fans then remove the inert fumes from the chamber into two scrubbers that contain water and serve as a neutralizing agent.
      i) The neutralizing process takes approximately 30 minutes from the time the offender's death is determined.
   g) Death is estimated to usually occur within 6 to 18 minutes of the lethal gas emissions.

2) History
   a) The use of a gas chamber for execution was inspired by the use of poisonous gas in World War I, as well as the popularity of the gas oven as a means of suicide.
   b) Nevada became the first state to adopt execution by lethal gas in 1924 and carried out the first execution in the same year.
   c) Lethal gas was seen as an improvement over other forms of execution, because it was less violent and did not disfigure or mutilate the body. The last execution by lethal gas took place in Arizona in 1999.

3) Current application
   a) Only four states (Arizona, California, Missouri, and Wyoming) currently authorize lethal gas as a method of execution as an alternative to lethal injection, depending on the choice of the inmate, the date of the execution or sentence, or the possibility of lethal injection's being held unconstitutional.

HANGING

1) Procedure
   a) Prior to any execution, the gallows area trapdoor and release mechanisms are inspected for proper operation.
   b) The rope, which is made of manila hemp at least 3/4 inch and not more than 1 1/4 inches in diameter and approximately 30 feet in length, is soaked and then stretched while drying to eliminate any spring, stiffness, or tendency to coil.
       i) The hangman's knot, which is tied pursuant to military regulations, is treated with wax, soap, or clear oil, to ensure that the rope slides smoothly through it.
       ii) The end of the rope that doesn't contain the noose is tied to a grommet in the ceiling and then is tied off to a metal T-shaped bracket, which takes the force delivered by the offender's drop.
   c) Prior to an execution, the condemned offender's file is reviewed to determine if there are any unusual characteristics he possesses that might warrant deviation from field instructions on hanging.
   d) A physical examination and measuring process are conducted to ensure almost instant death and a minimum of bruising.
       i) If careful measuring and planning are not done, strangulation, obstructed blood flow, or beheading could result.
   e) At the appropriate time on execution day, the inmate, in restraints, is escorted to the gallows area and is placed standing on a hinged trapdoor through which he will be dropped.
   f) Following the offender's last statement, a hood is placed over his head. Restraints are also applied. If the offender refuses to stand or cannot stand, he is placed on a collapse board.
   g) A determination of the proper amount of drop for the offender through the trapdoor is calculated using a standard military execution chart for hanging.
       i) The "drop" must be based on the prisoner's weight, to deliver 1,260 foot-pounds of force to the neck.
       ii) The noose is then placed snugly around the convict's neck, behind his left ear, which will cause the neck to snap. The trapdoor then opens, and the convict drops.
       iii) If the hanging is properly done, death is caused by dislocation of the third and fourth cervical vertebrae or by asphyxiation.
       iv) A button mechanically releases the trapdoor, and escorts then move to the lower floor location to assist in the removal of the body.

2) History
   a) Hanging is the oldest method of execution in the United States but fell into disfavor in the 20th century after many botched attempts and was replaced by electrocution as the most common method.
   b) There have been only three executions by hanging since 1977: Westley Dodd (Washington, 1993), Charles Campbell (Washington, 1994), and Billy Bailey (Delaware, 1998).

3) Current application
    a) Only three states (Delaware, New Hampshire, and Washington) currently authorize hanging as a method of execution as an alternative to lethal injection, depending on the choice of the inmate, whether injection is "impractical," or the possibility of lethal injection's being held unconstitutional.

FIRING SQUAD

1) Procedure
    a) Shooting can be carried out by a single executioner, who fires from short range at the back of the head or neck as in China.
    b) The traditional firing squad is made up of three to six shooters per prisoner. They stand or kneel opposite the condemned person, who is usually tied to a chair or stake.
    c) Normally, the shooters aim at the chest because this is easier to hit than the head. A chest shot causes rupture of the heart, great vessels, and lungs so that the condemned person dies of hemorrhage and shock.
        i) It is not unusual for the officer in charge to have to give the prisoner a pistol shot to the head to finish him off after the initial volley has failed to kill him.
    d) The Utah statute authorizing execution by firing squad only provides that "if the judgment of death is to be carried out by shooting, the executive director of the department or his designee shall select a five-person firing squad of peace officers."
        i) At the appropriate time, the condemned offender is led to the execution area or chamber, which is used for both lethal injection and firing squad executions.
        ii) The offender is placed in a specially designed chair, which has a pan beneath it to catch and conceal blood and other fluids.
        iii) Restraints are applied to the offender's arms, legs, chest, and head.
        iv) A head restraint is applied loosely around the offender's neck to hold his neck and head in an upright position.
        v) The offender is dressed in a dark blue outfit with a white cloth circle attached by Velcro to the area over his heart.
        vi) Sandbags are placed behind the offender to absorb the volley and prevent ricochets.
        vii) Approximately 20 feet directly in front of the offender is a wall with firing ports for each member of the firing squad. The weapons used are .30-30 caliber rifles. No special ammunition is used.
        viii) Following the offender's statement, a hood is placed over his head, and the warden leaves the room. The firing squad members stand in the firing position and support their rifles on the platform rests. With their rifle barrels in the firing ports, they sight through open sights on the white cloth circle on the offender's chest. On the command to fire, the squad fires simultaneously. One squad member has a blank charge in his weapon, but no member knows which member is designated to receive this blank charge.

2) History
    a) In recent history only two inmates have been executed by firing squad, both in Utah: Gary Gilmore in 1977 and John Albert Taylor in 1996.
    b) Although execution by firing squad was popular with the military in times of war, there has been one such execution since the Civil War: Private Eddie Slovik in World War II.

3) Current application

    a) Only three states (Idaho, Oklahoma, and Utah) currently authorize shooting as a method of execution, all as an alternative to lethal injection, depending on the choice of the inmate, whether injection is "impractical," or the possibility of lethal injection's being held unconstitutional.

LEGAL ASPECTS OF HOMICIDE

1)   Homicide is the killing of one human being by another. The term *homicide* does not reflect the moral or legal implications of the act. Homicide is not necessarily a crime. For legal purposes, homicide falls into two broad categories:

      a) Justifiable homicide results from some unavoidable circumstance without any will, intention, desire, or negligence on the part of the person who committed the act.

      b) Felonious homicide is the wrongful killing of another human being without justification in law. There are two types of homicides that fall within this category:

         i) Murder is the unlawful killing of a human being by another with intent or knowledge or during an attempt to commit, or during the commission of, a forcible felony. The person who committed the crime must be of sound mind and discretion (i.e., of sufficient age and mental capacity to form and execute a criminal design) and must commit this murder in the peace of the state and without any warrant, justification, or excuse in law.

            (1) To establish the felony of murder, the evidence must demonstrate that the suspect, without any proper reason, killed another person and, at the time of the killing, one of the following conditions existed:

              (a) The suspect intended to kill the victim or another person.

              (b) The suspect intended to seriously injure the victim or another person.

              (c) The suspect knew that the act was practically certain to cause the death of the victim or another person.

              (d) The suspect knew that the act created a strong possibility of death or serious injury to the victim or another person.

              (e) The suspect was attempting to commit, or was committing, a forcible felony other than voluntary manslaughter. A homicide committed during the perpetration (or attempt) of a forcible felony (e.g., treason, murder, rape, robbery, burglary, arson, kidnapping, aggravated battery, and any other felonies involving the use or threat of physical force or violence against an individual) is considered a murder even though the killing may have been unintentional or even accidental.

            (2) The taking of the human life must be consciously intended. It must be the purpose of the objective.

            (3) A well-laid plan is not essential. The killing may be conceived and executed in a short interval.

            (4) Premeditation is not required in cases where an act is considered practically certain to result in death or great bodily harm.

            (5) To kill while engaged in an act inherently dangerous and evidencing a wanton disregard of human life can constitute murder.

            (6) For proof of murder the following elements must be established:

              (a) The victim named or described is dead.

(b) The death was the result of an act of the accused.

(c) The circumstances show the accused had a premeditated design to kill or intended to kill or inflict great bodily harm; or was engaged in an act inherently dangerous to others and evidencing a wanton disregard for human life; or was engaged in the perpetration or attempted perpetration of a forcible felony.

ii) Manslaughter is the unlawful killing of another with or without intent or knowledge. There are two types of manslaughter:

(1) Voluntary

(a) A homicide committed with an intent and sufficient provocation under a sudden heat of passion. It is recognized that a person may be so overcome with sudden passion he may cause a fatal injury before he can resume self-control.

(b) The provocation must not only create an intense passion in the accused, but also must be conduct that would excite an intense reaction of passion involving a reasonable person.

(c) The provocation may have come from the victim or another person whom the accused meant to kill when he accidentally or negligently killed the victim.

(d) Mere words or gestures, no matter how abusive, are not adequate provocation.

(e) After the provocation, the heat of the passion must immediately have led to the fatal act.

(f) With an unreasonable belief the act was justified. The accused believes his act is necessary to prevent:

(i) Imminent death or serious injury to the accused or another.

(ii) The commission of a forcible felony.

(iii) The escape from arrest of a person who commits or attempts a forcible felony or indicates that he will endanger human lives unless arrested without delay.

(iv) An assault upon him or another person within a home, when the victim enters or attempts to enter the home in a violent, riotous manner.

(v) The death is referred to as "voluntary" because the death is an intended act.

(2) Involuntary

(a) A person who kills an individual without lawful justification commits involuntary manslaughter if that person's acts, whether lawful or unlawful, cause the death or are such that they likely cause the death or great bodily harm to some individual, if the person commits the acts recklessly.

(b) It is an unintentional killing that is neither murder nor voluntary manslaughter and is not justifiable (if the accused knew his acts were practically certain to cause death or serious injury or that his acts created a strong probability of producing that result).

(3) Proving manslaughter

(a) The victim named or described is dead.

(b) Death was the result of an act or omission of the accused.

(c) The facts and circumstances show that the homicide amounted in law to the type of manslaughter involved.

..

NOTE: This index is found in the back of all three volumes. Pages 1–132 appear in Volume 1; pages 133–648 in Volume 2; pages 649–976 in Volume 3.

C

I

T

ABOUT THE AUTHOR

Louis N. Eliopulos has 25 years of experience in death investigations. Currently, he is a senior homicide investigations analyst with the Naval Criminal Investigative Service (NCIS), where he reviews, consults, and suggests investigative analysis and strategy on active and cold-case homicide investigations from all over the world. He also consults on homicide investigations for other criminal justice agencies. Before being employed by NCIS, Eliopulos was chief forensic investigator for the Medical Examiner's Office in Jacksonville, Florida, where he created, hired and trained the investigative staff, as well as serving as the special investigator in the Capital Crimes Division for the Florida Public Defender's Office. He also was a forensic consultant for the teams responsible for recovering the remains from the Pentagon after the September 11, 2001, terrorist attack.

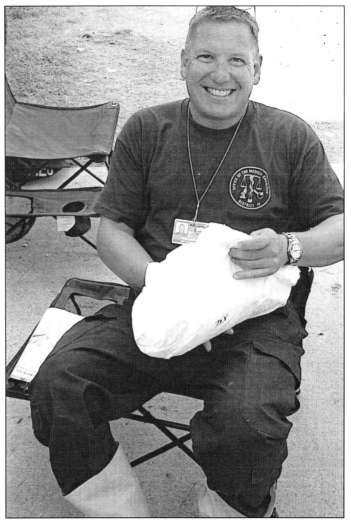